Careers in Creative Industrie

Routledge Advances in Management and Business Studies

Full a full list of titles, please visit: www.routledge.com

Careers in Creative Industries

Edited by Chris Mathieu

Routledge
Taylor & Francis Group

LONDON AND NEW YORK

First published 2012
by Routledge

Published 2014 by Routledge
711 Third Avenue, New York, NY 10017

Simultaneously published in the UK
by Routledge
2 Park Square, Milton Park, Abingdon, Oxfordshire OX14 4RN

Routledge is an imprint of the Taylor and Francis Group,
an informa business

First issued in paperback 2015

Typeset in Sabon by IBT Global.

Library of Congress Cataloging-in-Publication Data
    Careers in creative industries / edited by Chris Mathieu.
        p. cm. — (Routledge advances in management and business studies ; 49)
Includes bibliographical references and index.
    1. Cultural industries. 2. Arts. 3. Career development. 4. Creation
(Literary, artistic, etc.) I. Mathieu, Chris.
    HD9999.C9472C37 2011
    700.23—dc23
    2011029799

ISBN 978-0-415-80826-2 (hbk)
ISBN 978-1-138-96061-9 (pbk)
ISBN 978-0-203-13616-4 (ebk)

Contents

PART III
Architecture

PART IV
Music

PART V
Visual Arts and Fashion Design

Figures

Tables

Part I
Overviews

1 Careers in Creative Industries
An Analytic Overview

Chris Mathieu

FOUNDATIONS OF THE BOOK

This volume collects empirical studies of aspects of career-making in several creative industries from around the world. These studies focus on what are often referred to as the 'creative' roles, jobs, and occupations in creative industries, leaving largely aside the essential and numerous roles, jobs, and occupations in creative industries that Caves (2000) calls 'humdrum' and Becker (1982) refers to as 'support.' The reason for this focus is that the primary and general interest in creative industries is usually associated with understanding the creative work, workers, and careers found in these industries. These are the roles and work that draw our attention to creative industries, as researchers and potential or active participants in these industries. A second reason for this choice is that there frequently are important differences in the manners in which 'creatives' versus 'humdrums' are employed in creative industries, with creatives more often hired on a project or freelance basis, whereas humdrums (from lawyers and accountants to cleaners and caterers) are often more stably employed by durable companies in creative industries or the companies that they contract with. This choice by no account underplays or marginalizes the importance of these roles in the production processes in creative industries—they are vital and in many respects no less interesting—it merely sharpens the focus of this book to one, albeit broad and often difficult to precisely define, class of occupations and activities. We return to definition issues below, and Chapter 2 by Bille is largely devoted to them.

The reason for compiling empirical studies from several different industries in different national and institutional contexts is to facilitate the contrasting of both common and unique factors and processes, and the identification of specific, easily overlooked, and even nascent processes and mechanisms that usually are sacrificed at the level of theoretical generalization. This does not sacrifice theory-building ambitions but rather provides theory building with further empirical foundations to construct 'deep analogies' (Stinchcombe 1978). Another reason for collecting empirical studies is that both creative industries and recent career research have recently gone through similar cycles of celebrating the positive, self-realization, and even emancipatory dimensions of work in creative industries and 'new' or 'boundaryless' careers, with the promise of self-guided employment in stimulating work and an attractive spectrum of material and intrinsic rewards. These initial pronouncements were met with critical backlashes emphasizing the negative or dark sides of boundarylessness and work in creative industries (Hesmondhalgh and Baker 2011). At the moment we are at a more or less reasoned reconciliation between the positive and negative portrayals of both, where most parties admit both positive and negative dimensions of creative industries work and boundarylessness. Work and careers in these industries are not unequivocally positive or negative, and these dimensions are often inextricably intertwined. Empirical studies give us the opportunity to examine the mixed and ambiguous manners in which these things converge in practice and how such judgments or assessments are made.

The studies found here not only examine a wide variety of creative industries in several national and institutional contexts, they also do so from a variety of methodological and disciplinary informed styles, spanning management and business, organizational theory, work and career studies, to the classical disciplines of sociology and anthropology. This diversity includes wide methodological variation, as well as theoretical traditions, concepts applied, and levels of investigation. This means that the authors seek to accomplish different goals by different means. What they do have in common is an ambition to increase our understanding of general career issues and problems by drawing out the complexities and intricacies of particular cases or processes (Stolte et al. 2001). The selections in this volume open up new avenues of research, as well as contribute to more sophisticated understandings within established areas of research, contributing to theory building, concept development, and question framing via empirical analysis that can be transferred to other and broader contexts. Here, the words of Stinchcombe (1978, 115–116) are again relevant: 'the dilemma between synthetic reasoned generality, tested against the facts, and historical uniqueness, a portrait of the facts is a false dilemma. The way out of the dilemma is that portraits of the facts, combined with an intellectual operation of carefully drawn analogies, are roads to generality.' Keeping with the creative and artistic tone of this book, we recommend putting the 'portraits of the facts' found here on larger theoretical and paradigmatic canvases and see how they reinforce or alter the images that come forth. The various authors assist in this process of overlaying their findings on some relevant canvases, but there naturally are several other canvases on which these findings and questions can be fruitfully applied.

CAREERS AND CREATIVE INDUSTRIES

This volume draws on and integrates two areas of research and literatures—research and theorizing on career, and research and theorizing on creative industries. In the following section both fields are introduced. As two theories or conceptual points of departure—'boundaryless careers' and 'art worlds'—regularly recur in the following chapters, both are briefly introduced in this section as well. Both theories and concepts have two qualities that make them appealing to empirical researchers. One is a spaciousness that allows for broad interpretation and application, and the other is that they make juxtapositions that lead understanding away from hitherto conventional understandings.

Career studies is the more established field, broad and multidisciplinary, extending back to at least the 1930s as a distinct field of academic study (see Abbott 2005; Barley 1989 for concise, insightful analyses of the development of the sociology of work, occupations, professions, and careers; and Moore et al. 2007 on the historical origins of career theory from an organization studies perspective). Rather than review this historical development, which as noted is done insightfully elsewhere, it should suffice to set the stage for the studies presented here by contextualizing some of the most relevant current career theories for the studies in this volume. First, it is important to acknowledge that there are both academic and popular definitions of career, and that the latter are influenced by the former, often with a significant time lag. This means that a widespread current popular conception of career as a planned, linear, sequential escalation from well-defined position to well-defined position based on training and skill development with corresponding increases in authority, prestige, and remuneration within a single firm corresponds well with the classic academic concept of the 'organizational' (Kanter 1977) or 'orderly' career that Wilensky (1961, 523) defines as 'a succession of related jobs, arranged in a hierarchy of prestige, through which persons move in an ordered (more-or-less predictable) sequence.' Worth noting here is that in this sociological definition, the career as a structure is prior to the individuals who move through them.

As actual careers or 'work histories' have changed, academic definitions of career have also changed. They have tended to go from strong or rich conceptions such as the 'organizational' or 'orderly' definition of career to leaner definitions that can encompass the increasing heterogeneity of how work sequences actually play out in the contemporary world. We also see a shift from an emphasis on career structure to career agency (Tams and Arthur 2010), emphasizing the activities and strategies of individuals in *accomplishing* careers in less stable and traditionally structured environments. The leaner or more stripped down definitions of career drop the previous stipulations of 'succession,' 'order,' 'predictability,' and even 'related jobs.' This can be seen in the highly influential definition of career by Arthur et al. (1989, 8) as 'the evolving sequence of a person's work experiences over time' that fits well with the 'boundaryless' or 'new career' paradigm. Worth noting here is the notion of 'work experiences' that can be interpreted in terms of both concrete, objective experiences (i.e., what one has done), as well as with subjective experience (i.e., how it is felt), and that it privileges neither structure nor agency by avoiding the question of what governs the 'evolving sequence.'

On this topic, Barley (1989) speaks of the 'Janus-faced' nature of career, which simultaneously regards the 'objective' features of work or job history, such as holding various positions and turning points, and the 'subjective' dimension, which has to do with 'the meanings individuals attributed to their careers, to the sense they made of their becoming' (p. 49). The subjective and objective inhere in each other at the individual level, with subjective understandings 'enabl[ing] individuals to align themselves with the events of their biographies' (p. 49). This dual approach to career mitigates an either/or in favor of a both/and perception, which links concepts of the one dimension with concepts of the other in mutually constitutive pairs: objective-subjective, structure-agency, institution-individual, role-identity, history-experience, and so on. Tracing this approach back to the Chicago School of Sociology, Barley (1989, 50) elaborates on one of these conceptual pairings, role and identity: 'Whereas roles referenced the setting's interaction structure, identities referred to the stable definitions of self that enabled persons to enact their roles. Role looked outward towards a pattern of situated activity, whereas identity looked inward toward the actor's subjective experience of that situated being.' Barley succinctly sums up this perspective in the following passage:

> To be sure, careers remained something that only individuals could experience, but they were not solely of the individuals' making. Persons might willfully choose between different courses of action as they progressed through a career. . . . But the options they foresaw and the choices they made were always limited by contextually defined possibilities. Careers, then, were pieced together from the string of alternatives and the set of interpretive resources offered individuals at any point in time by the collectivities to which they belong. (Barley 1989, 51)

Thus, changes at the industry or societal levels provide the contextually defined possibilities, or what Abbott (2005) calls the 'labor opportunity structure' for individual careers. A means whereby the labor opportunity structure is seen, interpreted, and made subjectively relevant is via identification with reference groups that provide actors with models of career paths available, with cues for judging career progress, and with a terminology for staking down one's identity and making sense of one's position. In periods of stability, the identification of relevant reference groups is easier, as is the identification of both career patterns and the mechanisms that contribute to these patterns. In periods of instability, the opposite is the case, but the search for and identification of guiding reference groups or individuals is arguably equally, if not more, important under periods of instability for the processes of identifying career paths based on the histories of others, judging progress, and identity creation, as the resources for these largely socially based activities are less institutionalized. I will now turn to one theory that focuses on careers under the latter conditions.

Boundaryless Careers

'Boundaryless careers' is a nonsensical and absurd term but a meaningful and significant concept. Taken literally and applied to empirical reality, the term is nonsensical. As Gunz et al (2007) argue, work and career, as social life in general, is shot through with boundaries and only possible through the existence of boundaries. Even in its initial formulation and use by its originators (see the following quote by Arthur and Rousseau 1996), what is highlighted is the transcendence and permeability of boundaries rather than the non-existence of boundaries. Why then does the 'boundaryless career' concept continue to be so influential, even among its theoretical and empirical critics (Rodrigues and Guest 2010), and especially in creative industries research? Inkson (2006) argues that the concept serves well as a metaphor and a label. As a label, it allows us to conveniently and selectively refer to a number of phenomena and tendencies at once. If we look at the full, early exposition of the concept, we can see why it has resonated with analyses of careers in creative industries.

> Within the general meaning of boundaryless careers—as being the opposite of organizational careers—lie several specific meanings, or emphases. The most prominent of these is a case where a career, like the stereotypical Silicon Valley career, moves across the boundaries of separate employers. A second meaning occurs when a career, like that of an academic or a carpenter, draws validation—and marketability—from outside the present employer. A third meaning is involved when a career, like that of a real-estate agent, is sustained by external networks or information. A fourth meaning occurs when traditional organizational career boundaries, notably those involving hierarchical reporting and advancement principles, are broken. A fifth meaning occurs when a person rejects existing career opportunities for personal or family reasons. A sixth meaning depends on the interpretation of the career actor, who may perceive a boundaryless future regardless of structural constraints. A common factor in the occurrence of all these meanings is one of independence from, rather than dependence on, traditional organizational career arrangements. (Arthur and Rousseau 1996, 6)

The first and most obvious point is that in industries where it is readily apparent that careers play out far more often across, rather than within, organizations (Jones 1996), the 'boundaryless' notion seems readily applicable. Two common conditions in many creative industries lead to careers across, rather than within, organizations. One is that even when employed in a durable organization, such as a theatre company, contracts are frequently of short duration (see Eikhof et al., Chapter 3, this volume) and that promotion or vertical mobility is usually not secured by progression but open competition (see Faulkner 1973 for an example from symphony orchestras). The other is that production in creative industries is often project-based. Durable companies may exist and even organize or commission production, but the bulk of creative production often takes place in temporally delimited project organizations largely staffed by freelance or contract personnel. As these project-based organizations cease to exist after the completion of a specific project, some of the significant and most visible 'boundaries' around these temporary organizations disappear at the same time. In this sense, in accord with the boundaryless career concept, one can argue that boundaries do disappear along with the temporary project organizations that provided impermanent employment. Paradoxically, such conditions are at variance with the meaning of boundaryless careers in the sense of transitioning across organizational boundaries. However, the more elementary process of mobility identified in the boundaryless career concept as central to work and career is accessed here. It is also worth noting that what has come to be termed creative industries have long been characterized by, and more recently reference points for, boundaryless career-making and thinking (see e.g., Faulkner and Anderson 1987; Jones 1996; even Wilensky [1961, 524] noted that careers in 'entertainment' are generally disorderly).

The second and third points in the previous quote are also frequently picked up by researchers on work and careers in creative industries. If careers are built across organizations or in a series of temporary project organizations, then one's skills and abilities need to be recognizable and recognized in wider circles than just one's current employer. Likewise, one is reliant on information from a wide range of sources about employment opportunities, just as one also needs to send information, directly or vicariously, about one's ability and availability to a large number of potential employers, patrons, buyers, clients, and so on. These processes are closely associated with the concept of reputation, which is extensively dealt with in the coming chapters. In summary, a great deal of the appeal of the boundaryless career concept has to do with its emphasis on mobility, networks, reputation, and individual responsibility for career-making, opening up for a range of issues under a single conceptual banner.

One point on which the concept as developed by its proponents is routinely questioned, especially by creative industries researchers, has to do with boundarylessness as a structural condition rather than a choice. The initial and much continued application of the boundaryless career concept emphasizes the subjective, agency, and voluntaristic dimensions of career-making against the backdrop of the declining salience or prevalence of traditionally structured environments. However, in project-based industries or industries where whole occupational categories only are employed on freelance bases, mobility is a structural demand and not an individual choice. That is to say, there are no organizational or orderly careers to be had for many occupational groups in creative industries, radically altering the parameters of the debate. Another critical issue has to do with moving beyond the mere inter- contra intra-organizational dimension of career and focusing on other boundaries and barriers. One argument, also found in many places in this book, is that structural constraints and facilitation have certainly not ceased and probably not even diminished; it is just that the traditional structuring forms have decreased. It might be better to think in terms of structurally transformed rather than less structured environments (i.e., that there are new structural imperatives that are possibly equally as rigid and obliging, but rather in different manners, that we are only now beginning to identify as structuring and obliging rather than opening and liberating). This multidimensional tension is a central aspect of several studies collected in this volume, as we will see later, especially with regard to the cluster of concepts that include uncertainty, insecurity, freedom, and precariousness.

CREATIVE INDUSTRIES

Research and policymaking on what has come to be known as 'creative industries' have grown exponentially since the end of the 1990s. The publication of Richard Caves' (2000) book, *Creative Industries*, along with the work of Richard Florida (2002, 2005) have made creative industries research a growing field largely due to framing them as increasingly significant sectors of advanced, post-industrial capitalist economies in a way that the sociology and even economics of 'the arts, culture, and entertainment' never managed (or intended) to accomplish. Although there is no universal definition of creative industries or agreement on this label,[1] a frequently invoked list of which industries are classified under this label is that given by the British Department of Culture, Media, and Sports (2001). This list comprises: advertising; architecture; art and antiques; computer games (interactive leisure software); crafts; design; designer fashion; film and video; music; performing arts; publishing; software; and TV and radio.

The perils and intricacies of defining creative industries, creative work, occupations, activities, and creative workers are the subject of Chapter 2 by Bille (this volume), so I will not dwell on this matter here. However, I would like to concur with Bille on one issue and then extend this point to illuminate its bearing on the content of this book. Bille, as others before, contends that at the core of creative industries are activities and work strongly related to art. As creativity can also be primarily of scientific, economic, or everyday natures (Joas 1996; Sawyer 2006), it is important to recognize the concentricity with artistic and aesthetic-based industries in most definitions of creative industries. If one takes the artistic dimension to be at the core of creative industries and looks at the work and occupations covered in this book, virtually all have close associations with artistic and aesthetic-based activities—architects, composers, film editors and cinematographers, visual artists, fashion designers, actors, dramaturges, and so on.

The creative industries are indisputably attractive sectors to work in. This can be seen in terms of the chronic and vast 'oversupply' of available labor to these sectors (Menger 1999), indicating that far more people train themselves for and seek to enter careers in these industries (especially, but not exclusively, in their core creative jobs and occupations) than these industries can employ. Much of the attraction of these industries has to do with the highly visible and fabulous 'F' rewards made available in these industries—fame, fortune, and fulfillment (Menger 1999; Ursell 2000; and nearly all chapters in this book take up the lures, as well as the pitfalls, of work in various creative industries). As expanded on later and throughout this book, this often creates extreme competition for roles offering these rewards. The empirical focuses of the following chapters ranging from the 'consecrated' elite in film and architecture, to aspirants in music and theatre, to the abjectly 'unsuccessful' visual artists portray careers all along the objective success–failure spectrum—from those who obtain and for a prolonged period enjoy fame, fortune, and fulfillment, to those whose careers remarkably resemble Hobbes' famous description of life in the 'state of nature'—solitary, poor, nasty, brutish, and short.

Art Worlds

Becker's (1982) book *Art Worlds* is a landmark treatise and was radical in its approach to artistic creation at the time of its publication. It brought profane and mundane academic tools from the sociology of work and occupations to the study of the then sacred territory of artistic production.[2] As Becker brought mainstream sociology to the study of the arts and artistic production, he paved the way for mainstream sociology and other social sciences to no longer treat this realm of activity as forebodingly atypical and encouraged us to see artists as subjected and responsive to many of the same dependencies and social forces as other occupational groups.

The enduring impact of this work can be seen in the fact that it is still, after 30 years, the most prominent theoretical orientation invoked in the following chapters for exploring the workings of creative industries. For Becker (1982, X), art worlds 'denote the network of people whose cooperative activity, organized via their joint knowledge of conventional means of doing things, produce[s] the kind of art works that art world is noted for.' What generally gets picked up from Becker's concept is the coordinated, collective action on the part of an extensive network to produce the art works or creative products associated with this sphere. There are two important dimensions to this. The first dimension is the recognition of the wide range of occupations, individuals, groups, and organizations that are necessary for sustained artistic, creative, or cultural production. Becker also underscores the influence of, and even dependence on, things such as distribution systems and the state for artistic production, further distancing his perspective from the 'inspiration' paradigm of artistic production with bold claims such as, 'Artists produce what the distribution system can and will carry' (129). The second dimension has to do with what coordinates these occupations, individuals, groups, and organizations. Here, knowledge of the conventions on which the coordination of production rests is primary. Whereas the first points to the social integration of artists into wider networks and systems required to materially bring artworks into existence, the latter emphasizes the cognitive and normative integration of artists into wider communities, impacting the content of artistic production. Within this framework, questions such as how art worlds hang together, evolve, or mutate, on the one hand, and how actors penetrate, navigate, and interpret at least parts of the art worlds they seek to or actually participate in, on the other hand, can be addressed. Art worlds becomes a conceptual means of short-handedly referring to a complex agglomeration of actors, sites, materials, knowledge, and processes, which are both demarcated and diffuse and overlapping, allowing for both the exploration and comparison of specific art worlds.

To sum up this section and foreshadow the coming content of the book, most of the studies in this volume look at careers in creative industries in terms of the conditions, strategies, barriers, challenges, and so on for obtaining and remaining in work within a given 'creative' occupation or industry over a *prolonged period* of time, of which both the subjective and objective dimensions of work and non-work (remunerated and non-remunerated) are the central components. Here one can say that both the present (one's actual career history) and the absent career (the career history one has not had, as well as the career one intends to have in the future) are of importance. What differentiates this volume with a focus on careers in creative industries from, for example, studies of work in creative industries is the centrality of protractedness, duration or extension over time, and attention to what hasn't been and may in the future transpire, as well as what has actually been experienced.

SUMMARIES AND SYNTHESES: THE PRIMARY ISSUES, WHERE THEY ARE FOUND, HOW THEY ARE TREATED

The chapters in the book are arranged by industry. However, themes and issues cross-cut the chapters, industries, occupations, historical periods, and geographic locations. In the chapters, we find convergence, that is, similarities across contexts, as well as divergence or differences across contexts. In the following, I present the chapters contained in the book not on a chapter-by-chapter basis but rather based on how the chapters treat and contribute insight into specific topics or issues. Some topics, such as networks, are so pervasive that they will not be treated here as topics in themselves.

Career Management

Each chapter deals with career management in some form or another. Career management can be seen as a deliberate, conscious, planning activity or a largely unconscious, surreptitious process where 'management' takes place through engagement in, relating to, and coordination of discrete opportunities rather than explicit planning and evaluation of longer trajectories. Classically, career management was a shared responsibility between employer and employee. Under conditions of extensive freelance work, self-employment, individual production and promotion of artistic products, and short-term project-based contract work, this classically shared responsibility has radically tipped toward becoming the sole responsibility of the creative worker. As Menger (1999, 569) notes, 'Through short-term contractual ties, employers take no responsibility for most of the elements that constitute a career.' In contemporary career research, this figures under the rubric of career self-management (King 2004; Sturges 2008). As the term implies, career self-management entails a primary or total responsibility for career-making activities resting on the individual.

This entails knowledge of both self and environmental factors and how these combine. Knowledge about self includes understanding one's personal desires, ambitions, and goals, as well as knowledge about one's abilities and potential both in one's own estimation and the estimation of others. Thus, with regard to the latter factors, understanding of self goes beyond self-assessment, including also external assessments of one's standing and relative rank in relation to others. So, in this sense, the knowledge of self that is vital to career self-management includes identity, but it also goes beyond identity. Beyond self-knowledge in both of the previously mentioned dimensions, career self-management also requires knowledge about the terrain of the employment and occupational landscape or pertinent aspects of what Abbott (2005) calls the 'labor opportunity structure.'

Several points central to career self-management are made in the chapters in this book. Pralong et al. (Chapter 11) deal explicitly with career self-management, focusing on the mindsets, knowledge, and actual capacities to produce career-advancing behaviors. On the matter of obtaining the requisite knowledge to comprehend and function effectively within particular art worlds, they indicate that proximity and attention to key insiders is essential: 'Agents of art worlds—art galleries, critics, collectors, museums, media, audiences, etc.—play an essential role in helping artists with this awareness and defining where boundaries are; hence it is important that artists should be close to the agents.' Even when not playing the role of product intermediaries per se, such agents are both strategically placed observers with different positional vantage points and conduits of important knowledge or opinions that may be jealously guarded or freely dispensed to intimate or broad publics in truthful, partial, or distorted manners. Similarly, Eikhof et al. (Chapter 3) comment on the sources, and indirectly also the quality, of information when noting that information and advice come from the individuals whom one consults, 'rather than organizational pastoral care.'

It would be misleading to portray career self-management as exclusively a matter of knowledge, a point made in several chapters. As a practice, career self-management relies not just on knowledge but also on the capacity to produce contextually appropriate behaviors even in challenging situations. Career management entails not only broad but also intimate emotional and personal dimensions of sometimes curiously infantile situations and environments. Skov (Chapter 13), for example, writes of having to deal with personal attacks, jealousy, and mudslinging, which her informants describe as all too frequently characterizing interpersonal relations in their workplaces in the Danish fashion industry. The personal nature of much work in creative industries—investing of self, putting self on display, longing to be loved as Matthias puts it in Eikhof et al. (Chapter 13), and working through personal networks and on personal recommendations—highlights the intimate and personal nature of career management as an activity. As both work projects and the manner in which discrete projects frequently lead to repeat collaboration, career management often means relationship management—as Skov (Chapter 13), Eikhof et al. (Chapter 3), Wagner (Chapter 9), and Mathieu and Stjerne (Chapter 6) make clear. The interesting question in this regard that Jones (Chapter 7) raises in the case of Frank Lloyd Wright is how he succeeded in managing relationships in a manner that trained credit exclusively toward himself. As discussed below in the section on 'rethinking the individualization of career,' there is also evidence in some chapters that career management may still in some cases be a joint or collective endeavor.

Ultimately, career management, even with comprehensive and accurate knowledge and an ability to produce appropriate behavior, may not be sufficient to attain success. As Stoyanova and Grugulis (Chapter 4) state, 'We would like to demonstrate that, given the nature of the labor market, career development and destruction were also caused by factors over which freelancers had little control and which ran independently of their strategies.'

Temporal Issues

Temporal issues surface recurrently and in different guises in analyzing careers in creative industries. One of the most fundamental temporal questions is, when is a creative worker a creative worker? This question is bookended by the two questions: When does one become a creative worker, and when does one cease to be a creative worker? Complicating the first question is Menger's (1999, 551–52) assertion that 'many creative artists and performers produce serious work and get credits before their formal training is complete.' This blurs the generally visible and significant demarcation between student and worker. With regard to the latter question, does one first cease to be a creative worker when one no longer intends to engage in creative activity or after the final episode of practical engagement in creative work? Between these bookends are the questions arising from the fact that creative workers are seldom in continuous employment and frequently take employment in other occupations and sectors that are not generally classified as 'creative' or 'cultural.' These issues bring us back to Bille's (Chapter 2) recurrent question: Who decides? Researchers or census designers or the individuals in question? Here identity and identification play central roles—personal identity and the identification made by external assessors, subjective or objective criteria—with the temporal question remaining at what point, on the basis of either subjective or objective criteria, are persons to be included or excluded from this population?

The pace and fixed-term project nature of much production in creative industries also impacts career development. As Stoyanova and Grugulis (Chapter 4) show, when vacancies arise during television production (much the same holds for film as well), rather than turning to the external labor market, the best option is frequently the best readily available candidate (i.e., 'promoting' someone who is already on set). Even when hiring from outside of a production team, they find that compressed schedules means that an ability to 'start on Monday' becomes 'a prime qualification for the job.' Additionally, the form and pace of current TV production in the UK makes it, in their words, a 'young person's game,' premised on young mind-sets and lifestyles.

In keeping with the theme of the intertwining of personal and occupational dimensions of temporal issues, Lincoln and Allen (Chapter 5) make at least two central points with regard to evaluating film careers and consecration processes. The first is that they find it significant to differentiate career age and biological age and not conflate the two. When doing so, they find that career length prior to first nominations for men and women is almost identical in a single year comparison and, at first, second and third nominations for Oscars. This brings them to the second point—'that acting nominations are not simply based on innate talent.' Instead, this finding suggests that it 'takes time to develop acting talent and secure entry into networks that gives access to the roles that have the most chance of garnering critical acclaim.'

Using a study of three cohorts of formally educated fashion designers, Skov makes evident the obvious but frequently overlooked point that history matters. She shows how persons with the same training, background, and presence in and around the same industry can have vastly different experiences due to the period of entry into the Danish garment and fashion industry that has changed greatly over the past 30 years.

A backdrop issue for many of the studies here (particularly Wagner [Chapter 9], Skov [Chapter 13], Boutinot [Chapter 8], and Lincoln and Allen [Chapter 5]) has to do with the cyclical and seasonal nature of both work and recognition in creative industries. With regard to work and production, seasons impact everything from advertising campaigns to release periods for creative products and events, annual cycles impact genre productions from fall fashion collections to summer novels and movies, to back-to-school advertising campaigns, to New Years concerts, and so on, which can create feast and famine conditions for both specialized individual creative workers and organizations. Likewise the annual nature of events such as festivals, awards, and prizes have the potential and often actual effect of reconfiguring if not fields then at least certain hierarchies and patterns of production and consumption within fields on a regular basis.

Locational Issues

Location can be interpreted in terms of both geographic and social place-ment. Both understandings are employed in the chapters in this book. One prominent geographic locational issue in some of the chapters has to do with the industrial restructuring that takes place in given locations or jurisdictions at particular times. Although ostensibly 'local' in this sense, restructuring frequently reacts to wider, even global, political, and eco-nomic factors, as both pressures and opportunities. Such restructurings are prominent backdrops to the chapters written by Stoyanova and Grugulis (Chapter 4) and Skov (Chapter 13). Stoyanova and Grugulis argue that the labor market in the UK television industry has been radically trans-formed by a reconfiguration of the sector from in-house production at large hierarchical and vertically integrated terrestrial broadcasters to outsourced production from a myriad of independent production companies of various sizes. This fragmentation brought with it a vast reduction in staff positions, a vast rise in freelance work, as well as a talent drain to major hubs such as London, having detrimental effects on regional production environments.

Skov also sets her findings in terms of the restructuring of the Danish fashion and apparel industry. The first of Skov's cohorts entered an industry that was in crisis and decline but in which all phases of garment production took place in Denmark. As the process of deindustrialization, outsourcing, and off-shoring continued, the employment prospects for trained designers altered radically. As Skov argues,

'Paradoxically, we find that although Danish fashion is now acknowl-edged to have sustained growth during deindustrialization, it is actu-ally harder for fashion designers to launch their careers now than it was 20 years ago when the industry was considered to be in a crisis. The total dependence on outsourcing that characterizes the Danish fashion sector today has brought with it an extensive industrial restructuring

that has also reconfigured the role of fashion designers. Their supporting role in manufacturing has been replaced by a focus on collection
development at an ever-increasing pace.'

Eikhof et al. (Chapter 3) underscore both the importance of location
for visibility, as well as the demand for physical mobility on German theatre actors. On the first issue, they find an increased polarization between
'cultural metropolises and provincial areas,' with the latter falling further
behind the former with regard to visibility and career and pay prospects.
As careers for most actors is comprised of freelance work on a project-by-
project basis or short one- to two-year contracts at best, geographic mobility is also a necessity for having a career in German theatre. This leads to
nomadic lives for those bent on a career in theatre, and a lifestyle follows
accordingly, characterized by an unwillingness to put down roots—personal, social, material, and financial—in any given place.

Physical mobility is also a central feature in Wagner's chapter (Chapter 9),
where ambitious violin students often move internationally to take instruction from eminent teachers, following them to international competitions and
even following them on holiday so as not to miss lessons. As Wagner argues,
while mobility is common and central, ideas and conceptions about place of
origin and associated characteristics and demands play decisive roles in career
opportunities and development. This leads her to formulate the significance
of 'transnationalism' for violin virtuosos who 'construct their careers in several countries,' as this construction is premised on and continuously informed
by traces of national and ethnic origin, as well as social placement.

With regard to the social conception of location, as organizational placement becomes less relevant, other forms of placement rise in significance—
network or field placement. Following up on this dimension of Wagner's
study, both the social placement of violin students and masters are mutually intertwined, with students initially being placed based on their collaboration with famous masters, whereas the placement of masters is in part
impacted by the subsequent fates of their former students. Social placement
and national origin are also intertwined, with regard to 'fear of Russian
passports' expressed by participants at international youth violin competitions and the rise and fall of fads such as 'the Russian prodigy,' which can
elevate or sink the career prospects of talented violinists with the right or
wrong ethnic or national origins.

Social placement is a major theme in the Pralong et al. chapter (Chapter 11), focusing on both peripheral geographic and social location for the
'unsuccessful' artists studied. Their 'outsider' position is investigated not just
socially but also in terms of the cognitive structures that can arise and cement
this standing. Other studies take their point of departure at the other end
of the social locational spectrum. Jones (Chapter 7) examines the network
work of one of the most successful architects of the past century, Frank Lloyd
Wright. Boutinot (Chapter 8) examines the attainment of social recognition

and standing among elite French architects and the process of reputation building among different audiences. Lincoln and Allen (Chapter 5) also look at career developments among elite actors in French and American film, as well as their focal interest in the operation of the 'consecration processes' on which elite social placement frequently relies. Mathieu and Stjerne (Chapter 6) also use a sample of elite Danish filmworkers to explore how they both exploit and can be captive to success and elite standing. They find that these elite filmworkers do not just elect to work on high-prestige, high external rewards projects but use their social standing and cultivated reputation to engage in work on smaller, less prestigious projects of interest to them, sometimes even on a voluntary basis, also with a strategic intent to counterbalance the detrimental effects of stamps of exclusivity. Because social placement impacts and is impacted by many of the factors discussed next, I defer further comment to the following discussions.

Vertical Mobility

Vertical or hierarchical mobility can be seen to be associated with some of the locational issues discussed earlir but is of sufficient interest that it should not be buried under a wider heading. Despite the decline of strictly organizational careers, and hence organizational hierarchies, creative industries are filled with hierarchies and gradations of both formal and informal characters. Hierarchical mobility can be seen in terms of objective positions, such as moving from being a staff architect to a partner, a camera operator to director of photography, a supporting to a lead actor, playing principal versus second chair in an orchestra, or in terms of ascribed status—such as moving from 'B-list' to 'A-list' status. Thus, hierarchical mobility needs to be seen in terms of the various arenas in which it can take place, as well as the possible declining salience of hierarchic gradations in some contexts and for some individuals as a result of less rigid, visible, and immediately consequential hierarchies. That is, some hierarchies may be becoming more ambiguous and have a looser rather than a tighter structuring effect (i.e., those associated with formal titles), whereas other more 'subjectively' sustained hierarchies may be increasing in salience.

Combining hierarchical mobility with the temporal dimension, mobility opportunities in creative industries can be periodized in radically different manners. The common project-oriented view of work in creative industries leads to the impression of regularly occurring openings and opportunities of comparable quality. However, as Faulkner (1973) notes with regard to symphony orchestra musicians, there are also once in a lifetime openings, as well as 'schedules' of career progression rates indicating at which ages various positions should be attained in order to continue on an elite career path or reconcile with a lower level career. Similarly, Lincoln and Allen (Chapter 5) explore progression rates in terms of first and subsequent nominations for César and Academy Awards. As mentioned earlier with regard to temporality and later with regard to recognition processes, the annual nature of awards and prizes impacts vertical mobility by regularly opening up the reorganization of field-level rankings based on the outcomes of such processes. In most creative industries, reaching the top or even the next level does not ensure enduring standing but merely temporary occupation of a given position. Stoyanova and Grugulis (Chapter 4) highlight this in terms of both failure and downward mobility associated with tournament career structures.

Skov (Chapter 13) argues that much of the horizontal mobility she finds in her sample is a result of blocked vertical mobility within companies. While not the only motivation behind job-hopping—horizontal mobility is also a way of attaining employment security in a volatile industry as well as a means of obtaining professional challenge—an industry structure with small companies often run by owner-proprietors, exacerbated by an orientation toward novelty and innovation, and 'poor interpersonal relations' or bad organizational management leads to restricted vertical mobility and ultimately to other forms of mobility.

Whereas much of the literature on vertical mobility in project-based and creative industry research focuses on processes of moving up 'between projects' (Ebbers and Wijnberg 2009; O'Mahoney and Bechky 2006), Stoyanova and Grugulis (Chapter 4) find that vertical mobility frequently occurs within as well as between projects, especially for more junior positions. Much of this type of mobility has to do with 'being at the right place at the right time'—that is to say, being on set or part of the production when illness or other causes lead to spontaneous vacancies. As noted earlier, the pace of production leads to the necessity of filling positions quickly and with proven or known staff, leading frequently to 'internal promotions.' Another form of pseudo-vertical mobility they note that can have career building implications is 'title inflation,' a process whereby a worker is given or credited with a higher title than the work actually carried out, sometimes as a means of compensating for meager financial compensation. As this process becomes more common, however, and the mechanisms for title standardization break down with industry fragmentation, this practice leads to 'title skepticism' within the industry, further increasing uncertainty in the industry.

In contrast with the relatively dynamic vertical mobility processes discussed earlier, Dowd and Kelly (Chapter 10) remind us that some powerful stratification processes take and endure over long periods of time but are not entirely static. Finally, and in line with what we explore regarding uncertainty, sometimes it isn't clear what the next level is. Sometimes its a matter of collecting multiple accolades—nominations or prizes, as Lincoln and Allen (Chapter 5) discuss, that leads to consecration, or the canonization that Dowd and Kelly discuss, or what might be called 'coronation' as 'the greatest living architect' that Frank Lloyd Wright was elevated to by many commentators according to Jones (Chapter 7).

Recognition Processes

Recognition and its more extended and durable form—reputation—are central to work in creative industries for both subjective and objective purposes. This is why so many of the chapters in this volume treat recognition processes in one way or another. Two primary orientations are found here. One focuses on how recognition processes function and the other on what effects they have. These are often explored simultaneously. Recognition processes can be seen on a continuum from the intimate and fleeting to the grandest dimension—from spontaneous comments during work processes (Bechky 2006) to things like the Nobel Prize in literature, which is given in global competition, across literary genres, for lifetime production of a *corpus* of work.

Boutinot (Chapter 8) and Lincoln and Allen (Chapter 5) examine the structural dimensions of formal recognition processes. Boutinot argues that the elite recognition, or consecration, to use Lincoln and Allen's term, entailed in receiving the *Grand Prix National d'Architecture* (GPNA), the highest French architectural prize, is the result of successful and similar patterns of sequentially building reputation in specific audiences or publics that in turn establish one's reputation in subsequent audiences. Boutinot argues that these publics apply different but not contradictory criteria in evaluating architectural merit. Lincoln and Allen compare two national recognition or consecration processes and find both similarities and differences in the operation and effects of these processes within the French and American film industries. One similarity that Lincoln and Allen find is that in both cases it takes roughly the same amount of time in terms of career age to garner a first nomination, indicating that it takes time to develop one's artistic ability and gain both significant roles that accord one the opportunity to display one's capacity and obtain the attention of electors.

Jones (Chapter 7) also focuses explicitly on recognition processes. She takes issue with the previous tendency to conflate or at least assume that collaborative networks are more or less synonymous with promotional networks. That is to say, those who one works with are those who build and promote one's reputation and promote one's work and employment opportunities. Jones shows that this isn't necessarily the case—that separate and specialized networks can exist for particular purposes and look radically different.

At the more intimate end of the continuum, Mathieu and Stjerne (Chapter 6) discuss the tremendous significance of the mutual recognition between artistic collaboration partners that fosters and sustains trust, a constructively critical context, and respect. This has significance both for their mutual objective career progression as it intimately impacts the creative process, as well as for their subjective satisfaction and experience of their work and collaboration, and thereby also their disposition toward further collaboration.

Beyond individual recognition, Ooi (Chapter 12) takes up the centrality of recognition of spheres or classes of creative production and creative producers. This, he argues, is embedded in the educational system, as well as the pronouncements and activities of the state and its agencies, and it has tremendous implications for the opportunities of Singaporean visual artists to both domestically market their products and enjoy social esteem.

Competition

In the absence of succession processes such as senority for moving from one position or level to the next, as was a feature of 'orderly' or organizational careers, almost all mobility for creative workers is premised on competition, frequently intense competition. The most extreme formulation of this is the concept employed by Stoyanova and Grugulis (Chapter 4) of tournament careers. The tournament concept implies that gaining work is a continuous competitive process, with winners and losers, and that winning is not a permanent state but usually merely allows one to work on a single, temporally restricted project and then compete again at the same or possibly a higher level. A particularly insidious aspect of competition in creative industries is that the rules of competition or decision-making processes are not always transparent, nor are decisions usually justified or explained. As discussed previously, this compounds uncertainty and can lead to ascriptions of arbitrariness and chance, even if this is not in fact the case.

Complicating matters further, as Stoyanova and Grugulis (Chapter 4), among others, point out, different genres or realms of the same field or industry can have different competitive or tournament rules. This is a common point; both the rules and levels of competition in creative industries are not 'natural' but rather institutionally set and dynamic. Skov (Chapter 13) shows how both levels of competition among designers and what types of jobs they can compete for in Denmark radically alters over the 30-year span of her cohort analysis in concert with the industrial restructuring that the Danish fashion and garment industry has gone through under the impact of economic globalization. Stoyanova and Grugulis show how the fragmentation of the British television industry as a result of political directives creates a situation of perennial external competition, where competition was previously concentrated to the ports of entry (Osterman and Burton 2005) of large producer-broadcasters such as the BBC. Previously, those who succeeded in gaining entry to such organizations could then pursue Wilenskian (1961) 'orderly careers' with skill and organizational and industry knowledge acquisition and career progression proceeding in a rather coherent package. These political directives created the current situation of competition around every corner, with increased interfirm competition between production companies competing for contracts from commissioning bodies, and creative workers competing with each other for work on temporally limited projects. This, a consequence of a new form and level of competition, they argue, squeezes out not just the predictability of career progression but also the requisite stability for skill and knowledge acquisition, as the discontinuous nature of work and the tournament process of work acquisition means that less time is actually spent in and on work and thus acquiring on-the-job training and skill development. In such situations, job acquisition skills are honed and required to the detriment of developing occupational skills.

As argued by Menger (1999) and explored in this volume by Ooi (Chapter 12), Pralong et al. (Chapter 11), Dowd and Kelly (Chapter 10), Skov (Chapter 13), and Eikhof et al. (Chapter 3), what impacts levels of competition is both the 'oversupply' of artists, as well as the underdimensioned demand or markets, and there are multiple contributory factors to both.[3] These range from market economic factors to public policy factors, ranging from education policy, to arts, culture, industry, and employment policy, to taxation policy that impacts the commercial and noncommercial dimensions of creative industries in various manners. The extreme competition that can result from the interplay of oversupply of labor and underdimensioned markets, especially at particular levels in creative industries, makes it ripe for exploitative practices, which have received increasing attention both in terms of 'self-exploitation' and organizational exploitation. In this volume, Skov deals tellingly with unhealthful and degrading working conditions where owner-managers remind employees of the myriad of hopefuls outside the door ready to take the jobs of current employees. This leads employees to accept conditions of long hours and no overtime pay and to 'cry into the computer because of stress and pressure.'

As mentioned, a central dimension of competition is failure, which Stoyanova and Grugulis (Chapter 4) and Pralong et al. (Chapter 11) investigate. Success receives most of our attention because it is what we strive for, and the successful are the attractive, rapidly identifiable role models. We look at them and trace their paths and actions to see what should be emulated. But success and failure are inextricably linked, and if they are only differentiated or decided by chance or serendipity, we probably should spend more time paying attention to both lots in order to truly see what in fact differentiates them in competitive processes with regard to more than just outcome. In creative industries research, we have conceptions that steer our attention toward the 'winners' in terms of talent, hard work, and persistence, but the frequency with which one hears the term 'lucky break' or the like indicates that the margins of difference and what tips in one direction rather than the other might be both small and arbitrary. Ultimately, to truly understand competitive processes, we should pay significant and simultaneous regard to both winners and losers, rather than to just one or the other as we tend to do for a variety of reasons.

Even in the hyper-competitive environments that creative industries tend to be, there are exceptions to the general rule of competition. Mathieu and Stjerne (Chapter 6) indicate that established relationships not only set open competition out of play when recruiting for key roles in film projects but also suggest that there is good reason to rethink, at least in certain cases, the general expectation of competitive external hiring practices in project-based production, even where freelance personnel are involved. Thus, competition should not be a presupposition associated with given production forms, but the qualitative nature of the relational infrastructure needs to be brought into the equation. In Pralong et al. (Chapter 11) and other studies, we see examples of artistic production based on non-competitively acquired resources, products that may filter into the markets of various creative industries. This can range from no and low budget, self-financed or student films to 'hobby' or intended commercial products that are financed outside the commercial realm of creative industries via unemployment benefits, social security, other jobs, or spousal income. Even where this is found, most of those producing in this manner seek to produce on and for the labor or art markets and earn an income or a living from their artistic or creative activities.

Boutinot (Chapter 8) makes the important point that competition among the architects she studies is reliant on collegial reputation, as colleagues are those who recommend architects to competitions and selection committees. Thus, competition is premised on a form of mediated peer selection. A similar point can be made about the Academy Awards, although members of the Academy span several occupational categories and are thus not strictly peer-competitors.

Finally, as Dowd and Kelly (Chapter 10) argue, competition is not just a fight among the living and active but also against the dead. In the realm of classical music, the dead continue to beat the daylights out of the living because, as they argue with reference to Burkholder (2006, 410), 'It is a contest in which the reigning champions have an overwhelming advantage, for the orchestral repertoire is very crowded and the classics have enormous prestige'

Uncertainty: Insecurity and Freedom

A central and well-acknowledged feature of work in creative industries is uncertainty. This is due to the largely discontinuous nature of much work in creative industries. Uncertainty has several sources—competition, as named earlier, economic fluctuations, the collective nature of many production processes, the opacity of many judgment and decision-making processes, as well as things such as political decisions. The capricious antagonists producing or contributing to uncertainty can be all from consumers to employers to critics and prize juries to politicians to competitors. Uncertainty is thus a multi-source and perennial condition and consideration. As Menger (1999, 560) notes, 'Uncertainty plays a major role not only during the early part of a career but throughout the whole span of the professional lifetime.' As both condition and consideration we revisit here the objective–subjective issue. As a condition, the origins and some of the outcomes of uncertainty can be analyzed. However, conditions do not give us thoughts and feelings in an unmediated way, leaving an openness for interpretation, which may depend on psychic disposition or social position. This opens the possibility for uncertainty to be subjectively felt and considered in even diametrically opposed manners.

In the following chapters we see examples where the uncertainty of freelance work is the preferred or ultimate career dream and where a more stable, embedded form of employment is either a mark of failure or settling for a second-best option. Wagner's (Chapter 9) violin virtuosos are quite clear in their aspirations for a career as transnational guest concert violinists and consider having to take a permanent job in even a leading symphony orchestra as failure: 'In this world, the elite path means intensive mobility and a permanent position in the musical ensemble is perceived as failure.' The theatre actors in Eikhof et al. (Chapter 3) also rate the leading role freelance guest player as the preferred career trajectory, although their informants are more reconciled with the idea of a career as a member of a preferably elite theatre ensemble. These are contexts where both totally freelance and more stable employment arrangements are available for individuals in the same occupations, where uncertainty at the high end is preferred due to its association with choice—of roles, pieces to be played, and so on; of context; of collaboration partners; and of time—and material, social, and intrinsic rewards. A more stable employment situation may be the result of a failure to attain elite status or actively choosing to accommodate other aspects of one's personal or professional life (see also Faulkner 1973).

In other contexts, there is not a choice between freelance and stable work for particular occupational categories. For the film editors and cinematographers included in Mathieu and Stjerne (Chapter 6), freelance work is the only option, a basic condition that is subjectively reacted to in a variety of different manners even by the same person, from appreciation of the freedom to choose to the continuous concern about when the next project will come along and with whom. Sometimes, as in the case of Martin found in Skov's chapter (Chapter 13), insecurity about future work as a designer, resulting in worry about financial uncertainty, is interpreted as a *personal weakness* and ultimately leads to choosing a more stable career path outside of the fashion industry per se. Such 'choices' are also found among a number of the artists in Ooi's (Chapter 12) study. Pralong et al. (Chapter 11) reiterate the subjective dimension of uncertainty as a potentially crippling poly-dimensional cognitive frame, comprising concern with not just income and career matters but also artistic production and creation opportunities and ability.

This perennial subjective existential uncertainty surfaces clearly even among those enjoying a relatively extended period of employment. Again, the words of Matthias from the Eikhof et al. chapter (Chapter 3) display this fear: 'You are always afraid that you will be cast for too few or too small roles—you are always afraid that theatre management and audience will not love you enough.' Although currently enjoying a relatively high degree of employment stability (on a one- or two-year contract), he knows he will soon be facing the open market but also that there is the internal competition that Faulkner (1973) also found among orchestral musicians. While it doesn't go away, uncertainty may lessen in periods due to attained status and oscillate in character between two basic dimensions: the temporal dimension of 'when' something expected will come about, and a more fundamental form of uncertainty revolving around whether something will materialize or transpire, at lest in its expected form—'if' it will happen or not. As Menger (1999) argues, there is uncertainty right up to the end of careers in creative industries and often uncertainty about the end of one's career. As Bille (Chapter 2) shows, many careers in creative industries are short-lived, and much uncertainty revolves not just around when a career will end but also how—voluntarily, involuntarily, or, as we often hear, quasi-voluntarily as a deliberate withdrawal from an occupation or industry due to no longer being able or willing to cope with the conditions of work, of which a primary factor is uncertainty itself.

Another important aspect of uncertainty and insecurity on the part of employers, theatre directors, film producers, and those who can choose their collaborators is that it tends to lead to conservatism (i.e., choices are based on previous experience and using the known vs. taking a chance on the unknown). We see this in the homophilious choices made by the violin masters in Wagner's chapter (Chapter 9), where assumptions about ethnic origin and work ethics guide collaborator selection; the decision making in German theatre discussed by Eikhof et al. (Chapter 3); in Mathieu and Stjerne's (Chapter 6) cinematic collaboration constellations; throughout Stoyanova and Grugulis' chapter (Chapter 4); and arguably most evident in Dowd and Kelly's chapter (Chapter 10) on canon in classical music repertoires.

Gender

Creative workers, it should be remembered, are not abstract entities but are embodied like all humans, and a central dimension of our embodiment is gender (Wainwright and Turner 2006). Again, this has both subjective and objective implications, and career experiences and outcomes are frequently impacted by gender. On the objective side, Eikhof et al. (Chapter 3) display how gender impacts everything from admission to the most coveted drama schools in Germany, to how a long list of decisions affecting males, but most often females, are made by anticipating wants and demands further down the production chain, leading to an ever narrowing gender stereotyping. They also display how gendered opportunities lie in the repertoire material, the 'literary material that forms the basis of theatrical production,' in terms of the number and types of roles available to men versus women, older versus younger, and on down to physical appearance factors.

In general, the combination of these factors from theatre school to roles in the plays that frequently get performed leads to higher competition among women for roles. Lincoln and Allen (Chapter 5) also explicitly investigate gender in their samples of elite film actors in France and the US and find similarly that even among the most consecrated (i.e., those actors with the most prestige and status), men get far more film roles. The degree of this also varies from industry to industry, with much more pronounced gender difference in the US than in France.

The monitoring and evaluation of the private life choices of women are also displayed in the chapters, as well as the ways in which industry work conditions impact private lives. Eikhof et al. (Chapter 3) find skepticism toward female (but not male) actors with children, not due to artistic evaluations, but rather imputed assumptions about levels of commitment to their work and profession. Skov (Chapter 13) reports pressures on female designers to wear the company's products rather than being able to express her own clothing style. Stoyanova and Grugulis (Chapter 4) find that women often dropped out earlier, in their 30s, than male counterparts from the British TV industry. They are often faced with a choice between having children or continuing their TV career because the erratically long hours of freelance work is difficult to combine with most forms of childcare, for which women culturally are still held primarily responsible. On the previously mentioned issue of insecurity, they find that both men and women leave the British TV industry due to employment and income instability.

Gender segregation of occupations and status levels in creative industries can also be seen in some of the sample populations of the studies. For example, we see a mix of male and female film editors in Mathieu and Stjerne's (Chapter 6) sample and the absence of female cinematographers, which are global norms. There is a crack in the male-dominated façade of classical music composers, at least among the living in Dowd and Kelly's (Chapter 10) population, and Bille's (Chapter 2) data also give clear indications of gender segregated and mixed occupations and industries in Denmark.

Chance, Randomness, Arbitrariness, Serendipity

Like uncertainty, chance, randomness, arbitrariness, serendipity, and so on are conditions and considerations or ascriptions. As a condition, arbitrariness in terms of the sovereignty and legitimacy of the choices of consumers and key decision makers is part of the terrain of creative industries. This is exemplified in the Eikhof et al. (Chapter 3) discussion of the unquestionability of 'artistic reasons' as an ultimate and unassailable justification for selections made by positioned authorities in German theatre. As Stoyanova and Grugulis (Chapter 4) point out, chance, randomness and arbitrariness, while always a matter of uncertainty, can work to either one's advantage or disadvantage, spurring both optimism and pessimism as resulting considerations. As a consideration, belief in chance, randomness, arbitrariness,

serendipity, and so on appears to a certain extent to be a function of settings where one does not know on a reasonably secure basis what the criteria of evaluation in force are and what one's own skill level and that of others are. Likewise, the impression of arbitrariness increases as standards and allocation transparency are inadequate to validate outcomes. In such settings, actors may over- or under-estimate their skills, capabilities, and attractiveness according to whether they tend to win or lose.

Another central finding in many of the chapters is that chance, randomness, arbitrariness, serendipity, and so on are not entirely random but appear stratified. Contrasting the chapters by Boutinot (Chapter 8) and Stoyanova and Grugulis (Chapter 4), one finds more randomness at lower or entry levels of the occupational and prestige hierarchies. This may seem innocuous and inconsequential, but if this is, as Stoyanova and Grugulis argue, what makes it possible to compete in further tournaments, this may be excising talented individuals from the outset on inappropriate grounds. In contrast, Boutinot argues that there are strong similarities in the trajectories of the elite architects in her sample, leading to the impression that the higher one gets in 'consecration' processes, the less chance and arbitrariness appear to be at play. Whether this is primarily a condition or an ascribed factor is ambiguous. It may be the case that decisions at higher levels are more deliberate, cautious, and judicious, marginalizing chance, arbitrariness, and randomness as more is at stake than at lower levels. Or it may also be the case that either the criteria for selection and decision making are clearer and consistent over cases, or more detailed justifications are offered couched in legitimate and legitimating terms, mitigating the impression and ascription of arbitrariness and chance to such decisions.

Chance and randomness also appear less arbitrary the deeper one looks into the contextual situation of those who just 'happened to be in the right place at the right time.' In the chapters by Stoyanova and Grugulis (Chapter 4), Mathieu and Stjerne (Chapter 6), and Skov (Chapter 13), for example, the amount of work in positioning oneself to be in a selectable position can be great. In other words, serendipity is seldom truly random but tends to fall on people in well-positioned pools. Ultimately, however, one can place oneself as best as one can and attempt to foresee what the selectors want, but you can't be sure that this will suffice. As Stoyanova and Grugulis conclude, 'For many in the [TV] industry, successes were as much a product of good luck as good judgment and it was the interplay of the random and serendipitous events with freelancers' conscious efforts and strategies that shaped careers.' Many creative workers are continuously at the mercy of fateful decisions couched in unassailable 'artistic reasons' or 'consumer preferences.'

Education to Work in Creative Industries

Another recurrent theme in the book is the connection between formal education and work and careers in creative industries. The most prominent issue is the frequent lack of occupational or professional socialization as part of the formal training of students in creative or artistic educational programs. Bille (Chapter 2) shows the consequences of this disjuncture statistically with regard to unemployment among those with 'creative educations' as compared with others with educational backgrounds of comparable duration, and the presence, or more strikingly relative absence, of persons with creative educations both in creative industries and jobs with creative job content. In the chapters by Ooi (Chapter 12), Pralong et al. (Chapter 11), and Skov (Chapter 13), all of which focus on persons with formal arts or design training, a recurrent complaint is the lack of preparation they received during their educations for entering into and meeting the challenges of their work and art worlds. Skov deals extensively with this issue of being unprepared for the transition and the 'shock' that all three cohort generations experienced but in different manners. These exposed deficiencies of formal creative and artistic education programs stand in stark contrast to the deep and poly-contextual professional socialization that accompanies the content training found in the education process of violin virtuosos in Wagner's chapter (Chapter 9). In addition to the issues of content training and socialization, Wagner, Mathieu and Stjerne (Chapter 6), and Eikhof et al. (Chapter 3) all touch on the significance of how elite education programs actively or passive promote their students in the industry by staging events attracting industry attention where student productions are spotlighted or actively work to place their students in high visibility projects, competitions, and contexts and the way this facilitates entry for students from certain institutions into the industry over others. Likewise, Wagner implies that elite violin students take 'master classes' with teachers other than their own for content reasons but also because many of those who teach such classes sit on selection committees and juries at major international competitions.

Formal education systems also play wider roles impacting the career opportunities for artists and creative workers by developing or suppressing markets and appreciation for certain creative products and occupations. Ooi (Chapter 12) displays how the general educational system in Singapore stratifies occupations, leading to discouraging potentially talented artists from pursuing artistic careers, low social status for artists, and a generally less appreciative environment and market for especially contemporary Singaporean-produced art. As Ooi concludes, 'The streaming processes in the Singaporean education system perpetuate a low status for artists in Singapore and, by association, a low regard for art in general.' Again, this impacts not only the production of artists but also their work and life conditions—their market opportunities for selling their work to a local audience appreciative of their work and wider social prestige. On the same theme, Dowd and Kelly (Chapter 10) also note that a 'large population with highly educated individuals' is almost a prerequisite for a consumption base for especially sophisticated creative, artistic, or cultural production. Thus, education in general, and not just arts education programs in particular, is of central importance for the careers of creative workers.

Mediators

Mediation can be carried out by humans, objects, and print or electronic images and texts. Mediators can play several different roles, from market creation, to intervening between or connecting employers and employees or buyers and sellers, to introducing and counseling novices in entering elite environments. They can range from holding specialist remunerated positions such as an agent, to a voluntary promotional role played for example by fans, to art collectors who may engage in promotional activities for ideal or identity reasons or to increase the value of works that they possess. It may require specialist environmental and social knowledge and skills or merely knowledge or opinions about the individual or group promoted.

In Wagner's chapter (Chapter 9), we see violin masters playing several mediation roles from content training to elite behavioral socialization, as well as introducing their students to and coaching them through elite competitive environments. As Wagner also makes clear, the fusion of the names and reputations of the teacher and student plays a significant passive mediation role in the environment she studies. Likewise, when a former student attains success and recognition as a violin virtuoso, his or her association with a given teacher plays an important mediating role between the teacher and potential students. As Wagner writes figuratively, 'These protégés are "business cards" ' for their teachers.

Pralong et al. (Chapter 11) discuss the question of the absence or inability of unsuccessful artists to access intermediaries. In their sample, there is an expressed desire for contact with intermediaries possessing the knowledge or social contacts that the artists recognize they lack, and the interesting issue here is what blocks or inhibits contact with potentially helpful intermediaries.

Dowd and Kelly (Chapter 10) and Eikhof et al. (Chapter 3) in different ways examine how 'canon' is used in mediation. Dowd and Kelly argue that, ' "Canon" refers to ongoing explanations by important intermediaries about what constitutes great art. In offering such explanations—which are evolving, if not contested—these intermediaries often emphasize a select number of creators from an earlier era, showing how such individuals have both stood the test of time and have fundamentally shaped their art's historical development.' Eikhof et al. also emphasize the role of authoritative ideas in programming choices, arguing in turn that the plays that regularly get selected for performance have profound structuring impacts on the labor market for theatre actors in Germany.

Dowd and Kelly also note collective efforts on the part of composers and proponents of contemporary classical music to create promotional organizations and activities for composers in the form of organizations, festivals, and publishing periodicals to increase visibility, legitimacy, and a market in order to generate interest and demand for their output. Interestingly, as Lincoln and Allen (Chapter 5) point out, it is as such an endeavor that the Academy Awards started out. The Academy Awards now consecrates a select number of its members for not only the industry community but also the general populace. Jones (Chapter 7) also deals explicitly with the role of intermediaries in the career of Frank Lloyd Wright—in human terms with regard to his promotional network but also in material terms with regard to her emphasis on the significance of his buildings and images (pictures and drawings) found in the writings by and about Lloyd Wright for promotional purposes.

Rethinking the 'Individualization' of Career

One of the primary objectives of this book is to unearth and analyze divergent tendencies, even when they occur within the same phenomenon. While we have hitherto primarily noted the individualization of career-making in creative industries, highlighting individual competition for jobs and vertical mobility and the centrality of career self-management, evidence in the studies collected here lead us to question whether this is an unequivocal trend in all respects. It may also be instructive to divide career responsibility into moral and practical realms. In the moral realm, there does seem to be an acceptance of increased or sole ultimate individual responsibility for career-making. At the practical level, however, responsibility, and especially the ability to govern career development, appears more complicated.

At the field level, Eikhof et al. (Chapter 3) examine German theatre as an 'employment system' that places strong and powerful demands and constraints on individual agency. They argue that, 'While careers are the individual actor's responsibility, the structures of the employment system leave little scope for shaping them in a genuinely individual, personal way.' Even in the theoretically conducive setting of German theatre, truly individualized, or 'customized' careers (Valcour et al. 2007) are difficult to produce due to innumerable systemic forces. Here we see a clear disjuncture between moral responsibility and practical ability to fashion individualized careers. How this disjuncture between 'ought' and 'can' plays out is not just an issue for those involved in German theatre but creative industries in general. Similar tensions come to expression in Stoyanova and Grugulis' chapter (Chapter 4), as well as the psychological dimensions of this conflict in Skov's chapter (Chapter 13). Also at the field level, other studies of creative industries indicate that as organizations shed responsibility, ability, and authority, these are picked up by other collective actors or mechanisms, such as 'latent organization' (Ebbers and Wijnberg 2009; Starkey et al. 2000) or the 'semi-permanent work groups' identified by Blair et al. (2003).

There are also strong indications that practical responsibility for career making is shared at the interpersonal level in two chapters in this book.

This point is in line with the nascent acknowledgment and exploration of social constellations and units between the individual and organization, or individual and network, as exemplified in the work of Alvarez and Svejenova (2005). The concept of career coupling explored by Wagner (Chapter 9) and Mathieu and Stjerne (Chapter 6) shows that mutual interest but also a strong dimension of mutual identification binds actors together in extended periods of collective career development. Interestingly, these two chapters find career coupling processes in different types of constellations. Wagner finds it in master–student relationships, whereas Mathieu and Stjerne find it in elite collegial relationships. Both Wagner's and Mathieu and Stjerne's chapters indicate the significance of career coupling and collaborative career-making for the objective as well as the subjective dimensions of work and career. While in accord with the idea that careers can only be experienced individually, it should also be conceded that frequently what one experiences, both objectively and subjectively, depends on how one's collaborators act, think, and feel.

Jones (Chapter 7) runs partially countercurrent to these arguments in showing how luminary status can be created by resisting or denying collaborative attachments while still dependent on enlisting others in one's promotional network and activities.

But perhaps there is one sense in which work and careers are undeniably individualized. As Barley (1989) writes, careers can only be experienced individually but are not solely of an individual's making. The experience of career can have to do with everything from the elation and fulfillment of individually receiving accolades, such as Césars, Academy Awards, or the *GPNA* for accomplishments that are, as we have seen, in significant respects collective products influenced by structural circumstances (Rossman et al. 2010), to having to personally bear the brunt of and pay the costs for work conditions far beyond the capacities of individuals to remediate or modify them. We hear this echoed at the end of a long theatre career on the theme of loneliness and abandonment by the industry that one has invested in self- and social engagement rather than family and friends in Eikhof et al. (Chapter 3) and in the words of the burnt-out fashion designers in Skov's chapter (Chapter 13). Again, the sweet and sour of careers can only be individually experienced, but the objective structural conditions pervasive in specific industries seem to mass produce particular subjective experiences.

OMISSIONS BIG AND SMALL

The limited scope of this single volume and the choice of presenting focused empirical studies, as opposed to review essays or theoretical critiques or syntheses in such a vast field lead to strengths but also weaknesses. Under such circumstances, the studies presented here can inevitably only be partial contributions to wider debates, investigations, and theory building.

There are several significant dimensions of careers in creative industries that are only cursorily or not covered at all. One of the most significant career-impacting factors that is not treated by the selections here has to do with how economic fluctuations increase or decrease demand for creative works and thereby also workers. Partially linked to this, but also to issues of technological change, is the issue of which occupations are expanding or contracting and why. The issue of the terms and conditions under which creative work is carried out is touched on in several of the studies, but there is no comparative or historical mapping of such developments. Gender, life-course matters, and the impact of cultural or creative industries policies on careers surface intermittently but naturally also merit more concerted attention.

Neither does the vast issue of occupational selection, revision, and especially departure from creative work and careers receive extended attention. Focus in this volume lies rather on making it and persistence in creative work, although as Bille (Chapter 2) shows this is far from the predominant process despite intentions to the contrary. Focus in such studies would be on voluntary and involuntary disengagement with creative work and careers and the reasons for both. Many careers in creative industries are sustained by various 'straddling processes,' whereby work (or other forms of financial support) in several different sectors or even occupations under different contractual forms are used to patch together a career. Many levels and patterns of 'disorderliness' of careers are found among creative workers and merit focused exploration. However, one point that the chapters in this volume implicitly demonstrate is the frequency with which creative workers insist on and persist in pursuing progressive single occupation careers. In other words, the boundaryless, disorderly career is a pattern seen, but apparently in most cases it is an involuntary outcome of an inability to attain primary career ambitions. The overall impression from the selections presented in this volume is a predominant preference for occupational expansion into different genres and experimentation from an occupationally anchored position, rather than voluntary transversing occupations and sectors. What this volume cumulatively affords is an opportunity to ascertain what is voluntary and involuntary, what is experienced as opportunity and beneficial versus what is experienced as constraining and harmful across creative industries, at both the individual and systemic or industrial levels.

USING THE BOOK AS A PRACTICAL GUIDE

Although this book is not written manifestly nor intended to be a practical guide or manual in 'how to navigate the sometimes turbulent, oft unknown waters of work and career in creative industries,' the empirical nature of the chapters in this book afford possibilities for interpreting findings as advice. Lurking between the lines in many of the contributions are statements addressing the issue of what may well be partial determinants of success and failure.

The most basic and prominent piece of 'advice' is to attempt to understand at least the proximate areas of the industry or art world in which one intends to participate. Here the concepts, theories, and empirical methods used in this book can supply inspiration about what to look for, where to look, as well as practical tools for systematically approaching these activities. Part and parcel to this is attention to the specificity of given contexts. Contexts are unique (locational issues) and can change rapidly (temporal issues), which means that assessments need to be made locally and updated.

In settings where older structures are breaking or have broken down, attempt to identify the new emerging integration mechanisms or navigational tools (especially those used by employers). They are there. They may be nascent and difficult to identify, but they should be apparent to those who use them and possibly also to those who they are used on or impacted by them. They may be difficult to articulate, and the primary and ultimately successful ones might be hard to pick out in the crowd of pretenders or soon to be discarded options.

The book is also laden with first-hand reports from practitioners in various creative industries in several national contexts who offer both observations about their environments, as well as explicit prescriptive advice. One such example is found in Skov's chapter (Chapter 13): 'I could have done with some guidance after I finished school. I didn't know what I could do, but I still believed that when I was employed I should show the world—or the company—that they couldn't do without me. So I worked so hard for a three-month trial period. I thought when I had permanent employment, I could calm down and then they would know what I can do. But by that time, I had created an identity as the girl who was always there. My advice to fresh graduates is this: Find out what role you want to play and play it from day one.'

Another central point that runs through the book is that elsewhere, but especially in creative industries, what you can know and learn largely depends on who you know. That is, the most relevant information runs largely through personal communication channels. Because multiple processes take place simultaneously, it is beneficial to have access to observers spread throughout the field rather than clustered if one needs an overarching view. Likewise, all individuals present in situations are potential observers, evaluators, and mediators of information to wider circles, and their opinions may matter in the short or long run.

As noted throughout the book, memory—individual and collective—is often pivotal to career-making, but etching memories often requires situationally appropriate work to establish and preserve what is favorable and of strategic importance. That is, be aware of and use mechanisms of collective memory and forgetting (if possible). Recognition and preservation are important to reputation, so not just getting but also preserving, sustaining, and spreading positive recognition is essential and should be done in contextually appropriate manners.

A related point is that talent alone is rarely enough. As Lincoln and Allen (Chapter 5) argue, both talent and the opportunity to move into positions to display talent take time to develop. Occupational skills, talent, and ability are important, but to a significant extent, employment acquisition skills (one's own or in some cases those of an agent or a collaborator) are the vehicles that carry creative workers and their talent and ability through careers.

Finally, it is important to recognize, but not get overwhelmed by, the complexity of work and career-making in creative industries. Knowledge can be acquired and used constructively, and one should investigate the environments in which one intends to work in a sophisticated manner. However, much of what researchers uncover, study, and analyze is surreptitiously managed or managed at a less deliberate or conscious level by practitioners in a field with greater or lesser degrees of success. Uncovering and systematizing knowledge is often helpful for both subjective and objective career purposes as Barley (1989) notes but should be seen as only part of the practical capacity to employ both intuitive and explicit knowledge in social settings.

NOTES

1. Hesmondhalgh (2007) prefers the term 'cultural industries,' whereas Howkins (2002) prefers 'the creative economy.'
2. This is not surprising because Becker was a student of the famous sociologist of work, occupations, and professions, C. Everett Hughes, at the University of Chicago.
3. 'Oversupply' of labor and 'underdimensioned' markets are interrelated and relative to each other (especially in the sense of 'over' and 'under'), but labor supply and dimensions of markets have discrete causes.

REFERENCES

Abbott, A. 2005. "Sociology of Work and Occupations." In *The Handbook of Economic Sociology*, edited by N. Smelser and R. Swedberg, 307–30. Princeton: Princeton University Press.

Alvarez, J., and S. Svejenova. 2005. *Sharing Executive Power: Roles and Relationships at the Top*. Cambridge: Cambridge University Press.

Arthur, M., D. Hall, and B. Lawrence. 1989. "Generating New Directions in Career Theory: The Case for a Transdisciplinary Approach." In *The Handbook of Career Theory*, edited by M. Arthur, T. Hall, and B. Lawrence, 7–25. Cambridge: Cambridge University Press.

Arthur, M., and D. Rousseau. 1996. *The Boundaryless Career: A New Employment Principle for a New Era*. New York: Oxford University Press.

Barley, S. 1989. "Careers, Identities, and Institutions: The Legacy of the Chicago School of Sociology." In *The Handbook of Career Theory*, edited by M. Arthur, T. Hall, and B. Lawrence, 41–65. Cambridge: Cambridge University Press.

Bechky, B. 2006. "Gaffers, Gofers, and Grips: Role-Based Coordination in Temporary Organizations." *Organization Science* 17: 3–21.

Becker, H. 1982. *Art Worlds*. Berkeley: University of California Press.

Blair, H., N. Culkin, and K. Randle. 2003. "From London to Los Angeles: A Comparison of Local Labour Market Processes in the US and UK Film Industries." *International Journal of Human Resource Management* 14: 619–33.

Burkholder, P. J. 2006. "The Twentieth Century and the Orchestra as Museum." In *The Orchestra*, edited by J. Peyser, 409–32. Milwaukee: Hal Leonard.

Caves, R. 2000. *Creative Industries: Contracts Between Art and Commerce*. Cambridge, MA: Harvard University Press.

Department of Culture, Media and Sport. 2001. *Creative Industries Mapping Document 2001* (2nd ed.). London, UK: Department of Culture, Media and Sport, http://www.culture.gov.uk/reference_library/publications/4632.aspx, last accessed February 2011.

Ebbers, J., and N. Wijnberg. 2009. "Latent Organizations in the Film Industry: Contracts, Rewards and Resources." *Human Relations* 62: 987–1009.

Faulkner, R. 1973. "Career Concerns and Mobility Motivations of Orchestra Musicians." *The Sociological Quarterly* 14: 334–49

Faulkner, R., and A. Anderson. 1987. "Short-Term Projects and Emergent Careers: Evidence from Hollywood." *American Journal of Sociology* 92: 879–909.

Florida, R. 2002. *The Rise of the Creative Class*. New York: Basic Books.

Florida, R. 2005. *The Flight of the Creative Class*. London: HarperCollins.

Gunz, H., M. Peiperl, and D. Tzabbar. 2007. "Boundaries in the Study of Career." In *The Handbook of Career Theory*, edited by H. Gunz and M. Peiperl, 471–94. Los Angeles: Sage.

Hesmondhalgh, D. 2007 . *The Cultural Industries*. London: Sage.

Hesmondhalgh, D., and S. Baker. 2011. *Creative Labour: Media Work in Three Cultural Industries*. London: Routledge.

Howkins, J. 2002. *The Creative Economy: How People Make Money From Ideas*. London: Penguin.

Inkson, K. 2006. "Protean and Boundarlyess Careers as Metaphors." *Journal of Vocational Behavior* 69: 48–63.

Joas, H. 1996. *The Creativity of Action*. Chicago: University of Chicago Press.

Jones, C. 1996. "Careers in Project Networks: The Case of the Film Industry." In *The Boundaryless Career: A New Employment Principle for a New Era*, edited by M. Arthur and D. Rousseau, 58–75. New York: Oxford University Press.

Kanter, R. 1977. *Men and Women of the Corporation*. New York: Basic Books

King, Z. 2004. "Career Self-Management: Its Nature, Causes and Consequences." *Journal of Vocational Behavior* 65: 112–33.

Menger, P.-M. 1999. "Artistic Labor Markets and Careers." *Annual Review of Sociology* 25: 541–74.

Moore, C., H. Gunz, and D. Hall. 2007. "Tracing the Historical Roots of Career Theory in Management and Organization Studies." In *The Handbook of Career Theory*, edited by H. Gunz and M. Peiperl, 13–38. Los Angeles: Sage.

O'Mahoney, S., and B. Bechky. 2006. "Stretchwork: Managing the Career Progression Paradox in External Labor Markets." *Academy of Management Journal* 49: 918–41.

Osterman, P., and D. Burton. 2005. "Ports and Ladders: The Nature and Relevance of Internal Labor Markets in a Changing World." In *The Oxford Handbook of Work and Organization*, edited by S. Ackroyd, R. Batt, P. Thompson, and P. Tolbert, 425–45. Oxford: Oxford University Press.

Rodrigues, R., and D. Guest. 2010. "Have Careers Become Boundaryless?" *Human Relations* 63: 1157–75.

Rossman, G., N. Esparza, and P. Bonacich. 2010. "I'd Like to Thank the Academy, Team Spillovers, and Network Centrality." *American Sociological Review* 75: 31–51.

Sawyer, R. 2006. *Explaining Creativity. The Science of Human Innovation.* Oxford: Oxford University Press.

Starkey, K., C. Barnatt, and S. Tempest. 2000. "Beyond Networks and Hierarchies: Latent Organizations in the U.K. Television Industry." *Organization Science* 11: 299–305.

Stinchcombe, A. 1978. *Theoretical Methods in Social History.* New York: Academic Press.

Stolte, J., G. Fine, and K. Cook. 2001. "Sociological Miniaturism: Seeing the Big Through the Small in Social Psychology." *Annual Review of Sociology* 27: 387–413.

Sturges, J. 2008. "All in a Day's Work? Career Self-Management and Management of the Boundary Between Work and Non-Work." *Human Resource Management Journal* 18: 118–34.

Tams, S., and M. Arthur. 2010. "New Directions for Boundaryless Careers: Agency and Interdependence in a Changing World." *Journal of Organizational Behavior* 31: 629–46.

Ursell, G. 2000. "Television Production: Issues of Exploitation, Commodification and Subjectivity in UK Television Labour Markets." *Media, Culture & Society* 22: 805–25.

Valcour, M., L. Bailyn, and M. Quijada. 2007. "Customized Careers." In *The Handbook of Career Theory*, edited by H. Gunz and M. Peiperl, 188–210. Los Angeles: Sage.

Wainwright, S., and B. Turner. 2006. "Just Crumbling to Bits? An Exploration of the Body, Ageing, Injury and Career in Classical Ballet Dancers." *Sociology* 40: 237–55.

Wilensky, H. 1961. "Orderly Careers and Social Participation: The Impact of Work History on Social Integration in the Middle Class." *American Sociological Review* 26: 521–39.

2 Creative Labor

Who Are They? What Do They Do? Where Do They Work? A Discussion Based on a Quantitative Study from Denmark

Trine Bille

INTRODUCTION

This chapter focuses on three main questions: Who are the creative workers? What do they do? Where do they work?

Most studies of the creative labor market have been done with the purpose of obtaining knowledge on the creative workers' employment, working conditions, income, and so on. In this context, it is of course important to bear in mind that the results can be dependent on the definitions and approaches used. To analyze the creative labor market, the research population must be defined and delimitated. There can be many different approaches to this, and we know from the literature that there is no a priori correct definition.

Creative labor will by most definitions be delimitated broader than artists, but most definitions will place the artists in the core of creative labor and no doubt include them in the definition. But even for artists, no universal correct solution to the problem of definitions exists. In their review of the criteria for being an artist, Frey and Pommerehne (1989) come to the conclusion that no "right" definition of artists exists. No definition would qualify everywhere. The authors suggest that the criteria be selected contextually: with regard to the purpose of the study and the availability of data. They also emphasize that the choice of the criteria for the definition of artists has major consequences for the research findings, ranging from the number of artists arrived at to the assessment of their economic conditions. See also Higgs, Cunningham, and Bakhshi (2008) for a discussion.

Quite different approaches and methodologies can be used when studying creative labor. One dominant approach is the *qualitative approach* to the social and political dimensions of creative labor, focusing among other things on the experience of work, "good work," the conception of work and normative criteria for evaluation work (see e.g., Hesmondhalgh 2010). Another dominant approach is the more *quantitative research* on artists and the creative labor market, focusing on the working conditions of the creative workers, for example, their income conditions, employment status, and so on (e.g., Alper and Wassall 2006). The two different kinds of research can supplement each other, making different contributions to the knowledge of creative labor.

This chapter takes a quantitative approach and takes advantage of the vast amount of information gathered by Statistics Denmark to make methodological and empirical points. Compared with many other countries, Denmark has quite a unique position based on the official registers on the inhabitants of Denmark, which can be used for research purposes. This information can be used to study creative labor and their working and living conditions. In this chapter, different definitions of creative labor and artists are discussed on the basis of the available data and categories from Statistics Denmark.

This chapter looks at three different criteria for the delimitation of creative labor and artists: 1) creative job functions, 2) creative educations, and 3) creative industries. This makes it possible to get a more holistic picture of the creative labor market, and it means that the chapter will answer important questions such as: How important is a formal education for obtaining jobs in the creative industries? Do those with formal 'creative' educations work in the creative industries or outside the creative industries? What is the profile of the jobs within the creative industries (are they creative or humdrum)?

As soon as we have definitions of the relevant groups of creative laborers, the data from Statistics Denmark can be used to answer many questions about the different groups. For the selected groups, it will be possible to look at their socioeconomic status and job conditions including: age, gender, job mobility, unemployment rates, income, and so on. It is also possible to compare different definitions of creative labor as well as different creative industries.

BACKGROUND

What do we know about the creative labor market from the quantitative and economic perspective? Creative labor is not a well-defined concept, but there has been some research on the labor market for artists.

Alper and Wassall (2006) present a review of some of the most important empirical economic research done on labor markets for artists, where the overall purpose has been to generate knowledge of artists' employment and income conditions and compare them with other professionals and technical occupations. The most important research questions that have been analyzed in these studies include: As working professionals, to what extent have artists fared less well than comparably educated persons in other disciplines? Has the often reported disparity in earnings between artists and comparably educated groups grown or shrunk over time? Is this apparent 'earnings penalty' due to the characteristics inherent in the nature of the artistic labor market?

Some of the main findings of these studies are:

- Artists are found to work fewer hours, suffer higher unemployment, and earn less than members of the reference group.
- Disparities in unemployment and annual hours worked are found to shrink somewhat over time, but disparities in earnings do not.
- Artist earned less across all years even when only members working full time year round of each group are compared.
- The earnings of artists are found to display greater variability than those of other professional and technical workers.
- Many people participate in the artistic labor market, but few succeed to the point that enables them to develop a career in the arts.
- In part due to their relatively high educational levels, artists are found to be able to transition from forays into arts occupations or jobs in professional and managerial occupations, not into service occupations as artists' 'mythology' might suggest.
- When artists are young and struggling to make it, they do work in various service occupations that tend to provide greater work schedule flexibility.
- Many people explore the arts as an occupation, but few remain as artists for significant periods of time.

According to Alper and Wassall (2006), the most striking findings are related to the consistently poorer labor market outcomes of artists (see also Abbing, 2002). Alper and Wassall summarize several hypotheses that have been advanced to explain what makes the artist labor market unique (see also Menger 2006): Throsby's (1994) 'work preference' model of artist behavior, which postulates that the artist is driven to create, and will maximize time spent working as an artist subject to constraints of earning sufficient income, form either inside or outside the arts, to finance an acceptable level of consumption. Another set of theories lies in the roles of risk-taking among artists and the rewards to those who rise to the top of their profession. Although these theories were mainly used to explain income distributions among artists, they also have implications for labor supply. A related theory is found in the literature on the earning of superstars (Adler 2006; Rosen 1981) and 'winner-take-all markets.'

In general, in the empirical studies concerning artists' careers, different methodologies have been used. *Quantitative studies* often utilize existing information on a group of artists obtained from a variety of sources to develop an understanding of an aspect of artists' careers. Sometimes the data for this research are anecdotal. *Retrospective studies* often employ surveys of artists, asking them to re-create their careers by responding to written questionnaires or personal interviews. *Panel data based on surveys* are usually 'quasi-panels.' where they follow a group of artists, many of whom are likely to be the same from survey to survey over time, but exactly the same group of people/artists are not followed from the start to the end of a multiyear period, such as would be the case in true panel studies.

Alper and Wassall's (2000) studies are some of the most extended empirical studies on artists' employment and earning conditions in the US. For Australia, a large survey has been done by Throsby and Hollister (2003). Much research, such as Alper and Wassall (2000) for the US and O'Brien and Feist (1995) for the UK, is based on US census data, which obviously have some drawbacks. The US census requires the person filling out its long form to choose a single occupation. This choice is based on time spent at work during a single reference week. This means among other things that census definitions result in a bias toward including only those who achieve the most success in their art form as artists, and that many artists also hold non-artistic jobs (i.e., they are multiple jobholders). This aspect cannot be studied using census data.

As Karttunen (2001, 284) remarks, there can be serious problems with this: "The census definition of occupation as the primary work done by a person in order to obtain income violate the ideology according to which art is not made for the sake of money. More importantly, it does not accord with how artistic work is actually carried out in our society. Time after time, it has been empirically established that many people who perceive themselves as artists, or whom arts policy makers might consider as such, cannot live from their art. If self-defined artists earn most of their income as taxi-drivers or waiters, they are counted as such in the census."

Wassall and Alper (1992) have further established that many disagreements between researchers on artists actually derive from the use of different data sources, in particular census or other government sources, versus surveys conducted by the researchers themselves. This chapter takes this discussion a step further.

DEFINITIONS OF CREATIVE LABOR

There is no clear or uniform definition of creative labor. In the literature, there are almost as many definitions as there are studies, and there is no consensus on which criteria base the definition.[1] There is a continuing discussion about the definition of artists (e.g., Frey and Pommerehne 1989). The delimitation of creative labor is even broader and harder to define. Depending on the definition of creativity, the definition of creative labor can range from Richard Florida's (2002) broad definition of the creative class to more elitist definitions of artists.

Problems of Defining Creativity

To deal with and delimitate creative labor, one needs a definition of creativity. Creativity is something inherent in human beings and can be used in many contexts, and no clear definition of creativity exists. The literature on this issue is growing fast, and it is not possible to do justice to this vast literature here (see e.g., Kaufman and Sternberg 2010). However, some definition is needed. The KEA European Affairs report (2006, 41) defines creativity in this manner: "Creativity refers to the ability to create something new. It derives from the verb 'to create' initially used exclusively in relation to God and referring to making something/someone exist, ex-nihilo."

The concept of creativity is often used in connection with the creation of works of art, and it is therefore often used synonymously with 'artistic creativity' (see Throsby 2001 for a discussion of artistic creativity). In the UNCTAD (2008, 9) report, four creativity areas are suggested: 'Artistic creativity' involves imagination and a capacity to generate original ideas and novel ways of interpreting the work, expressed in text, sound, and image. 'Scientific creativity' involves curiosity and a willingness to experiment and make new connections in problem solving, and 'economic creativity' is a dynamic process leading toward innovation in technology, business practices, marketing, and so on, and it is closely linked to gaining competitive advantages in the economy. 'Technological' creativity is involved to a greater or lesser extent in the other three kinds of creativity and is interrelated with them.

In this chapter, creativity is used synonymously with 'artistic creativity.' For a full elaboration of the concept of artistic creativity, even though this concept is not fully explained either, see Throsby (2001).

DEFINITION OF ARTISTS

According to Frey and Pommerehne (1989), there are at least eight criteria that might be applied in order to determine who is an artist:

1. the amount of time spent on artistic work
2. the amount of income derived from artistic activities
3. the reputation as an artist among the general public
4. the recognition among other artists
5. the quality of the artistic work produced (which means that artistic 'quality' must be defined somehow)
6. membership in a professional artists' group or association
7. professional qualifications (graduation in arts schools)
8. the subjective self-evaluation of being an artist.

Frey and Pommerehne (1989) emphasize that in the study of artists, the methods of data collection and analysis may have especially wide implications on the findings.

Looking at the criteria listed by Frey and Pommerehne (1989), it is obvious that they will lead to quite different results because the groups of artists that will be delimited by the different criteria will be different.

The most *"objective"* criteria are 1, 2, 6, and 7 because they do not directly relate to the quality of the work but rather to the amount of time spent on artistic work, the amount of income derived from artistic activities, membership in a professional artists' group or association, and professional qualifications (graduation from arts schools). Membership in a professional artists' group or association is an often used criterion. Graduation from arts schools and income from artistic activities are commonly used criteria as well (see below), while time spent on artistic work is often hard to assess and use as a criterion.

Some of the criteria are more *subjective* and relate to the *quality* of the artistic work (i.e., reputation as an artist among the general public, recognition among other artists, and the quality of the artistic work produced, which means that artistic 'quality' must be defined somehow). Reputation, recognition, and quality are subjective criteria, whereas the last one, namely, 'the subjective self-evaluation of being an artist,' is even more subjective. As Karttunen (1998, 3–4) points out, "The difficulties of the criteria is due to the fact that anybody at all is free to call himself an artist without a formal degree or any officially recognized demonstration of competence. . . . And their income from it may be insubstantial, or even turn negative."

Another problem is that the criteria may actually be contradictive. Karttunen (1998) presents a good example from a Finish 'status-of-the-artists study' where—among others—the group of 'photographic artists' had to be delimitated. Starting with the members of the Union of Artists in Photography, this was considered too limited with only about 60 members. Using the 'reputational method,' they ended up with a group of 200 people, which was still limited and biased toward more avant-garde and artistic photographers. After publication of the report, advertising and press photographers criticized the study population for being biased. If they had played a greater role in the study population, the income level of photographic artists would have been much higher.

Membership in professional artists' groups or associations can to some degree be interpreted as artistic quality. The membership associations for different artists' groups (musicians, visual artists, actors, etc.) do, however, have different criteria for membership: Some of them are quite elitist, whereas others have open criteria.

It is therefore quite clear that different selection criteria will give different results. The census and register data are based on one's main income source, while the artists' associations are often based on high professional standard. As Karttunen (2001) notices, the different definitions will have a partial overlap, but the census definition will exclude an avant-garde artist who lives on service jobs yet include a 'low reputation' artist who lives on the sale of his/her work. The census data actually force a market test of who should be counted as an artist.

A few studies have systematically compared the workings of alternative definitions within their own data. Jeffri and Throsby (1994) concluded that the majority of self-described visual artists in both the US and Australia could be considered professional by training and/or peer recognition, but only a minority would satisfy the conventional marked-based definition of professionalism.

FROM THE CREATIVE CLASS TO ARTISTS

In this section, some of the most common definitions of creative labor are discussed, starting with the broad definition of the creative class by Richard Florida (2002) and ending with more elitist definitions of artists.

A broad definition of creative labor is put forward by Florida (2002) in his book *The Rise of the Creative Class*. According to Florida, the creative class is the class that, through their creativity, creates the most economic value. Florida divides the workforce into four classes: the creative class, the service class, the working class, and people working in agriculture. The creative class is further divided into two classes according to the degree of creativity entailed in their occupation—namely, the creative core and the creative professionals. The class to whom Florida assigns the most creativity he calls the *creative core*—a core that is defined by virtue of their creation of new forms or designs, which can improve future working practices and can be widely applied. Examples of people included within this core are those employed in IT and mathematical branches, architects and engineers, researchers, artists, designers, people employed in the entertainment business, as well as in sports, media, and advertising. The creative class also includes *creative professionals*. The work carried out by this group is characterized by problem solving, and their jobs most often demand a high level of education. Examples of people falling under this category are business and financial managers, legal professionals (e.g., lawyers, medical professionals, and people employed in high-tech industries). *The working class* comprises people working in various trades, the construction and extraction industries, installation, maintenance, production, and transport, and *the service class* is primarily composed of nurses, care assistants, people employed in the restaurant branch, and cleaning staff. *Agricultural workers* comprise fishermen, forestry workers, and farmers. Florida's definition of creative labor as equal to the creative class is, on the one hand, broad and comprises about one third of the total population. On the other hand, creativity is attached to special occupations, and in this regard, the definition can be seen as limiting, which is also one of the points Florida has been criticized for. Creativity is inherent in all human beings and can be used in most occupations.

Another definition of creative labor could be 'artistic professions,' a kind of definition used in many studies. Alper and Wassall (2006) include: 1) actors and directors; 2) announcers; 3) architects; 4) post-secondary art, drama, and music teachers; 5) authors; 6) dancers; 7) designers; 8) musicians and composers; 9) painters, sculptors, craft artists, and printmakers; 10) photographers; and 11) artists not elsewhere classified. Although the production of art demands many kinds of support personnel, the title 'creative labor' is usually reserved to the creative core occupation, excluding technical or routine kind of work. Sometimes art teachers in higher education may, nevertheless, be included in artist occupations (see Alper and Wassall 2006).

If creative labor is defined as artists, another common approach is to select the research population on the basis of membership of selected labor market organizations for selected groups of artists, such as The Danish Association of Visual Artists and the Danish Musicians' Union (e.g., Elstad and Pedersen 1996; Heian, Løyland, and Mangset 2008), and collect data by means of surveys. These studies tend to focus on people who function within the bounds of the established art worlds and who also describe themselves as artists. Such people normally join the artists' associations. One problem with this approach is that it will only create knowledge about those artists who are members of such organizations. If most artists are members of these kinds of organizations and the degree of organization is high, the problem will be small. But we do not know very much about the degree of organization among artists and different groups of artists and how this has changed over time. Besides, as mentioned earlier, different arts organizations often have different criteria for membership.

It is also possible to select people with 'a creative or artistic education.' The first problem is to make the selection of the relevant educations as the basis for the analysis (see below). By focusing on those persons with 'an artistic or creative education,' another problem could be that many artists or people working with creative content do not have a formal education that qualifies them for this work. Many artists are self-taught (Alper and Wassall 2006). By only looking at persons with some kind of artistic or creative education, one excludes the group of artists and other creative people who are doing the same kind of creative work but do not have a qualifying formal education.

Bearing this in mind, it is, however, an interesting empirical question to focus on those persons who have an artistic or a creative education and see what they are doing. In which industries do they work? Which job functions do they occupy? What is their degree of unemployment, their income, and their wages? This can then be compared with others at the same educational level.[2]

DATA FROM STATISTICS DENMARK

In this chapter, the definitions of creative labor are made on the basis of the possibilities in the register data from Statistics Denmark.[3]

The register contains, among other things, detailed information about the person's social background (age, gender, family, education, etc.), income (annual personal income, households income, earnings per hour, etc.), employment (industry, job function, primary job, secondary job, degree of unemployment, etc.), as well as many other variables. Using these data, it is possible to explore the careers of creative people and artists. This chapter is based on data from a single year—namely, 2007.[4]

The main advantage of register data is their unique horizontal and vertical comparability (Karttunen 2001),[5] whereas their major limitation concerns the identification of the population, which affects the basic enumeration. When using register data, researchers have little influence on the categories used by Statistics Denmark, which have initially been determined with other objectives in mind.

The overall procedure of assigning people an occupation has important implications for who will be defined as a creative or an artist in the register. The fact that only the employed labor force is assigned occupations may have specific implications for the enumeration of artists. Occupation is the activity or work done by a person in order to obtain income. Statistics Denmark assigns people the occupation from which they receive most or most recent income. The employed labor force is divided into employees (wage and salary earners) and entrepreneurs. The income data for the register are derived from the national tax register that is maintained for determining and collecting taxes.

Delimitation of Creative Workers Based on Data from Statistics Denmark—Who Are They? What Do They Do?

As discussed earlier, there is no 'correct' definition of creative labor. In this chapter, the broad definition of the creative class used by Florida (2002) is not used, but instead a quite narrow definition is chosen, defining creativity as artistic creativity, and creative labor is therefore defined close to the definition of artists. The reasons for choosing the quite narrow perspective is to make it possible to make the conclusions as sharp as possible on labor market conditions for artistic creativity and production.

The first step has been to select the areas of creative content (domains), which should be included in the study. Because creativity is defined as 'artistic creativity' (see above), the following fields are included: performing arts, music, film, media, architecture, design, crafts, visual arts, advertising, and photography.

The next step is to delimitate the creative labor working in these areas. Using register data from Statistics Denmark to define the creative workers, two different criteria can be used for delimitation: job function and education.

By means of the register data, it is possible to select a range of job functions that are creative in the sense that their main input is artistic creativity to the production of an art product/service or a creative product/service in the creative fields mentioned earlier. This is an intuitively correct definition. The creative workers are defined by what they do. For example, if they work as actors, they are actors. But there are also problems with this definition. Job category normally signifies the most important position the person in question has on the Danish labor market (i.e., giving the highest income). The person may also have other jobs and may receive income from other sources (e.g., company profit). Relating to the criteria of Frey and Pommerehne (1989), this criterion is related to "The amount of income derived from artistic activities."

This could—in some cases—be seen as a problem, as discussed earlier, because we know that a number of persons work part time with their creative activities but also have other jobs—for earning a living. If the other jobs are the most important (i.e., their primary income), they may be registered under other job codes and do not become part of the data set. Such persons are difficult to locate or draw out of the statistics. Besides, the quality of the creative work (the artistic standard) is not taken into account in this delimitation of the group.

Another problem with the definition is that only those who actually practice the creative work are counted. In this way, it is not possible to define a certain group of people who are 'artists' and follow their career, look at their unemployment rates, and so on. Because who does this group consist of? Should everybody who had creative work for one year count as a creative worker? In many cases it would not make sense because a lot of people probably do some creative work for one year and then do something completely different—because they want to. They do not regard themselves as artists and should not be counted as such.

The definition of jobs with creative content used in this chapter is found in Appendix 2.A.

It is also possible to select people with 'an artistic or creative education.' The first problem is to make the selection of the relevant educations as the basis for the analysis. The educations should be within the creative fields selected earlier, and the educations should lead to skills for the *production* of creative content within these fields. But in practice, there are a lot of borderline cases and 'grey' areas. For instance, there are a lot of short-term educations and labor market educations and courses within the creative areas more broadly, especially concerning the media and technical skills. These are not included. Additionally, educations for the protection and dissemination of cultural heritage, such as library schools, museum curator educations, and so on, are not included. There are also a lot of master's degrees in the humanities at the university level, which are directed at knowledge and interpretation of creative work of arts but not the production of creative content. Neither are these educations are included. The choice of creative educations is listed in Appendix 2.B.

The impact of education on artists' earnings has been the subject of different studies. Towse (2006) discusses human capital theory and argues that it applies only weakly to artists' decisions about investment in schooling and training and about occupational choice.

Earning functions can be used to explore possible differences in the rewards to education, training, and other labor market attributes between artists and a reference group. Results show that artists do not seem to fit the standard earnings model as well as other workers, and earnings functions for them have poorer goodness-of-fit. Also results shows no or a negative correlation of education with artistic earnings and a positive correlation with non-artistic earnings (Alper and Wassall 2006). Rengers (2002) found that characteristics of the artist's education had little or no impact on the artist's career. Self-educated artists have the same earnings and the same supply behavior as those with formal arts education, and the prestige of the arts college attended does not have long-lasting effects. However, Filer (1989) found, looking at three-digit occupations, that measures of earnings inequality for occupations where individual talent and performance are important determinants of earnings tend to be similar to those for artists, making the arts similar to 'equal' occupations.

Where Do They Work?

Where do the creative laborers work? The first hypothesis is that they work within the creative industries.[6] But again we have a problem of definition.

There is no universal or general accepted definition of *creative industries*. As Throsby (2007) points out, different delimitations have been used in different studies primarily depending on the purpose of the studies. In this chapter, the following industries (based on six-digit NACE codes) have been selected: independent artists, performing arts, music, film, media, architecture and design, advertising, photography, and crafts. Because the idea is to look at *artists* and *creative* industries, the choice is made only to include those areas, which have *production with artistic creativity as the main input in the production process, with an arts product or a creative product as the main output*. This delimitation is only possible to a certain degree, but it implies, for instance, that museums and libraries as well as distribution, sale of arts, and creative products in general are not included in the analyses. This is a narrow definition, compared with other definitions of creative industries (see e.g., Bille and Lorenzen 2008; Birch 2008; Throsby 2007), but again it is chosen to make the focus as sharp as possible on the labor market conditions for artistic creativity and production.

The definition of creative industries used in this chapter is found in Appendix 2.C.

Looking at the labor market for the selected creative industries, we find people working there with a creative job function and people working with 'ordinary' job and humdrum functions (Caves 2000), such as office work, technical support, and so on. Likewise, we will probably find creative labor, either with a creative job function or a creative education, working outside the creative industries.

DESCRIPTIVE RESULTS

In this section, some descriptive results are presented concerning creative labor, answering questions such as: Who are they? What do they do? Where are they working? This is done by looking at creative labor from the three perspectives: creative industries, creative job functions, and creative educations. The numbers can be compared to a total workforce in Denmark of 2,800,250 persons (2007).

Creative Job Functions

Creative job functions are a way of defining creative labor by what they do.

A total number of about 42,000 persons in Denmark have a creative job function, as it is defined in this chapter (see Appendix 2.A). Of these people, about 50 percent work in the creative industries. The rest is working in other industries. The variation among the creative job functions shows that the largest numbers of creative jobs are found in architecture (17,583), 'writing' (9,204), 'craft and design' (5,961), and 'photographers including image and sound recording equipment operators' (3,271). It is obvious that these job categories also are those with the broadest scope compared with the more artistic specific occupations in the visual arts, dance, acting, and music.

However, it is among the creative jobs within the visual arts, dance, acting, and music that we find the largest shares of jobs within the creative industries: 95 percent of the creative jobs for 'choreographers and dancers' are within the creative industries, 89 percent of the creative jobs for 'sculptures, painters, and related artists' are within the creative industries, and 78 percent of the creative jobs for 'film, stage, and related actors and directors' as well as 'photographers and image and sound operators' are within the creative industries. Compared with this, only 28 percent of the architects are found within the creative industries. The rest of the architects are in other industries. The same applies to craft and design, where 46 percent of the creative job functions are within the creative industries.

Table 2.1 shows the share and number of people with a creative job function working outside the creative industries. Most of these jobs are in 'finance and business activities,' 'manufacturing,' 'public and private services,' and 'wholesale and retail trade; hotels and restaurants.' For example, many people working with craft and design work in wholesale and retail trade with cloth; writers work in press bureaus, banks, labor unions, software development industries, and business consulting; while architects work in the consulting engineering industry and in different kinds of manufacturing industries.

Table 2.2 shows the numbers of persons with a creative job function who have a creative education. In total, 28 percent of the persons with a creative job function have a creative education. The share is highest among musicians, where 46 percent of those with a creative job function have a

Table 2.1 Persons with a Creative Job Function, Distributed by Industry, Denmark, 2007

Job function / Industry	Visual artists	Dancers	Actors and directors	Musicians	Photographers etc.	Writers	Architects	Craft and design	Total
Creative industries (pct.)	89	95	78	70	78	68	28	46	51 (21,134)
Other industries (pct.)	11	5	2	30	22	32	72	54	49 (20,460)
Agriculture, fishing, and quarrying (pct.)	0	0	0	0	0	0	0	0	0 (27)
Manufacturing (pct.)	25	0	4	1	7	10	31	12	23 (4,764)
Electricity, gas, and water supply (pct.)	0	0	0	0	0	1	1	0	1 (132)
Constructing (pct.)	0	0	3	0	1	1	6	0	4 (749)
Ws. and retail trade; hotels, restaurants (pct.)	20	14	27	4	15	8	4	68	16 (3,197)
Transport, post, and telecommunication (pct.)	0	0	6	1	3	6	2	1	2 (445)
Finance and business activities (pct.)	25	0	20	3	18	27	41	16	33 (6,768)
Public and private services (pct.)	30	86	39	92	56	48	15	2	21 (4,367)
Activity not stated (pct.)	0	0	1	0	0	0	0	0	0 (11)
Total (pct.)	100	100	100	100	100	100	100	100	100
Total	2,827	133	1,407	1,208	3,271	9,204	17,583	5,961	41,594

Table 2.2 Persons with a Creative Job Function, Distributed by Education, Denmark, 2007

Job function Industry	Visual artists	Dancers	Actors and directors	Musicians	Photographers etc.	Writers	Architects	Craft and design	Total
Creative education (pct.)	16	0	31	46	25	39	25	26	28 (11,770)
Non-creative education (pct.)	81	58	59	42	72	59	71	70	68 (28,135)
Short	44	78	68	42	63	34	11	39	29 (8,031)
Short-cycle higher education	33	7	14	12	23	12	11	39	18 (5,089)
Medium-cycle higher education	16	14	13	26	10	27	52	18	34 (9,530)
Long-cycle higher education	6	3	5	19	4	26	26	4	18 (5,128)
PhD degree or higher	0	0	0	0	0	0	0	0	0 (357)
No or unknown (pct.)	3	42	10	12	3	2	5	4	4 (1,689)
Total (pct.)	100	100	100	100	100	100	100	100	100
Total	2,827	133	1,407	1,208	3,271	9,204	17,583	5,961	41,594

creative education. In visual arts, it is 16 percent. This confirms former results that in some art forms, such as music (especially classical music), training is a prerequisite for sustaining a career, whereas among painters (by comparison), autodidacts are quite common (Karttunen 1998).

Table 2.2 also shows which kinds of education those people have who have a creative job function but not a creative education. About half of them have a short education. The share of people with a short education is largest among 'photographers and image and sound recording equipment operators,' film, stage, and related actors and directors' and 'dancers.' These data show that these occupations can be occupied without a high level of formal training. But also among 'craft and designers' and 'sculptures, painters, and related artists,' a high share of people have a short education. Of those with a short education, many do not have further education than elementary or high school. Some people have some kind of technical education or a short graphics education or an education within commerce or office work. About one third have a medium-cycle higher education, and 18 percent have a long-cycle higher education. Of those with a non-creative higher education, most have a technical or language education.

Artistic or Creative Educations

In Denmark, 60,363 persons have a creative education as it is defined in this chapter, and about half of them are educated within graphics and craft and design. About 9,000 to 10,000 are educated as architects and journalists, respectively, and about 5,000 have an education within music. About 3,700 are educated within photography, and only minor proportions are educated within film and TV, theatre, dance, and the visual arts.

Of those with a creative education, Table 2.3 shows that 25 percent are working within the creative industries, almost half of them are working outside the creative industries, and 30 percent are somehow outside industries (most of them are on pension [almost 80 percent], and some are unemployed). The largest share of those people who have a creative education and work within the creative industries have a film or television education, where 63 percent work within the creative industries. By comparison, only 15 percent with a graphics education and 16 percent with a craft and design education work within creative industries. The reason for these relatively small shares is probably that the educations within graphics as well as craft and design are quite broad and therefore do not relate to specific industries.

Of the persons with a creative education who are not working in the creative industries, most people work in 'public and private services' but also to some extent in 'finance and business services,' 'wholesale and retail trade, hotels, and restaurants,' and 'manufacturing.' Only a small share of those with an education in music work in the creative industries, and most of them work in 'public and private services,' mainly engaging in teaching activities at all levels, at university, high school, and elementary school

Table 2.3   Persons with a Creative Education, Distributed by Industry, Denmark, 2007

Job function / Industry	Photography education	Film and television education	Graphic education	Journalist education	Theater education	Dancer education	Music education	Art education	Craft and design education	Architecture education	Total
Creative industries (pct.)	25	63	15	39	55	49	17	19	16	41	25 (15,174)
Other industries (pct.)	32	20	59	27	24	43	70	28	45	39	46 (27,693)
Agriculture, fishing, and quarrying (pct.)	1	0	0	1	0	0	0	1	1	0	1 (142)
Manufacturing (pct.)	19	1	27	5	1	0	1	5	13	5	15 (4,162)
Electricity, gas, and water supply (pct.)	0	0	0	0	0	0	0	0	0	1	0 (72)
Constructing (pct.)	2	0	2	1	3	0	0	2	3	4	2 (542)
Ws. and retail trade; hotels, restaurants (pct.)	13	2	14	7	10	31	3	7	34	6	15 (4,118)
Transport, post, and tele-communication (pct.)	7	1	5	5	4	0	1	2	3	4	4 (1,146)
Finance and business activities (pct.)	13	27	16	22	20	0	6	10	12	24	15 (4,264)
Public and private services (pct.)	44	69	36	58	61	69	88	73	33	57	48 (13,245)
Outside industries (pct.)	43	17	25	34	21	8	14	54	39	20	29 (17,496)
Total (pct.)	100	100	100	100	100	100	100	100	100	100	100
Total	3,734	417	18,097	9,876	1,182	37	5,114	767	12,039	9,100	60,363

Table 2.4 Persons with a Creative Education, Distributed by Job Functions, Denmark, 2007

Education / Job function	Photography education	Film and television education	Graphic education	Journalist education	Theater education	Dancer education	Music education	Art education	Craft and design education	Architecture education	Total
Creative job function (pct.)	17	19	4	36	33	5	12	5	11	50	20 (11,770)
Other job function (pct.)	25	29	52	16	23	38	57	30	39	25	37 (22,511)
Management at highest level in firms, organizations, and the public sector (pct.)	4	5	3	15	4	0	2	0	3	15	5 (1,154)
Work that assumes knowledge at highest level within field (pct.)	10	30	7	32	31	0	77	58	11	55	25 (5,561)
Work that assumes knowledge at medium level (pct.)	25	57	23	22	32	21	7	7	29	16	22 (4,879)
Office work (pct.)	14	2	22	19	7	14	4	8	9	4	14 (3,133)
Retailing, service, and care work (pct.)	15	1	9	6	11	50	4	13	17	5	10 (2,168)
Work within agriculture, market gardening, forestry, and fishing industry (pct.)	1	0	0	1	0	0	0	1	0	1	0 (62)
Crafts and related trade workers (pct.)	13	2	21	1	4	0	1	3	19	3	14 (3,164)
Plant and machine operators and assemblers (pct.)	8	0	7	1	2	7	0	2	4	1	4 (961)
Other occupations (pct.)	12	2	8	4	7	7	4	8	7	2	6 (1,429)
Unknown job function (pct.)	58	52	44	48	44	57	31	65	50	25	43 (26,082)
Total (pct.)	100	100	100	100	100	100	100	100	100	100	100
Total	3,734	417	18,097	9,876	1,182	37	5,114	767	12,039	9,100	60,363

Table 2.5 Degree of Unemployment for Persons with a Creative Education, Denmark, 2007

Education / Degree of unemployment	Photography education	Film and television education	Graphic education	Journalist education	Theater education	Dancer education	Music education	Art education	Craft and design education	Architecture education	Total
Full-time employed	92	66	85	91	61	28	80	85	84	87	86 (50,849)
1–50 percent unemployment	6	23	12	7	31	42	16	9	12	9	12 (6,653)
51–99 percent unemployment	3	10	3	2	10	31	5	7	4	3	3 (1,906)
Full unemployed	0	0	0	0	0	0	0	0	0	0	0 (54)
Total (pct.)	100	100	100	100	100	100	100	100	100	100	100
Total	3,658	416	17,816	9,740	1,169	36	749	11,838	8,988	8,988	59,462

Table 2.6 Degree of Unemployment for All Other Educations, Denmark, 2007

Education / Degree of unemployment	Short	Short-cycle higher education	Medium-cycle higher education	Long-cycle higher education	PhD degree or higher	No or unknown	Total
Full-time employed	91	90	90	89	93	98	91 (4,277,073)
1–50 percent unemployment	8	9	9	9	6	2	8 (377,281)
51–99 percent unemployment	1	1	1	2	1	0	1 (52,936)
Full unemployed	0	0	0	0	0	0	0 (3,711)
Total (pct.)	100	100	100	100	100	100	100
Total	1,942,751	1,392,919	542,724	216,774	12,225	570,308	4,677,701

levels. Many people with a music education also work within religious institutions (e.g., the church). People with a graphics education are work-ing within different kind of printing industries and foundations but also institutions such as hospitals, schools, and institutions for old people. The same goes for people with an education within craft and design. Many of these people also work in hospitals, schools, and institutions for old people, but the majority work in wholesale and retail with cloth. Architects mainly work in public administration and education.

Of the persons with a creative education, Table 2.4 shows that 20 per-cent have a creative job function, 37 percent have other job functions (hum-drum), and 43 percent have unknown job functions. Few with a creative education within art, dance, or graphics have a creative job function (4–5 percent). But also few with an education within craft and design or music have creative job functions (11–12 percent). This means that many with a creative education do not have creative jobs (as defined in this chapter).

Of those people with a creative education who have non-creative job functions, most are doing work that assumes knowledge at the highest or medium level within the field. This includes teaching. There are especially many with a music or an architect degree doing work that assumes knowl-edge at a high level, mainly teaching. Journalists frequently also teach and do business consulting, whereas people with a graphics education often do ordinary office work, and people with an education within craft and design are doing work that assumes knowledge at medium level, such as sales.

The 43 percent with unknown job functions are either on pension or unemployed or their job functions are for some reason not stated. Many are on pension (see above), but there is also a group that is unemployed. For a well-defined group like people with a creative education, it is possible to look at things like unemployment rates etc. Table 2.5 shows the degree of unem-ployment for persons with a creative education. Eighty-six percent of those with creative educations are employed full time, compared with 91 percent for all other educations (Table 2.6). With a dance education, only 28 percent are working full time, and for theater education, the percentage is 61.

Of course, there are many more possibilities in the data for looking at the working conditions and the careers of creative labor with a creative education. But this is out of the scope of this chapter.

Creative Industries—Where Do They Work?

In Denmark, 132,412 persons are working in the creative industries as defined in this chapter.

The largest number of jobs in the creative industries is found in advertis-ing, design, and publishing. The smallest number of jobs is found in music and the visual arts.

Table 2.7 shows the proportion of those employed in the creative indus-tries who have a creative job function. On average, 16 percent of those

Table 2.7 Persons Employed in the Creative Industries, Distributed by Job Functions, Denmark, 2007

Industry / Job function	Independent artists	Visual artists	Theatre	Music	Film	Publishing	Radio and television	Architecture	Design	Advertising	Photography	Total
Creative job function (pct.)	7	47	20	1	23	16	30	52	8	7	38	16 (21,134)
Other job function (pct.)	82	19	49	71	45	47	40	27	73	24	25	45 (58,979)
Management at highest level in firms, organizations, and the public sector (pct.)	1	7	2	3	5	5	9	10	5	7	5	6 (3,401)
Work that assumes knowledge at highest level within field (pct.)	94	26	22	69	10	10	15	19	2	7	3	10 (5,932)
Work that assumes knowledge at medium level (pct.)	2	18	20	11	61	28	35	43	11	31	10	23 (13,397)
Office work (pct.)	2	21	15	11	13	21	23	16	10	18	33	15 (9,057)
Retailing, service, and care work (pct.)	0	12	14	3	5	5	4	3	2	8	35	5 (2,991)
Work within agriculture, market gardening, forestry, and fishing industry (pct.)	0	0	0	0	0	0	0	0	0	0		0 (25)
Crafts and related trade workers (pct.)	1	2	9	2	2	8	7	4	35	5	3	17 (10,156)
Plant and machine operators and assemblers (pct.)	0	1	0	0	0	6	3	0	21	1	4	10 (5,714)
Other occupations (pct.)	1	12	18	1	4	17	4	5	13	22	7	14 (8,306)
Unknown job function (pct.)	11	35	31	28	32	37	30	21	20	69	37	40 (52,299)
Total (pct.)	100	100	100	100	100	100	100	100	100	100	100	100
Total	1,627	654	7,767	536	4,486	26,719	9,152	9,421	31,309	37,390	3.351	132,412

Table 2.8   Persons Employed in the Creative Industries, Distributed by Education, Denmark, 2007

Industry Job function	Independent artists	Visual artists	Theatre	Music	Film	Publishing	Radio and television	Architecture	Design	Advertising	Photography	Total
Creative education (pct.)	19	7	16	7	12	15	17	36	6	4	21	11 (15,174)
Other education (pct.)	77	89	72	88	78	61	76	58	87	43	72	65 (85,922)
Short	48	41	56	54	60	46	46	28	49	56	54	49 (42,282)
Short-cycle higher education	20	35	24	23	18	30	28	19	41	26	37	31 (26,641)
Medium-cycle higher education	20	18	14	16	13	14	16	44	8	11	7	14 (11,666)
Long-cycle higher education	11	6	6	7	8	9	10	8	2	7	2	6 (5,278)
PhD degree or higher	1	0	0	0	0	0	0	0	0	0	0	0 (59)
No or unknown (pct.)	4	4	12	5	10	24	6	6	7	53	7	24 (31,312)
Total (pct.)	100	100	100	100	100	100	100	100	100	100	100	100
Total	1,627	654	7,767	536	4,486	26,719	9,152	9,421	31,309	37,390	3,351	132,412

working in the creative industries have a creative job function, 45 percent have other (humdrum) job functions, and 40 percent have unknown job functions. Again there are variations among the industries, where the largest proportion of creative jobs is found in architecture, the visual arts, and photography. The music industry,[7] independent artists,[8] advertising, and design have the lowest proportion of creative job functions.

Table 2.8 shows that among those people working in the creative industries, 11 percent have a creative education. The largest part of those with

Table 2.9   Socioeconomic Distribution for Three Different Criteria for Defining Actors (Percent)

	Job function as an actor	Membership of actors association	Acting education
Income	2007	2007*	2007
0–100.000	20.9	40.3	39.9
100.000–200.000	19.6	21.6	18.8
200–300.000	14.1	15.8	15.3
300–400.000	13.5	10.8	11.6
400–500.000	10.5	5.7	6.7
500–600.000	4.8	2.0	2.8
>600.000	2.0	3.7	4.9
Total N	1,457	1,987	973
Industry			
Theatre, film, and TV	37.5	31.3	34.0
Other industries	45.0	38.3	28.0
Out of industry or unknown	17.2	30.3	37.8
Total N	1,457	2,204	984
Actor union			
Member	36	100	75
Non-member	64	0	25
Total N	1,457	2,204	985
Age			
18–27	25.6	16.1	4.2
28–37	35.1	27.9	25.3
38–47	21.1	22.2	20.5
48–57	9.7	17.4	17.6
58–67	6.5	10.6	16.1
68+	1.9	5.9	16.4
Total N	1,276	2,005	985
Gender			
Men	54.2	46.0	47.6
Women	45.8	54.0	52.4
Total N	1,457	2,005	985
Education			
Actor education	21.3	37.7	100
Other education	78.7	64.3	0
Total	1,457	2,005	985

*Membership data from the Danish Actors Association are from 2010.

another education (49 percent) has a short education (most of them have only graduated from elementary or high school), 14 percent have a non-creative medium-cycle higher education, and 6 percent have a non-creative long-cycle higher education.

Again there are variations among industries, with the largest share of those working in architecture having a creative education (36 percent). Twenty-one percent of the photographers have a creative education, and about 19 percent of the independent artists.

The largest share of persons with a short educational background is found in film, theatre, advertising, music, and photography. The lowest share is found in architecture.

Having selected the relevant research population, it is quite easy to use the data from Statistics Denmark to obtain all kind of socioeconomic information of this group. This is out of the scope of this chapter, but an example is given next.

ACTORS: AN EXAMPLE

In Table 2.9, actors are delimitated in three different ways: 1) having a job as an actor,[9] 2) membership with the Danish Actors Association, or 3) having an acting education. Looking at the socioeconomic characteristics of these three groups, it is quite clear that they are different.

The income distribution shows a much higher income for those who have a job as an actor compared with those who are members of the Danish Actors Association or those with an acting education. It tell us that the two latter groups probably define themselves as artists but are out of the acting business and do not satisfy the conventional market-based definition of professionalism. There is also a larger share from the first group that are working in the creative industries and a smaller share that are out of industry compared with the two other groups. It is also interesting to notice that only 36 percent of those with a job as an actor are a member of the Danish Actor Association, whereas 75 percent of those with an actor education are members of the Danish Actor Association. The age distribution tells us that those who have a job as an actor are young, whereas the population with an acting education are much older, and those who are members of the Danish Actor Association are somewhere in between. There are also more men than women with a job as an actor, whereas the two other groups have a higher proportion of women.

Table 2.10 also shows some interesting results. If we look at career length in the total panel dataset 1996–2007, it shows us that of those who have a job as an actor in 2007, 43 percent only have the job for one year, and they also had a small income. Those with a longer career as an actor have on average a much higher income. The results show us that few can sustain a long career as an actor, but many try out the opportunity with a low

Table 2.10   Career Length and Income for Actors (Percent)

Income (1,000 DKKK) Career length	0–100	100–200	200–300	300–400	400–500	500+	Total
1 actore year	40.2	21.2	17.5	12.0	4.0	5.0	452 (43 percent)
2 actor years	28.3	23.5	20.0	14.5	6.2	7.6	145 (14 percent)
3–5 actor years withour "in betweens"	11.5	21.5	25.3	25.3	6.9	9.3	130 (12 percent)
3–5 actor years with one "in between"	13.9	23.6	22.2	19.4	9.7	11.1	72 (6 percent)
6–7 actor years without "in betweens"	0.0	6.5	16.1	35.5	6.5	35.5	31 (3 percent)
6–7 actor years with one "in between"	4.0	8.0	28.0	36.0	16.0	8.0	25 (2 percent)
8 actor years without 'in betweens'	5.0	10.0	12.5	35.0	32.5	5	40 (4 percent)
8–11 actor years with one "in between"	17.5	7.5	22.5	22.5	17.5	12.5	40 (4 percent)
12 actor years without "in betweens"	0.0	13.3	17.3	22.7	33.3	13.3	75 (7 percent)
12 actor years with one "in between"	2.3	4.6	31.8	20.5	22.7	18.2	44 (4 percent)
Total	259 24.6	198 18.8	210 19.9	191 18.1	104 9.9	92 8.8	1,054

income. If we include those people with only one year in the acting busi-ness, the income distribution looks much different than if we only include those people with a longer career. These people are not necessarily found among those with an actor education or those who are members of the Danish Actors Association. Besides, many of those who are members of the Danish Actors Association do not have a job as an actor.

CONCLUSION

This chapter has focused on three main questions: Who are the creative workers? What do they do? Where do they work?

The categories from Statistics Denmark are used for delimitation, and this makes it possible to analyze creative labor from three different per-spectives: creative industries, creative job function, and creative educa-tion. A quite narrow definition has been used in all three perspectives focusing on the production of culture and creative content, making the conclusions as sharp as possible on labor market conditions for artistic creativity and production.

Who are the creative workers? There is no clear definition here. In this chapter, two criteria are used: creative job function and creative education.

If we delimit the population of creative workers by creative job function, we get a definition of creative labor saying 'you are what you do.' Another possibility is creative education.

What do they do? If we use creative education to define creative labor, it is possible to look at what those people with a creative education are actually doing. Other questions can be answered as well. Where do they work? What is their unemployment rate? What is their income level? What do their career patterns look like and why?

Where do they work? Using data from Statistics Denmark, it is possible to see in which industries creative laborers work. The descriptive results presented in this chapter show us that there is a huge amount of non-creative jobs in the creative industries (only 16 percent of the persons working in the creative industries have a creative job function), and many of the persons working in these industries only have a short education. About one third of the people working in the creative industries have a short education (only elementary, high school, or the like).

Creative workers can be defined by either creative job function or education. Defined in these ways, the analysis shows that most creative workers are working in industries other than the creative industries. In terms of job function, about 50 percent work outside the creative industries, whereas in terms of creative education, only 25 percent work in the creative industries when using this chapter's delimitation. This means that the creative economy is much broader than the creative industries, and creativity in the form of creative labor is largely spread to other industries.

The results also tell us that there is not much of an overlap among the different definition criteria. Depending on whether creative labor is defined

Table 2.11 Delimitation of Creative Labor by Industry Job Function and Education, Denmark, 2007

	Creative job function	Creative industries	Creative education
Creative education	28 (32) pct.	12 (12) pct.	—
Other education	72 (68) pct.	88 (88) pct.	—
Total oct.	100 pct.	100 pct.	—
Creative job function	—	16 (7) pct.	20 pct.
Other job function or unknown	—	84 (93) pct.	80 pct.
Total pct.	—	100 pct.	100 pct.
Creative industry	51 pct.	—	25 pct.
Other industry or outside industry	49 pct.	—	75 pct.
Total pct.	100 pct.	—	100 pct.
Total	41,594	132,412	60,363
Total (The Danish Enterprise and Construction Authority, 2008)	46,248	266,448	

Note. The numbers in brackets are from the Danish Enterprise and Construction Authority (2008).

by industry, job function, or creative education, the research population will be different and following that also the research results. The categories developed in this chapter can be further developed by refining the register categorizations by cross-analysis. For instance, we can delimitate the people who have a certain creative job function and at the same time work in some selected, specified industries.

The analyses have shown a lot of variation among different creative industries, different kinds of creative job functions, and different kinds of creative educations. This means that it does not make much sense to study the creative industries in total. The creative labor market looks different for the different creative industries.

The highest number of jobs is found in architecture, craft and design, authors and writers (including journalists), and photography (including image and sound recording equipment operators). Compared with this, the more art-related and specialized jobs, such as in the performing arts, music, and the visual arts, are smaller in number, and, besides, the relation among the creative jobs, the creative educations, and the creative industries is much closer in these fields.

The findings in this chapter suffer from the serious drawback mentioned in the beginning of this chapter: Different definitions give different results. The criteria used in the chapter concerning creative job function, creative educations, and creative industries are subjective and could have been defined differently. In a report from 2008, the Danish Enterprise and Construction Authority (*Erhvervs—og Byggestyrelsen*) has looked at almost the same problem using data from 2005. The results of this analysis are shown in brackets in Table 2.11. Although some broader definitions have been used by the Danish Enterprise and Construction Authority, compared with the definitions chosen in this chapter, the results are not too different. In the report from the Danish Enterprise and Construction Authority, twice as many people are working in the creative industries, compared with the findings in this chapter. This is of course a result of the broader definition used by the Danish Enterprise and Construction Authority. However, it is interesting that the shares of people working in the creative industries and having a creative job function or a creative education are almost identical.

This chapter is based on register data from Statistics Denmark from 2007, and it should be emphasized that there are good reasons to believe that the more generic results obtained can to a large degree be generalized. The analyses have shown different problems connected to the delimitation of creative labor, which is also true for other countries and other years.

This chapter has mainly looked at the delimitation of creative labor and artists, and it has shown some descriptive results based on industries, job function, and education. The results make it clear: No uniform definition of creative labor exists. The results also show much variation among creative industries, and it is clear that each industry deserves to be studied in much more details, but this is out of the scope of this chapter. However, it is clear that the data from Statistics Denmark used in this chapter make it possible to do further research on the labor market conditions for creative labor and artists. Questions such as job mobility, inflow and outflow to different industries, and especially income conditions for the different groups of creative labor can be the subject for further research based on the data presented here. The panel structure in the data has not been used in this chapter, where only results based on one single year—namely, 2007—were presented. But using the whole dataset from 1994 to 2007, research on career patterns is possible. Selecting the 'right' group of artists and creative labor is a big challenge. Having selected a group of artists or creative labor, it is possible to use the register data from Statistics Denmark to create more knowledge about the creative labor market (see e.g., Bille et al. 2010).

NOTES

1. The same applies to the definition of 'creative industries.' No general definition exists, and every country has its own definition (see e.g., Birch 2008).
2. A report from the Danish Ministry for Cultural Affairs (2009) focuses on wages, unemployment rates, and so on among graduates from the 18 artistic and cultural educational institutions in Denmark.
3. Finland is one of the few other countries that have had the same data possibilities for several years.
4. Our data from Statistics Denmark are real panel data—namely, register data for the total Danish population from 1994 to 2007. Real panel data mean that each person (in anonymous form) can be traced over time. People are identified by their unique personal code (CPR number); hence, it is possible to track particular individuals or cohorts over time. It is interesting to notice that none of the empirical studies mentioned by Alper and Wassall (2006) is based on real panel data possibly because Denmark has unique possibilities.
5. Looking at employment and income conditions for creative labor and artists, in most cases we need a reference population. As Alper and Wassall (2006) observe, most census-based studies have compared artists' labor market outcomes to a reference population. But the choice of reference population has not been consistent, ranging from specific occupations with comparable educational attainment to specific professional occupations, to all workers, and to all managerial, professional, and technical workers. Based on data from Statistics Denmark, it is possible to select the reference population that suits the analyses best. The reference population can be the total workforce in Denmark, the persons with an education on similar level, and so on.
6. Among others, Hesmondhalgh (2007) has argued that 'cultural industries' is a better term than 'creative industries.' There is, however, no consensus on either of the concepts.
7. This is probably because the music industry consists of two industries: 'Publishing of sound recording' and 'Music agency and other services.' This means that musicians are included elsewhere.
8. This mainly consisting of journalist writing.
9. A broader definition is used here because, besides film, stage, and related actors and directors, it also includes choreographers and dancers; street, night-club, and related musicians; singers and dancers; plus clowns, magicians, acrobats, and related associate professionals.

REFERENCES

Abbing, H. 2002. *Why Are Artists Poor? The Exceptional Economy of the Arts.* Amsterdam: Amsterdam University Press.

Adler, M. 2006. "Stardom and Talent." In *Handbook of the Economics of Arts and Culture,* edited by V. A. Ginsburgh and D. Thorsby (Series: Handbook of Economics 25). Amsterdam: North-Holland.

Alper, N. O., and G. H. Wassall. 2000. *More than Once in the Blue Moon: Multiple Job Holdings by American Artists.* Washington, DC: National Endowments for the Arts.

Alper, N. O., and G. H. Wassall. 2006. "Artist's Careers and Their Labor Markets." In *Handbook of the Economics of Arts and Culture,* edited by V. A. Ginsburgh and D. Thorsby (Series: Handbook of Economics 25). Amsterdam: North-Holland.

Bille, T., and M. Lorenzen. 2008. *Den danske oplevelsesøkonomi—afgrænsning, økonomisk betydning og vækstmuligheder.* Copenhagen: Forlaget Samfundslitteratur.

Bille, T., F. Agersnap, S. Jensen, and T. Vestergaard. 2010. *Performing Artists' Income Conditions and Careers in Denmark.* Working paper Creative Encounters no. 49. Copenhagen: Copenhagen Business School.

Birch, S. 2008. *The Political Promotion of the Experience Economy and the Creative Industries—Cases from UK, New Zealand, Singapore, Norway, Sweden and Denmark.* Copenhagen: Forlaget Samfundslitteratur.

Caves, R. 2000. *Economics of the Creative Industries.* Cambridge, MA: Harvard University Press.

Danish Enterprise and Construction Authority (Erhvervs—og Byggestyrelsen). 2008. *Vækst via oplevelser—en analyse af Danmark i oplevelsesøkonomien.* Copenhagen: Author.

Danish Ministry for Cultural Affairs. 2009. *Beskæftigelsesrapport* (Employment report). Copenhagen: Author.

Elstad, J. I., and K. R. Pedersen. 1996. *Kunstnernes økonomiske vilkår. Rapport fra Inntekts- og yrkesundersøkelsen brandt kunstnere 1993–94* (INAS report). Oslo: Institut for Socialforskning.

Filer, R. K. 1989. "The Economic Condition of Artists in America." In *Cultural Economis 88: An American Perspective,* edited by D. V. Shaw et al. Akron: Association for Cultural Economics.

Florida, R. 2002. *The Rice of the Creative Class—And How It's Transforming Work, Leisure, Community and Everyday Life.* New York: Basic Books.

Frey, B. S., and W. W. Pommerehne. 1989. *Muses and Markets. Explorations in the Economics of the Arts.* Oxford: Basil Blackwell.

Heian, M. T., K. Løyland, and P. Mangset. 2008. *Kunstnernes aktivitet, arbeids—og inntektsforhold, 2006* (Report no. 241). Bø: Telemarksforskning-Bø.

Hesmondhalgh, D. 2007, January. Creative Industries Critique: Possibilities and Problems. Paper presented at the Cultural Industries Network: New Directions in Research: Substance, Method, and Critique conference, Edinburgh, Scotland.

Hesmondhalgh, D. 2010. "Normativity and Social Justice in the Analysis of Creative Labour." *Journal for Cultural Research* 14: 231–49.

Higgs, P., S. Cunningham, and H. Bakhshi. 2008. *Beyond the Creative Industries: Mapping the Creative Economy in the United Kingdom.* London: National Endowment for Science, Technology, and the Arts.

Jeffri, J., and D. Throsby. 1994. "Professionalism and the Visual Artists." *European Journal for Cultural Policy*1: 99–108.

Karttunen, S. 1998. "How to Identify Artists? Defining the Population for 'Status-of-the-Artists' Studies." *Poetics* 26: 1–19.

Karttunen, S. 2001. "How to Make Use of Census Data in Status-of-the-Artist Studies: Advantages and Shortcomings of the Finnish Register-Based Census." *Poetics* 28: 273–90.

Kaufmand, , and Sternberg, eds. 2010. *The Cambridge Handbook of Creativity*. Cambridge: Cambridge University Press.

KEA European Affairs. 2006. *The Economy of Culture in Europe*. Brussels: European Commission.

Menger, P.-M. 2006. "Artistic Labor Markets: Contingent Work, Excess Supply and Occupational Risk Management." In *Handbook of the Economics of Arts and Culture*, edited by V. A. Ginsburgh and D. Thorsby (Series: Handbook of Economics 25). Amsterdam: North-Holland.

O'Brien, J., and A. Feist. 1995. *Employment in the Arts and Cultural Industries: An Analysis of the 1991 Census*. London: Arts Council of England.

Rengers, M. 2002. *Economic Lives of Artists; Studies into Careers and the Labour Market in the Cultural Sector*. Utrecht: Utrecht University, Interuniversity Center for Social Science Theory and Methodology.

Rosen, S. 1981. "The Economics of Superstars." *American Economic Review* 71: 845–58.

Throsby, D. 1994. "Work-Preference Model of Artist Behavior." In *Cultural Economics and Cultural Policies*, edited by A. Peacock and I. Rizzo, 69–80. Boston, MA: Kluwer Academic.

Throsby, D. 2001. *Economics and Culture*. Cambridge: Cambridge University Press.

Throsby, D. 2007, January. Modelling the Creative/Cultural Industries. Paper presented at the Cultural Industries Seminar Network: New Directions in Research: Substance, Method, and Critique conference, Edinburgh, Scotland.

Throsby, D., and V. Hollister. 2003. *Don't Give Up Your Day Job Yet: An Economic Study of Professional Artists in Australia*. Sydney: Australia Council.

Towse, R. 2006. "Human Capital and Artists' Labor Markets." In *Handbook of the Economics of Arts and Culture*, edited by V. A. Ginsburgh and D. Thorsby (Series: Handbook of Economics 25), Amsterdam: North-Holland.

UNCTAD. 2008. *Creative Economy Report 2008: The Challenge of Assessing the Creative Economy: Towards Informed Policy-making*. Geneva: Author.

Wassall, G. H., and N. O. Alper. 1992. "Toward a Unified Theory of the Determinants of the Earnings of Artists." In *Cultural Economics*, edited by R. Topwse, 187–200. Berlin: Springer.

Table 2.A   Creative Job Functions

Creative jobs within	Disco code	Creative jobs
Visual artists	2453	Sculptures, painters, and related artists
Dancers	2454	Choreographers and dancers
Actors and directors	2455	Film, stage, and related actors and directors
Musicians	2453	Composers, musicians, and singers
Photographers	3131	Photographers and image and sound recording equipment operators
Writers	2451	Authors, journalists, and other writers
Architects	2141	Architects, and town and traffic planners
	2149	Architects, engineers, and related professionals not elsewhere classified
Craft and design	3471	Decorators and commercial designers

Table 2.B   Creative Educations

Creative education within	HFUDD Creative educations
Photograph educations	4461, 4462, 4474, 4864, 4865, 4866, 4867, 4869, 9757
Film and television educations	5801, 5802, 5803, 5804, 5805, 5806, 5807, 5816, 5817, 6724, 9167, 9830
Graphic educations	4451, 4453, 4454, 4458, 4465, 4472, 4473, 4475, 4703, 5082, 5083, 5087, 5758, 5759, 5813, 5820, 6452, 9706
Journalist educations	5735, 5736, 6147, 6665, 9144
Theater educations	4315, 5846, 5847, 5848, 5849, 5850, 5852, 5855
Dancer educations	5856
Music educations	5602, 5603, 5611, 5615, 5618, 5619, 5620, 5895, 5901, 5902, 5904, 5909, 5918, 5919, 5921, 5922, 5923, 5925, 5995, 5996, 6586, 6587, 6786, 6787, 7873, 9171, 9172
Art educations	5811, 5812, 5814, 5821, 5822, 5823, 5825, 9176
Craft and design educations	5057, 2421, 4037, 4055, 4070, 4071, 4072, 4073, 4074, 4075, 4076, 4257, 4258, 4268, 4308, 4339, 4341, 4342, 4343, 4481, 4485, 4491, 4493, 4501, 4506, 4507, 4508, 4509, 4528, 5056, 5058, 5059, 5062, 5131, 9197, 9704, 9739, 9788, 9815
Architect educations	5470, 5480

Table 2.C   Creative Industries

Creative industries within	NACE Code Creative educations
Independent artists	92.31.20
Visual arts	52.48.35
Theatre	92.31.10, 92.32.00
Music	22.14.00, 74.84.90
Film	92.11.00
Publishing	22.11.10, 22.11.20, 22.12.10, 22.12.20, 22.13.10, 22.13.20, 22.13.30, 22.13.40, 22.15.00
Radio and television	22.31.00, 22.32.00, 92.20.00, 92.20.10, 92.20.20
Architecture	74.20.40, 74.20.50, 74.87.10
Design	74.84.10, 74.84.20, 17.40.20, 17.40.90, 28.73.00, 17.51.00, 17.71.00, 17.72.00, 17.73.00, 17.74.00, 17.75.00, 18.10.00, 18.21.00, 18.22.00, 18.22.10, 18.22.20, 18.22.30, 18.23.10, 18.23.90, 18.24.10, 18.24.90, 18.30.00, 19.10.00, 19.20.00, 19.30.10, 36.11.10, 36.12.00, 36.13.00, 36.14.10, 36.21.00, 36.22.10, 36.22.20, 74.87.20
Advertising	74.40.10, 74.40.90
Photography	74.81.10, 52.48.25, 74.81.20

Part II
Theatre, Television, and Film

3 Behind the Scenes of Boundarylessness
Careers in German Theatre

*Doris Ruth Eikhof, Axel Haunschild,
and Franziska Schößler*

INTRODUCTION

A career in the creative industries is a desired goal for many: an opportunity to express oneself in creative activities, to work flexibly, with interesting people and on exciting projects. Around the world, talent shows such as *The X Factor* and *Pop Idol* both document and perpetuate the appeal of working in a job as glamorous and intrinsically fulfilling as that described by Matthias, an ensemble actor at one of Germany's most prestigious theatres: *"Being on stage every night, doing what you are best at and being rewarded with applause and, even, money—that's just the best thing ever."* In his opinion, this *"best thing ever"* makes up for those difficulties and disadvantages of a career in the creative industries that are less in the spotlight of public attention and culminate in a constant pressure to perform: *"You are not only exposed to external judgement all the time, you also constantly monitor your own work [. . .] There is a low barrier to panic and you are always afraid that you will be cast for too few or too small roles—you are always afraid that theatre management and audience will not love you enough."*

In the career and creative industries literature, this continuous oscillating between *"best thing ever"* on the one hand and *"panic"* on the other hand has predominantly been analyzed through the lens of project-based employment and boundaryless careers. As creative workers move from project to project, their careers transcend the boundaries of organizations and the field or industry becomes the main frame of reference. Some writers have emphasized the opportunity that such careers hold for workers to mold careers according to their own preferences and to align personal and professional aims over the life course. Elsewhere, the difficulties of sustaining oneself through periods of unemployment and the overall precariousness of such careers have been the focus of attention. Both debates emphasize that careers have become individualized. Career trajectories are particular to the individual worker, and the responsibility for successfully shaping these trajectories is an individual one as well—for better or worse.

Based on evidence from German theatre, this chapter takes a look behind the scenes of such boundaryless, project-based, and individualized careers. In so doing, it explores a range of more nested and hidden but nevertheless powerful features of theatre as an employment system that constrain individual agency in career development. Although careers are the individual actor's responsibility, the structures of the employment system leave little scope for shaping them in a genuinely individual, personal way. Instead, career trajectories are marked by typical patterns. Based on several in-depth studies into theatre as an employment system, this chapter shows how careers can be boundaryless but still bound by a variety of factors.

CAREERS IN THE CREATIVE INDUSTRIES

Across industries and national employment systems, creative production is dominated by project work. Whether in film, theatre, advertising, or new media (e.g. Blair 2001; Dempster 2006; Grabher 2002; Jones 1996; Pratt 2009), production is organized in 'motley crews' (Caves 2000, 6) of diverse talent. Teams are brought together for a certain period of time to achieve a specific output—curate an exhibition, stage an opera, produce a TV show—and disband once that output is delivered. This specific organization of creative production leads to a perception of careers in the creative industries as sequences of projects in two important ways.

First, careers are understood as the series of discreet artistic or creative achievements an individual has been involved in. These achievements are observed and evaluated within the respective creative industry—formally, for instance, with awards and prizes such as the Oscar or César in film (see Chapter 5, this volume) or the Turner Prize in visual arts and informally, through conversations and recommendations within the industry. Such collective evaluation within the industry constitutes a creative worker's reputation (e.g. Chapter 8, this volume; Jones 2002, Chapter 7, this volume). On the one hand, such evaluation is essential for individual self esteem: "*You can walk down the street with the thrill of knowing that you are considered worthy by other creative people in the business*" (music producer on receiving a Grammy Award; cited in Anand and Watson 2004, 67). Collective recognition of one's work also calms the constant panic described by actor Matthias: "*Did I play often enough? Did I play enough main roles? Are there any signs of the theatre manager wanting to keep me on? Or worse, that he wants to get rid of me?*" On the other hand, reputation has a direct impact on a creative worker's chance of participating in future projects: the higher the industry's collective evaluation of a creative worker's artistic capabilities, the higher their chance of being asked not only to participate in future projects but also to participate in a prominent—and artistically interesting—capacity. The phrase "You're only as good as your last job" (Blair 2001) describes evaluation practices throughout the creative industries: Future project participation crucially depends on how peers and the public view the last project a creative worker was involved in.

Second, careers in the creative industries are also perceived as sequences of projects because creative production as well as employment tend to be project-based (Blair 2001; Jones 1996; Randle and Culkin 2009). Instead of climbing a hierarchy of organizational positions, creative workers' career trajectories consist of participation in different projects underpinned by a sequence of employment contracts. Creative workers tend to fulfill similar roles on projects (e.g. as an actor, light designer, or web designer), but the quality and responsibility of their contributions may evolve over time (e.g. they may move from support to lead acts or from lighting assistant to head of lighting department), similar to upward moves in a more traditional organizational hierarchy.

Such project-focused careers have been describes as boundaryless (Arthur and Rousseau 1996; Jones 1996): Organizational boundaries lose their relevance for both individual career moves and the recognition of careers within a field. Not only do careers take place in projects dotted across the respective industry, they are also evaluated and validated by significant others beyond a specific employing organization, for instance, via industry-wide processes of constructing reputation. Changes from organizational to boundaryless careers enhance individual agency (Arthur 2008) and provide the opportunity for individuals to deliberately shape their professional trajectories (Arthur et al. 1999; Hall et al. 2002).

The freedom of shaping one's career according to individual aims and preferences goes hand in hand with an individual responsibility for translating career aims into career reality (see Chapter 11, this volume, on similar pressures for visual artists). To this end, creative workers need to actively market their labor, in particular through networking and utilizing personal contacts across their industry (e.g. Eikhof and Haunschild 2006, 2007; Grugulis and Stoyanova 2009; Jackson 1996; Jones and DeFillippi 1996; Randle and Culkin 2009). Across different industries, creative workers strategically develop and use contacts to find work. Although traditional recruitment processes may exist, personal networks of both recruiters and recruitees are paramount: "*I have never gotten a job off sending my resumé cold. Never, ever, and I have sent out hundreds of resumés, and I've never gotten a job that way ever. I have only gotten jobs because I knew someone in the office who could walk my resumé in*" (makeup artist cited in Blair et al. 2003, 629).

Studies focusing on the precariousness of project-focused or boundaryless careers have emphasized a less positive aspect of the individualization of careers: Project-based employment puts creative workers under considerable pressure to economically sustain themselves (Randle and Culkin 2009; Skillset 2008). With projects at times only lasting a handful of days (e.g. Blair 2001; Skillset 2008), project-based employment often leaves creative workers spending more time searching for work than actually working: "*Finding and negotiating work is the hardest part. Doing the work is the fun. Finding the work is the job"* (script supervisor cited in Randle and Culkin 2009, 101). In addition to finding employment, creative workers have to sustain themselves through periods of unemployment and bear training costs, professional development, insurance, sick pay and maternity leave (Gill 2002; Skillset 2008; Warhurst and Eikhof 2010). Depending on personal preferences and circumstances, such pressures can become too much to bear: *"My partner and I have both decided that as 'late thirty-somethings with children', in independent production, we are getting too old for this insecurity and uncertainty"* (company owner cited in Dex et al. 2000, 299).

Across these studies and regardless of whether they focus on the positive or the precarious aspects of project-focused and boundaryless careers, three features of employment systems are commonly emphasized as career-relevant: (temporary) employment contracts or their absence, an individual's reputation within the industry and personal networks. Embedded in these structures, careers in the creative industries are understood as an individualized matter, with career trajectories particular to each individual creative worker. Using the German theatre industry as an example, the following sections widen this perspective and explore a range of additional features that influence project-focused and boundaryless careers (see Chapter 4, this volume, for an analysis of similar issues in the UK TV industry).

EMPIRICAL STUDY

Data used in our analysis comprise qualitative empirical data and secondary data both collected by the authors. Primary data includes 51 semi-structured in-depth interviews conducted between 2000 and 2003 and in 2009. The first set of interviews (10 interviews) was carried out in a German theatre (Staatstheater) financed by public subsidies and situated in a city with approximately 500,000 inhabitants. Interview partners here included the theatre manager (artistic director), a senior administration manager, a director, a project coordinator and several actors linked to the theatre by different contractual arrangements. The second set of interviews (five interviews) was conducted with representatives of inter-firm institutions: the national employers' and employees' associations, the state-run work agency for actors and a state-run theatre school (see also Haunschild 2003). A third set of interviews (16 interviews) was conducted with theatre actors, dramaturges,[1] a director and a theatre manager in two repertoire theatres situated in a city with approximately 2 million inhabitants. The interviewees comprised ensemble members (actors on one- to two-year contracts) as well as self-employed theatre artists. A fourth set of interviews (20 interviews) covered actors, theatre managers, dramaturges and directors affiliated with three German theatres of different sizes and degrees of reputation within the theatre community.

Depending on the interviewees, the interview schedules covered motivation to become or be an actor, career ambitions and trajectories, career planning, the role of self-marketing and personal networks, everyday experiences of work and employment in theatre, the relationship between 'work' and 'life,' the (perceived) problem of aging, employment relations (e.g. pay and terms of contract), structural aspects of theatre as an employment system (e.g. education, labour markets, industrial relations), HR practices (in particular recruitment), gender-related work conditions of theatre artists (in particular aesthetic demands and role requirements) and the impact of growing economic pressure after the German reunification in 1989. Interviews were analyzed by teams of researchers, and findings triangulated with secondary information and data. During all phases of data collection, additional informal discussions with theatre artists and other members of the industry as well as participation in industry events such as premiere celebrations provided further information. Secondary data used include interviews with theatre artists in newspapers and practitioner journals, statistical reports and information given on theatres' and inter-firm institutions' websites.

EMPLOYMENT AND PRODUCTION IN GERMAN THEATRE

Compared with the performing arts internationally, the German theatre industry constitutes an idiosyncratic context for creative workers' careers (for more details see Eikhof 2009; Haunschild 2003). Nearly all German theatres of artistic relevance are public theatres owned by cities or local states. Surprisingly unharmed by 200 years of changing political systems, German theatre developed from royal theatre groups at court and free citizens' theatres into an industry that now comprises around 150 publicly funded theatres. The respective local governments finance up to 95 percent of these theatres' annual budgets via income tax. Private theatres are not of significant artistic relevance and artistic reputation within the public-funded theatres mainly concentrates on a group of approximately 10 'A-houses' and 'B-houses.' In theory, a theatre's reputation depends on the theatre manager of the moment. Theatre managers are responsible for a theatre's overall artistic output and are hired—on five-year contracts—to bring their particular take on theatre as art to the post. In practice, A-houses and B-houses tend to be those theatres in cities with more than 500,000 inhabitants, as only larger communities provide the local governments with budgets big enough to offer reputed theatre managers artistically attractive organizational budgets and personal conditions.

Germany's public theatres employ a standing group of actors, the ensemble. At medium- to large-sized theatres, ensembles consist of approximately 25 to 40 actors. Their employment contracts are 12-month contracts embedded in the 'Normalvertrag Bühne' (NV Bühne), which is the result of collective bargaining between employer association and union. Despite being temporary, ensemble contracts grant actors some job security. However, less than one third of the estimated 9,000–10,000 professional actors in Germany work as ensemble actors at one of the 150 public theatres. The remaining two thirds work either (a) as 'guests' employed as freelancers for a certain play; (b) as contractors employed for part of the season; (c) in private, commercial or 'free' theatres on various contracts; and (d) across the acting profession (e.g. in film, TV, and radio productions) or they are unemployed actors (Haunschild 2004). This oversupply of labour makes the labour market for theatre actors in Germany competitive and the competition for ensemble contracts is most intense (see Chapter 2, this volume, for an analysis of the comparatively high unemployment rates in the performing arts).

In addition to the ensemble members other key artistic staff members are employed on a project-by-project basis. Directors, who lead productions artistically, are typically freelance and work for several theatres throughout a season, both consecutively and in parallel. Costume and stage designers tend to be freelance as well. Together with directors they often form comparatively stable teams that move from project to project in a similar fashion to the 'semi-permanent work groups' in film described by Blair (2001). Production teams also frequently comprise guest actors hired on a freelance basis for that particular production. Freelance guests can usually command higher wages, but they are also exposed to higher job insecurity. For the duration of a production, freelance directors, stage and costume designers and actors are integrated into the respective theatre's rehearsal and show schedule. They constitute an important personified link between internal and external labor markets as well as between the respective theatre and the overall theatre community in Germany. At A- and B-houses, guests are often cast for particularly prestigious roles. Consequently, ensemble actors find themselves in direct competition not only with ensemble colleagues but also with actors from the 'external' labour market. Moreover, freelance theatre artists moving from one project to the next contribute to the permanent exchange of ideas, opinions and information within the theatre industry.

Public theatres in Germany are repertoire theatres and offer a different drama every night, drawing on a repertoire of 15 to 30 plays for a season. Although some of these plays will be productions developed in previous seasons, new plays are developed at any given time during the theatre season. This development takes place during daytime rehearsals and in dedicated teams of actors, directors, stage designers, costume designers and other support staff. Development phases usually last eight weeks and at a medium-sized to large theatre up to four plays are developed in parallel. For each evening's performance, actors re-assemble in a team that once worked together in development and play the respective show. Typically, the actors on stage at night will have worked with one or more development teams during the day. Therefore, a reasonably busy ensemble actor usually works on at least two plays and with two different teams of colleagues on any given day.

Ensemble employment at publicly funded repertoire theatres and production in constantly changing teams of temporarily employed and freelance artists are the key characteristics of work and production in German theatres. The following sections explore how these key characteristics combine with a range of other features of the theatrical employment system to influence actors' careers.

A CAREER IN ACTING

The dominant career aim among German actors is ensemble membership at an A- or a B-theatre. Ensemble membership at an A- or a B-theatre offers the opportunity to be involved with the production of art at a highly recognized and artistically interesting level. Moreover, it contributes to individual reputation and makes it more likely that an actor will be approached to star as a guest in other productions or in film or TV. Ensemble actors are frequently involved in such freelance work in parallel to their ensemble projects, which brings not only additional income but broadens their artistic horizons and enhances their reputation and their contacts within the industry (see also Haunschild and Eikhof 2009). Several interviewees confessed that the absolutely ideal career situation would be to work freelance but predominantly as a guest with one specific (ideally an A-) theatre. Compared with ensemble membership, such a situation gives actors more choice and control over the projects they want to be involved in and the nature of the involvement (read: the role) combined with higher wages, but they are able to still maintain close links with a local community of trusted and valued colleagues. However, our interviewees also admitted that only a few, exceptionally good actors achieved this desirable career stage. Ensemble membership at an A- or (preferably better) B-theatre is a much more realistic career aim and therefore the dominant aspiration among established actors as well as drama school graduates. However, only 400 of the approximately 2,350 ensemble contracts in Germany at the time of our study were located at A- and B- theatres. Even achieving this more realistic career aim therefore means beating tough competition and because contracts are only temporary, maintaining employment at an A- or a B-theatre is equally difficult. This section explores in more detail the structural constraints and influences that shape actors' careers.

DRAMA SCHOOLS

In theory, anybody can work as an actor in Germany—there are no mandatory exams or degrees or other entry requirements. Acting can be 'studied' at a host of private drama schools, which, on average, are not overly selective in their admission decisions. However, the majority of private drama school graduates go into musical theatre and TV. A- or B-theatres hardly ever recruit actors from private institutions but from one of the 15 public drama schools. In A- and B-theatre ensembles, actors who have come through any other educational route than a public drama school are a rare exception. Actors as well as theatre managers, directors, dramaturges and other industry experts confirmed that a degree from a public drama school was not a legal but a de facto requirement for a successful career in acting. Public drama schools are part of the German university system and, unlike private schools, charge no or only nominal fees. However, admission processes are psychologically tough and extraordinarily competitive, with selection ratios in some cases below five percent. Applicants usually complete a series of auditions at various schools. Subjecting oneself to the subjective scrutiny of admissions panels is an intimidating and humiliating experience and only applicants who possess the rare combination of genuine talent and real determination to become a serious actor succeed at this stage.

Beyond selecting for talent and determination, admission into drama school creates two important early career effects. First, the reputation of the respective drama school significantly impacts on a graduate's first job. Drama schools usually collaborate with local theatres which will include students' projects as part of their regular program. Such real-life productions increase the quality of the students' practical experience and skills but also give students ample opportunity to recommend themselves directly to key decision makers at these theatres. Obviously, A- and B-theatres offer better quality of practical experience and more valuable personal contacts, but they tend to collaborate only with a handful of renowned drama schools. In addition, reputed public drama schools hold graduation shows, which theatre managers, dramaturges and agents from all across Germany attend to scout talent. Less reputed schools have to travel with their graduation classes to potential employers and the format of these auditions makes it much more difficult for graduates to favorably exhibit their talent. Collaborations with local theatres during degree programs and different forms of presenting graduates to potential employers structure the transition from university to employment in a powerful, near-rigid way. Together these specific features of the theatre industry create a significant early career effect that, for better or worse, is difficult to shake off in the subsequent years (see also Chapter 12, this volume, for an account of Singapore's arts schools and see Chapter 13, this volume, for fashion designers' transition from school to work).

Second, admission policies at drama schools contribute to significant gender differences in actors' career experiences. Theatres employ approximately 60 percent male and 40 percent female actors as ensembles members, but public drama schools usually accept at least as many women as men. Consequently, career prospects for female actors are, right from the start, lower than those for male actors. This disadvantage for aspiring female actors is compounded by the fact that more women than men apply to drama schools and our interviewees unilaterally described female applicants as, on average, more talented than males. Moreover, in their admission decisions, drama schools anticipate theatre managers', directors', spectators' and critics' aesthetic norms regarding body shapes and looks for actors performing certain (classic) roles. These norms are significantly narrower for women than for men, boiling down to an almost binary classification of 'young, naïve girl' versus 'tough, energetic, more mature woman' (see also Dean 2005). As a consequence, entry into acting—via drama school and then via ensemble jobs—is gendered and considerably more difficult for women than for men.

RECRUITMENT AND STAFFING DECISIONS

Once graduated from drama school, actors' careers depend on staffing and casting decisions. These decisions occur on two levels:

1. *Recruitment decisions on ensemble membership*: Theatre managers have to recruit an ensemble with which they can staff the season's repertoire. While guest actors are frequently used as flexible supplements, most of the productions have to be staged with ensemble actors. Theatre managers' recruitment decisions are therefore influenced by the need to secure a varied pool of talent and corporeal aesthetics. Decisions on ensemble membership either take the form of recruiting a new ensemble member or extending/not extending an existing ensemble member's temporary contract. The latter decision has to be made on all ensemble contracts at the beginning of each theatre season. As a consequence of the ensemble system, actors' careers in German theatre are evaluated not solely as a sequence of projects but also with respect to the ensemble membership an actor has held (e.g. A-/B-theatre vs. provincial theatre). Decisions on ensemble membership therefore have a significant impact on actors' careers.

2. *Casting decisions for plays (i.e. allocating roles)*: In close collaboration with directors and dramaturges, theatre managers allocate roles for new productions. These decisions are mainly driven by artistic concerns (i.e. which actor the decision makers can best imagine to play a certain role, although see below on the importance of personal likes and dislikes). While the key idea of ensemble theatres is, of course, to staff plays with ensemble members, it is common practice to hire guest actors. In particular at A- and B-theatres, guest actors are regularly allocated lead roles and thus constitute real competition for ensemble members. Roles are crucial for actors' careers for two reasons. First, because career opportunities and moves are usually based on an actor's reputation within the industry. Because performance can be directly observed, visibility is essential for gaining

reputation. Lead or artistically interesting roles offer such visibility, and it is therefore imperative that an actor be allocated such roles. Second, ensemble members continuously compete against each other for roles. Casting decisions, which generally are authoritarian decisions, are therefore the most important organizational feedback actors receive on their previous performance(s) and are decisive for generating career opportunities.

Underlying recruitment and casting decisions and therefore influencing actors' careers is another key feature of the theatre industry: the plays' scripts. While German repertoire theatres do stage contemporary plays, more than half of the productions in a theatre season are classical dramas (i.e. written before 1900). Consequently, actors' jobs and career opportunities are significantly influenced by the roles offered in this particular type of literary material (for a similar effect see Chapter 10, this volume, on contemporary and classical composers). In comparison with contemporary plays, classical dramas typically offer only a few lead roles, supported by a cast of artistically less attractive smaller roles. In contemporary plays, artistic contribution tends to be more evenly distributed among all (or at least a larger share) of the characters on stage. The focus on classical dramas therefore enhances competition among actors for roles that give the opportunity to enhance and demonstrate their artistic talent. In addition, classical dramas offer considerably more lead roles for men than for women, which further increase competition among female actors. Indeed, the competition among actresses is commonly referred to as 'the vipers' nest' throughout the theatre industry. Moreover, the limited range of female characters essentially perpetuates traditional gender roles and the near-binary aesthetic norms for actresses (Schößler 2008). In summary, the literary material forms the basis of a specifically structured labour demand that results in high competition and, in particular, in unequal work conditions and career prospects for female and male actors. However, this discrimination is regarded as artistically legitimized and as a consequence of the constitutionally guaranteed 'freedom of the arts' (*Kunstfreiheit*; see Eikhof 2009 for more details) artistic considerations supersede equal opportunity employment laws in theatre.

Finally, careers in theatre are to a large extent influenced by individual, subjective preferences of key deciders. It is widely accepted in the industry and was openly admitted by our interviewees that theatre managers, directors and dramaturges recruit and staff plays on the basis of personal preferences. Personal preferences may relate to artistic aspects and it is common understanding that artistic views are subjective and often inexplicable. Even the industry-wide union contract recognizes 'artistic reasons' as a legitimate justification for decisions on role allocation and ensemble membership—and as one that, even in a legal dispute, literally does not require any further explanation beyond the words 'for artistic reasons'. Moreover, personal artistic preferences are subject to more general fashions in the industry: Styles of acting can gain or lose artistic currency depending on the industry's taste at the time. 'Chemistry' between team members was another often cited rationale behind recruitment and staffing decisions. Although by no means an objective criterion either, chemistry among team members is, in the views of many interviewees, essential not only for a pleasant work environment but for artistically excellent outputs. It is considered a functional requirement of creative production and team members expect decision makers to, for art's sake, explicitly consider it. Nevertheless, and again openly admitted by actors as well as theatre managers, dramaturges, directors and other industry experts, recruitment and staffing decision are always—although to different extents—down to who likes whom as a person. Ensemble actor Matthias was therefore not exaggerating when he talked about being *"loved enough"* by theatre management. Personal likes and dislikes, friendships and love relationships between actors, on the one hand, and directors, theatre managers and dramaturges, on the other hand, can make or break role allocations and recruitment decisions. Because artistic persona and individual personality are closely intertwined in theatre, few decisions will ever be purely personal. However, throughout the industry, interviewees reported a tendency to defend decisions as 'artistically motivated' that were—at least to a considerable extent—due to team chemistry considerations or personality issues or both.

While the forms of production and employment described in the previous section are undoubtedly relevant for actors' careers, this section has explored career influences resulting from the interplay of various more nested and hidden, but nevertheless powerful, features of the theatrical employment system: the link between drama schools and industry entry, between the literary material and recruitment decisions and between staffing decisions and personal preferences that are particular to the decision makers, but the existence of which is collectively accepted and justified (for an employment system perspective on the theatre industry see also Haunschild 2004). The following section shows how these career influences result in careers that are individualized but exhibit typical patterns rather than distinct, personalized trajectories.

ARTISTIC CAREERS: INDIVIDUALIZED BUT PATTERNED

Artistic careers in German theatre are boundaryless in the sense that actors do not move up the hierarchy within one organization but rather move from one theatre to the next (albeit almost exclusively within the German-speaking countries; for more international careers see Chapter 9, this volume, on violin soloists). In addition, both ensemble and freelance actors regularly work for more than one employer in parallel, for instance, when ensemble actors star in TV series in addition to their ensemble work or when freelance actors work as guests for two theatres at the same time.

As a sequence of (ensemble or project-based) contracts, careers in theatre thus transgress organizational boundaries both sequentially and simultaneously. As described earlier for boundaryless careers in general, freelance and temporary employment contracts, transorganizational social networks and industry-wide individual reputation play an important role for actors' careers as well.

Because theatrical production takes place within organizations and ensembles members are temporary members of organizations, 'boundarylessness' does not imply that organizations are irrelevant for actors' careers. However, organizational Human Resource Management (HRM) practices are essentially limited to recruitment and staffing decisions and, as explained earlier, even these practices are to a large extent down to the individual decision maker. In contrast to more traditional industries, where HRM departments aim to increase the objectivity of recruitment decisions, the theatre industry accepts that artistic decisions are subjective. Moreover, theatres do not engage in traditional HRM practices, such as career or succession planning or personnel development (see also Haunschild 2003). Theatre managers, directors, dramaturges or senior actors may offer advice to younger actors, but such advice is informal, based on personal likes and dislikes and, again, by no means limited to members of the same organization. On the contrary: friendships and professional alliances are formed and maintained across organizational boundaries.

Given the absence of organizational or otherwise institutionalized career support, theatre actors are entirely individually responsible for their careers. The key aim for both ensemble and freelance actors is to be cast for prestigious roles, which not only satisfies the intrinsic motivation to act but also increases one's artistic reputation. As we have described in more detail elsewhere (Eikhof and Haunschild 2006, 2007; Haunschild and Eikhof 2009), actors pursue these aims by strategically marketing their labour power through personal networks, calculating the costs and benefits of participating in particular projects and evaluating and disseminating industry information—be it reviews, awards or simply gossip.

Careers in German theatre are therefore not just boundaryless in the prior sense but also individualized. However, in the remainder of this section, we demonstrate how far from developing genuinely individual or even personalized trajectories, actors careers still exhibit typical patterns and how these patterns are notably gendered.

MOBILITY AND FLEXIBILITY

Whereas it is theoretically possible (and was common in East Germany before reunification) to stay at one theatre for one's entire career, a credible artistic career has to develop across organizational boundaries both sequentially and simultaneously. Partly, actors take the initiative in changing employers. In addition, theatre managers hold fixed-term contracts too and move from one theatre to the next after usually 5- or 10-year periods. Moving on with the theatre director or being made redundant because neither the previous nor the succeeding theatre manager offers employment are further typical reasons for crossing organizational boundaries. In addition, actors often simultaneously work on several projects in theatre, film or TV. Sequentially and simultaneously transgressing organizational boundaries requires considerable spatial mobility and flexibility. Such requirements are even more pronounced for actors working as freelance guests on project-based contracts and often in different cities.

Germany is a geographically compact country and only a comparatively small and relatively constant number of organizations and individuals are of real relevance for a successful career in acting. These factors should, in theory, enhance mobility within the industry and facilitate boundaryless careers. However, changes to public funding have restrained the opportunities for successfully pursuing boundaryless careers. Since the German reunification (1989), overall economic pressures have led to budget cuts and even theatre closures (a new phenomenon in Germany's highly subsidized theatre landscape, East and West), putting existing theatres under considerable pressure (see also Chapter 13, this volume, for increasing labor market pressures on fashion designers in the last decades). These economic strains have impacted careers in two ways. First, theatres try to reduce fixed costs by employing a higher share of actors as freelance guests. Such HRM strategies reduce the prospect of successful career moves into ensemble membership. Second, the divide between cultural metropolises and provincial areas has become (even) more pronounced. Working at a provincial theatre (i.e. out of the sight of the most crucial decision makers) reduces visibility and thus negatively impacts careers and pay. Changes as small as moving to a theatre in a city not served by Germany's express train network can therefore reduce career prospects significantly.

Actors respond to these mobility and flexibility requirements with several typical practices. First, to enable career moves across the industry, they lead deliberately nomadic lifestyles. They typically do not buy property, they prioritise spatial mobility over their and their families' local ties, and some even reported only owning furniture that can easily be adapted to constantly changing rental accommodations. Second, and in particular in response to budget cuts, actors often provide accommodations for each other so that theatres do not have to pay freelancers' accommodation costs, which makes actors' labour cheaper and thus increases their likelihood of getting a (freelance) job. Such 'sleeping with the competitors'[2] contributes to actors confining their social relationships to the art world: Actors' friends and lovers tend to be other actors or artists who share a similar (nomadic and work-centred) lifestyle. Third, and in response to the geographical dispersal of attractive jobs, more and more actors move to Berlin, where a high number of theatres provide comparatively more job opportunities—but where the increasing labour supply does not necessarily make it more likely to get a paid job.

In summary, although at first sight seemingly enabling boundaryless careers, the theatre industry is marked by significant spatial restrictions for those who work at a provincial theatre and/or who lack mobility. As a response, actors shape their career trajectories and lifestyles in a way that is individualized but by no means individually idiosyncratic.

WORK-LIFE BALANCE AND GENDER

In the same way that recruitment and career development are not embedded in explicit human resource (HR) policies in theatre, 'work-life balance' issues are left to the individual artists. Not only is there a high (social) pressure to attend all rehearsals and not to miss a single performance (unless indisputably severe health conditions get in the way, which often does *not* include a broken bone), actors are allowed only eight days of annual leave on which they cannot be called in at short notice to, for instance, substitute a sick colleague. On all other days, the evening show takes precedence over any personal matters—be they birthday parties, weddings or holidays. The task of balancing such demanding working conditions with non-work concerns is solely left to the individual actors. Again, any advice from senior actors, dramaturges, theatre managers or directors is informal and borne out of personal preferences for certain actors rather than organizational pastoral care.

As the ability to cope with mobility and flexibility requirements is much greater for independent singles than it is for parents or those with other care responsibilities, we now take a closer look at gender-related consequences of boundaryless careers. Gendered working conditions for actors have a long tradition in Germany. From historical accounts, we know that, for example, in the 18th and 19th centuries, actresses had to pay for their costumes themselves and they were expected to present the newest fashion on stage (Kord 1992; Möhrmann 2000). This put female actors into a precarious economic situation and made them dependent on well-off male favorers whose interest—as, for example, Schnitzler picks up in his play 'Freiwild' (1896)—was often not limited to sponsoring the arts.

While such extreme discrimination between male and female actors does not exist today, inequality is still prevalent, although often less visible. Role availability and narrow norms regarding corporeal aesthetics disadvantage, as outlined earlier, female actors in comparison with their male colleagues. In addition, higher competition between actresses makes sustaining a successful career more difficult. Such problems are particularly salient for 'middle-aged' actresses, which in theatre means an age of above approximately 35 years (i.e. a time when personal issues such as family tend to be a prime concern). At this age, role availability not only rapidly diminishes, but actresses are typically viewed as predestined for 'mother roles'. Because such roles heavily stigmatize if played too young (i.e., before an actress is in her mid-40s) and such stigma hinders careers, actresses try to avoid playing them. However, too often the decision is between mother roles or no roles at all. Job opportunities (roles and the chances to get a new job offer as an ensemble member) diminish significantly for actresses in these age brackets.

A further career constraint is motherhood. Parental responsibilities are particularly difficult to reconcile with work demands in theatre, due to both the intense physical nature of the work and the long and unsocial working hours. These pressures are so severe that one actress who fell pregnant at the same time as she finally received a long desired offer to star in a TV soap seriously considered an abortion so as not to jeopardize this career opportunity. Our female interviewees frequently stated that (male) theatre managers and directors regarded them as less employable because of their non-work responsibilities, which allegedly resulted in them having 'lost their bite.'

Such perceptions of actresses' reduced employability are not based on artistic quality and talent but on the fact that non-work responsibilities render a lifestyle that is entirely work-focused less viable. It is this combination of artistic, aesthetic and lifestyle-related factors that makes middle-aged actresses less 'interesting' for directors and theatre managers. Such interest, however, is crucial for being offered bigger and demanding roles that enable actors to demonstrate and further develop their talent.

In response to these constraints, actresses' careers are far from individual but typically follow one of two patterns: The worker either remains childless and mimics the male career path or she compromises her career significantly—accepting smaller roles, working freelance or withdrawing from the labour market.

CONCLUDING DISCUSSION

Careers in the creative industries are described as boundaryless: Workers move from one project to another and their trajectories are validated in industry-wide processes of ascribing reputation. While some authors see such situations as liberating workers to take control over their careers and align them with personal aims (e.g. Arthur 2008; Hall et al. 2002), others have emphasized the precariousness that project-based employment and individualized career responsibility entail (e.g. Dex et al. 2000; Gill 2002; Randle and Culkin 2009). Acknowledging both of these potential outcomes of boundaryless careers, this chapter has widened the perspective beyond the common focus on project-based employment, industry-wide reputation and personal networks. In doing so, we have shown how careers in German theatre are boundaryless and at the same time bound by a range of influences.

Careers in German theatre are indeed, as described by the literature on boundaryless careers (Arthur et al. 1999; Currie et al. 2006), individualized. Organizational HRM strategies or procedures in the traditional sense are absent, employment is temporary or freelance and personal contacts and individual reputations are paramount for recruitment. Consequently, the onus is on each actor to plan, develop and maintain their career. In theory, the German theatre industry should be conducive to developing boundaryless careers according to individual preferences: Germany is geographically compact and the number of influential individuals and organizations a successful artist needs to keep in contact with is comparatively manageable. In addition, one third of the workforce work on temporary but project-transcending contracts, which reduce employment insecurities. However, in reality a range of factors constrain individual agency in career development. First, drama schools exert significant early career effects both with respect to reputation and gendered career experiences. Second, recruitment and staffing decisions are not based on individual artistic brilliance but are constrained by the literary material that forms the basis of theatrical production. Key decision makers' subjective perceptions further influence recruitment and staffing decisions and thus careers. Third, actors have to respond to mobility and flexibility demands, which, in the past two decades, have been further intensified by an increasing economic pressure on theatres.

None of these aspects inevitably shapes careers in a particular way. However, they combine as a set of conditions under which individual agency in career development centers on maintaining a constant state of readiness, of constantly being able to respond to the needs of the industry. Typical patterns of enacting careers in theatre therefore include living a nomadic life, reducing family and social commitments and subjecting life to work requirements (Eikhof and Haunschild 2006; Haunschild and Eikhof 2009). Such patterns are significantly more difficult to enact for older actors, actors with family commitments and women than for single and/or younger actors. While getting older is non-negotiable, actors undertake considerable effort to fight off signs of aging and many either decide against family commitments or involuntarily find themselves left by partners unable to cope with the work-life overspill. As one actress on the eve of retirement stated, *"You live for theatre only, and in the end you are alone. Friends and relations have died or live far away. Living in and for the theatre is only non-problematic when you are young."*

Her statement stands in stark contrast to the common portrait of creative workers as self-managing free spirits 'unfettered by tradition' who move in and out of working alliances and exploit market opportunities to make money (Banks 2006, 457). Although the details may vary, studies from other creative industries hint at similar boundaries for boundaryless careers, in particular with respect to gender and life course issues. In new media, for instance, corporeal aesthetics are far less influential for female workers' careers than for actresses. Nevertheless, as Gill (2002) has shown, the lack of transparency prevailing in the 'clubby atmosphere' of new media networking fosters discrimination against women and leads to gendered career trajectories. While in theatre it is the spatial and temporal availability that leads to actors foregoing family commitments, in other industries it is income uncertainty that forces career versus family decisions (e.g. Dex et al. 2000; Skillset 2008). Such industry-specific influences on careers need to be understood in far more detail and beyond the dualism of empowerment and precariousness, in particular for discussions with those academics, think tanks and politicians who herald the creative industries as offering 'life beyond permanent employment' (Friebe and Lobo 2008) and 'a new world of work' (Leadbetter and Oakley 2005).

In particular, we would suggest a more detailed exploration is needed of when, how and why creative workers pursue and quit careers. Although ensemble actor Matthias' boundaryless career not only earned him 'best actor' nominations and awards, but also a painful divorce, he still described being on stage unreservedly as *"the best thing ever."* By contrast, his very successful colleague, Elena, was much more conscious of her career's potential negative impacts: *"I am happy to internalize my employers' mobility and flexibility requirements, but I'm not prepared to let those requirements choke me to death."* Changing importance of work and life over an individual's life course is likely to be relevant for career decisions but also the strength of an individual's commitment to art for art's sake and the influence of supporting bohemian values and lifestyles (Eikhof and Haunschild 2006). Similarly, developments on the industry level, for instance in terms of funding or parental leave legislation, will play a role. The creative industries rely on creative workers making creativity available as a key resource. It would therefore be of both academic and practical interest to continue the exploration of individualized careers beyond boundarylessness and into the more intricate and complex interplay between structure and agency that shapes the careers and lives of workers like Matthias and Elena—and with and through them, the creative industries a whole.

NOTES

1. Within the German-speaking theatre world, dramaturges act as artistic consultants with varying job definitions, but they are key players in staffing and recruiting decisions in every theatre.
2. We would like to thank Chris Mathieu for this phrase.

REFERENCES

Anand, N., and M. R. Watson. 2004. "Tournament Rituals in the Evolution of Fields: The Case of the Grammy Awards." *Academy of Management Journal* 47: 59–80.

Arthur, M. B. 2008. "Examining Contemporary Careers: A Call for Interdisciplinary Inquiry." *Human Relations* 61: 163–86.

Arthur, M. B., and D. M. Rousseau, eds. 1996. *The Boundaryless Career.* Oxford: Oxford University Press.

Arthur, M.B., K. Inkson, and J. Pringle. 1999. *The New Careers.* London: Sage.

Banks, M. (2006) "Moral Economy and Cultural Work." *Sociology* 40(3) 455–472.

Blair, H. 2001. "'You're Only as Good as Your Last Job': The Labour Process and Labour Market in the British Film Industry." *Work, Employment and Society* 125: 149–69.

Blair, H., N. Culkin, and K. Randle. 2003. "From London to Los Angeles: A Comparison of Local Labour Market Processes in the US and UK Film Industries." *International Journal of Human Resource Management* 14: 619–33.

Caves, R. E. 2000. *Creative Industries.* Cambridge, MA: Harvard University Press.

Currie, G., S. Tempest, and K. Starkey. 2006. "New Careers for Old? Organizational and Individual Responses to Changing Boundaries." *International Journal of Human Resource Management* 17: 755–74.

Dean, D. 2005. "Recruiting a Self: Women performers and Aesthetic Labour." *Work, Employment and Society* 19: 761–74.

Dempster, A. 2006. "Managing Uncertainty in the Creative Industries: Lessons from *Jerry Springer the Opera.*" *Creativity and Innovation Management* 15: 224–33.

Dex, S., J. Willis, R. Paterson, and E. Sheppard. 2000. "Freelance Workers and Contract Uncertainty: The Effects of Contractual Changes in the Television Industry." *Work, Employment and Society* 14: 283–305.

Eikhof, D. R. 2009. "Does Hamlet Have to Be Naked? Creativity Between Tradition and Innovation in German Theatres." In *Creativity and Innovation in the Cultural Economy*, edited by P. Jeffcutt and A. Pratt, 241–261. London: Routledge.

Eikhof, D. R., and A. Haunschild. 2006. "Lifestyle Meets Market. Bohemian Entrepreneurs in Creative Industries." *Creativity and Innovation Management* 15: 234–41.

Eikhof, D. R., and A. Haunschild. 2007. "For Art's Sake! Managing Artistic and Economic Logics in Creative Production." *Journal for Organizational Behavior* 28: 523–38.

Friebe, H., and S. Lobo. 2008. *Wir nennen es Arbeit.* Updated edition. München: Heyne.

Gill, R. 2002. "Cool, Creative and Egalitarian? Exploring Gender in Project-Based New Media Work in Europe." *Information, Communication and Society* 5: 70–89.

Grabher, G. 2002. "The Project Ecology of Advertising: Tasks, Talents and Teams." *Regional Studies* 36: 245–62.

Grugulis, I., and D. Stoyanova. 2009. " 'I Don't Know Where You Learn Them': Skills in Film and TV." In *Creative Labour*, edited by A. McKinlay, and C. Smith, 135–155. Basingstoke: Palgrave.

Hall, D. T., G. Zhu, and A. Yan. 2002. "Career Creativity as Protean Identity Transformation." In *Career Creativity*, edited by M. A. Peiperl, M. B. Arthur, and N. Anand, 159–79. Oxford: Oxford University Press.

Haunschild, A. 2003. "Managing Employment Relation in Flexible Labour Markets: The Case of German Repertory Theatres." *Human Relations* 56: 899–929.

Haunschild, A. 2004. "Employment Rules in German Theatres: An Application and Evaluation of the Theory of Employment Systems." *British Journal of Industrial Relations* 42: 685–703.

Haunschild, A., and D. Eikhof. 2009. "Bringing Creativity to Market: Actors as Self-Employed Employees." In *Creative Labour*, edited by A. McKinlay, and C. Smith, 156–173. Basingstoke: Palgrave.

Jackson, C. 1996. "Managing and Developing a Boundaryless Career: Lessons from Dance and Drama." *European Journal of Work and Organizational Psychology* 5: 617–28.

Jones, C. 1996. "Careers in Project Networks: The Case of the Film Industry." In *The Boundaryless Career*, edited by M. B. Arthur, and D. M. Rousseau, 58–75. Oxford: Oxford University Press.

Jones, C. 2002. "Signaling Expertise: How Signals Shape Careers in Creative Industries." In *Career Creativity*, edited by M. Peiperl, M. Arthur, and N. Anand. Oxford: Oxford University Press.

Jones, C., and R. J. DeFillippi. 1996. "Back to the Future in Film: Combining Industry and Self-Knowledge to Meet the Career Challenges of the 21st Century." *Academy of Management Executive* 10: 89–103.

Kord, S. 1992. *Ein Blick hinter die Kulissen. Deutschsprachige Dramatikerinnen im 18. und 19. Jahrhundert.* Stuttgart: Metzler.

Leadbeater, C., and K. Oakley. 2005. "Why Cultural Entrepreneurs Matter." In *Creative Industries*, edited by J. Hartley, 299–311. Oxford: Blackwell.

Möhrmann, M. 2000. "Die Herren zahlen die Kostüme. Mädchen vom Theater am Rande der Prostitution." In *Die Schauspielerin—Eine Kulturgeschichte*, edited by R. Möhrmann, 292–317. Frankfurt a.M.: Insel.

Pratt, A. 2009. "Situating the Production of New Media: The Case of San Francisco (1995–2000)." In *Creative Labour*, edited by A. McKinlay and C. Smith, 195–209. Basingstoke: Palgrave.

Randle, K., and N. Culkin. 2009. "Getting in and Getting on in Hollywood: Freelance Careers in an Uncertain Industry." In *Creative Labour*, edited by A. McKinlay and C. Smith, 93–115. Basingstoke: Palgrave.

Schößler, F. 2008. *Einführung in das bürgerliche Trauerspiel und das soziale Drama.* 2. Aufl. Darmstadt: WBG.

Skillset. 2008. *Feature Film Production, Workforce Survey Report 2008.* London: Skillset.

Warhurst, C., and D. R. Eikhof. 2010. *The Creative Industries: You Don't Have to be Male, White and Middle Class to Work Here—But It Helps.* Paper presented at the Work, Employment, and Society Conference, September, Brighton, England.

4 Tournament Careers
Working in UK Television

Dimitrinka Stoyanova and Irena Grugulis

In the contemporary world, organizations and work are being fragmented. People change jobs more often, and their working lives are made up of 'chunks of labour' (Sennett 1998). This has implications not only for the way they work and the way they learn skills but also for lives outside work. There is a great deal of variation between sectors in the extent to which work and organizations are fragmented. Many areas have changed little over the last few decades, whereas others outsource peripheral tasks such as cleaning, security, or supplement existing workforces with temporary staff. However, there are some, and UK television production is one of these, in which the changes have been dramatic. Here the process of fragmentation was initiated in the 1980s, and the sector changed from one dominated by large vertically integrated organizations, such as the BBC and ITV, to one composed of a large number of small independent production companies and a small number of large ones working on commissions from the broadcasters.

This chapter considers the implications of these changes for careers in the UK television sector. It observes the uncertainty, serendipity, and pitfalls which the new structure fosters. Freelance careers are driven by individuals, but, particularly in a labor market where those seeking employment far outnumber the jobs available, these individuals often face tough competition in 'tournaments' rather than straightforward progression. Too often the careers literature assumes that individuals' influence is unrestricted and that progression is natural. Yet boundaryless careers (Arthur 1994) depend on both individual agency (Blair et al. 2003; Jones 1996; Tams and Arthur 2010) and macro-level factors (Jones 2010), and the former are often responsive to the latter (Baumann 2002; Platman 2004). This chapter gives due weight to the acts of individuals but also reveals the ways in which individuals are acted on. We introduce the concept of 'tournament careers' to capture the tenuous character of failure and exit as well as success and progression. Tournaments suggest competing for a desired prize; they involve effort, preparation, building strategies, and winning or losing independently of those. The winners are always outnumbered significantly by those competing. They may drop out at each stage of the tournament, so winning is always temporary. These are all aspects of the way freelancers in the UK television build their working path. In the fluid institutional environment of contemporary television, there is a strong element of chance and arbitrariness beyond the reach of freelancers' strategies. In this labor market, the random chance can work either in favor of or against freelance career progression, adding to the experience of insecurity and making careers more tenuous than much of the literature suggests.

TELEVISION CAREERS

In film and television, careers are usually project-based. As Faulkner and Anderson (1987, 883) observe:

> Career lines are forged as participants on both sides of the market move from film to film, from opportunity point to opportunity point. Career attributes are accumulated as people move from credit to credit. Sustained participation in this structure of contracts, credits, and attributes is the requirement for continued success.

Faulkner and Anderson (1987, 887) also indicate:

> Building a career line is an uncertain and often erratic process, with quite a range of outcomes possible in the form of (a) continuity of contracts over a period of time and (b) a range of recurrent ties with many and different kinds of people in the business.

Following the boundaryless career approach, Jones (1996) developed a project-based career model using US film industry data. She distinguished four stages: beginning, crafting, navigating, and maintaining the career. Beginning a career in film is challenging because the environment is highly competitive, and there are no established entry paths. The process of 'crafting' one's career involves acquiring technical skills through on-the-job training while being socialized into the values and culture of the industry. The next stage, navigating, involves establishing a reputation (by creating good work), developing skills, and establishing a network of industry contacts based on relationships. So it is essential to produce good quality work in order to be able to secure further projects. Jones' (1996) respondents associated their individual reputation with the reputation of the final product (e.g., the success of the film they worked on). Careers then become really precarious because the success of any film, as the author herself points out, depends on a large number of external factors. The final stage of the film career is maintaining it. Jones highlights two main challenges at this stage: sustaining and extending one's network and balancing professional and personal lives. In this way, the focus is shifted to developing others and maintaining presence in the industry.

In a working life constructed between organizations and jobs, there is also a tension between skills development and career development, which previously, in an organizational context, used to run in parallel. This is reflected in the 'career progression paradox' (O'Mahony and Bechky 2006). The concept problematizes the ways in which freelance professionals expand their skills in order to take their next career step. In this type of employment, such moves depend largely on the previous project role. In fragmented and external labor markets, there is a higher risk for employers hiring people with the right skills. When applying for a job, a freelancer would be looking for positions similar to the last one held, and employers would hire individuals who have experience in similar positions (i.e., use credits as an indicator of skills). Because there is a risk in hiring 'external' individuals anyway, it is highly improbable that a freelancer would be engaged for a position different or 'higher' than the one (s)he had held previously. So there is a paradox, which freelancers can overcome by explicit tactics to enable them gain additional skills and progress ('stretchwork').

CAREERS AS TOURNAMENTS

Boundaryless careers can be conceptualized as tournaments, a term used by Marsden (2007) to describe entry into labor markets dominated by project-based employment. The idea of a tournament is highly relevant to UK television careers. First, a tournament is an activity that can be won but may also be lost. Accounts of the 'new careers' usually focus on the ways they unfold, and the idea of failure is either not explored or given far less emphasis than is accorded to success. Conceptualizing 'careers as tournaments,' however, allows for attention to be paid to the notion of failure and discontinuity: both important and influential aspects of creative careers. Second, tournament suggests a certain degree of preparation, of conscious effort to equip oneself with the skills, contacts, and behaviors that can lead to success. At the same time, it also suggests that there is a strong element of chance, of things 'beyond one's control,' which can have a powerful influence on the outcome. Finally, tournaments imply competing for a prize, something desirable and prestigious. This is also an element of work in television: a career perceived to be one of glamour and fame. Thus, conceptualizing careers as tournaments captures the delicate dynamics between effort and outcome in a way that is sensible to the often random way in which project-based careers unfold or, rather, 'happen.'

The notion of tournament has been applied to careers before. Rosenbaum (1979) suggested a tournament mobility model that introduced the idea of career as a chain of competitions, "*each* of which has implications for an individual's mobility chances in all subsequent selections" (222–23). It particularly stresses the importance of the initial stage of the 'competitions' for all subsequent results. This model is helpful in its distinction between 'winners' and 'losers' at each stage, whereby, "Winners have the opportunity to compete for high levels, but they have no assurance of attaining them; losers are permitted to compete only for low levels or are denied the opportunity to compete any further at all" (Rosenbaum 1979, 223). Contemporary television careers resemble such tournaments; however, they are tournaments whose outcomes are marked by ever increasing levels of ambiguity and uncertainty.

Not only is success uncertain at each career step, but the desired outcome or direction is tentative, too. Each step is thus a provisional one and is linked to a number of potential opportunities. A key feature of this type of career is its arbitrariness and the lack of clear steps of progression. Thus,

> Unlike in organisational careers where jobs are often organised into different career tracks which may be known in broad terms *ex ante*, in this example, there are few such guide posts. Workers know about their previous and present jobs or assignments *ex post*, but can only surmise where they are leading. (Marsden 2007, 979)

In addition to individual effort and strategies, macro-level factors also influence the career outcomes of creative professionals (Jones 2010). When television production was dominated by bureaucratic organizations and their internal labor markets, career steps were linked to the skills and experience required at each stage, which were clearly set out in the professional community. De-regulation, outsourcing, the decline of trade unions, and the rise of freelance labor and small independent firms changed all that. Entry was no longer limited, progression routes were far more fluid, and the link between job titles and expertise was greatly weakened. This is the environment in which we conducted our study and in which our informants worked. They could certainly influence their own careers, and many went to great lengths to do so. However, as they explained, this fractured labor market worked differently than the ordered, organizational systems that had preceded it. While individuals could still carve out progression routes (as Jones [1996] reveals), the absence of clear labor market structures meant that such development was uncertain. For many in the industry, successes were as much a product of good luck as good judgment, and it was the interplay of the random and serendipitous events with freelancers' conscious efforts and strategies that shaped careers.

UK TELEVISION CAREERS

Until 1990, the TV sector in the UK was dominated by four major terrestrial broadcasters, all of which were large bureaucratic organizations with strong internal labor markets. Entry to the industry was usually through one of them. Once hired, people would expect to progress through the hierarchy building their skills and enriching their knowledge in a relatively structured and predictable way. Trade unions were strong and ensured that only skilled and experienced people were hired on projects. The changes in the 1980s and 1990s led to the establishment of a new sectoral configuration, a prominent feature of which was the growth in independent production and increase in outsourcing relationships (Saundry 2001). This in turn led to considerable reductions in staff positions and a corresponding growth in the number of freelance workers (Dex et al. 2000; Thynne 2000; Tunstall 1993). The old vertically integrated and hierarchical production structures were replaced by a network of small companies (Barnatt and Starkey 1994; Davis and Scase 2000; Saundry 1998; Starkey et al. 2000; Tunstall 1993). As the sector fractured, new integrating mechanisms were created. External networks of professionals were set up, and small companies had to build links with broadcasters in order to get commissions. The labor market also changed: staff jobs were reduced, and freelance employment became widespread (Skillset 2007). Numerous media degrees emerged, and trade unions weakened. The numbers of people entering the industry both grew and became more varied because the major broadcasters no longer acted as gatekeepers, restricting entry to a small number, and progression became unregulated. The television industry fragmented into individual freelancers and independent companies. This created challenges for both. Jobs became potentially more diverse with greater individual control over employment, but they also became more uncertain and irregular.

These changes had a considerable influence on the ways in which careers evolved. They were experienced in different ways across the occupational 'generations' who were at various stages in their careers at the time of the reforms. Research showed that there was a shift in the value system of the industry, and the efforts to find employment took priority over all other activities (Paterson 2001). Insecurity rose significantly, leading to an increased emphasis on job search. This change of focus altered the balance between the types of skills individuals needed in order to progress in their working lives, increasing the importance of networking and social capital (Blair 2000; DeFillippi and Arthur 1994). This shift was similar to the one that occurred in the Hollywood film industry following the abandonment of the old studio system (see Christopherson and Storper 1989).

The outcomes of the shift from long-term employment within a single large organization associated with in-house training and progression through well-defined structures and clearly set out grades and roles to short-term contracts based on reputation, on-the-job and freelance training, and ambiguous, fluid job roles, raise a number of concerns (Tempest et al. 2004). One of them is the increasingly blurred association between job titles and previous experience, mainly found in cases when less experienced workers were offered an enhanced title in order to compensate for lower pay. Fragmentation also affected the social capital that both individuals and firms acquired. At individual level, many established freelancers had developed their social capital and established a network of contacts while working full time for one of the major terrestrials, that is, in the course of their organizational career, which preceded the freelance one. This process was facilitated by regular employment, greater opportunities to meet a range of specialists, and the (often significantly) larger organizational size. Irregular and brief periods of work during which professionals rarely get the opportunity to meet many of their fellows and a labor market dominated by small companies and small projects offer far fewer opportunities to engage. This raised concerns as to where social capital might be acquired in the future; an acquisition further complicated by the erosion of trust in the sector, with the shift to flexible employment patterns in the industry: "The short-term frame of contemporary business and the constant reconfiguration of flexible capitalism limit the ripening of informal trust" (Tempest et al. 2004, 1541). This resonates with Sennett's (1998) concern about contemporary working lives being fragmented and based on short-term relationships that undermine trust and mutual commitment. Such careers do not create a continuous narrative of one's life and have a destabilizing effect on people, 'corroding their character.' Hence, 'careering alone' (i.e., the fragmentation of career paths and individualization) is likely to have negative consequences for both professionals (Tempest et al. 2004, 1542) and their personal lives.

The changes in career patterns in the UK television were experienced differently by the various age groups of professionals (Paterson 2001). While those who entered the industry before the early 1980s had been 'seeking a career that had purpose, status and good earnings' (Paterson 2001, 498), the careers of later recruits were marked by uncertainty, which they disliked and responded to with various strategies (Dex et al. 2000; Paterson 2001). Thus, freelancers sought additional income from working outside television, dedicated time and effort building and maintaining networks, and relied predominantly on people they knew for work. These studies on UK television demonstrate how the new commercial pressures introduced in the sector resulted in increased employment insecurity for the freelance creatives, effectively limiting their work and career choices and setting boundaries on boundaryless careers. As Langham (1996, 49) summarizes:

> Anyone who wants a career in film, television or video . . . must understand the new structure (or lack of structure) in the industry and the implications of the changes for employment opportunities. . . . A career in film, television or video demanded great resources of emotional stamina to accept the uncertainty and even enjoy the roller-coaster atmosphere of the industry increasingly subject to rapid change.

METHODOLOGY

This chapter draws on a qualitative study of UK television conducted between 2005 and 2007. The study had two main components: 71 face-to-face or telephone semi-structured interviews with industry freelance professionals and key informants. The interviews with freelancers revolved around informants' work histories and explored the main stages of their working lives as well as their views and experiences of work. The second component of the study was three months of participant observation in a small production company in the North of England, during which one of the authors shadowed the making of a one-hour science documentary while observing the day-to-day work in the office of the company. In addition, we participated in industry events and shadowed a one-day shoot for a BBC food program.

All interviews were recorded and transcribed. The average length of the transcribed interviews was 21 pages. Field notes were taken close to the time, and a research diary was kept. The field notes amounted to 160 pages.

RANDOM WALK: UNPREDICTABLE TOURNAMENTS

A prominent characteristic of television careers is the lack of either a clear structure or easily identifiable career stages. Our interviewees indicated that there were no systems in place to guide them (see also Skov, Chapter 13, this volume; Pralong et al., Chapter 11, this volume). This was different to the situation before de-regulation and older professionals often contrasted the two. Alexander, an experienced producer-director, described the way in which organizational careers in television had developed, as skills did, on the job:

> The problem is that it is . . . there is no career paths anymore for people. . . . What we used to . . . I mean there used to be, it wasn't exactly formal structure, but we used to say that you know, most people who start as a researcher, say as a junior researcher, we would expect them to do probably three years as a researcher, you know, working their way up to become a senior researcher. . . . And then once they could do that and they had been an assistant producer for a few years, probably again another three years, then we would think about making them into producers. . . . Well, it is still the same now. It is still the same in terms of the skills that are required and the amount of time that is needed. But you don't have any sort of formal structure.

The changes on the technical side were similar, albeit perhaps not to the same extent. Arthur, a lighting cameraman, reflected on the implications that this lack of clear structure had on the current freelancers:

I think, you know, the thing to remember is in today's world it is much more difficult to go through a structured sort of regime of moving up the ladder which I am sure is why you are doing this research in the first place. It used to be, in the sort of days when the studios were much more in control, you used to very much join as a camera trainee, and then a clapper loader and then a focus puller and then an operator and then a DP [Director of Photography]; and it was a set way of doing things and you would generally do it over a set amount of time but that doesn't really exist anymore. So I think it's very difficult for people to know which direction to come in to . . . and I think the most common question I'm asked by people starting in the industry is 'what should I do next?' It is difficult.

Moves between jobs or chances to learn and join a network often depended on circumstances: 'being at the right place at the right time' or simply knowing the right people and being available to work. For example, Hugh, a camera operator, managed to build his reputation in commercials by standing in for a friend:

Quite often John was busy and couldn't do those jobs, so I would; so Peter would ask me to go and do them and that, and then from that you build up a reputation.

The way Sandra got her first production manager position was also telling:

My first up to production in, in production manager in television was when I was employed as a production co-ordinator. They said 'Yes, come in'; I went in for the interview on the Thursday and they said 'Right, see you Monday'. I turned up Monday morning and my production manager had been hospitalised with pre-eclampsia of pregnancy so I got promoted to production manager. So sometimes it is by accident. Sometimes it literally is by accident. (Sandra, production manager)

In the case of Oliver, it was a 'lucky break' six months after a period of persistently attempting to find his first job after a traineeship:

I went back to work at the Gap [a clothing store]. . . . I did that thing that I am sure thousands of people do is just send out . . . get the local directory/production directory for wherever you are living and just go through it with a pen. Go 'OK, I am going to write to them' and then put together a CV and just send out letters and get no replies. Because you never do. And finally my letter arrived on the desk of somebody the day that the person whose job I ended up taking had handed in their notice. So I got a job as a runner at a production company (Oliver, producer)

Abigail, who had also benefitted from her CV landing on someone's desk at the right time, summarized the situation:

> I don't know, I would say that everyone has a different experience in television. It is just so random, there is no control. It is so like . . . you know, someone will say how they got into it and it is so totally different to you and you are like, 'Oh, that is interesting.' (Abigail, producer-director)

Such random chances were confirmed by the recruiters. Experiencing the pressures of commissioning, Alan, an independent company producer, remembered hiring a 'second choice' candidate simply because she could start immediately:

> But it happened at relatively short notice so I was stuck because, again, the whole way the production is to just suddenly leap into action. So, you are not hiring someone for a month's time, you are recruiting someone because 'we want someone to start on Monday' . . . and so that became a prime qualification for the job. (Alan, producer)

Moving upward in this labor market sometimes seemed easier within rather than between jobs. Project-based career models assume that career steps occur between jobs. This research suggested that previous work with an employer, and 'being known,' could be a factor facilitating 'stepping up' in the course of a project. This was particularly so in the low grades where people had not succeeded to build a substantial portfolio or valuable contacts. Chance had a role to play here, too. Ciru was promoted to researcher on the same production on which she had been employed as a runner:

> To be honest, it was purely by luck. . . . I had been there by that point about sort of 6/7 weeks or something. And they said . . . would I be interested in looking after this element. So they came and asked me to do it. But that was actually . . . I mean, that was purely, purely luck. Well, no, not all luck, but, you know, it was very much I was in the right place and they sort of said 'look, there she is, let's give it to her.' And anyone . . . they could have employed someone else to do it but it was almost easier because I had already been on it for 6/7 weeks to just say 'look she can look after that area'. . . . I mean, I have been really lucky because I was only a runner for, like, a month, you know. And I know people who have been runners for 2 years, you know. So, I was really, really lucky to be . . . it is just about being in the right place and someone giving me the opportunity to move up. (Ciru, researcher/associate producer)

The fact that there were many different routes to success meant that free-lancers had a rich diversity of opportunities to take advantage of. But such choice could also be actively misleading. Even successful freelancers spent the majority of their time out of work (Randle et al. 2008), and many started their careers working for little or no pay in firms or on projects that might generate opportunities for future work (Holgate and McKay 2007; see also Chapter 13, this volume). But paying these industry dues was no guarantee of later employment, and the freedoms that permitted many different paths to progress on also allowed many more hopefuls to enter the industry than would ever find work (Marsden 2007). This absence of organizational gatekeepers could be confusing, and young people might continue applying for jobs hoping for career breaks long after their more experienced colleagues had effectively written them off. Such individuals were given few clear signals of when to stop, and there was a danger that many would not realize that they had failed to establish a career in television until it was too late to start building one elsewhere (Marsden 2007).

Career moves based on chance also meant that there was greater variability in the skills people in notionally identical positions (and certainly with the same job title) might have. Respondents were careful not to read too much into job titles. The signals they would otherwise have provided for levels of experience and competence were distorted, and their function at the labor market was undermined (Dex et al. 2000).

Another aspect of the serendipity or happenstance that influenced progress was the availability of more senior colleagues to help and support television freelancers. Mentoring, skills development, advice, or simply expressions of good will are important support mechanisms in freelance lives. A number of interviewees emphasized the crucial role that such people played in their careers and again stressed the role of chance:

> The [show] was just coming to the end and the lady I was working with in the music department came back upstairs one day and said, 'Oh, I've done you a really good favour' and I sort of, said, 'What, you know, I don't know what you are talking about'. And then I got a call from the HR ladies and I got offered an interview to be a production secretary on [another show]. . . . I was very lucky in that the production manager at the time was very good friends with the production co-ordinator at the time. So they were a really nice friendly pair, and I sort of luckily sort of slotted in quite well with them. Half way through the production co-ordinator was made into the production manager as the production manager left, and they brought in a different co-ordinator who also was fantastic. (Grace, researcher)

This collegial good benefitted Grace further in her career, when a co-worker suggested she e-mailed a particular person at a terrestrial broadcaster:

> And I was very lucky she . . . it was just at the right time again when the [programme] were looking for researchers and I literally sent my CV to

her, got a response saying 'Thank you for sending your CV' and then I think the day after got a call saying would I come in for an interview. . . . So I went for that, again didn't think I would get it because I didn't think I had enough experience. And I got it and started the week after! (Grace, researcher)

In line with previous research on 'getting on' in such 'tournament' environments (Barley and Kunda 2004; Baumann 2002; Blair 2001; Blair et al. 2003; Saundry 2001; Ursell 1998), interviewees emphasized the importance of building relationships. This was a 'rule' or a 'factor' where one could exercise some control over the outcome of the tournament without fundamentally changing its random nature.

I mean, the whole of TV is completely just if you are in the right place at the right time. There is no . . . well, I mean obviously it is to do with skill as well but it is like, who you make friends with and I . . . you know, I know some runners who will, you know, make friends with everybody and, you know, and stay in contact with everyone and after jobs and everything and they get on really well. . . . I know people who have been runners who you know, have spent a long time trying to get somewhere but not getting anywhere at all even though they are really good. Whereas other people who aren't so good just happen to have a lucky lucky break, so you know it makes them get there and I think a lot of it is to do with making friends with the right people. (Susan, production manager)

Sometimes circumstances would open up opportunities for skills development by making people take on more responsibilities, usually within a production they had been working on. This could be a prerequisite for a positive career move. However, such a step also presumed that individuals were already working on a project. As mentioned earlier, moves within jobs or companies were often much easier ways for the freelancers to progress to different job roles than moves between them. This was particularly so in the cases of junior freelancers and in cases where professionals were trying to change or expand on their specialism ('stretchwork'). Trust, established through continuous work, played an important part. Often just being present was sufficient to create an opportunity, especially for junior freelancers, because their presence on set legitimized their standing as worthy members of the community. Other strategies involved building a reputation as pleasant, reliable, hard-working, and friendly. Partly serendipitous factors were, for example, the knowledge of a language or expertise in a narrow specialism that could benefit a production (as in the science documentary, which sought out science graduates to do the administrative tasks). Sometimes structures were available to support this: Some regional independent production companies combined their efforts in order to identify job opportunities for freelancers and thus keep them available as a resource in the region. But these too relied on the human factor, and telephone calls notifying other companies of good people about to come on to the market were irregular and far more likely to be prompted by good performance or personable behavior (plus the originating company's belief in future relevant contracts).

Different genres also seemed to have different tournament rules. Moves between them were sometimes difficult, and the individual's very presence in one genre could mean tournament failure in another. For example, a producer in community television was unlikely to become a sought after freelancer working for regional independent production companies, and a creative doing TV spots was unlikely to be accepted as a drama professional. There is a hierarchy of genres based on prestige within the community, and moves from a less to a more prestigious genre are rather difficult.

In emphasizing the element of randomness, we are not suggesting that freelancers did not try and actively 'position' themselves, build strategies for finding the 'right' place and time at the different phases of their career (Jones 1996), or obtain 'stretchwork' (O'Mahony and Bechky 2006). They did with varying degrees of energy, enthusiasm, and talent. Rather, we would like to demonstrate that, given the nature of the labor market, career development and destruction were also caused by factors over which freelancers had little control and which ran independently of their strategies.

TENUOUS CAREERS

Working in television does not mean enjoying a lifetime career. Freelance working lives were permeated by an acceptance that careers were fragile and futures uncertain. Careers evolved around various projects, but project-based work is inherently finite, so there was an ever-present uncertainty about whether such employment would be continued, whether there would be a next project, and where or when the end of the working life would come. Many interviewees, at all stages in their careers, told us of the moments of doubt or fear of whether there was ever going to be another job for them in television. As Claire, a production manager, remarked, 'I think everybody has those moments where they think, "Oh, God, I am going to have to get a bar job!"' This was a constant feature of the freelance working life and in some cases seemed to result in an erosion of the idea that a working life could be identical with a career. Rather, freelancers had doubts about the continuity and the length of their television work. Anna, a producer-director, recalled that she felt the uncertainty even when the result of her application had been positive:

There was an advert in the Media Guardian [newspaper] while I was unemployed so I sent my CV and didn't hear anything and thought, 'I am never going to get a job' you know, the Media Guardian, it goes to millions of people. And they rang me up about a month later and said 'Yes, come in for an interview,' and I got it like that, through the Media Guardian!

Freelance careers in television were characterized by a persisting idea of a secondary career elsewhere, of a 'fall back' option. Respondents spoke of training as therapist, doing organic farming, or setting up their own small business, often related to their TV work. For example, one location manager established a location library, which she made available to colleagues for a fee; a production manager set up a website with her card designs, which she hoped to develop into a small business. Sometimes the parallel work would be a 'filler' rather than a secondary career. Periods of unemployment meant that people did part-time jobs in offices or bars in order to earn their living between projects.

Television is known to be a 'young person's game.' There were few respondents in their 40s, and even this pattern was gendered. Women often dropped out earlier, in their 30s, and for them it would often be a choice between having children, because the erratically long hours of freelance work was difficult to combine with most forms of childcare, or continuing to work in television.

> It is awful to say, but when people get to about 50 or 55, they often get less employed. I do still think it's more of a younger person's industry, and that is not deadly so because I do have a lot of . . . know a lot of older location managers. But I think they are just not as employed as much at that age which I think must be quite tricky for them. And they don't like to say their age, a friend of mine, Ralf, who is a location manager, and he is about 50 and you wouldn't know it but he is like, 'Don't tell anyone my age, they might not employ me.' . . . I think it's tough that is why I think they need to sort of plan ahead, really. (Laura, location manager)

Amber, another location manager, was uncertain whether she would be able to sustain the intensity of the work:

> I don't know, 15 years time, no, probably . . . probably still doing this or completely go out of the industry and do something completely different. I think it is such a fast industry that a lot of people don't live in it all the time. I think a lot of people burn out and just drop and do maybe something.

Claire had similar doubts:

> I do have this kind of feeling that I shouldn't be doing this when I am 50. I really do feel . . . our industry is now, it is so young! I think

production managers: there are several areas where you can be older and still get work, and still get respect. But I do think there is a lot of the industry that expects you to be young. And I think that is really bad. But I really can't see that I would be doing this when I turn 50 so I have got to come up with some game plan. Because you know, by the time I am . . . in the next few years I need to be thinking how . . . what on earth could I do, how could I retrain, what could I afford to be doing. . . . Once you get to your 40s I would have thought in an awful lot of areas in our industry people are thinking, 'What do I do now?' Whether we manage to get out or not I don't know. My colleague, my business partner Jacky is now, she is probably 54 and she is a producer/director and she can't get work. (Claire, production manager)

The early cut-off point and the short working lives put additional pressure and present additional challenges to those who want to build their careers in television. As Simon, a Trade Union representative, ironically remarked, 'You are 21, but there are plenty of 18-year-olds and 17-year-olds coming up behind, you know.'

An important feature of the end of the career is the unknown termination. In the words of Brian, a producer-director, 'You don't leave television, television leaves you.' There was a clear concern about the later working life. But freelance television careers were not just short in duration. Their end point was unclear, and people had to realize when that point comes because the only external prompt is that invitations to work on projects cease. Given the erratic and uncertain gaps between work for active freelancers, this can be difficult to identify. Chris, an executive producer, elaborated:

I think the biggest pressure . . . is that at some point over the next few years I won't be able to get work because I will be too old. In this industry I won't be able to do what I do at some point. Anywhere between three weeks and 15 years time but I won't know when that point is. No one will tell me when that point is. It will just emerge that I am not getting work.

Freelance careers were tenuous and uncertain at least in three ways. First, as our informants agreed, a career in television was not a continuous occupation. The uncertainty of freelance employment meant that individuals faced potential 'discontinuities' at any stage of their working lives. Second, working in television usually involved having a secondary job: either to sustain individuals between projects or to gradually replace the insecure work on productions. Third, these careers were much shortened by their association with youth and energy. This meant that people would exit television, voluntarily or otherwise, fairly young, and that those in work were never aware of the precise moment when their working lives would come to an end.

DISCUSSION AND CONCLUSIONS

Positioned in the continually moving gap between projects and organizations, careers in television were both accidental and fragile. Degrees and definitions of success were varied, and individual experiences differed greatly. But all accounts, even when informants had achieved a great deal and progressed or enjoyed regular work, were permeated by an emphasis on temporariness and chance.

Such careers raise problems in at least three respects. First, with regard to skills development and career progression. Because skills development in television is mainly done on the job (Grugulis and Stoyanova 2009), random career moves or moves based on accumulation of experience and credentials meant that skills and skills development were highly varied. Identical job titles could denote quite variable experience and expertise, especially on the production and editorial side. As a result, job titles and positions were far less useful at denoting individual expertise, and employers found it hard to judge competence based only on past credits. This increased the importance of social mechanisms still further (Baumann 2002) because these are used for verifying and selecting reliable candidates.

Second, this dynamic environment was not inherently conducive to building trust. In many cases, freelancers took career steps within rather than between jobs. This saved costs by eliminating the need to search outside of the immediate project team and was a way of solving the 'career progression paradox' (O'Mahony and Bechky 2006), which reduced the risk of hiring incompetent people.

Third, the career tournaments had a profound effect on freelancers' experiences of work. They reinforced the lure of varied possibilities while increasing the levels of uncertainty. The combination of these nurtured and at the same time undermined individual success strategies to make tournament outcomes often a function of chance, particularly as the number of those competing significantly exceeded the jobs available.

In discussing some of the aspects of contemporary careers in television, this chapter has emphasized the uncertainty and randomness in the way that freelancers' working paths unfold. Contemporary careers are increasingly 'boundaryless' (Arthur 1994) as opposed to 'organisational' (Watson 2003). Career paths are no longer linear and static but dynamic and multidirectional (Baruch 2004). This shift also implies that careers are now owned by the individual, with individuals adapting, learning, and improvising in the changed career environment (Arthur et al. 1999). In them, freelancers are liberated from structural straitjackets to pursue portfolios of work, themed areas of interest, or simply make time for life outside work.

Such inter-organizational careers can also be conceptualized as ongoing or extended tournaments (Marsden 2007, 2010), the outcome of which is only partly dependent on the explicit strategies and efforts of the competitors. As with other tournaments, chance has a role to play. This notion does not feature as strongly in the careers literature as it did in the stories of our respondents, and here we drew the attention to this characteristic of the new fragmented labor markets.

This study allows us to make a few further suggestions about issues related to making career progressions in freelance labor markets. The first one relates to skills development and career moves. As O'Mahony and Bechky (2006) showed, freelancers need to make a number of compromises in order to overcome the 'career progression paradox.' All of these assume that moves are made between rather than within jobs. However, our findings suggest that, especially for junior freelancers, such steps were sometimes easier to make in the course of a single project. A few factors influence and condition this. In lower level jobs, the risks associated with promoting people may be lower, and so decisions about promotions are easier to make. This, combined with the often significant time pressures in sourcing crew members, makes promoting an already present junior person an efficient solution for companies. The fact that these young people were already on set both made them immediately available and 'legitimized' them as reliable candidates. As Dex et al. (2000) also observe, in some cases, such promotions were 'rewards' for junior staff members often not matched by financial benefit. So business pressures as well as the rather fluid rules for promotion made 'being at the right place at the right time' a decisive factor in making a positive career step. The fluid institutional environment made such serendipitous moves perfectly possible.

A point that should also be emphasized is that in the contemporary television labor market, such steps are not necessarily a part of an overall career. As Rosenbaum (1979) noted in relation to the tournament mobility model, those who 'won' only won the opportunity to compete at the next level.

Our study also allows us to provide three insights about the tournament nature of freelance careers. First, these relate to the possible variety of tournament rules for the various genres. The different status attached to the different genres as well as the different social networks meant that freelancers would have different opportunities to progress. An aspect of this was the extent to which a genre was subjected to job conversions. In some, such as factual television, the number of people engaged in a production has been considerably reduced. Job roles are often merged, and it is not uncommon for people to be 'sound recording producer-directors' or 'shooting producer-directors.' In others, such as television drama, the demands of the production process have prevented this tendency, and one still finds larger crews with more intermediate job positions.

Second, the tournament rules are different for the freelancers at the different stages in their careers. Artistic labor markets based on project-based work organization and freelance employment are segmented (Christopherson 2009; Faulkner 1983). We would like to suggest that the different segments of freelancers are competing under different tournament rules. The more junior (or aspiring) professionals are more likely to experience the random element of the tournament in their career progression or, at least, are more likely to benefit from it in sourcing a new position. It is at that level that an opportunity stands out because of the large number of junior aspirants competing for a relatively small number of positions (Marsden 2010).

One could (quite rightly) argue that chance has always had a role to play in artistic careers. What research such as this shows, however, is that in an institutionally fluid environment where entry is largely unrestricted and a vast number of people are aspiring to make a career in the field, serendipitous moves become the structurally determined and legitimate rule for working lives to evolve. This is particularly so outside the small core of well-established professionals.

Third, we would like to suggest that the tournament rules had a regional dimension. The labor markets outside of the big hubs of the television industry (e.g., London) face the challenge of retaining people, especially young professionals. In them the rules of competing can sometimes be less ruthless, and young people may find some support from the companies in securing a further position, obtaining more exposure or getting credits.

In conclusion, we need to point out that our research, in common with most work on careers, exaggerates the success of its informants. Indeed, in this study, the very fact of an individual's presence in the labor market (and our sample) meant that they had been successful in at least some of the tournaments. We heard of many who had dropped out, some to related work (PhDs in drama, teaching in university departments, working for tertiary bodies associated with the television industry), whereas others embarked on completely unrelated fields (driving taxis, fitting bathrooms). However, although we can note their presence and the implications of such turnover for the labor market, our work cannot represent their views or experiences. Indeed, identifying them would be a major methodological challenge but could add valuable insights into the realities of the tournament careers and the individuals who live and work with them.

REFERENCES

Arthur, M. 1994. "The Boundaryless Career: A New Perspective for Organizational Inquiry." *Journal of Organizational Behavior* 15: 295–306.

Arthur, M., K. Inkson, and J. Pringle. 1999. *The New Careers: Individual Action and Economic Change.* London: Sage Publications.

Barley, S., and G. Kunda. 2004. *Gurus, Hired Guns and Warm Bodies: Itinerant Experts in a Knowledge Economy.* Princeton and Oxford: Princeton University Press.

Barnatt, C., and K. Starkey. 1994. "The Emergence of Flexible Networks in the UK Television Industry." *British Journal of Management* 5: 251–60.

Baruch, Y. 2004. "Transforming Careers: From Linear to Multidirectional Career Paths: Organisational and Individual Perspectives." *Career Development International* 9: 58–73.

Baumann, A. 2002. "Informal Labour Market Governance: The Case of the British and German Media Production Industries." *Work Employment Society* 16: 27–46.

Blair, H. 2000. "Active Networking: The Role of Networks and Hierarchy in the Operation of the Labour Market in the British Film Industry." *Management Research News, Patrington* 23: 20–21.

Blair, H. 2001. " 'You're Only as Good as Your Last Job': The Labour Process and Labour Market in the British Film Industry." *Work Employment Society* 15: 149–69.

Blair, H., N. Culkin, and K. Randle. 2003. "From London to Los Angeles: A Comparison of Local Labour Market Processes in the US and UK Film Industries." *International Journal of Human Resource Management* 14: 619–33.

Christopherson, S. 2009. Working in the Creative Economy: Risk, Adaptation and the Presence of Exclusionary Networks. In *Creative Labour. Working in the Creative Industries*, edited by A. McKinlay and C. Smith, 71–90. Basingstoke: Palgrave Macmillan.

Christopherson, S., and M. Storper. 1989. "The Effects of Flexible Specialization on Industrial Politics and the Labor Market: The Motion Picture Industry." *Industrial and Labor Relations Review* 42: 331–47.

Davis, H., and R. Scase. 2000. *Managing Creativity: The Dynamics of Work and Organization*. Buckingham: Oxford University Press.

DeFillippi, R., and M. Arthur. 1994. "The Boundaryless Career: A Competency-Based Perspective. *Journal or Organizaional Behavior* 15: 307–24.

Dex, S., J. Willis, R. Paterson, and E. Sheppard. 2000. "Freelance Workers and Contract Uncertainty: The Effects of Contractual Changes in the Television Industry." *Work Employment Society* 14: 283–305.

Faulkner, R. 1983. *Music on Demand. Composers and Careers in the Hollywood Film Industry*. New Brunswick and London: Transaction Publishers.

Faulkner, R., and A. Anderson. 1987. "Short-Term Projects and Emergent Careers: Evidence from Hollywood." *American Journal of Sociology* 92: 879–909.

Grugulis, I., and D. Stoyanova. 2009. " 'I Don't Know Where You Learn Them': Skills in Film and TV." In *Creative Labour. Working in the Creative Industries*, edited by A. McKinlay and C. Smith, 135–55. Basingstoke: Palgrave Macmillan.

Holgate, J., and S. McKay. 2007. *Institutional Barriers to Recruitment and Employment in the Audio Visual Industries. The Effect on Black and Minority Ethnic Workers*. London: Working Lives Research Institute.

Jones, C. 1996. "Careers in Project Networks: The Case of the Film Industry." In *The Boundaryless Career: A New Employment Principle for a New Organizational Era*, edited by M. Arthur and D. Rousseau, 58–75. New York: Oxford University Press.

Jones, C. 2010. "Finding a Place in History: Symbolic and Social Networks in Creative Careers and Collective Memory." *Journal of Organizational Behavior* 31: 726–48.

Langham, J. 1996. *Lights, Camera, Action: Working in Film, Television and Video*. 2nd revised edition. London: British Film Institute.

Marsden, D. 2007. "Labour Market Segmentation in Britain: The Decline of Occupational Labour Markets and the Spread of Entry Tournaments." *Economies et Societés* 28: 963–98.

Marsden, D. 2010. "The Growth of Extended 'Entry Tournaments' and the Decline of Institutionalised Occupational Labour Markets in Britain." *CEP Discussion Paper No 989*. London: LSE.

O'Mahony, S., and B. Bechky. 2006. "Stretchwork: Managing the Career Progression Paradox in External Labor Markets." *Academy of Management Journal* 49: 918–41.

Paterson, R. 2001. "Work Histories in Television." *Media Culture and Society* 23: 495–520.

Platman, K. 2004. " 'Portfolio Careers' and the Search for Flexibility in Later Life." *Work Employment and Society* 18: 573–99.

Randle, K., L. Wing-Fai, and J. Kurian. 2008. *Creating Difference: Overcoming Barriers to Diversity in UK Film and Television Employment.* Hatfied, Hertfordshire: Creative Industries Research and Consultancy Unit, University of Hertfordshire.

Rosenbaum, R. 1979. "Tournament Mobility: Career Patterns in a Corporation." *Administrative Science Quarterly* 24: 220–41.

Saundry, R. 1998. "The Limits of Flexibility: The Case of UK Television." *British Journal of Management* 9: 151–62.

Saundry, R. 2001. "Employee Relations in British Television-Regulation, Fragmentation and Flexibility." *Industrial Relations Journal* 32: 22–36.

Sennett, R. 1998. *The Corrosion of Character: The Personal Consequences of Work in the New Capitalism.* New York: W. W. Norton.

Skillset. 2007. *Employment Census 2006: The Results of the Sixth Census of the Audio Visual Industries.* London: Author.

Starkey, K., C. Barnatt, and S. Tempest. 2000. "Beyond Networks and Hierarchies: Latent Organizations in the U.K. Television Industry." *Organization Science* 11: 299–305.

Tams, S., and M. Arthur. 2010. "New Directions for Boundaryless Careers: Agency and Interdependence in a Changing World." *Journal of Organizational Behavior* 31: 629–46.

Tempest, S., A. McKinlay, and K. Starkey. 2004. "Careering Alone: Careers and Social Capital in the Financial Services and Television Industries." *Human Relations* 57: 1523–45.

Thynne, L. 2000. "Women in Television in the Multi-Channel Age." *Feminist Review* 64: 65–82.

Tunstall, J. 1993. *Television Producers.* London: Routledge.

Ursell, G. 1998. "Labour Flexibility in the UK Commercial Television Sector." *Media Culture and Society* 20: 129–53.

Watson, T. 2003. "Occupational Careers." In *Sociology, Work and Industry*, edited by T. Watson, 163–64. London: Routledge.

5 Oscar et César
Deep Consecration in French and American Film Acting Careers

Anne E. Lincoln and Michael P. Allen

Several chapters in this volume deal with the relevance of reputation and bonds between artists and cultural careers. Boutinot explores the relevance of reputation among artistic peers, clients, and the public to French architectural careers. Similarly, Jones explores the influential career relationships the architect Frank Lloyd Wright had with a limited number of people late in his career. She finds that becoming known and incorporated into the profession and culture, a "sparse collaborative network," may not be detrimental to artists' success; rather, that the extensiveness of an artist's promotional network is a crucial factor. The present chapter explores the process of 'deep consecration' in the careers of film actors who have received *repeated* critical recognition for their performances in two film industries: French cinema and Hollywood.

THE VALUE OF ACTORS

As 'valuable commodities,' actors are generally understood to be important to the commercial success of a film and crucial for its identity, promotion, and exhibition (Vincendeau 2000). It is equally true that the success of a film as an artistic achievement depends on the talents of its actors. Most of the films that possess any degree of artistic merit employ skilled actors who are dedicated to the art of acting. Because the commercial success of a film is typically measured by its box office receipts, its artistic success can be measured by the number and type of awards that it receives. One of the most important measures of the symbolic value of a film as art is the professional recognition it receives from members of the film industry. Similarly, the contributions of individuals to the production of such a film can be measured by the recognition bestowed by their peers in the film industry.

One of the paradoxes in the study of culture industries is that film acting is both heavily scrutinized and woefully understudied—and unquestionably under-theorized. Certainly, actors today draw popular attention for their personalities and off-screen exploits, although students new to this literature may be surprised to learn this was not true in the early days of

Hollywood, when stars went unnamed and unknown on the silver screen. Indeed, during the Silent Era, stars went unnamed by the studios for fear that they would demand higher wages if their identities became known and their fame grew. Thus, Florence Lawrence was simply known as the 'Biograph Girl' through her employer, Biograph Studios. Actors who receive critical acclaim in the form of awards and prizes typically receive the most scholarly attention as well.

As we outline in greater detail elsewhere (Lincoln and Allen 2004), cultural consecration is the action of creating distinctions by institutions that have the cultural legitimacy to do so. Yet there is woefully little comparative work that explores the 'consecration projects' of different film industries. Given the importance of actors to the value of films, in this chapter, we explore the enactment of these distinctions on the most decorated film actors in France and the United States and their implications for film acting careers.

BACKGROUND

The Academy of Motion Picture Arts and Sciences was formed in Hollywood in 1927. One of the goals of this organization was to promote the recognition of motion pictures as an art form. The first president of the Academy, Douglas Fairbanks, proposed that the Academy bestow 'awards of merit for distinctive achievement' to films and film professionals each year. In addition to recognizing excellence in film production, the Awards sought to elevate the image of film from mindless entertainment to that of art (Sands 1973).

These professional honors, known popularly as Oscars, have been awarded every year, beginning with the first annual Academy Awards banquet in 1928. In the ensuing years, the Academy Awards have grown to become one of the best known and prestigious cultural consecration projects in the world. An Academy Award nomination represents a collective affirmation of the talent of an actor by his/her peers, one that only a few actors ever receive in their entire career.

The success of the Academy Awards has spawned parallel awards in numerous other countries, including the Genies in Canada, the Goyas in Spain, and the Donatellos in Italy (English 2005). In 1974, the Academy of Cinema Arts and Techniques (French: *Académie des Arts et Techniques du Cinema*) established the César as the national film award of France. The first awards were bestowed in 1976.

Short of winning, the highest honor for an actor is to be nominated for one of these awards. As part of this process, in both the US and France, five actors are nominated each year in each of four categories stratified by sex and role: Best Actor, Best Actress, Best Supporting Actor, and Best Supporting Actress (French: *César du meilleur acteur, César du meilleur second rôle masculine, César de la meilleure actrice, César du meilleur second rôle feminine*). In this chapter, we use the term 'actor' to refer to men and women alike except when referring to the official title of an award.

The American Academy Awards follow a business model, a "cultural prize as trademarked property, publicity vehicle, and profitable media franchise" (English 2005, 84). Indeed, films that win Academy Awards for Best Picture are typically box office successes (Ginsburgh 2003). Moreover, films that receive a Best Actor or Best Actress nomination are also rewarded at the box office (Nelson et al. 2001). Beyond the documented commercial effects, Oscar recipients draw a great deal of both popular and academic scrutiny for other reasons—not only from the discipline of film studies but also from the disciplines of psychology, sociology, and even medicine. For example, psychologists have compared the types of roles that Oscar-nominated women and men receive (Simonton 2004), sociologists have examined networks between collaborators (Rossman, Esparza, and Bonacich 2010), and physicians have examined the mortality of Oscar nominees and winners (Redelmeier and Singh 2001; Sylvestre et al. 2006). Yet in the 35 years since the inception of parallel awards in France, César recipients have remained remarkably understudied. In this chapter, we compare the careers of Oscar and César nominees. Building on our previous work on gender differences in career longevity in American film acting (Lincoln and Allen 2004), we focus on 'deep' consecration projects, the careers of the most elite performers who are nominated more than once for leading or supporting role awards in France or the US.

Data

To compare the effects of award nominations on the careers of actors in two of the most influential film industries, we collected data on the careers of all actors who have received at least two nominations from their respective film academies, either the American Academy of Motion Picture Arts and Sciences or the French Académie des Arts et Techniques du Cinéma (see Appendix 5.A). We deliberately set out to construct two cohorts of performers that were maximally comparable. Although the Academy of Motion Picture Arts and Sciences began presenting awards in 1929, the Académie des Arts et Techniques du Cinéma did not bestow its first awards until 1976. Therefore, both samples include only those individuals who received multiple nominations between 1976 and 2010. To ensure the comparability of the careers of these actors, each sample includes only those actors who were part of the cohort that was born between 1940 and 1959.

A relatively large number of actors have received at least one nomination in their careers, but a relatively select few have received two or more nominations. Many one-time nominees go on to have relatively undistinguished careers or leave acting altogether. Following Lincoln (2004, 2007), we purposely excluded actors who produced only one celebrated performance in their careers and restricted the sample to actors who received at least two

Oscar or César nominations by 2010. We also limited the samples to actors with 'typical' careers and included only French performers whose careers were primarily in France and American actors who had careers mainly in the US. Consequently, we excluded a few nominees, such as Ben Kingsley, who got his start in English films before moving into American films, and Charlotte Rampling, an English actress who also performed in French films. We also excluded child stars such as Jodie Foster and Brigitte Fossey (those whose careers began prior to age 18). In our counts of the number of film performances, we only included screen performances in full-length films, excluding voice roles, shorts, uncredited roles, and television roles. These criteria produced a sample of 61 French and 43 American actors who performed in 4,990 films during their careers. Of these films, 3,344 were French and 1,646 were produced in Hollywood.

Results

Important differences are immediately apparent between the French and American film industries. First and foremost, the 61 French actors appear in more films than their American counterparts. Historically, these César nominees have performed in an average of 1.6 films per year, whereas Oscar nominees have averaged 1.1 films, significantly fewer. This finding suggests that, although many more films are produced in the US than are produced in France each year, the key roles in these films are distributed more widely in the US than they are in France. For example, 699 films were released in the US in 2005 compared with 240 in France that year (Lorenzen 2009).

In the film industry, producers often cast actors who are stars in order to ensure their commercial success. Using the same logic, producers cast talented actors in their films as a means of ensuring their critical success. Between 1976 and 2010, 180 French films were nominated for the César Award for Best Film. Table 5.1 presents the number of times that the performers appeared in these 180 films. These totals include only those actors who had already been venerated by the time they were cast in a film. Even a conservative analysis of the 37 most highly consecrated French actors of this period—those who have received *three* nominations—shows that France has a more closely knit industry. In all, 99 of these 180 films, or 55 percent, employed at least 1 of these 37 most elite performers in their casts, and 51, or 28.3 percent, had more than 1 of the 37 most highly consecrated French actors in their casts.

By comparison, during the same period, 180 films were also nominated for the Academy Award for Best Picture. Table 5.1 presents the number of times that our 43 consecrated American actors appeared in these 180 films. As before, these totals include only those actors who had been nominated once by the time they were cast in a film. Only 51 of these 180 films, or 28 percent, employed at least 1 of these 43 consecrated actors in their cast. In addition, only nine of these films, or 5 percent, employed 2 of these 43 American stars

Table 5.1   Percentage of Best Picture-Nominated Films Employing Two-Time César- and Two-Time Oscar-Nominated Actors, 1976–2010

Number of Consecrated Actors	France	US
0	45.0	71.7
	(81)	(129)
1	26.7	23.3
	(48)	(42)
2	21.7	5.0
	(39)	(9)
3–5	6.7	0.0
	(12)	(0)
n	180	180

Note: Number of films is in parentheses.

in their casts, and none employed three or more performers. Consequently, it is clear from this comparison that the relationship between venerable actors and film is much weaker in the US than in France. Other research argues that in cultural labor markets, artistic achievement is the result of collaborative creative effort (Rossman, Esparza, and Bonacich 2010). In film acting, then, a small group of actors receives most of the awards, gets more of the best roles, and works with the best people, elsewhere identified as the "Matthew Effect" (Merton 1968). This observation, however, is clearly more reflective of French cinema than that of Hollywood.

The descriptive statistics for the two samples of actors reveal interesting differences between the two industries. César nominees are younger when they begin their film careers, have performed in more films at several key

Table 5.2   Descriptive Statistics for César and Oscar Nominees, 1976–2010

	César	Oscar
Female (percentage)	41.0	60.5*
Age at first film	24.9	26.1
Films in career	54.8	38.3***
Career nominations	4.1	3.4
Age at first nomination	34.5	33.8
Films by first nomination	17.0	7.7***
Years to first nomination	10.7	7.7*
Age at second nomination	39.8	39.2
Films by second nomination	26.2	15.1***
Years between first and second nominations	5.2	5.4
Films between first and second nominations	9.2	7.4
n	61	43

*$p < .05$ ***$p < .001$ (two-tailed tests)

stages of their careers, and are more decorated than their Oscar counterparts (Table 5.2). However, one key distinction that emerges is that Oscar nominees are recognized three years earlier in their careers than César nominees. Also striking is the gender differences between the samples. César nominees are somewhat more likely to be male, whereas the opposite is true for Oscar nominees. The latter finding is consistent with our research that found a sort of 'revolving door' for young women in Hollywood (Lincoln and Allen 2004). We turn now to explore these differences in greater detail.

GENDER DIFFERENCES BETWEEN FRANCE AND THE US

A large body of research finds disparities between the careers of men and women in Hollywood in terms of length, quality and number of roles, and age of performers. These findings generally hold true for these multiple César and Oscar nominees. In the two samples combined, the 51 female stars performed in 2,087 roles during their careers, whereas the 53 men performed in 2,903 roles. On its face, gender differences are starker in France. Indeed, the 36 French men performed in 2,072 films, whereas the 25 French women appeared in only 1,272 films, whereas American men and women (n = 17 and 26, respectively) were more evenly matched with 831 and 815 performances, respectively. However, a few French men in our sample have had extraordinary careers that inflate the number of acting performances for consecrated men in France. Two men in particular, François Berléand and Gerard Depardieu, performed in a staggering 249 films in the period under study. In fact, 24 of our 61 French actors performed in more than 60 roles in the period under study. By comparison, the largest number of performances by an American in our sample was 82 by Christopher Walken, and only two American actors in the sample have performed in more than 60 films.

Despite the large difference in number of roles for French nominees, further scrutiny reveals that gender differences in number of career performances are actually greater for Americans than for the French actors in our sample. American women performed in roughly 31 films during their careers, whereas American men averaged nearly 49 films or nearly 18 more films (Table 5.3). The gender difference is substantially smaller in France. The French female nominees averaged 50.9 films during their careers compared with 57.6 films for the consecrated male actors, a difference of 6.7 films that is not statistically significant. The largest difference in the number of career performances is actually between women in the two countries. French women performed in nearly 20 more films than American women during the period under study. Figure 5.1 graphically presents the annual number of performances of men and women in each country through their entire career. Perhaps most striking are the national differences in career

Table 5.3 Average Number of Career Film Roles for Consecrated Actors

	France	US	Difference
Men	57.6	48.9	8.7
	(36)	(25)	
Women	50.9	31.3	19.5***
	(17)	(26)	
Difference	6.7	17.5***	

***p < .001 (two-tailed tests)
Note: Number in parentheses is the number of actors.

US

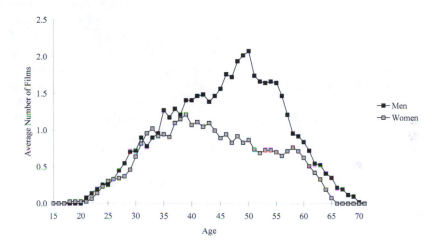

France

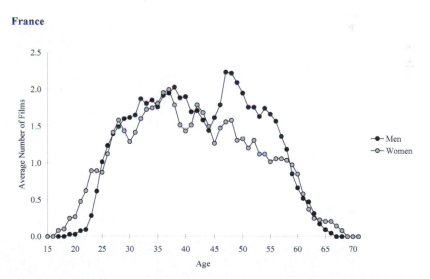

Figure 5.1 Average number of annual film roles for major film actors.

trend lines for these consecrated stars. Women's careers wane more quickly than those of men, with the decline beginning as early as age 39 for American women, whereas French women's careers do not diverge from men's until they are in their late 40s. However, the decline associated with age is less pronounced for American women.

Is There a Paradox for Best Actresses?

Prior research on American Academy Award recipients has asserted the existence of a 'Best Actress paradox,' the observation that male leading role nominees are twice as likely to appear in films that are simultaneously recognized with a nomination for Best Picture, whereas the leading roles for which women are nominated occur in films that do not (Simonton 2004). We find no support for this contention among these elite actors. In our data, American men were nominated on 21 occasions for a leading role performance in Best Picture-nominated films, whereas women were similarly nominated in 34 instances. Considering that there are different numbers of women and men in our American sample, this means that women are nominated for a lead role performance about 6 percent more frequently than are men (Table 5.4).

Although we find no evidence for it in our American sample, does a 'Best Actress paradox' exist for French actors in César-nominated films? We conclude against this possibility also. French men made 114 appearances in films that were nominated for a Best Picture César award and were nominated for Best Actor in these films on 56 occasions, whereas French women appeared in Best Picture-nominated films on 79 occasions and were nominated for Best Actress in 48 of those films. While the sample is too small to test for statistical differences, these figures mean that the French men in our sample were nominated for Best Actor in a Best Picture-nominated film an average of 2.7 times, whereas French women were nominated for Best Actress in consecrated films somewhat more often—3.0 times. Considering that there are more men than women in our French sample, women are nominated for a leading role in films that are simultaneously nominated for Best Picture roughly 12 percent more often than French men. In short, there is no support for the 'Best Actress paradox' in either French of American film acting in our highly selective sample of multiple nominees.

Table 5.4 Number of Leading Role Nominees in French and American Best Picture-Nominated Films

Nomination type	César		Oscar	
	Men	Women	Men	Women
Lead role	56	48	21	34
No lead role	58	31	29	16

Why, then, unlike other scholars, do we not find a 'Best Actress paradox?' While we do not pursue this finding further in this chapter, it is possible that the paradox is an artifact related to one-time nominees. In other research, Lincoln (2004, 2007) found that women and men are roughly equally likely to be nominated only once for a leading role during the course of the acting career. Consequently, it may be that the paradox is biased by the types of roles that one-time nominees receive. That is, women who are nominated only once for the Best Actress award may be more likely than one-time male leads to appear in films that are not nominated for Best Picture. Future research should explore this distinction.

Are Oscar and César in "Double Jeopardy?"

In previous research on a pool of 318 leading 20th-century Hollywood actors, we found evidence for 'double jeopardy,' the idea that two characteristics, such as age and gender, have a multiplicative rather than an additive effect. In the case of film acting, double jeopardy disadvantages older women in particular (Lincoln and Allen 2004). Specifically, we found that women in Hollywood are younger than men when they begin their acting careers, they appear in fewer films than men even early in their careers, and their film acting careers are shorter than men's careers. However, the gendered age differences observed among Oscar nominees are somewhat more complicated than those of the broader pool of actors we examined. Research by Lincoln (2004, 2007) clarifies the observation made by scholars and public commentators alike that women are nominated for Oscars at younger ages than are men (e.g., Markson and Taylor 1993; Stark 2000). Rather, the disparity is not only a result of women's earlier career launches but also a statistical artifact resulting from the conflation of first and subsequent nominations. Put another way, other research has not only equated biological age with 'career age' but also compared nominees at different career stages, resulting in the comparison of seasoned actors—sometimes significantly so—with those who are more junior.

The nominees for acting performances at the 2002 Academy Awards provide a convenient demonstration of these issues. The average age of the 10 male nominees that year was 52.2 years, whereas the 10 women were nearly 13 years younger, 39.5 years of age. Closer analysis reveals that seven of the men were multiple nominees, and four had previously received more than three nominations, including Jack Nicholson, who received his 12th nomination for *About Schmidt*. The women nominated that year were also highly accomplished—six had been nominated more than once and two had received more than three nominations, including Meryl Streep, who earned a 13th nomination for her performance in *Adaptation*. When comparing only the first-time nominees that year, however, a different picture emerges. First, the age gap is substantially narrower—the average age of the men is 39.0, whereas the women are 34.5 years old—a 4.5-year difference. What about the length of their careers prior to 'promotion?' The nominees' filmographies reveal that the length of women and men's film acting careers prior to the first nomination is roughly the same. That is, the career length of men at their first nomination was 13.7 years, whereas women were nominated at 13.5 years into their acting careers, a negligible difference for annual awards.

More broadly, the tenure of women and men is roughly equivalent when they are nominated for a first, second, and even third Academy Award (Lincoln 2004, 2007). This implies that acting nominations are not simply based on innate talent. Instead, this finding suggests the possibility that it takes time to develop acting talent and secure entry into networks that gives access to the roles that have the most chance of garnering critical acclaim. We revisit these implications shortly, but first we compare French film careers to Hollywood careers at several key points (Table 5.5).

Strong similarities between both the US and France in age at first Oscar or César nomination are readily evident. Being in their early 30s, both French and American women are younger than their male counterparts when nominated for their first leading role award, whereas men typically are first nominated at the exact same age, when they are 35. Between the women, there is less than a one-year difference. Because these awards are conferred on an annual basis, this difference should be interpreted as negligible. In addition, due to the small sample size, these differences are not statistically significant; however, because this is a population of consecrated stars, rather than a sample, these differences can be interpreted as real and important. In particular, due to the annual award cycle, this point is particularly true for any differences greater than one year.

Table 5.5   Career Statistics for César and Oscar Nominees

	Age at first nomination	Age at first film	Years to first nomination	Age at second nomination	Years between first and second nominations	Years between first film and second nominations
César						
Men	35.1	25.7	10.4	41.0	5.9	16.3
Women	33.8	23.7	11.0	38.0	4.3	15.3
Oscar						
Men	35.1	26.8	8.4	42.7	7.6	15.9
Women	32.9	25.7	7.2	36.9	4.0	11.2

***p < .001 (two-tailed tests)
Note: Number in parentheses is the number of actors.

Following the finding that women's earlier career starts explain gender differences in age at first Oscar nomination (Lincoln 2004, 2007), we examine whether the beginning of these elite actors' careers explains the age differences at first nomination. That is, does the age difference at the beginning of the career match the disparities at nomination? On its face, it does not. American women are two years older than French women at their first screen performance, whereas at nearly 27 years of age, American men are a little more than one year older than their French counterparts. Moreover, distinct gender differences are apparent within each country. In Hollywood, women are about one year younger than men at the beginning of their careers, whereas French women are two years younger than French men. In general, American men tend to be the oldest at the start of their careers and French women the youngest, whereas American women and French men tend to begin their careers at the same age.

That French men are first nominated when they are the same age as American men—in their mid-30s—means that it actually takes French men more than two years *longer* than American men to receive the first nomination. Similarly, although French women are two years younger than American women at their first film appearance, they perform nearly four years longer before being nominated for a first César. The fact that American women are first nominated slightly more than one year earlier in their careers than American men roughly corresponds to their age advantage at career start. In contrast, French men recoup the two-year deficit at career start to earn their first nomination at about the same point in their careers as do French women.

In all, despite being the youngest when they begin their film careers, French women require the most time of the four groups to earn their first César nomination, whereas American women require the least. In all, Hollywood actors earn a first Oscar nomination more quickly than their counterparts in French cinema. These differences suggest distinct national differences in the process to securing professional recognition. Indeed, if the development of acting talent or networks is required for the crucial roles, the process appears to differ somewhat between France and the US.

On the whole, the analysis suggests that there are two distinct points to be made about time to recognition between the American and French film systems. First, if we regard a César or an Oscar as a form of career advancement, it is clear that Hollywood initially 'promotes' its stars more quickly than does French cinema. However, because the gender difference in time required for French actors' first 'promotion' is relatively negligible, French cinema appears to be rather more egalitarian than Oscar in meting out recognition. These findings suggest that the consecration processes of each system operate under somewhat different rubrics. We explore these implications further below.

After discerning distinct industry differences at first nomination, we compared the time required to achieve the second nomination. Among men, we

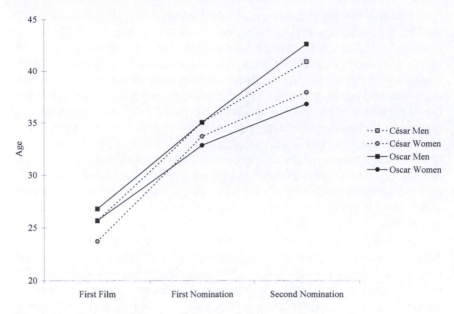

Figure 5.2   Career trajectories of César and Oscar nominees.

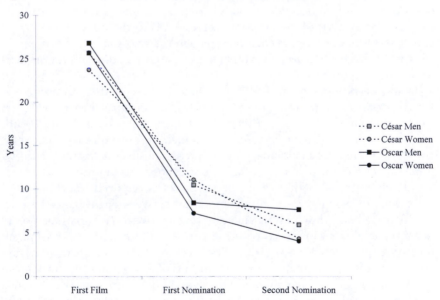

Figure 5.3   Duration to first and second César and Oscar nominations.

find that the 'promotion' advantage switches to César nominees. French men earn a second nomination less than six years after their first nomination, whereas American men are not recognized a second time for another 7.6 years. All in all, French men have been performing for about 15 years when they receive a second nomination, whereas American men have been in film acting for about 16 years before reaching the same point. Women in both countries are recognized a second time about four years after a first nomination. Ultimately, women have been performing in French cinema for more than 14.3 years when they receive a second César nomination, whereas the careers of American women are on average only 11.2 years long at the same point. Consequently, the disparity between French and American women is attributable to the length of time it takes to earn a first nomination.

How should we make sense of these results? Are acting careers influenced more by gender or industry structure? Graphical representation is a useful way to summarize the findings. Generally, the women in our sample are younger than men at the key points in the first 15 years of their careers—first film, first nomination, and second nomination (Figure 5.2). In Figure 5.2, the more horizontal a line segment, the smaller the difference in age between the two points that is implied. So, for example, the steeper first segment for French women as compared with the second segment indicates that French women receive their second César nomination more quickly than they do their first. Of the four groups, the trajectory of American men is the most linear, indicating the greatest equivalence in duration to first and second nomination. In comparison, the trajectory of the second segment of the other three groups is distinctly flatter than the first, indicating speedier second nominations.

Of course, biological age should not be used as a proxy for career experience. We therefore graphed the length of career from first screen appearance to first and second Oscar or César nomination (Figure 5.3). In Figure 5.3, steeper lines indicate shorter periods of time. From this figure, it is clear that Hollywood initially 'promotes' actors somewhat more quickly, but that the French system moves much more swiftly for second nominations.

Different Award Systems?

Earlier, we saw that that French actors earn more nominations during their careers than their American counterparts—on average, these consecrated French actors receive roughly four nominations compared with three nominations for Americans. This nominations gap is gendered; women are nominated for one more film than their male counterparts in both Hollywood and French cinema (Table 5.6). Certainly, outliers exist. Gerard Depardieu, a Frenchman, and Meryl Streep, an American, both have received the most nominations of the 104 performers—15 each. Generally, however, American actors receive fewer nominations during their careers than the French, and women receive more recognition than men. Yet these national differences cannot be related to the differences in the number of films produced in each country. Recall that Hollywood released nearly three times the number of films as the Cinema of France in 2005 (Lorenzen 2009), yet the French actors in our sample performed in more than 16 additional films compared

Table 5.6   Average Number of Career Nominations

	Men	Women	*Difference*
France	3.7	4.8	1.0
US	2.9	3.7	0.8
Difference	0.8	1.1	

with their Hollywood counterparts. Consequently, to better compare the two industries, we turn to multivariate regression analysis.

Table 5.7 examines the relationship between the characteristics of actors' careers and the number of César and Oscar nominations received during that career using ordinary least squares (OLS) regression. Statistical procedures such as t-tests are a premature measure of interpretation because they do not take into account any additional differences between, for example, men and women or Oscar and César nominees. OLS regression allows estimates of the relationship between two variables while adjusting for multiple other predictor variables. Thus, in finding that American men perform in more films in their careers than do women (Table 5.3), OLS regression permits comparison of men and women on key variables of interest like years to nomination while statistically equalizing their filmographies. We report the regression analyses as standardized regression coefficients, which means that all variables have been transformed to standard scores with mean = 0 and standard deviation = 1 and are thus directly comparable to each other in terms of strength and direction. All analyses were conducted with the statistical program STATA version 10 from StataCorp, College Station, TX, US. Variable correlations are reported in Appendix 5.B.

We conducted independent analyses for César and Oscar nominees because the samples were constructed separately and represent different industries within distinct cultures. In the analyses, we assess the effects of sex, the year of each actor's first film, age at career start, number of films in the career, and years to first and second nominations on number of career nominations received. We expect that actors who begin their careers at earlier ages have more time to accumulate nominations than those who enter the acting profession later in life. We also expect that actors who have performed in more films will have more nominations, *ceteris paribus*.

As expected, the more time actors require to receive a first and second César nomination, the fewer nominations they receive, whereas in Hollywood, only duration between first and second Oscar nominations has a significant effect on career nominations. As Figure 5.3 hints, there are national differences in the time actors require to earn a nomination. Recall that the trajectory to first nomination was flatter, and thus slower, for César nominees. Consequently, actors who linger before reaching the first César nomination ultimately have less decorated careers than peers who are nominated more quickly, net of the number of performances they enjoy. The time that

Table 5.7   Standardized Regression Coefficients of Number of Career Nominations on Actor Characteristics

Number of nominations in career	César	Oscar
Female	0.162	0.267
Years of first film	−0.025	−0.022
Age at first film	−0.194	−0.012
Films in career	0.421***	0.437*
Years to first nomination	−0.372**	−0.281
Years between first and second nominations	−0.260*	−0.398*
n	61	43
R^2	0.437	0.243
Adjusted R^2	0.374	0.117

*p < .05 **p < .01 ***p < .001 (two-tailed tests)

elapses between first and second nominations is slightly more influential in predicting fewer subsequent Oscar nominations. There is no significant difference between men and women in career nominations earned, nor is there a significant effect of age at career start on nominations, indicating that actors who are older when they make their first appearances are not unduly disadvantaged, nor is there an interaction of gender and age at career start (results not shown).

Importantly, the number of performances is significantly predictive of the number of nominations actors earn in their careers—simply put, the more performances by an actor, the greater the number of nominations accrued. The size of the effect, however, is nearly equivalent between Hollywood and French cinema. As a control variable, this variable has the effect of equalizing the length of French and American filmographies. Practically speaking, the coefficient on this variable means that each additional film in an actor's filmography has roughly the same effect on the number of career nominations in Hollywood as it does in French cinema. Thus, performances in the French cinema do not carry more weight than they do in Hollywood in terms of apparent propensity to have acting roles worthy of nomination. Consequently, the nomination disparity between France and the US is a result of the French cinema's tendency for César nominees to be more heavily utilized than their Oscar peers. The French model provides a stronger account of actor consecration than does the Hollywood model because it explains more than one third of the variation in the number of career nominations for French actors compared with roughly 12 percent for that of Oscar nominees.

Thus far, the analysis has shown that the length of time to first nomination is crucial to the number of career César nominations, whereas time to second nomination is somewhat more predictive of career Oscar nominations, net of the number of performances in an actor's filmography. What factors, then, are predictive of the length of these two career periods, and are there national differences? We have put forward earlier the idea that actors are developing social capital as well as acting talent during their careers (Rossman, Esparza, and Bonacich 2010). We therefore assess the effect of the number of performances on duration to first and second nominations and employ sex and age at career start as controls (Table 5.8). As can be expected, the number of screen performances is strongly predictive of duration to nomination for both Oscar and César nominees: Actors who have accepted more roles prior to first nomination will generally have longer careers. The coefficient on this variable is more than 50 percent larger for Oscar nominees, reflecting the fewer roles that Oscar nominees receive prior to nomination and thus the greater weight of these roles in the regression. Put another way, a larger number of roles is associated with a longer duration to first nomination, and thus the strength of the effect is larger for Oscar nominees than for César nominees. This latter point highlights the differences in how the American and French cinemas utilize consecrated actors. There is no gender difference in years to first nomination, but actors who are older at career start earn a first nomination more quickly than their younger peers. Although the results are not presented for the sake of brevity, there is no significant interaction of gender and age at beginning of career.

With these findings in mind, we then turn to examine influences on the duration between the first and second nominations. We carry over all variables from the previous analysis and add the number of film roles between the first and second nominations, as well as the dependent variable from the previous model as a control. The number of films actors add to their

Table 5.8 Standardized Regression Coefficients of Years to First Nomination and Between First and Second Nominations on Nominee Career Characteristics

	Years to first nomination		Years between first and second nomination	
	César	Oscar	César	Oscar
Female	0.029	0.128	−0.054	−0.023
Age at first film	−0.263*	−0.181*	0.073	−0.082
Films by first nomination	0.499***	0.820***	−1.398***	−0.599***
Years to first nomination			0.072	−0.073
Films between first and second nominations	—	—	1.497***	1.131***
n	61	43	61	43
R^2	0.372	0.685	0.669	0.824
Adjusted R^2	0.338	0.660	0.639	0.800

*p < .05 **p < .01 ***p < .001 (two-tailed tests)

filmographies is predictive of the time period between nominations; as before, more roles typically require time to accumulate and are indicative of a longer duration between first and second nominations. Importantly, however, in this model, the direction on the coefficient for films by first nomination has changed direction and become negative. This indicates that the number of films accumulated by first nomination *reduces* the time it takes actors to earn a second nomination. However, the time to first nomination—the dependent variable in the first model and a control variable in the second model—has no effect on the time to the second nomination. This implies that it is not a general process of career maturation that benefits actors, but rather that some aspect of accumulated performances paves the way for a second nomination. These performances may point to developing acting talent, social networks, or some combination of the two. If so, the acquisition of these skills or networks as actors' careers progress appears to subsequently provide strong benefits by reducing the time required for a second recognition. Moreover, the effect is twice as large in French cinema as in Hollywood.

DISCUSSION

This chapter has compared aspects of the careers of the most highly consecrated film actors in French and American cinema, performers in the cohort of actors born between 1940 and 1959 who earned two or more César or Oscar nominations between 1976 and 2010. We found no evidence that women are more likely than men to be nominated for performances in otherwise undistinguished films, the 'Best Actress paradox.' Moreover, although women perform in fewer roles than men as they age, we found no evidence for a 'double jeopardy' effect among these highly consecrated actors. We did, however, uncover key differences between the two countries' consecration systems. In terms of career performances and recognitions, César nominees record many more film performances than their Hollywood counterparts, as well as earn more recognition in the form of César nominations. However, our analysis confirms that it is simply these additional performances that are what yields more nominations for French actors. Indeed, we found the effect of filmography length on nominations to be essentially equivalent between French cinema and Hollywood. Consequently, the number of screen performances by actors largely explains the national difference in career nominations during their careers. Moreover, that performances have the effect of reducing the length of time required to reaching a second recognition once an actor initially produces a celebrated performance suggests that each additional performance may generate social capital—through building relationships and networks with directors, screenwriters, and other creative producers (Rossman, Esparza, and Bonacich 2010).

We close this chapter with the observation that consecrated French performers appear in many more films than their American counterparts. Why might this be? It is possible that the French system is more 'closed' than the American system, and thus rewards are concentrated among a smaller number of actors. The data also suggest that French producers rely on consecrated actors more than American producers perhaps because 'artistic merit' is more important in France. The French government provides financial assistance to producers in the form of loans that are typically only repaid if a film recoups its production expenses. Consequently, there is less emphasis on the economic value of a film than on its cultural or symbolic value. In this sense, French producers may be more 'conservative' and less 'innovative' in terms of using 'new' acting talent than American producers. The result is a small group of highly celebrated actors who receive more opportunities than the larger group of less highly renowned actors in America. This interpretation would explain why the duration to first nomination is more important for predicting the number of nominations for French actors than American actors. Once French stars enter the coronation circle, their talents are heavily utilized, whereas in Hollywood actors have fewer such assurances.

The discoveries in this chapter highlight the benefits to be found in comparative research on culture industries and point to important directions for future research and theory development. While providing evidence of structural differences—and similarities—between industries, this research permits comparison of mechanisms across institutional contexts and the refinement of theory. Certainly, we are left with more questions than we answered, such as why French cinema delays initial recognition of its celebrated actors and why Hollywood under-utilizes its elites. Future research on the study of careers in culture industries should make comparative analysis a priority.

REFERENCES

English, J. F. 2005. *The Economy of Prestige: Prizes, Awards, and the Circulation of Cultural Value.* Cambridge, MA: Harvard University Press.

Ginsburgh, V. 2003. "Awards, Success, and Aesthetic Quality in the Arts." *Journal of Economic Perspectives* 17: 99–111.

Lincoln, A. E. 2004. "Sex and Experience in the Academy Award Nomination Process." *Psychological Reports* 95: 589–92.

Lincoln, A. E. 2007. "Cultural Honours and Career Events: Re-conceptualizing Prizes in the Field of Cultural Production." *Cultural Trends* 16: 3–15.

Lincoln, A. E., and M. P. Allen. 2004. "Double Jeopardy in Hollywood: Age and Gender in the Careers of Film Actors, 1926–1999." *Sociological Forum* 19: 611–31.

Lorenzen, M. 2009. "Creativity in Context: Content, Cost, Chance and Collection in the Organization of the Film Industry." In *Creativity, Innovation and the Cultural Economy*, edited by A. C. Pratt and P. Jeffcutt, 93–118. New York: Routledge.

Markson, E. W., and C. A. Taylor. 1993. "Real Versus Reel World: Older Women and the Academy Awards." *Women and Therapy* 14: 157–72.

Merton, R. K. 1968. "The Matthew Effect in Science: The Reward and Communication Systems of Science Are Considered." *Science* 159: 56–63.

Nelson, R. A., M. R. Donihue, D. M. Waldman, and C. Wheaton. 2001. "What's An Oscar Worth?" *Economic Inquiry* 39: 1–6.

Redelmeier, D. A., and S. M. Singh. 2001. "Survival in Academy Award-Winning Actors and Actresses." *Annals of Internal Medicine* 134: 955–62.

Rossman, G., N. Esparza, and P. Bonacich. 2010. "I'd Like to Thank the Academy, Team Spillovers, and Network Centrality." *American Sociological Review* 75: 31–51.

Sands, P. N. 1973. *A Historical Study of the Academy of Motion Picture Arts and Sciences (1927–1947)*. New York: Arno Press.

Simonton, D. K. 2004. "The 'Best Actress' Paradox: Outstanding Feature Films Versus Exceptional Performances by Women." *Sex Roles* 50: 781–94.

Stark, J. 2000. "Age and the Academy." March 13. Available at http://www.salon.com/entertainment/log/2000/03/13/oscar_age

Sylvestre, M.-P., E. Huszti, and J. A. Hanley. 2006. "Do Oscar Winners Live Longer than Less Successful Peers? A Reanalysis of the Evidence." *Annals of Internal Medicine* 145: 361–63.

Vincendeau, G. 2000. *Stars and Stardom in French Cinema*. New York: Continuum.

Table 5.A César and Oscar Nominees

France	United States
Isabelle Adjani	Joan Allen
Richard Anconina	Kathy Bates
Anémone	Annette Bening
Jean-Hugues Anglade	Jeff Bridges
Fanny Ardant	Cher
Pierre Arditi	Jill Clayburgh
Niels Arestrup	Glenn Close
Ariane Ascaride	Willem Dafoe
Daniel Auteuil	Geena Davis
Sabine Azéma	Richard Dreyfuss
Jean-Pierre Bacri	Sally Field
Josiane Balasko	Whoopi Goldberg
Nathalie Baye	Tom Hanks
Francois Berleand	Ed Harris
Charles Berling	Holly Hunter
Dominique Blanc	William Hurt
Michel Blanc	Anjelica Huston
Richard Bohringer	Tommy Lee Jones
Michel Boujenah	Madeline Kahn
Carole Bouquet	Diane Keaton
Myriam Boyer	Jessica Lange
Clementine Celarie	John Lithgow

Continued

Table 5.A Continued

France	United States
Carole Cellier	John Malkovich
Alain Chabat	Marsha Mason
Patrick Chesnais	Mary McDonnel
Francois Cluzet	Frances McDormand
Gerard Darmon	Bette Midler
Jean-Pierre Darroussin	Nick Nolte
Catherine Denueve	Joe Pesci
Gerard Depardieu	Michelle Pfeiffer
Andre Dussollier	Susan Sarandon
Jacques Dutronc	Talia Shire
Andrea Ferreol	Sissy Spacek
Catherine Frot	Kevin Spacey
Jacques Gamblin	Meryl Streep
Nicole Garcia	John Travolta
Hippolyte Girardot	Christopher Walken
Bernard Giraudeau	DenzelWashington
Pascal Greggory	Sigourney Weaver
Joseph "Ticky" Holgado	Dianne Wiest
Isabelle Huppert	Robin Williams
Catherine Jacob	Debra Winger
Gerard Jugnot	James Woods
Gerard Lanvin	
Dominique Lavanant	
Bernard Le Coq	
Philippe Leotard	
Vincent Lindon	
Therese Liotard	
Fabrice Luchini	
Christophe Malavoy	
Miou-Miou	
Eddy Mitchell	
Yolande Moreau	
Marie-France Pisier	
Jean Reno	
Alain Souchon	
Patrick Timsit	
Jacques Villeret	
Helene Vincent	
Lambert Wilson	

Table 5.B Variable Correlations

France

	1	2	3	4	5	6	7	8
1	1.0000							
2	−0.0937	1.0000						
3	0.0450	−0.1734	1.0000					
4	−0.3736	0.0085	−0.1628	1.0000				
5	−0.3669	0.1396	−0.1897	0.6342	1.0000			
6	0.1690	−0.1229	−0.1387	−0.3875	−0.3730	1.0000		
7	0.5490	−0.1029	−0.0673	−0.2498	−0.1982	0.4740	1.0000	
8	−0.0417	0.7958	−0.1513	−0.0338	0.0566	0.2435	0.0706	1.0000

US

	1	2	3	4	5	6	7	8
1	1.0000							
2	−0.0236	1.0000						
3	−0.1150	−0.3402	1.0000					
4	−0.4015	−0.1518	−0.0562	1.0000				
5	−0.2671	−0.1177	−0.1303	0.5704	1.0000			
6	0.1526	0.4694	−0.5807	−0.1444	−0.0547	1.0000		
7	0.7937	0.0618	−0.3254	−0.1684	−0.0841	0.4169	1.0000	
8	0.0724	0.8990	−0.3929	−0.1151	−0.0692	0.6592	0.1737	1.0000

1. Years between first film and first nomination
2. Years between first and second nominations
3. Sex
4. Year of first film
5. Age at first film
6. Number of films in career
7. Number of films by first nomination
8. Number of films between first and second nominations

6 Central Collaborative Relationships in Career-Making

Chris Mathieu and Iben Sandal Stjerne

INTRODUCTION

This chapter analyzes subjective and objective dimensions of developing careers largely based on strong dyadic relationships and the personal and professional advantages and dilemmas encountered in this process. Focus is on the two-fold dimension of the processes of association. On the one hand, we look at dynamics inherent in the dyadic relationship because these are central to the subjective experience of one's career (i.e., meaningfulness, quality of working life, ambitions, and accomplishments), as well as its more objective trajectories. On the other hand, we look at how the perceptions and actions of persons external to the dyadic relationship are informed by the existence of the given dyadic association (i.e., the reputational dimensions of a dyadic collaboration). Empirically, the chapter uses data gathered from Danish film editors and cinematographers about their relationships with directors.

Structural and individual-based factors play into these processes. On the structural side, cinematography, directing, and editing are distinct roles in the production process, distinct aesthetic and knowledge spheres, areas of distinct technical competence, and distinct leadership roles, but they are also mutually interdependent, making full autonomy rarely granted or experienced and bi-directional exchange of ideas and judgments the rule. Although producers do the ultimate hiring, and along with financiers they may make suggestions or demands, directors are often given a large role in choosing these key collaboration partners. This hiring dimension further exacerbates asymmetric power and dependence relations, in addition to the structural and cultural privileging of the director in relation to cinematographers and editors, as discussed later.

The director role is central to the filmmaking process. Especially in European productions, directors are frequently originators on projects, or they are brought in early in project development and thereby invited, expected, and able to form the project in accordance with their wishes and visions. In general, the director role entails the prerogative to make the ultimate creative and artistic decisions. Auteur theory encapsulates the most extreme form of cultural and structural privileging of the director (Caughie 1996; Hicks and Petrova 2006). Although auteur theory still exists as a privileging discourse and an operative ideology in several contexts, there is also wide recognition that filmmaking is a complex team process requiring specialist contributions from a myriad of technical, managerial, and artistic persons and occupations.

The orientation of this chapter is more elementary than a team perspective. Focus is on the dyadic dimension of collaboration, which is more intimate, immediately interpersonal, intensive, and face-to-face (Turner 2002) than broader teamwork, and it recognizes the general and particular hierarchies and dependence between occupational roles and artistic professions, as well as the role that personal resources, whether personality or socially based (such as esteem, reputation, authority), play in informing the ongoing interaction and specific events in dyadic interactions.

This study is based on in-depth career history interviews with eight Danish cinematographers and 10 editors. The interviews were carried out in Danish, and all quotes are translated by the first author. All 18 are among the elite in their profession, in terms of longevity (remaining in work over a prolonged period of time), frequency (working regularly—at least two feature films a year), and the prestige of the projects on which they work (major productions of an artistic and/or commercial nature), with the primary part of their career based in feature filmmaking. The sample was generated by both analyzing who had worked on the most critically acclaimed and popular (box office) Danish films over the past 10 years, as well as collegial recommendations. Shortlists based on these criteria were produced for both occupations, with 15 cinematographers and 19 editors. Elite filmworkers were purposely selected on the assumption that they can say the most about career development and success and changes in the industry. Interviews lasted between one-and-a-half to four hours, with most between two to three hours. The gender composition of the sample generally reflects the gender ratio in these occupations, with a roughly 50–50 split among editors and an overwhelming majority of male cinematographers. Because the Danish film industry is quite small and intimate, protecting the promised anonymity of the participants is difficult. In order to do so, we use only the terms 'an editor' or 'a cinematographer' throughout the chapter because giving them fictitious names or designations such as 'editor A' would quickly lead to building profiles of the individual respondents, which would make them easy to identify. Likewise, we use the term 's/he' and the gender-neutral third-person possessive 'their' instead of the gender-indicative first-person possessives 'his' and 'her' in order to mask the sex of the respondent for the same reasons.

CAREER COUPLING AND REPEAT COLLABORATION

Terms such as 'coat-tailing' and 'piggybacking' are used in academic and everyday discourses to connote processes whereby an individual or group 'rides' its association with another individual or group for better or for worse. In studies of creative industries, the phenomenon is primarily explored in terms of 'career coupling' (Wagner 2006) as well as repeat collaboration.

Wagner (2006, Chapter 9, this volume) explores how careers are made through collaboration and the coupling of reputation in asymmetric dyads, analyzing the process whereby violin and scientific-research students form formal associations with 'masters'—violin teachers or established research scientists. She examines the processes of both formal 'content training'— violin and performance technique, and the scientific craft—and what she calls elite socialization and the building of social capital and reputation coupling. In the career coupling process, she identifies three phases: 1) the selection and matching process, wherein masters and students find each other, usually based on the reputation of the master and the evidenced ability and character of the student, and initiate enduring dyadic relations; 2) active collaboration, in which the master and student work together, and their cooperation becomes known to the wider environment; and 3) passive collaboration, wherein the names and reputations of the master and student continue to be linked despite cessation of active collaboration, although relationships are often maintained. Summarily, Wagner's career coupling concept focuses on long-term dyadic relationships, the long shadow of collaborative relationships even after active collaboration, the transfer of social and technical knowledge, the inseparability of private emotions from professional work, and intertwined professional fates.

Some significant differences exist between the context that Wagner (2006) explores and that examined in this chapter. The most significant is that Wagner examines 'master–apprentice' relationships in the same occupation or discipline, whereas we look at collaboration and career coupling between professionals in different occupations at the same rank, so-called 'A' functions, although as noted earlier there is an asymmetry in the ranking of these occupations and thereby also the roles. Thus, in our case, there is not the inter-generational, intra-occupational, teacher–student dimension, but rather a situation of inter-occupational elite peer collaboration.

Repeat collaboration is dealt with from several perspectives in film industry research. Some studies focus on the economic performance of films produced by a stable core (Delmestri et al 2005; Simonton 2004), whereas others focus on building protective cocoons around talented, idiosyncratic, maverick filmmakers (Alvarez et al. 2005). Studies from a work and career perspective focus on serial re-employment, entailing a central theoretical challenge in what is supposed to be an open external labor market (Faulkner and Anderson 1987; Jones 1996; Jones and DeFillippi 1996; O'Mahoney and Bechky 2006; Zuckerman 2005). Blair and collaborators (Blair 2001, 2003; Blair and Rainnie 2000; Blair et al. 2001, 2003) look at labor market processes in primarily the British but also Hollywood film industries and note the prevalence of what they call 'semi-permanent work groups.' These groups comprise hierarchically organized 'work-gangs' within a single occupation or department, in which the leader, often a head of department, secures work from one project to the next for his or her 'crew.' Blair explains this as a logical response on the part of workers to the chronic insecurity and vagaries of continuously being challenged to find one's next job (Menger 1999), the convenience and security offered to producers by reducing the number of hiring activities and knowing that a crew has previously successfully collaborated, eliminating the need for even 'swift trust' (Meyerson, Weick, and Kramer 1996). Blair's work focuses on hierarchical collaboration within occupations. Others have looked at how repeat collaboration occurs across professional or occupational boundaries.

Bielby and Bielby (1999, 65) show how talent agencies impact career outcomes or, in their terms, 'how mediating organizations segment the labor market for a professionalized contingent workforce.' They examine how, in Hollywood, agencies 'package' whole groups of the individuals they represent—writers, producers, directors, and actors—into a team or unit that is then presented to a studio. Thus, repeat collaboration in this regime is a function of the same personnel often being at the disposal of a talent agency and the talent agency creating packages that group its clients into creative, cost, and status coherent packages. Faulkner and Anderson (1987) argue that repeat collaboration in Hollywood is due to labor market segmentation in terms of cumulative advantage accruing to the already successful—a feature of a narrowing market at the top of the industry for elite talent creating a small pool to select from, rather the active agency of individuals such as agents.

Zuckerman (2005) argues based on quantitative Hollywood feature film production data from 1935 to 1995 (comprising both the height of the studio system and the contemporary 'flexible specialization' [Christopherson and Storper 1989] eras) that collaboration patterns during the 'market' flexible specialization era belie what we would expect for outcomes from a classical market. Zuckerman (2005, 32) concludes that "little seems to change" with regard to repeat collaboration despite the transition from a firm to a market-based system. Zuckerman explains this in terms of markets being more structured than previously or widely conceived due primarily to restricted search processes based on beliefs that few or no better collaboration partners exist, leading to "(over) commitment" (Zuckerman 2005, 33) to one's former collaboration partners. Ebbers and Wijnberg (2009) highlight the role of the 'latent organization' and its capacity to promote and hold sufficient trust to facilitate delayed rewards as a central mechanism in repeat collaboration. In the relationships between producers and directors in the Dutch film industry, they find that full rewards for contributions are not paid for each transaction, or at least not up front, and that rewarding takes several forms and is temporally extended into the future: implicit promises of re-employment, 'promotions' in terms of wage levels, higher status ranks, bigger budgets, more prestigious projects, or projects of the director's own initiation. Thus, Ebbers and Wijnberg (2009, 1006) question the reality of the open, external labor market assumption in the (Dutch) film industry: 'We show that latent organizations allow for flexible contracting and rewarding practices, that create possibilities for "semi" internal labor markets and career paths.'

Film industries are generally understood and investigated as prototypical external labor market-based industries as if this were synonymous with being a project-based industry where projects are carried out in project-specific temporary organizations or inter-firm collaboration and where careers "move across rather than within firms" (Jones and Walsh 1997, 59). The basic assumption in the repeat collaboration literature is that *re-engagement*, as opposed to *dis-engagement*, is the basic process. This image is probably given by the physical, economic, and legal but not the social, emotional, or cognitive disbanding of concrete project groups. Although some of the studies noted earlier have begun to question the accuracy of the atomistic, individual, open, skill or human capital-driven external labor market conception, the more fundamental question about how to frame the basic question raised above hitherto remains unarticulated. Thus, at the basis of both this chapter and our understanding of the basic process are two rival possibilities. The current formulation of the issue is *why repeat collaboration takes place in an open market setting*. The alternative formulation is *why repeat collaboration breaks down in a context of intense, intimate social relations*. Film industries are rampant with dyadic and multi-actor constellations that are more resilient and result in living collaboration than 'network' concepts acknowledge. Blair (2001) shows the operation of durable work groups, Ebbers and Wijnberg (2009) display some of the mechanisms for recurrent collaboration, and Zuckerman (2005) declares 'over-commitment' between collaborators in a market setting. In the following, we show both the fact of and basis for enduring collaboration and their dissolutions and then thematically take up central aspects of collaboration.

RELATIONS AMONG CINEMATOGRAPHY, DIRECTING, AND FILM EDITING

Before going into the analysis of collaboration and career coupling, a brief presentation of these three roles is probably helpful.

The cinematographer, sometimes referred to as 'director of photography' (DP), does or plans the actual camerawork. The cinematographer heads the 'camera department,' which includes clapper/loaders, focus pullers, other camera operators, and grips. Because the camera is the central apparatus in the filming process, it, and the crew around it, are the hub of the filming process, and the cinematographer is a central figure on set. One cinematographer we interviewed explained the central role of their job: 'The cinematographer is the practical work-leader for everything that takes time,' such as deciding where to and moving the camera and lighting. Another cinematographer says, 'There isn't anything worse than a cinematographer who doesn't know what to do. They totally panic over that.' After each shot, the director and the cinematographer usually confer on their satisfaction with the shot and modifications to be made before possibly reshooting.

The director has the overarching authority and responsibility for the artistic direction and choices in the production process. The director heads the 'director's unit,' including assistant directors, script supervision/continuity, and the digital video monitor. He or she does the instruction of the actors and actresses, and her or his focus is on the story (including dialogue and sound), as well as the visual impression. The director is the 'general' on set who may devolve tasks in a mainstream or modified manner to the 'lieutenants' at his or her disposal. The 'commander-in-chief' role above the director may be held by one or several (executive) producers.

The editor puts sound and images together and then cuts the segments into a coherent and effective story. Today, most editing is done on a computer, with digitalization entailing radical changes in the timing, location, and physical and social settings of the editing process. Whereas the director and cinematographer work on set during principal photography (shooting the film), the editor works off set, sometimes in a trailer near the set, sometimes in an editing room thousands of kilometers away, possibly in close proximity to other editors, sound engineers, or composers, or in isolation—or even at home. The editing process can take place almost in real time as the film is shot or can begin once the shooting is over. According to the editors we interviewed, the editing process usually begins while the film is still being shot and may extend months after the principal photography is concluded. Although the editor does the actual cutting and sequencing of the film, the director and/or producer(s) can monitor or engage themselves deeply in the process and discuss or make choices.

Directors work first intensively with the cinematographer on set and then with the editor during the editing process. By most accounts, and preference, it is rare that editors visit the set and rarer that cinematographers visit the editing room. As one editor says, 'They [the editing-room and on-set shooting] are two different worlds. . . . I don't want to know how much bother they've had [with the filming]. . . . What is the picture and what does it say? That is what I need to know.' Cinematographers, in contrast, frequently comment that editors sit in dark rooms and miss all the action and adventure on set. In general, there is a great degree of respect across the three functions, and they recognize their mutual dependence and 'obligations.' In the words of a cinematographer, 'Editors are intelligent, reflexive people. My job is to make sure that in the editing process there are enough pictures [shots] so that the editor both for the film in general and within scenes can do things differently than in the script—so that flexibility is available.'

One cinematographer describes the essence of being a good cinematographer as being able 'to capture the visions of the director, both technically and artistically and be able to convey that vision through practical work that on the screen is the expression that the director wanted. One can heighten that expression, so as a collaborative partner the expression can be even better than what the director wanted.'

Although the director is the privileged role, and, as expressed in the previous quote, cinematographers seek to capture or enhance the director's vision, age and experience may play a role in both relations in general and in adjudicating specific situations. The fact that the director role is more comprehensive leads both to more and less authority in particular circumstances. As one cinematographer explains, 'In general directors make fewer films than we do as cinematographers and that means that we have a greater experience base to draw upon when we talk about things standing there during filming, so there are many directors, especially those making their first film, who rely enormously on us.'

A cinematographer describes the filmmaking process this way: 'A film is made three time, its made as a script, then in the filming a new process starts where we come in as cinematographers [along with] the world of reality because the sun is to shine and it doesn't that day so there is a redefinition of the story, actors suddenly have opinions, etc, etc. And then when it comes to the editing process it doesn't matter what's in the script because the only thing that exists is the material that is shot, and then a whole new process begins that's called make a film out of the material that is shot.'

PHASES IN THE COLLABORATION PROCESS

In this section, we schematically examine three junctures in the overall collaboration process: 1) commencing or initiating collaboration, 2) renewing collaboration, and 3) ending active collaboration. In later sections, we look in more detail thematically at the active collaboration process and its perceived implications on career and personal issues.

Collaboration is most accurately conceived as relationships rather than transactions. The terms used in the interviews drew more on marriage and domestic partnership analogies than employer–employee or workplace task collaboration descriptions. Work between cinematographers and editors and the director is intense, temporally extended, personal, and emotionally charged in contrast to a depersonalized exchange of qualified services for (economic) compensation. In such a situation, termination or disengagement becomes the primary and interesting question, rather than renewal. This is the case for collaborations that have been initiated. Where quasi-'market circumstances' can be taken to prevail is in the process of finding and initiating collaboration, which is the first process examined next.

Initiating Collaboration

Structurally we see different patterns in initiating collaboration based on a couple of parameters. One parameter has to do with collaboration within or across age/experience cohorts, and the other parameter has to do with how contact between parities is mediated. These parameters can be combined in all manners, but certain combinations are more prevalent due to biases among central actors in the film financing and greenlighting process.

Certain combinations are more prevalent than others for understandable reasons. One of the more frequent means by which a collaborative relationship is initiated is mediated contact between experienced cinematographers/editors and inexperienced directors. Because feature films are generally expensive and risky endeavors, both private and institutional producers seek to limit risks by making sure that experienced and reliable individuals are in key roles, especially with a less experienced director. Creating the right balance of experience in a constellation is why one finds a preponderance of inter-generational collaborative constellations or constellations with only experienced core personnel.

Sometimes young, talented directors actively seek out a particular experienced editor or cinematographer for a number of reasons. In one case, an experienced cinematographer who had worked with one of the most important directors in Danish film history explained that s/he was chosen by a young emerging director specifically because of working with this renowned director, and the young director used the cinematographer to establish a living lineage to that director. Likewise, an editor explained how s/he initiated collaboration with a primary partner, '[Director X] was an admirer of [director Y] and I was director Y's editor, so I think that it was that way around that I came to know director X, and director X came to know me as director Y's editor.' Another editor was chosen by an inexperienced director due to the editor's particular artistic reputation: 'I think it's so that people have a conception of what one is good at. I don't think [the inexperienced director] would have asked me if s/he was to do an action comedy, but s/he was going to do a film on sorrow and dealing with sorrow. So that is the reputation I have. The sensitive one.'

One also finds situations in which an experienced director searches for younger collaborators. Sometimes this is done via recommendations, viewing work, or promoting someone who had a junior role on their previous productions. A cinematographer states that a renowned director, who made early career films with an iconic cinematographer, 'was looking for young cinematographers' and initially asked another cinematographer who couldn't do the film, so the director chose this young cinematographer who was a couple years out of film school and 'was out as an assistant every summer' adding, 'We were only six [cinematographers] who come out [of the National Film School of Denmark] every other year so there weren't that many of us to choose from.' This cinematographer called this initial collaboration 'a revolution for me, both career-wise and expression-wise.' This quote also exemplifies the central role of the national film school in Denmark as an elite educational institution both in terms of restricting the numbers of entrants into the Danish film industry with this prestigious training which, as implied in the quote, makes only its graduates legitimate candidates for topflight positions. Serendipity is seldom truly random but falls on people in well-positioned pools. The other thing worth noting is the manner in which such collaboration literally sweeps the young entrants into the film industry both artistically and career-wise up to another level. This can occur when a previously established collaboration partnership breaks down (due to a falling out, a desire to try a new path, the partner retires or begins directing, etc.) and an opportunity for change presents itself. Several interviewees state that some directors feel a need to 'reinvent' themselves on occasion, either out of boredom, artistic stagnation, or a series of flops, and choosing a younger editor or cinematographer can be a means of revitalizing one's work. In other cases, the reasons can even have primarily to do with physical conditioning. One cinematographer explained that after working as an assistant for a director who liked to film running chase scenes and be highly mobile, he was hired as the 'A' cinematographer in part because he could literally keep up with the pace of the filming.

One also finds examples of situations where an agreement is made between an experienced director and an experienced editor and the latter cannot do the job so his or her assistant or protégé is given the primary responsibility, sometimes with the promise of supervision or consultation from the experienced editor. If the inexperienced editor proves capable, then the collaborative relationship can continue. One editor began their collaboration with the director who has been the cornerstone of their professional career by first being hired by the primary editor then vested with more work as the primary editor could see that there was too much work to be completed alone. The young editor noted that '[the director] and I really got on well from the very beginning. Since then I've done just about all their stuff, with the exception of [film's name] because I had a child then.'

Where relatively inexperienced crews are found is in low budget, talent development-oriented novella films, or 'outsider' projects. Sometimes these projects become either box-office or artistic hits, and then these young cohort constellations are sanctified (Lincoln and Allen, Chapter 5, this volume) and given the opportunity to continue with bigger budgets next time despite limited experience in terms of numbers of films done. One editor describes their career trajectory as an effect of being put in contact with a young director through a mediator on a film school project. The 'outsider' project that the young director and editor collaborated on turned out to be a great success, 'pav[ing] the way for everything I've done since. . . . When you come out [of film school] with such a big film as it became, then you end up somewhere other than if I'd edited something else. I became visible in that way.' Here we see multiple associations for this young editor—to an innovative young director, to a successful film, to a path-breaking style. This has solidified the relationship to the director and allowed the editor to be selective in subsequent projects undertaken, as well as granting direct admission to editing feature films directly out of film school, which is quite rare. In summing up career opportunities, this editor remarks, 'I don't know what is me and what is a result of having done [film title].' In such situations, one sees a same-generation cohort team emerge and usually remain intact over a prolonged period. Here we often find collaborations between classmates from the National Film School of Denmark, as classmates have experience in working with each other, strong social bonds, and low-stakes projects are often funded to give emerging talents an opportunity to try out their ideas and gain practical experience in an industry setting. As one editor explained how s/he started working with a former classmate at this level, 'I did [director's name] novella film because we went to school together and it's normal to ring each other.' Thus, some young cohort collaborations are already established prior to entering into the commercial realm of the industry, but they are usually only permitted on low-cost, low-risk projects in this realm.

Worth noting in the prior instances is that mediators are industry actors, producers (including the Danish Film Institute), other editors, and cinematographers as opposed to professional mediators (i.e., agents). Agents are used to gain entry into foreign feature film industries and advertising films but not for feature films in Denmark.

At one level, accepting work is merely gaining employment, 'to put butter on bread' as many said. However, taking work on feature films is also seen as a first step toward a more durable relationship and weighed seriously. One editor states that working with young directors on interesting projects that may not be high in wages or prestige is 'also an investment' as it may lead to an ongoing and rewarding partnership, while another editor explains the process of choosing projects with a new director as deliberate and personal:

> I choose [the projects I work on] based on joy. It doesn't have to be for the script. It can be for the person. 'Who could it be exciting to sit in a room with for a half year?' You get very close to someone when you work with them. Closer than with your [domestic] partner. One can choose based on seeing someone's film that's interesting, but I still wouldn't do it if when we meet the personal chemistry isn't right. You have to feel that there is a spark or something. If you don't know each other you have to meet. I'd never say yes to do something because it's just interesting in form or because there is prestige in it. If I don't really fancy sitting with that person.

Thus, we see that initiating collaboration is not taken lightly and is often viewed in terms of not just the given project but in terms of a potential extended relationship.

Renewing Collaboration

Renewing collaboration on subsequent projects can be everything from an active decision to a non-question. In this section, we look at affirmative answers to this question and how and why collaboration gets renewed; in the subsequent section, we examine how and why collaboration is broken. In many cases, renewing collaboration illustrates a central point of this study—that while we usually think of the film industry as a project-based industry and take the project as the tone-setting and steering unit of analysis, at least the Danish film industry, or significant dimensions of it, are relationship based, and thus continued collaboration across projects is only questioned if the relationship is questioned.

An editor explains how s/he was asked to work with an experienced director who had an established relationship with another editor, noting first, 'These relationships are so solid. Something violent has to happen if you are to change [editors],' before explaining that the opportunity arose because the director's previous editor started directing films.

Another editor explains the freedom to choose in this way: 'I get to try lots of different directors. I'm not obliged to only use one director, so I cannot oblige a director to use one editor. . . . I get challenged by working with different directors, why shouldn't they get it by working with different editors. With the exception of [this editor's long-time collaboration partner] because s/he's satisfied [with me].' Here a general disposition towards change and artistic challenge is offered, but the importance and vitality of a special relationship is also usually affirmed. Another editor stated that s/he would be 'very surprised if [a specific director] did not work with him/her on the next film.' Most other editors and cinematographers state likewise that at least with certain collaboration partners, whether one is going to work on their next film isn't even a question. In one long-term relationship between an editor and a director, renewed collaboration was never doubted, and a tinge of exclusivity pervaded the relationship; the editor states, 'It was just that I always checked with her/him when I was agreeing to edit something [for someone else].'

Despite the reasoning about free choices and looking for newness, when specific collaborations that are experienced as good are not renewed, feelings are hurt and questions raised. One editor states, 'I had done some films for [director's name], and at one point s/he did some films where s/he didn't ask me to edit them . . . and I was very sad. But I have gotten over it. . . . Of course one has the right to choose the editor one wants for a given project. Maybe you are making a film where the other editor is more appropriate or you just want to try something new.' This testifies to the strong implicit expectation of being 'renewed' especially after the intense interpersonal process of working intimately on one or several projects. In other words, the interpersonal experience of collaboration is strong enough to shift the perspective from transaction to relationship.

Why is this the case? In part it's because directors, editors, and cinematographers work hard to maintain good, stimulating relationships and see a value in these relationships and 'find[ing] each other and follow[ing] each other,' as one editor put it. But we would argue that a large part of the explanation comes from the intimate, extensive, and intense nature of the collaboration activities and process. Our interviewees talked of collaboration in terms of 'putting your hands in the heart blood' of the director, work in the editing room being 'as intimate as having sex,' 'coming closer to your collaborator than your domestic partner,' and often in terms of marriage, connoting intimacy, commitment, development, and fidelity. In addition to the internal dynamics of the process being extremely strong, external factors, such as meeting critical, artistic, or commercial success, can further solidify relationships.

Ending Collaboration: Divorce

From our perspective, why collaborations, especially enduring collaborations, end is of central interest. Interestingly, as illustrated earlier, both repeat collaboration and divorce are seen as natural, accepted, and understandable, although again we see a difference between 'in principle' and 'in our case—our specific or special relationship' reasoning.

Collaborations may end for several reasons: a partner may retire or change occupations (start directing), directors may simply not get more projects, partners may feel the previously mentioned need to move on and try something new, a relationship may sour, a partner may move into a different genre or type of film or geographic location, there might be scheduling conflicts (due to work or domestic situations) that make collaboration impossible, or a third party, usually a producer, may strongly suggest or demand a change.

Although one may go to great lengths to secure that one is available on the productions of central collaborators (often detrimental to other employment prospects), explanations for not continuing collaboration include falling out of sync with each other timing-wise. Schedules do not match and a project has to be passed up. This often entails a risk of new collaborative relationships being established on both parts.

Another frequently given reason is that one or both parties feels that the relationship is no longer productive and it's time to move on. This can take the form of dramatic bust-ups usually revolving around artistic differences or problems in the work relationship of an interpersonal nature, amicable partings, or merely moving on without a final discussion of the matter. One editor explained the termination of a long and successful relationship in terms of artistic dissatisfaction with the type of film that the director continued to choose to make: 'I got tired of that form of film. . . . I feel our Nordic films were good, but the international films . . . [were not],' adding that the two of them have not had a final reckoning on the termination of their collaboration, it just stopped. Illustrating the quality of the work relationship as a basis for dissolving a collaborative relationship, an editor described the director s/he collaborated with in early career work as 'very complicated and headstrong about what s/he wants and can be a pain in the ass.' The manifest reason for terminating collaboration with this director was that 'It wasn't fun to be on his/her films any longer. I wouldn't develop more by working with him/her.' Pleasure and growth are explicitly mentioned, but the fact that the editor had another major and extremely successful collaboration under way may also have influenced the decision. The dissolution of this active repeat collaborative relationship didn't mean that the two never worked again, as the editor was brought in at a late stage on a project several years later, but the unquestioned collaboration on projects was broken.

Relationships can even precede active collaboration. One cinematographer described being a 'temp' with a director who was waiting for a friend to become experienced enough to begin active collaboration. When the friend of the director had a few film under their belt, the director hired the friend and released the cinematographer we interviewed despite a fine working relationship.

The art and emotion of maintaining, balancing, and ending relationships is central to collaboration, as we see later, but to close this section in dramatic fashion, one interviewee describes a former collaborative partnership and the insight that emerges first when the relationship is over, or at least temporarily suspended as future collaboration was not ruled out, in this manner: 'It's a very unhealthy relationship we have or have had . . . we are almost symbiotic in a bad way.'

WHAT MAKES COLLABORATION WORK (AND ENDURE): COMMON LANGUAGE, UNIQUE UNDERSTANDINGS, PERSONAL CHEMISTRY

This section examines some of the central factors that lead to the solidification of dyadic ties between directors and cinematographers and editors. Two things are of paramount importance: personal chemistry and a common artistic understanding or, at least, an ability or vocabulary to discuss artistic matters.

Several of the previous quotes testify to the importance of the working relationship and personal chemistry issues—that 'clicking' or getting on together right from the start is important. However, this initial 'finding each other' instance needs to be followed up by a developed interpersonal relationship in which trust, respect, challenge, and developing a common collaborative framework are central, as well as 'having fun together.'

In explaining how a collaborative relationship between a novice director and an experienced editor was initiated, the editor stated:

> I insisted that [director's name] be here all the time at the beginning because I wanted to find that language together with him/her. I wanted to know what s/he likes and what s/he wanted. Instead of pursuing something really nice and then the director coming in and not feeling that it is right. It is much more fun to create it together. But now it's the case that s/he's almost never here because we have [through past collaboration] found a language together. I [now] clip long scenes and have long consultations and then it is in the last two intensive weeks that we make the big decisions together.

This same editor explains how a previous long-term relationship functioned:

> [Name of a famous Danish director] is the one who has seen the filming and if it takes place way out in the countryside we talk on the phone during the lunch break. There has to be confidence so that when I say that its OK it's based on [the director's] criteria that I say its OK. Or if I say the acting isn't good enough in a scene, and s/he won't be satisfied with it, s/he has to trust this and go back and shoot it again. It is the partnership that is built up. We know each other so well because we made so many films together that when I say so, s/he knows what it means.'

In other words, the partnership comprises a role separation, a physical and social separation that allows the editor to focus on the 'material itself' rather than being influenced by the difficulty or bother in getting the sequence actually shot and the reactions of those on set. However, as the editor makes clear, it is the director's wishes and criteria that the editor uses in evaluations and professional activity. This forms the bases of mutual trust and respect—the establishment of a common frame of reference and vocabulary to discuss matters, a desire to both innovate and build on what has previously been accomplished, as well as an acceptance of roles and the principle that it is the director's vision and desire that need to be met, and that the 'good of the film' must be paramount.

This doesn't mean that subservience on the part of the editor or cinematographer is what makes relationships work. One editor states, 'There is always a fight over who decides. And that's why it demands so much trust on part of the director because you are sitting alone so much. That is why it's difficult with those splinter new, fresh collaborations. It takes time to get to know each other. A long time. You really hold onto those who you find.' This is backed up by another editor: 'Getting on with the people you work with is decisive for whether they come back, but this doesn't mean that I sell out one centimeter. On the contrary, it's wrong. When you are the person you are and dare to stand by what you believe in people can feel that. And you get close to people when you sit in the editing room, incredibly close, it's just like being married.' Tempering these exchanges is what's often termed a professional code or principle—it's the story that matters—expressed in the 'kill your darlings' cliché. This means the individual accomplishment and flair has to be sublimated to the greater good, the best shots or daring editing may be beautiful and creative but might not work in the totality, and the shot or editing might be too beautiful, attract too much attention, and thus detract from the overall storytelling.

Sometimes it's less of a common language than a work routine or principle of practice that makes the collaboration function well. One editor who works steadfastly with one of the most innovative directors in Denmark describes the hows and whys of their way of editing in the following manner:

> And I also think that one of the reasons why people want to work with me is that things don't end up in conflicts; you shouldn't sit there and discuss things to death, you should just try it, do it. I learned this rather quickly and especially the new technology makes it possible. We have developed a way of working together, because it's exhausting for the director to turn it into a discussion club. And you never really know, often the really good solution lies right next to the really bad solution. With [the innovative director] we try it even if the other thinks it's a bad idea. And then you try it anyway and you think, yeah that was pretty bad, but just there, there was an element that was really great. And then you try something else. And precisely this aspect is really essential for making the collaboration much more pleasurable. . . . It's also the case that as an editor you need to create the space between the editor and the director where nothing is too stupid and everything can be tried. One isn't smarter than that. Often it's good, even though you don't think so initially, and you just have to be open to saying its good when it is good.

Thus, what is essential here is creating an openness whereby both the director and editor feel comfortable making any daft suggestion, a willingness to try it, give it an honest look, an interest in finding what is good and capable of being developed upon, even if it is just a minute aspect, and a willingness to recognize what is good despite initial skepticism.

What develops relationships is the surreptitious intense, emotional engagement that is pervasive in these dyadic work collaborations. As one editor says, 'One quickly comes to talk about private things in the film branch. . . . So it is a branch that is more based on friendship than others. And it is very intensive processes and you talk about human things when you talk about feelings in film. That is after all what you look for and have to relate to.' In other words, the strength of the relationships is integrally related to the nature of the work that these people carry out together.

(IN)DEPENDENT ATTENTION AND REPUTATION

Although stable partnerships play important roles in artistic and employment contexts, they are rarely sufficient in themselves to sustain an adequate livelihood or satisfying professional work life for cinematographers and editors. While enduring partnerships have a great deal of intrinsic value for both parties, especially for cinematographers and editors, these relationships are a form of capital that is parlayed into other opportunities. The nature of shorter work periods for these two occupations as compared with directing makes it essential for editors and cinematographers to work on more projects than directors. A cinematographer puts it this way: 'One is never hired for more than four months at a time, so it is important to get lots of telephone calls for all types of things.' All types of things usually means feature films, documentaries, and advertisement films.

Positive Aspects for One's Career of Enduring Relationships

Successful collaborations bring visibility, and in this regard both quality and quantity matter. Collaboration on strong, successful projects makes one visible in the film community, as such projects are more widely seen and discussed in the film community, and who is on the cast and crew becomes known and discussed widely. Likewise if one works with someone who does films fairly frequently, one is also at the center of attention more often as almost all films attain a degree of exposure when released, as well as physical opportunities to meet potential employers at premiers, press events, and parties. Here, one's name and work become discussed, if only for a fleeting moment, but more fleeting moments etch one's name in the minds of industry players. These opportunities and exposure are more by-products of collaborations and more linked to products than associative relationships per se. However, as we saw in the section on initiating collaboration, some editors and cinematographers are sought out primarily due to their association with a given director. Likewise, once a positive collaborative relationship is established, as witnessed already, contractual renewal and thus further work is almost automatically guaranteed. These are the primary manners in which objective careers are supported and propelled by collaborative association. These are no doubt significant, and formally the basis of subjective career considerations, but it is probably at the subjective level that enduring collaboration is most important. It is in these long-term, intimate relationships where our respondents reported making most of their masterpieces and having the most artistically and personally satisfying work experiences. In other words, these dyadic collaborations are the primary sources of artistic and work life satisfaction because these are the relationships where mutual respect, trust, and artistic and creative zeniths are reached.

Negative Career Development Consequences of Strong Associations

Enduring, successful collaborations can paradoxically also have negative impacts on objective career development. One editor with a long and successful collaboration explained the negative consequences of this highly successful, primary partnership:

> Two things happened. First, I had a reputation . . . of being a clever editor, and people wanted to [work with me] but they didn't because they thought, 's/he only makes films with [director's name], s/he doesn't have time.' . . . Producers and people in the industry say you can forget about calling [me] because [I] won't have time or won't be interested . . . and this was deeply irritating because you also have to have butter on your bread. We also need to earn money . . . [and] there were periods where I turned down offers for things because I couldn't get out of them later if the other film [the big productions with his/her primary collaborator] started and I'd rather do that film.

The two negative things described are the establishment of a supposition that one is either too busy with one's primary collaborator or other collaborators in the same league and that one wouldn't be interested in minor, less prestigious, lower budget, or domestic (as opposed to international) projects. Thus, an 'exclusive' and 'excluding' reputation gets built, due to no fault of one's own, and largely beyond one's ability to impact the reputation, due to one's association with a top-flight director. The second process is that one spends time and effort creating 'availability,' turning down other projects and probably even in this way exacerbating one's image of 'untouchable' in order to work on the projects of one's primary collaborator. This cuts into one's ability to earn a living. One strategy used by some is to say yes to a couple of projects that may overlap, hoping that one will be delayed or not materialize. Others are wary of this strategy. As one editor states: 'It's bad to say yes to two films that are slated for the same time. That's bad. You just don't do that. . . . If you do that to a director who you work with a lot, you can be quite sure that you won't work together again after that.'

The problem of being classified as 'out of our league' is fairly widespread in our elite sample. Both cinematographers and editors describe how they consciously keep themselves in the running for all sorts of projects by doing low-budget productions as well. One cinematographer states, 'I also try to do small-budget stuff. I know I have had a reputation for using a lot of resources, so I consciously choose to do small budget productions to show that I still could do good work on a small budget. That I could elevate the expression even on a small budget, I consciously choose to do this.' An editor employs the same strategy: 'It can be a disadvantage that they think I'm so fine, I've done so much, I'm so experienced that I'm surely not interested or I'd need a salary that they can't afford. I've heard that people have said that.' So this editor also deliberately takes work on small, low-, or no-budget films to correct that image.

CONCLUSION

This chapter has sought to accomplish two things. One is to explore the objective and subjective career dynamics of enduring collaborative relationships across occupational lines in 'A' functions on film projects. Here we find that enduring relationships provide the cornerstones for objective career progress via reputational and exposure effects. Such reputational effects were not entirely unproblematic, as association to elite film directors could bring a detrimental stamp of 'exclusivity' to cinematographers and editors, which hinder them from obtaining a broad range of employment offers. At the subjective level, we find that it is primarily within such collaborative constellations that the most satisfying professional experiences transpire, due both to the heightened quality of the work process as well as the films themselves. The second purpose has been, on the basis of some of the central findings of this study, to contribute to the debate about changing how we should look at the employment process in the film industry (at least in Denmark and similar contexts). How fluid or durable are the bases for collaboration, that is to say, the underlying social relations? Are they transactional in the economic sense—one-off exchange relationships or transactional in Emirbayer's (1997) sense—they transcend and span specific actions and episodes and comprise an enduring relationship where termination is the critical question not repetition?

Repeat collaboration among these central figures in the film production process is underpinned by several factors. The most significant of these appear to be the nature of the production process entailing intimate, temporally extensive, and intensive interaction and work. The nature of the content of at least a great deal of the films made in Denmark necessitates a high degree of discussion and debate of topics of a personal, human, and heartfelt nature. On a purely interpersonal level, this kind of contact can be expected to build close bonds that result in both interpersonal identification and respect and thereby also frequently renewed collaboration. We would venture to say that the nature of the *content* of the film, as well as the production process, plays a role in enduring partnerships, which apparently are based on strong, confiding, personal, and professional role relationships.

We probably need new terms for the relationships we see here, which are neither personal friendship relationships, as many of the people we interviewed state that they do not socially see their enduring partners outside of work, nor strictly professional relationships characterized by depersonalized detachment from the other on an emotional level. These relationships are characterized by their intensity of mutual affirmation and occasionally disagreement, respect and trust, and deeply personal confiding and exchange (Wagner, Chapter 9, this volume). So in order to fully understand the nature of this feature of career-making in film, we need to appreciate the unique character of the relations engendered by collaboration between these functions.

REFERENCES

Alvarez, J., C. Mazza, J. Pedersen, and S. Svejenova. 2005. "Shielding Idiosyncrasy from Isomorphic Pressures: Towards Optimal Distinctiveness in European Filmmaking." *Organization* 12: 863–88.
Bielby, W., and D. Bielby. 1999. "Organizational Mediation of Project-Based Labor Markets: Talent Agencies and the Careers of Screenwriters." *American Sociological Review* 64: 64–85.
Blair, H. 2001. " 'You Are Only as Good as Your Last Job:' The Labour Process and Labour Market in the British Film Industry." *Work, Employment and Society* 15: 149–69.
Blair, H. 2003. "Winning and Losing in Flexible Labour Markets." *Sociology* 37: 677–94.
Blair, H., N. Culkin, and K. Randle. 2003. "From London to Los Angeles: A Comparison of Local Labour Market Processes in the US and UK Film Industries." *International Journal of Human Resource Management* 14: 619–33.
Blair, H., S. Grey, and K. Randle. 2001. "Working in Film: Employment in a Project Based Industry." *Personnel Review* 30: 170–85.
Blair, H., and A. Rainnie. 2000. "Flexible Films?" *Media, Culture & Society* 22: 187–204.
Caughie, J., ed. 1996. *Theories of Authorship*. London: Routledge & Kegan Paul.
Christopherson, S., and M. Storper. 1989. "The Effects of Flexible Specialization on Industrial Politics and the Labor Market: The Motion Picture Industry." *Industrial and Labor Relations Review* 42: 331–347.
Delmestri, G., F. Montanari, and A. Usai. 2005. "Reputation and Strength of Ties in Predicting Commercial Success and Artistic Merit of Independents in the Italian Feature Film Industry." *Journal of Management Studies* 42: 975–1002.
Ebbers, J., and N. Wijnberg. 2009. "Latent Organizations in the Film Industry: Contracts, Rewards and Resources." *Human Relations* 62: 987–1009.
Emirbayer, M. 1997. "Manifesto for a Relational Sociology." *American Journal of Sociology* 103: 281–317.
Faulkner, R., and A. Anderson. 1987. "Short-Term Projects and Emergent Careers: Evidence from Hollywood." *American Journal of Sociology* 92: 879–909.
Hicks, A., and V. Petrova. 2006. "*Auteur* Discourse and the Cultural Consecration of American Films." *Poetics* 34: 180–203.
Jones, C. 1996. "Careers in Project Networks: The Case of the Film Industry." In *The Boundaryless Career: A New Employment Principle for a New Organizational Era*, edited by M. Arthur and D. M. Rousseau, 58–75. New York: Oxford University Press.
Jones, C., and R. DeFillippi. 1996. "Back to the Future in Film: Combining Industry and Self-Knowledge to Meet Career Challenges of the 21st Century." *Academy of Management Executive* 10: 89–104.
Jones, C., and K. Walsh. 1997. "Boundaryless Careers in the US Film Industry: Understanding Labor Market Dynamics of Network Organizations." *Industrielle Beizenhungen* 4: 58–73.

Menger, P.-M. 1999. "Artistic Labor Markets and Careers." *Annual Review of Sociology* 25: 541–74.

Meyerson, D., K. Weick, and R. Kramer. 1996. "Swift trust and temporary groups." In *Trust in organizations: Frontiers of theory and research*, edited by R. M. Kramer and T. R. Tyler, 166–195. Thousand Oaks, CA; Sage Publications.

O'Mahoney, S., and B. Bechky. 2006. "Stretchwork: Managing the Career Progression Paradox in External Labor Markets." *Academy of Management Journal* 49: 918–41.

Simonton, D. 2004. "Group Artistic Creativity: Creative Clusters and Cinematic Success in 1,327 Feature Films." *Journal of Applied Social Psychology* 34: 1494–520.

Turner, J. 2002. *Face to Face: Toward a Sociological Theory of Interpersonal Behavior*. Palo Alto: Stanford University Press.

Wagner, I. 2006. "Career Coupling: Career Making in the Elite World of Musicians and Scientists." *Qualitative Sociology Review* 2: 78–98.

Zuckerman, E. 2005. "Do Firms and Markets Look Different? Repeat Collaboration in the Feature Film Industry, 1935–1995?" Unpublished manuscript, MIT Sloan School of Management, http://web.mit.edu/ewzucker/www/look_different.pdf, last accessed January 22, 2011.

Part III
Architecture

7 Frank Lloyd Wright's Artistic Reputation
The Role of Networks and Creativity

Candace Jones

INTRODUCTION

> [Wright] bears in himself the marks of the late nineteenth century; yet isolated and singlehanded, without aid from his contemporaries among painters and sculptors, he has introduced the beginnings of a new conception.
>
> Sigfried Giedion (1940/1956)

Building an artistic reputation enacts a fundamental paradox: An artistic product demands collaboration and interdependence among skills and roles, but art worlds, artists, and critics such as Giedion, "systematically ignore . . . the contribution of others to the works on which reputations are based" (Becker 1982, 361). Organizational scholars increasingly argue that creativity is fundamentally social not primarily individual (Perry-Smith and Shalley 2003). For instance, Hargadon and Bechky (2006) focus on the moments of collective creativity, where help seeking, help giving, reflective reframing, and reinforcing are critical to the creative process but do not assess who gets credit for the creative product. In contrast, Fleming et al. (2007) analyzed both the creation and credit of patents, revealing that individual brokers were more likely to create new ideas but less likely to have these ideas used by others, whereas collaborative brokerage—individuals who formed cohesive groups to co-create—were less likely to generate new ideas but more likely to have those ideas used by others. These findings highlight the tension between individual and collective bases of reputation: Individuals are more likely to be more creative than collectives but less likely to be recognized for their creativity.

The case of Frank Lloyd Wright's reputation and career appears to present a puzzle to the tension between heightened individual creativity and less social recognition for that creativity. He rarely collaborated with other architects, but his ideas were picked up and used by architects, anchoring his reputation as a pioneer within the architecture profession. The research question explored in this chapter is: How did Wright navigate the tension between the social and individual bases of a reputation for creativity in an art world?

Art worlds vary in the degree of cooperation they require between art-ists. Some art worlds such as painting, sculpture, and etching rely on indi-vidual creativity and execution, whereas other artistic products such as films and buildings demand collective creativity—the input of many highly skilled contributors and roles—due to the complex nature of the artistic product. Even in highly individualistic artistic products such as etching, a phalanx of others ensures that an artist gains attention and a reputation (Becker 1982; Lang and Lang 1988). In art worlds where the artistic prod-uct is simple and depends on one person for execution, artists are better able to cleave their individual creative act from the collective support that ensures the creative product finds an audience and attention. In contrast, when an artistic product demands the contribution of and interdependence of skills such as film or building, then it is less clear how an artist creates a reputation independent of those who collaborate in making the complex artistic product.

Even in art worlds where interdependence is prerequisite, such as film, critics and fellow professionals often focus on the individual. For instance, auteur theory in film explains a movie's quality by the director's techni-cal competence, distinguishable personality, and interior meaning (Sarris 1962–1963). Auteur theory ignores and renders invisible the contributions of a myriad of interwoven roles that influence the quality of a movie, such as "front office, producers, writers, editors and the rest of them" (i.e., Kael 1963, 23; Schatz 1988). It is easier to see and understand the creative con-tributions of roles when they are visible to audiences such as how actors and set designers contribute to a film. Further, the collective nature of the artis-tic product is encoded in film credits. Even so, auteur theory still dominates the critical discourse in film, focusing on the director's role and contribu-tion. This situation is exacerbated when creative roles and contributions are invisible to audiences. Such is the case in architecture, where from the Renaissance onward a building has been attributed to an architect, such as Christopher Wren, Bramanti, or Brunelleschi (Becker 1982; King 2001), even though a myriad of skilled artisans, professionals, and quasi-profes-sionals are required to construct the building. Indeed, within the architec-tural profession, only the design architect is given 'credit' for a building (i.e., recorded in the profession's history and archival material), rendering invisible the contributions of others and signaling the status of design as the highest skill within the architectural profession (Jones 2010).

I seek to answer how Frank Lloyd Wright, who famously refused to acknowledge the contributions of others and was attributed as an individ-ual genius by critics, had his ideas accepted by the profession. To identify not only the generation of new ideas but also their usage when assessing creativity, scholars argue that we must examine creative success: recogni-tion of a creator's ideas or work by the larger society (Becker 1982; Fleming et al. 2007; Simonton 1984). Thus, I examine the creative success of Frank Lloyd Wright over his career stages and examine the role that his social networks played in building his reputation as an artist. Frank Lloyd Wright provides an appropriate case for assessing reputation. He is widely recognized by architectural historians as a 'pioneer' of modern architecture who laid the foundation for fellow architects (Giedion 1940/1956; Scully 1954), recognized by eminent architects such as Philip Johnson (1949) and considered one of the greatest architects of the 19th and 20th centuries because of how he reconceptualized space and shaped the open layout of modern buildings (Blake 1960/1996; Scully 1960). Next I describe the approach and data that I used.

DATA COLLECTION AND RESEARCH APPROACH

Data Collection

I use an inductive and multi-method study employing archival research methods (Ventresca and Mohr 2002) and using multiple data sources and multi-method triangulation (Jick 1979). To capture his success, that is, the attention to Wright by those within the architectural profession, I used the *Avery Index to Architectural Periodicals* to identify the number of articles written about Wright for each year of his career. These writings about Wright are indicators of recognition throughout his career and after his death—that is, sustained attention from critics and historians of the profession and being entered into collective memory of a culture (Collins 1998).

Wright's Artistic Products: Buildings and Writings

To measure Wright's artistic products, I focus on the two products that he consistently produced: his buildings and his writings. For Wright's *buildings*, I used the project index compiled by Anthony Alofsin in the *Frank Lloyd Wright: Taliesin Correspondence*. It is a complete listing of all Wright's building-related work—whether sketches and plans for clients listed as projects or completed buildings listed as executed. It captures Wright's productivity at various points within and over his entire career. I use the date of the first building to mark the beginning of Wright's career in architecture.

To identify Wright's *writings*, I used several data sources. For his journal articles, I used the *Avery Index to Architectural Periodicals*, a comprehensive listing of journal articles on architecture and design containing more than 440,000 entries surveying more than 700 American and international journals. To identify Wright's books, I first used WorldCat, an online database that identifies all holdings by or about a person in libraries all over the world. It is the world's largest network of library content and services (see www.worldcat.org/whatis/default.jsp). The initial search pulled up more than 670 entries; however, many of these were the same books under different entries (e.g., various editions, revisions, and translations) as well as books written about Wright's work rather than by Wright, his exhibitions, and some journal articles. Thus, I opted to cross-check the validity of WorldCat's entries against the Frank Lloyd Wright foundation, which identifies the books written by Wright (see http://www.franklloydwright.org). This cross-check identified 20 books written by Wright throughout his career.

By focusing on Wright's artistic products, I was able to trace two types of networks: collaborative and promotional.

Wright's Collaborative and Promotional Networks

Collaborative networks are those that involved joint credit for Wright's writing or buildings—that is, recognition of another's contribution to the artistic product whether by Wright or by historians, as indicated by joint design or co-authorship status. For buildings, I used *Contemporary Architects* (Emanuel 1980, 1994; Morgan and Naylor 1987), a reference book that identifies all buildings and artifacts designed and created by modern architects such as Wright as well as biographical data. In addition, *Contemporary Architects* identified who, if anyone, within the architectural profession collaborated with Wright on his buildings. For writings, many of the books and articles listed Wright as an author because he provided building schematics, plans, elevations, and photographs for the editors of the monographs or articles. I used the entry notes in WorldCat helped to parse out these two categories: books about Wright versus books in which Wright helped to edit and select works.

Books that are editions summarizing Wright's work are considered promotional networks. There were 54 books about Wright by others who promoted his buildings, writings, and architectural approach.

Promotional networks, in contrast to collaborative networks, were others who promoted Wright by writing about his artistic products, bringing him to the attention of key audiences. To assess those who helped to promote Wright's career by writing about his architecture, I used both the WorldCat entries and Avery articles. I cross-checked the monographs from WorldCat with the publication listing for Wright on the Frank Lloyd Wright Foundation website. Because the articles about Wright in professional journals in the Avery Architectural Index number in the thousands, I randomly sampled 5 percent of all Avery articles across early, mid, and late periods to capture a sense of his promotional networks. This resulted in 28 articles.

Because promotional networks are by definition positive, a PhD student and myself coded the tone of articles—positive, negative, and neutral. Neutral were primarily plans, drawings, and photographs that exposed Wright's work but did not provide positive commentary. The raters were forced to assign numbers to each category (e.g., 1 for presence of negative, neutral, or positive; 0 for absence); thus, the fixed multi-rater kappa coefficient was used (Brennan and Prediger 1981; Siegel and Castellan 1988). The kappa coefficient for percent of overall agreement was Po: 0.887641, and the kappa value of the fixed marginal was 0.738813, where values above .70 indicate adequate inter-rater agreement. Of the 28 articles, 3 were negative and thus not included in the promotional network. I combined the 25 positive articles in professional journals and the 54 monograph books about Wright to capture his promotional network.

These two networks—collaborative and promotional—showed little overlap, as the following figures reveal. Because few buildings received attention before their complete construction, the promotional networks rarely overlapped or were shaped by collaborative networks. A caveat is that many of Wright's Taliesin Fellows, who worked as apprentices for Wright, later became key promoters of Wright, such as Brooks Pfeiffer and Edgar Kaufmann, Jr. Thus, collaborative networks, if the fellows had been recognized as collaborators, would have preceded the promotional network. However, these apprentices to Wright were never given credit as co-designers or creative contributors to his buildings.

Finally, to understand Wright's career, I drew on the numerous biographies, articles, and books written about Wright. Those cited are included in the References.

Research Approach

I parsed Wright's career into three stages: early, mid, and late. Early careers were identified as 10 years from the first building listed for Wright; research has shown that 10 years is the time required to develop expertise in an area (Prietula and Simon 1989). This time period corresponds roughly with Wright's first building in 1885 at age 18 to 1896 when he was 29 years old. Mid career was defined as 11 to 39 years from first building, corresponding to ages 30 to 59 and the years 1897 to 1926. Late career was operationalized as 40 years from first building until his death, corresponding roughly from ages 60 to 90 (Wright died at age 90 while completing the Guggenheim Museum).

WRIGHT'S REPUTATION: COLLABORATIVE AND PROMOTIONAL NETWORKS

First, I present an overview of Wright's artistic productivity and his recognition by the profession to gauge which activities were most important at what career stages. Wright's buildings and writings capture his artistic products, whereas exhibits (attention from museums) and articles about Wright in professional journals are indicators of recognition from those within the architectural and artistic professions. Each measure has been standardized by dividing the number of creative products in each career stage by the number of years in that career stage.

As Figure 7.1 shows, Wright is most productive in terms of buildings. Both his buildings and recognition by professional journals increased with each career stage. In his late career stage, the recognition from professional journals finally outstrips his artistic productivity, receiving proportionally more recognition than the buildings that he is producing. Clearly, the late career stage captures the cumulative effect of a career that builds over time in terms of both his artistic productivity and recognition from the profession.

Next, I examine the two forms of networks: collaborative based on co-production of artistic products—either buildings or articles—and promotional networks of professional articles and book monographs about him that brought Wright to wider attention in the profession and society.

For his collaborative networks on artistic products, Wright rarely acknowledged the contributions of others in buildings. For instance, although every building had a supervising architect and his son-in-law, Wes Peters, often acted as engineer on his buildings (Freidland and Zellman 2006), these individuals are never credited as co-collaborators. His collaborative networks were sparse to almost non-existent as shown in Table 7.1. In Wright's first two career stages, he credits no one (nor do those who compiled the data) for contributing to his artistic products. In contrast, in his late career stage, he collaborated on buildings with only two people: his son, Lloyd Wright, and a former student, Albert McArthur. These comprise only 4 of the 248 (1.6 percent) of the buildings in Wright's late career, which is surprising given the highly interdependent and collective process of building construction.

In his writings, Wright also rarely acknowledged anyone else as a contributor. Three people are credited as co-producers: Baker Brownell, Frederick Gutheim, and Edgar Kaufmann, Jr. Baker Brownell was a former a reporter and editor for the *Chicago Tribune* and the *Chicago Daily News*

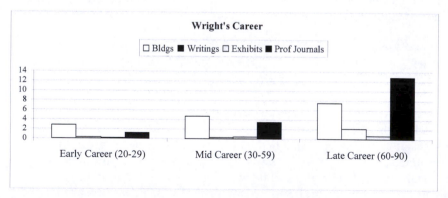

Figure 7.1   Wright's career: Artistic products (buildings and writings) and recognition (exhibits and reviews in professional journals).

Table 7.1   Collaborative Network by Career Stage: Building and Writing Collaborators

Career stage	Building collaborators	Writing collaborators
Early career (1885–1896)	None	None
Mid career (1897–1926)	None	None
Late career (1927–1959)	1923 Lloyd Wright, Sturer house 1924 Loyd Wright, Ennis House 1924 Lloyd Wright, Freeman House 1927 Albert McArthur, Arizona Biltmore Hotel	1937 "Architecture and Modern Life" with Baker Brownell 1941 "On Architecture" with Frederick Gutheim 1955 "An American Architecture" with Edgar Kaufmann, Jr

during the 1920s and later became a Professor of Philosophy at Northwestern University, as well as editor for Harper and Row during the 1940s. Frederick Gutheim was a prominentz urban planner, architect, and author. Edgar Kauffman, Jr. was the son of one of Wright's most important clients,

Figure 7.2   Wright's collaborative network (buildings and writings).

Edgar Kauffman, and for whom Wright built Fallingwater. Edgar Kauffman, Jr. was an architect, and he apprenticed with Frank Lloyd Wright at Taliesin from 1933 to 1934. He wrote many books on Wright throughout his career as an architect, critic, and Director of the Industrial Design for the Museum of Modern Art.

Figure 7.2 visualizes the collaborative network for easier comparison with the promotional network. His collaborative network is non-existent in early and mid career and quite sparse in late career.

Wright's promotional networks are far more extensive than his collaborative networks. Thus, I present these only in network visualization format to ease information load and enhance clarity and comparison.

As Figure 7.3 shows, Wright's promotional networks, in contrast to his sparse collaborative networks, were extensive. In his early career, Wright had few who sponsored him. In professional journals, Wright had two short and anonymous articles, comprised of photos and plans with no commentary, written about his building. In his mid career, he gathers promoters who actively and repeatedly select, edit, and write texts about his buildings. The two most active, who co-authored the books, were Yukio Futagawa and Bruce Brooks Pfeiffer, starting in 1900 and continuing through 1951—a 50-year span. He also had repeated ties with several key people, primarily in his late career, such as Henry Russell Hitchcock,

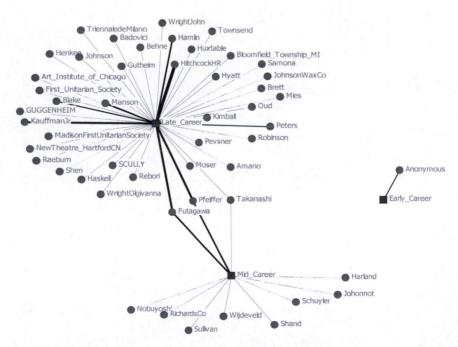

Figure 7.3 Wright's promotional network (books and articles).

who was initially critical of Wright's work. Henry Russell Hitchcock and Philip Johnson curated an exhibit on modern architecture at the Museum of Modern Art in 1932, and in their catalog to the exhibit they called Wright a 'half modern.' Both Hitchcock and Johnson later came to praise Wright as the greatest living architect at the end of his career. Another active promoter was Grant Manson, who wrote his dissertation at Harvard on Wright. Finally, Edgar Kauffman, Jr., an apprentice at Taliesin, was the son of Wright's important client, Edgar Kauffman, for whom he designed and built Fallingwater in 1935, one of Wright's most noted and important buildings. Wright's promotional network was peopled with clients, critics, and followers who promoted Wright's buildings and approach during his mid and primarily late career, through pamphlets, articles, and books or his writings through compilations or collected essays.

The drastic difference in Wright's collaborative and promotional networks helps to explain how an artist may not have repeated ties or even extensive ties in a collaborative network, which may facilitate artistic control and ensure that credit for a building goes to the designer. The data show that Wright's creative networks—those with whom he was actively engaged in producing creative products and whom he recognized as collaborators—were essentially non-existent; he collaborated with no one in his early and mid career, or at least he did not recognize their contributions, and in his late career he collaborated with only two people with whom he had high trust relationships—his son and a former apprentice. He actively collaborated with two co-authors who were highly influential, and thus to whom it was harder to deny credit, and can also actively promote him (Kaufmann and Gutheim). In contrast to the literature, a sparse collaborative network was not detrimental to Wright's artistic success—that is, becoming known and incorporated into the profession and culture. Wright actively used an extensive promotional network to get his name and work recognized.

DISCUSSION

Wright used two distinctively different networks to resolve the tension between artistic creation and artistic reputation or success through recognition. He collaborated with few others or at least did not acknowledge their contributions to his buildings, retaining control over and a singular artistic identity for himself. He built extensive promotional networks with others who actively promoted him, allowing his artistic ideals and visions to become recognized by and incorporated into the architectural profession and larger culture. Interestingly, his clients played an active role in this by publishing pamphlets about the buildings he designed and built for them. Wright was also extremely savvy in developing relationships with those who had access to the media, such as Baker Brownell, who, over his varied career, was a writer and editor for two of Chicago's most important papers, then for the book publisher Harper and

Row, as well as a professor at Northwestern University. Most of the literature on collective creativity and collaborative brokerage has focused on one type of tie content, and thus it may miss alternative means by which to resolve the tensions and tradeoffs between individual and collective action needed to create original ideas as well as disseminate them.

This research raises several issues for future research. One issue is how artists such as Wright can deny credit to lower level collaborators, such as his Taliesin Fellows, without alienating them and simultaneously engendering strong affective bonds that translate into a life long commitment to promote the artist. For Wright, this occurred with Edgar Kaufmann, Jr., Brooks Pfeiffer, and Wes Peters. An analysis of the personal correspondence and retrospective memories by these key promoters would help to identify the actions, events, and circumstances that engendered such strong affective commitment. This type of research also holds promise for identifying the content of networks and how this may shape future networks as well as the ability of an artist to translate one kind of network (i.e., training) into a distinctly different type of networks—that of promotion.

A second key issue is which audiences or more specifically networks are critical for promoting a reputation. Lang and Lang (1988) argued that it is primarily family members who promote an artist, ensuring recognition and renown. Wright's case revealed that family members were important (his wife wrote a book about him), but that apprentice and training networks were as or more important than family ties in securing an artist's recognition and renown. However, Boutinot's findings in Chapter 8 (this volume) argue that peer recognition is most central, then clients, and then the general public. She did not assess familial ties or roles; perhaps family becomes more important when a creative person has died as opposed to their networks while alive, which is Boutinot's focus. Wright, in contrast to Boutinot's findings, focused on clients. Without gaining opportunities from clients, there is little chance of recognition from architectural peers. A comparative study of French and American architects and the role of consecration by peers, similar to Lincoln and Allen's Chapter 5 (this volume), would be a useful next step to resolve and address the potential inconsistencies across time, constituents, and continents in reputation building.

A third future research issue is whether the dynamics of reputation and careers differs dramatically for creative endeavors that allow for individual recognition versus those that are fundamentally collective, such as orchestras (Dowd and Kelly 2011). This type of research would address the paradox and tensions noted in the introductory paragraph. Is creativity that is fundamentally collective and collaborative different in significant ways from forms of creativity where an individual's identity is central to the process of and reputation for creativity?

The findings from this study may help to explain how artists during their careers can cultivate a reputation for artistic and individual genius, even in art worlds that demand the contributions of many skilled people and roles to create the artistic product. By restricting credit for creative acts and simultaneously developing strong, long-term bonds with those who promote an artist's work, the artist can overcome the dilemma of lower quality but higher recognition of artistic product that occurs in collective brokerage and higher quality artistic product but lower recognition that occurs in individual brokerage. The complementarity of the two forms of social networks—collaborative and promotional—suggest that artists have options on how and with whom they manage their reputations.

REFERENCES

Alofsin, A. (ed). 1988. Frank lloyd Wright: An index to the Talisin Correspondence vol 1 and 2. New York: Garland Publishing Inc.

Avery Index to Architectural Periodicals. www.ebscohost.com/public/avery-index-to-architectural-periodicals. Downloaded September 2009.

Becker, H. 1982. *Art Worlds*. Berkeley, CA: University of California Press.

Blake, P. 1960/1996. *Masterbuilders: Le Corbusier, Mies van der Rohe, Frank Lloyd Wright*. New York: W. W. Norton.

Brennan, R., and D. Prediger. 1981. "Coefficient: Some Uses, Misuses, and Alternatives." *Educational and Psychological Measurement* 41: 687–99.

Collins, R. 1998. *The Sociology of Philosophies: A Global Theory of Intellectual Change*. Cambridge, MA: Belknap/Harvard University Press.

Emanuel, M., ed. 1980. *Contemporary Architects*. First edition. New York: St. James Press.

Emanuel, M., ed. 1980. *Contemporary Architects*. Third edition. New York: St. James Press.

Fleming, L., S. Mingo, and D. Chen. 2007. "Collaborative Brokerage: Generative Creativity and Creative Success." *Administrative Science Quarterly*, 52: 443–75.

Friedland, R. & Zellman, H. 2006. *The Fellowship: The Untold Story of Frank Lloyd Wright and the Taliesin Fellowship*. New York: Regan (Imprint of Harper & Row).

Giedion, S. 1940/1956. *Space, Time and Architecture: The Growth of a New Tradition*. Cambridge, MA: Harvard University Press.

Hargadon, A., and B. Bechky. 2006. "When Collections of Creatives Become Creative Collectives: A Field Study of Problem Solving at Work." *Organization Science* 17: 484–500.

Jick, T. 1979. "Mixing Qualitative and Quantitative Methods: Triangulation in Action." *Administrative Science Quarterly* 24: 602–11.

Johnson, P. 1949. "The Frontiersman." *Architectural Review* 106: 105–10.

Jones, C. 2010. "Finding a Place in History: Social and Symbolic Networks in Creative Careers." *Journal of Organizational Behavior* 31: 726–48.

Kael, P. 1963. "Circles and Squares." *Film Quarterly* 16: 12–26.

King, R. 2001. *Brunelleschi's Dome: How a Renaissance Genius Reinvented Architecture*. New York: Pengiun Books.

Lang, G., and K. Lang. 1988. "Recognition and Renown: The Survival of Artistic Reputation." *American Journal of Sociology* 94: 79–109.

Morgan, A., and L. Naylor, eds. 1987. *Contemporary Architects*. Second edition. New York: St. James Press.

Perry-Smith, J., and C. Shalley. 2003. "The Social Side of Creativity: A Static and Dynamic Social Network Perspective." *Academy of Management Review* 28: 89–106.

Prietula, M., and H. Simon. 1989. "Experts in Your Midst." *Harvard Business Review* 67: 120–24.

Sarris, A. 1962–1963. "Notes on the Auteur Theory." *Film Culture* 27: 1–8.

Schatz, T. 1988. *The Genius of the System: Hollywood Filmmaking in the Studio Era*. New York: Henry Holt and Co Inc.

Scully, V., Jr. 1954. "Wright vs the International Style." *ArtNews* 53: 32–5, 64–6.

Scully, V., Jr. 1960. *Frank Lloyd Wright*. New York: George Braziller, Inc.

Siegel, Sidney and N.J. Castellan, Jr. 1988. *Nonparametric Statistics for the Behavioral Sciences*. Second edition. McGraw-Hill.

Simonton, D. 1984. *Genius, Creativity and Leadership: Historiometric Inquiries*. Cambridge, MA: Harvard University Press.

Ventresca, M., and J. Mohr. 2002. "Archival Methods in Organization Studies." In *The Blackwell Companion to Organizations*, edited by J. Baum, 805–28. London, UK: Blackwell Publishing.

8 Reputation-Building in the French Architecture Field

Amélie Boutinot

"Many events helped me be an architect who builds, creates his own path and is called by clients from France or worldwide. . . . But for sure, the reputation constellation started with the peers' and public demand's validation. This is how an architect becomes interesting."

(French architect, interview notes 2009)

Not all the practitioners develop the same way in contemporary French architecture. Some became icon architects, being known among peers, governments, legal authorities, and even people at large. Others only acquire the respect of their peers for the quality and relevance of their architectural works—but the broader public may know neither their names nor their buildings.

Rindova et al. (2005) present a double view of reputation: an economic one (based on the quality and value of an organization's outcomes) and an institutional one (based on how widely an organization or individual is recognized among its organizational field). This chapter focuses on the latter to understand better how several reputations can be built by creative individuals within artistic fields and the roles of the audiences and the field in constructing those reputations.

The institutional view considers reputation as a global impression representing how an organization or an individual is perceived (Fombrun 1996; Rindova et al. 2005) by an audience. The term 'audience' here refers to a group of organizations or individuals who have the same role and characteristics within the same organizational field (DiMaggio and Powell 1983) and a common social identity (Ashforth and Mael 1989). Even if there may be some divergence in the audience members' thinking, they predominantly follow the same common logics due to a common framework of thoughts. Therefore, there is an internal consensus within an audience about how to assess individuals; a specific reputation is thus conferred within that audience. In creative industries, artists might expect talent and creativity from another artist, while potential clients might expect respect of procedures and potential visibility.

Previous studies have also highlighted the fact that reputation is established within an organizational field (Deephouse 2000; Fombrun et al. 2000; Rindova et al. 2005). An organizational field is a "set of organizations that, in the aggregate, constitutes a recognized area of institutional life: key suppliers, resource and product consumers, regulatory agencies, and other organizations that produce similar services or products" (DiMaggio and Powell 1983). It is thus an area of coherent and institutional life (Scott 2001) composed of several groups of organizations, which we consider as distinct audiences with different expectations and ways of assessing other field members (DiMaggio 1988). Applied to creative activities, a creative organizational field appears to be a plural space (Kraatz and Block 2008), where an individual will face multiple expectations at the same time, and where, therefore, he/she will build different reputations. Bringing the organizational field into the debate presents a puzzling gap in the reputation-building process: The very mechanisms of building and combining several different reputations remain quite obscure, especially in terms of the possible roles of the individual audiences, their potential consensus or divergence, and the creative field as a whole in this process.

Learning more about the process would help research about reputation in creative industries understand better the multiplicity of reputation-building. How does an individual actor proceed from gaining a reputation with one audience to gaining one with a whole creative organizational field? In other words, how do creative individuals build and combine reputations from several audiences to achieve a reputation at the field level?

I empirically investigate these mechanisms via a multiple case study of 11 already reputed French architects who have all won the Grand Prix National d'Architecture (GPNA), the most important French award in architecture. Besides offering the opportunity of becoming architectural icons, this award is particularly interesting for this study because the composition of its jury includes several 'profiles' related to architecture—critics, clients, and legal authorities as well as architects themselves—reflecting the potential variety of audiences that candidates must convince.

The chapter begins with a review of the relevant literature on the institutional view of the reputation-building process in creative industries, followed by an explanation of the chosen methodology, case selection, and analysis. It continues with the presentation of two mechanisms I found particularly interesting that answer the research question and concludes with possible contributions to reputation-building theory applied to creative industries.

REPUTATION IN A CREATIVE ORGANIZATIONAL FIELD

Reputation in One Audience

Core Characteristics of Reputation for an Audience

Institutional scholars working on reputation consider it to be a positive general impression that represents how a collective perceives an organization or individual (Fombrun 1996; Fombrun and Shanley 1990; Rao 1994).

I call such a collective an 'audience' in this chapter. An audience is under-stood as a group of organizations or individuals who belong to the same organizational field (DiMaggio and Powell 1983) and who have the same role within this area of social life. Thus, for example, producers are one audience, consumers are another. Each audience possesses a social identity (i.e., similar traits and a feeling of belonging to the same social group) (Ashforth and Mael 1989), which facilitates a consensus in the members' opinions. Even if some members may think differently, they predominantly tend to follow a common orientation of thoughts.

Such an audience assesses an organization and establishes its reputation compared to its peers, with a better-reputed organization being that which gives the impression of having a superior ability to create value compared with its competitors. On that account, King and Whetten (2008) state that—contrary to legitimacy, which corresponds to what conforms to an audience's expectations—reputation relates to what is judged as outstanding compared to peers. An actor or organization that reaches a minimum standard on a specific audience expectation is granted legitimacy; that which reaches a higher standard compared to their peers gains reputation with this audience.

But an audience does not confer reputation rapidly: Rather, based on several years of past actions (Weigelt and Camerer 1988), it extracts those who stand out over time (Fombrun and Shanley 1990). As a consequence (in contrast to the kind of status that may be unearned) (Washington and Zajac 2005), reputation definitely needs to be proven over time, be they financial, institutional, strategic, or less formal ones (Deephouse and Carter 2005; Fombrun 1996; Fombrun and Shanley 1990), to create a dialogue between the organization and the audience members. Such a dialogue is understood by theorization as a process of simplification and abstraction, which develops categories and identifies their properties and relationships (Greenwood et al. 2002). Thus, throughout their professional life, some types of organizations publish books or articles about their works, partici-pate in exhibitions and conferences, and so on.

Finally, this long-term characteristic means that reputation is not a static phenomenon: Its creation, building, and maintenance have been studied in previous research (Fombrun 1996; Fombrun et al. 2000; Fombrun and Shanley 1990; Rindova et al. 2005), as has its self-enforcement (Merton 1968), damage, and repair (Rhee and Valdez 2009). So an audience does not establish a reputation once and for all: Reputation-building is part of an evolution process that is never assured of its future.

Several Forms of Reputation in Creative Industries Depending on the Audience

Previous research has studied various possible audiences or forms for reputation. Fombrun and Shanley (1990) presented different audiences assessing an organization, such as employees, consumers, or media. Later, Rindova et al. (2005) established that consumers and local community could also be influential audiences assessing an organization, while Deephouse and Suchman (2008) noted how organizations or people can build their name across several publics, partners, media, and society at large. In the context of new ventures, Petkova, Rindova and Gupta (2008) demonstrated that reputation can be local (with a small audience that has direct experience of a company) or more generalized (with a larger audience that seeks to ascertain a company's reputation before entering into a relationship with it).

In the context of creative industries, such as art and entertainment (Caves 2000) or even research, whose dynamism is due to creative individuals,[1] who value talent, creativity, innovation, and merit, actors (generally) want "their reputation to increase as quickly as possible" (Becker 1988, 135). Being reputation-driven, the creative industries reveal the multiple forms of reputation: Artistic reputation is related to how creativity and talent are recognized by artistic societies, awards, or acceptance of works in juried exhibitions, for instance (Becker 1988; Lang and Lang 1988), whereas economic reputation is related to how well such individuals manage successful commercial projects, which can lead to mass success. In some cases, both kinds of reputation can be accrued: For instance, Italian film directors can have both artistic and economic reputations (Delmestri et al. 2005).

I draw on the idea of reputation taking several forms to elaborate how reputation in creative industries takes a specific form depending on the audience being addressed: Artistic reputation is established within the profession among peers, whereas economic reputation is established with a more general audience, related to clients or other people who do business with the organization or individual. But previous research also showed that reputation can be built within a broader space—an organizational field—and that an individual or organization desiring a field reputation may face a plurality of expectations that all need to be satisfied and exceeded. Literature on organizational fields may help us to better understand this point.

Facing Several Audiences: The Challenge of Reputation-Building in an Organizational Field

Creative Organizational Fields as Plural Spaces

Here I apply DiMaggio and Powell's (1983) definition of an organizational field to creative activities to create the notion of creative organizational fields, which are fields representing creative sectors such as arts and entertainment. The fact that various sets of organizations are integrated in one organizational field questions the way the reputation-building process has previously been addressed. Indeed, acquiring a reputation at the field level corresponds to a combination of several reputations with the field's several different audiences; it is thus necessary to draw on the notion of pluralism and understand an organizational field as a plural space, where actors face a heterogeneous set of groups at the same time (Kraatz and Block 2008). While it may be coherent in the sense of having common values, norms, and meanings (Scott 2001), its constituent groups of organizations (DiMaggio 1988)—here called audiences—will all have their own normative orders and logics that will dictate how to act and interpret reality (Thornton and Ocasio 1999). Thus, an organizational field is composed of multiple sources of authority, which may play different roles in reputation-building; be they central or peripheral (Greenwood and Hinings 1996; Leblebici et al. 1991), each audience has its own impact on the reputation-building process, although central actors, more integrated in the field (DiMaggio 1988; Scott 2001), are likely to play more important roles than peripheral ones.

Building Several Reputations in a Creative Organizational Field

Past research suggested some potential ways to deal with the plurality of expectations and logics within a field (DiMaggio 1988; Kraatz and Block 2008). First, Rao (1994) noted that there may be a dialogue between diverse audiences thanks to their own information systems that keep them aware of what is happening both within the group and in the wider field. In the same vein, Rindova, Petkova, and Kotha (2007) confirmed the importance of media, seeing them as institutional intermediaries for disseminating information among each audience and thus help reputation-building. Moreover, the individuals can manage this diversity by adapting their theorization depending on the audience (Rao et al. 2003; Svejenova et al. 2007); for instance, chefs will dialogue with other chefs through articles in the specialized press (such as *Restaurant* magazine) but with their clients via the mass press (i.e., the culture sections of newspapers like *The New York Times*, called the 'cultural press' in the rest of this chapter). Finally, Bowness (1989), who is also working on this plurality of expectations in creative industries, elaborated on the timing of how several audiences are integrated in building reputations. If artists face several kinds of audiences to build their reputation within their art field, such as peers, critics, potential clients, and the larger society (Becker 1988; Delmestri et al. 2005; Lang and Lang 1988), Bowness presents a clear progression by which artists become famous in a creative field: First they get reputed among their peers, then among specialist critics, then move outward to media and critics, and finally toward clients. Such a progression is established by the artist breaking himself/herself away from one audience ('dislocating') so as to settle in another one ('relocating').

But these previous studies don't address the actual mechanisms of the construction of various forms of reputation within a creative field and how they are combined. More specifically, we don't know the role that either the individual audiences or the field as a whole play in this reputation-building process. My research question is therefore: How do creative individuals build reputations with distinct audiences and combine them to achieve a field-level reputation?

METHODS

Research Context and Cases Selection

Given the exploratory and open-ended nature of the research question, a qualitative method was preferred. The field of French architecture was chosen because some of the theoretical points mentioned earlier are clearly visible in this field (Yin 2003). First, French architecture is a creative industry that is reputation-driven: Contemporary architects, in addition to conceptualizing and constructing buildings, want their names to be identified and remembered. More specifically, French architecture has been driven by individual reputation-seeking since the late 1970s, when the rules of the profession were modified. Before that, few architects could exercise and compete in their own name in France because the only architects who could participate in national architectural competitions[2] were those who had been awarded the Grand Prix de Rome, given by the Academy of the Beaux Arts of Paris (Champy 1999). No other school was delivering any diploma or award in architecture. But several architecture schools were created in France in the 1970s, enabling more people to become architects, to create their own architecture companies, and thus to enter in national competitions in their own name. In the early 1980s, French architects were allowed to participate in European and international competitions, creating an even higher distribution of the command and integrating the French community into the profession's international standards. Since then, excellence and innovation in architecture, but also individual reputation, have driven the dynamism of this sector in France.

Second, French architecture can be considered as a plural field, composed of several groups of organizations/individuals that we can take as representing the architects' diverse audiences: peers, clients, legal authorities, suppliers, educational administrations, and even people living or working in the buildings recently constructed. In this connection, architects' activity in general is varied enough that they will be linked to and dialogue with several audiences: They have diverse types of clients (public authorities, private firms, and private individuals); they give courses to students in architecture, design, and plastic arts schools; they write books and media articles about their recent building conceptualizations and their general aesthetic; and so on.

Finally, to answer the research question, I follow Anand and Watson's (2004) point and focus on awards because of their increasing role in establishing who is prominent in a field. Few French architects have received international awards, but many were recognized at a national level in several ways: for their first building (the *Prix de la Première Oeuvre*, awarded jointly by Le Moniteur—the main French architectural journal—and the French Ministry of Culture), for a single building (the *Equerre d'Argent*, given by the same two authorities), or for a set of architectural works (the GPNA, which is awarded by the French Ministry of Culture to architects practicing in France for architectural excellence and for both concrete and theoretical contributions to architecture, on the judgment of a jury composed of architects, public clients, journalists, and critics).

This study focuses on the GPNA as a good indicator of reputation in the French architectural field. First, echoing Becker's (1988) notion that the whole set of an artist's works needs to be taken into account to attest to their reputation, the GPNA recognizes whole bodies of architectural work that are exemplary and outstanding; it is not awarded to just single buildings. Second, this award attests to a collective validation of these works because its jury represents the several types of audiences that architects have to convince (peers, critics, and legal authorities, some of whom are also clients and users). Finally, each GPNA award recognizes the architects who are the 'best' compared to their peers, in terms of buildings and/or thoughts, as an agreement among the several members of the jury.

This GPNA was awarded annually between 1975 and 2004 and has been conferred bi-annually since then. Since its creation, it has been conferred 24 times—there was no award in 1988, 1994, 1995, 2000, 2001, 2002, 2003, and 2005 for unmentioned reasons. Twenty-eight architects have received the GPNA in that time, although they will remain anonymous in this chapter. To keep the data coherent and traceable, I have removed three categories of architects from the sample—those whose names are not included in their firms' brands (because reputation in architecture is considered here as a matter of individual name), those who are no longer practicing, and those who died before 2008—because they could not be interviewed. This left 11 comparable cases of architects who had won the GPNA (Appendix 8.A presents some biographical elements).

All of these architects have built their reputations on their names. Echoing Jones' study about Frank Lloyd Wright (Jones, Chapter 7, this volume), creativity is important for these architects who consider themselves 'auteurs.' They consider architecture more as a way of finding new solutions to societal matters than the provision of a service—and also as innovators, conceptualizing buildings, as one says, "that could not be done by someone else." In contrast to those other French architects who may also be both innovative and excellent but who remain less known, the GPNA winners communicate about their works and ideas willingly—they claim to theorize and want their ideas to be promoted.

Data Collection

The data collection focused on tracking what happened in these architects' career histories from the year they gained their architectural diplomas to when they won the GPNA. The primary data source was documents and archives about the 11 architects: Following the biographical data methodology (Roberts 2001), I first collected data about their lives through their websites, CVs, and books, but also websites about architecture. I also read the French architectural press and the French cultural press from 1975 to the year they won the GPNA to gather as much information as possible.[3]

I complemented this material by interviewing several kinds of actors from the French architecture field. I first interviewed the architects to make sense of the archives, to know why and how certain elements that had contributed to the construction of their reputation had occurred, and to learn which audiences were mobilized along the way. The interviews were performed between September 2008 and March 2009 and taped-recorded unless informants objected. I used the Merton et al. (1990) focused interview methodology to understand and question certain facts mentioned in the documents, about how they understand reputation in architecture, which audiences are involved and their link to the facts traced in their professional life, their tactics to manufacture their reputations, and whether there were some prerequisites for being a reputed architect. I also spoke to some of their clients, when possible, to know how they select architects for their buildings and what sources of information they use, among others. I finally interviewed French architecture school directors and journalists dedicated to architecture to have a clear view of the French architecture field. (All the quotations used in the following are taken from the interview transcripts.)

Data Analysis

I used a literal replication case study method (Yin 2003) to provide a detailed explanation of a situation and explore the common process of reputation-building among various audiences within the 11 cases. In the first stage, using both archives and interviews, I traced the architects' trajectories from gaining their diploma to their GPNA award. Drawing on literature on reputation and Strauss and Corbin's (1998) suggestions about coding, I elaborated on two categories of traces: 'actions,' which revealed the architects' proactivity in constructing their reputations, and 'events,' which represented involuntary positive or negative facts that occurred during their professional lives (Table 8.1).[4] The coding was first established for one case and then used for the others.

Each sub-category was refined. For instance, 'prestige of buildings' was divided into 'type of building' (cultural, housing, industrial, teaching, among others), 'type of contest' (open or by invitation), 'prestige of contests' (national, honorific—with high budgets, on fancy topics in French

Table 8.1   Categories of Traces in an Architect's Professional Trajectory

Categories of traces	Sub-categories of traces	Definition
Architect's actions	Prestige of buildings	Relevance of buildings for architecture and society
	Type of clients they work for	Public (governments, cities) or private (companies)
	Architect's writings	Books and articles written by the architect, in an architecture or mass edition
Events	Publications about the architects in media dedicated to architecture	Articles published in the top-five French magazines dedicated to architecture, and books published in a French architecture edition, written by other architects, critics, or journalists
	Publications about the architects in cultural media	Books published about the architects in a French cultural edition and articles published in the top-five French cultural journals (mass journals with a cultural section), written by critics or journalists dedicated to arts in general
	Awards	National or international architecture awards, such as the GPNA (national) and the Pritzker Prize (international)
	Honors	Public rewards, such as the Legion of Honor
	Partnerships	Works with other architects

Note: Exhibitions and conferences were other events that occurred in the architects' trajectories. However, they were removed from subsequent analysis because such data were difficult to gather because. no official records were available.

cities—or international), and 'place of construction' (French regions, Paris, and international cultural places) (Jones and Maoret 2010). While coding, I adapted the importance of each criterion depending on the period of time. For instance, in France, housing developments were prestigious in the 1970s but less so between the late 1980s and the mid-2000s, and they have subsequently regained their importance, in line with French government social housing policies.

In the second step, I analyzed the collected interviews with Nvivo, and in the third step, I triangulated the archive and interview data to understand the trajectory of each architect's career: Each trace sub-category was related to one or more audience based on the architects' words and some clients' opinions, so I could see which audiences were represented during the architects' professional trajectories. I gained further understanding by applying some theoretical reputation-building and creative organizational field characteristics to the data to see how architects and audiences 'played' with the rules of the field with a view to combining (or not) different reputations over time. Finally, to put this analysis into perspective, the GPNA winners' traces were compared to those from the first 20 years of some non-GPNAwinners[5] (as the GPNA is rewarded between 10 and 22 years after the architect's diploma), which enabled me to focus on similarities among GPNA winners' trajectories and compare to the others.

TOWARD A CUMULATIVE MODEL OF REPUTATION-BUILDING WITHIN THE FRENCH ARCHITECTURE FIELD

My results indicate that there are three main audiences that impact reputation-building in the French architecture field—peers, public clients, and intelligentsia—and that reputation is largely achieved via two mechanisms: 1) accumulation of activities among the three audiences, and 2) combination of three reputations over time.

Building Reputation among Three Audiences

> *"Everything starts with peers and public clients. It is fundamental. [. . .] And when my reputation was good enough, a larger public started to talk about me."*

Of the three main audiences that played a role in building the reputations of the 11 case-study architects, their peers are the other architects practicing in France who deliver an artistic reputation; public clients are those French State authorities (governments, municipalities, regions, and cities) who often commission new buildings and confer an economic reputation; the Intelligentsia represents all those French intellectuals and cultural critics who appreciate and disseminate arts and culture in general.

As the literature review mentioned, each audience possesses its own logic: Architects value peers who suggest innovative solutions for societal matters; governments, cities, and other State agencies search for improvement of urban spaces; and people at large search for beautiful buildings that answer their needs. Following these logics, each audience will have its expectations and thus has its own ways of assessing architects. Table 8.2 details the important criteria via which the GPNA winners gained reputation with each of the three audiences.

Table 8.2   Architects' Actions and Events to Get Reputed within Peers, Public Clients, and Society

	Peers	Public clients	Intelligentsia
Architects' actions	Talent and differentiation: *"One cannot be reputed without talent. Having talent here means that you differentiate yourself from the other architects, from what was done before."*	Being trustworthy by making regularly honorific public buildings: *"We wanted an architect who had already built several important projects."*	. . .
	Ability to theorize: *"Writing your own views on architecture positions you within your peers and thus helps you being identified."* Maintaining activity: *"The second element necessary to become reputed is a furious energy to go on."*	Ability to theorize: *"I selected them because I found their book very interesting; I thought they could do a great building for me."*	
Events	Being rewarded: *"Awards don't accelerate the construction of success as an architect; they consolidate it."* Being regularly published in the press dedicated to architecture: *"Being published a lot in architecture journals contributes to getting a high reputation among the other architects: they know if you did an interesting building, and if you explained it."*	Being regularly published in the press dedicated to architecture: *"Public clients spot architects by their frequent publications in architecture magazines."* Having already a reputation among architects: *"Clients invite architects to contests because their name is already known by other architects: this is a sort of co-opting the most talented ones."*	Regular publications in cultural journals
Indicator of achievement of reputation	Being regularly cited in architecture journals (compared to architects sending press releases)	Being regularly invited to public competitions (compared to participating only to open competitions)	Being regularly cited in cultural journals

Note: Quotations taken from the transcripts

While peers and public clients may look for different things, these two audiences assess architects in a similar way and evaluate them on the same traces while reading them differently. Thus, honorific buildings are important for the peers because they show evidence of the architects' ability to create innovative solutions for societal matters; in the same vein, this same trace is important for public clients because it reveals thatthe architects can be trusted to manage huge and beautiful projects.

Accumulating Traces for the Three Reputations: Self-Reinforcing Reputational Dynamics within and between Audiences

The first mechanism that helped these architects build a combined, field-level reputation was the accumulation of reputational traces with each individual audience. Accumulation is here understood as an accretion of elements (voluntary or not) that impact the actors' reputation in each audience more positively than negatively: I traced more positive elements than negative ones in these architects' trajectories, having demonstrated their legitimacy within each of them (Rao 1994). The architects built their reputations by playing with the rules of each audience; they designed and managed the construction of honorific and international buildings, and they also theorized about their works in books and articles, more or less intensively. Although the numbers of these elements differ from one trajectory to another, the 11 architects accumulated significantly more prestigious traces than did the professional trajectories of the non-GPNA winners. More specifically, and echoing the chapter by Pralong and his colleagues about unsuccessful artists (Pralong et al., Chapter 11, this volume), the accumulation process in these 11 trajectories exhibited some characteristics that were missing from those of the non-winners.

First, the accumulation was based on a mix of actions and events. The GPNA architects initiated dialogues with peers and clients—they participated in several competitions a year, and they wrote books and/or articles on a regular basis. Once architects act in ways that generate interest, architecture critics publish about them, reinforcing the diffusion of their reputations.

Second, their accumulation was based on regularity of traces: After their diploma years, the architects were invited to enter prestigious competitions several times, were mentioned at least once a year in the best architecture journals, and published books more or less regularly.

Third, this accumulation process is possible because the audiences' logics do not conflict. Thus, peers appreciate innovation in societal solutions, and public clients value the improvement of urban and social spaces while the intelligentsia values beautiful buildings that respond to societal needs. As such, the audiences complement rather than contradict each other—even if they read them differently, peers and public clients base their opinion on the same traces for reputation. As a consequence, there is a consensus within and between these audiences.

Table 8.3 Audiences' Internal Self-Reinforcement Mechanisms for Reputation-Building

Peers	Public clients	Intelligentsia
Being invited to competitions increases future invitations to competitions: *"Being invited to competitions creates a snow ball effect."*	Having built for prestigious clients increases invitations to honorific competitions: *"We know well [a French mayor]; we regularly win contests and make projects with them."*	Relationships between multiple cultural press sources increase the number of articles in such press: *"[An architect] communicated our decision to stop the competition to [a French cultural journal]. The next day, it was in [another French cultural journal], and the day after that it was in [two other French cultural journals]."*
Working with peers increases participation to competitions: *"Depending on your architecture choices, you belong to a family of architects who give you contacts."*		

Note: Quotations taken from the transcripts

Architects can talk to different audiences without either having to diversify their actions too much or relying on a too heterogeneous range of media.

Finally, accumulation is self-reinforcing, in that events help reputation-building in each audience (see Table 8.3), in line with the Matthew Effect (Merton 1968); the already reputed ones will become even more reputed and rewarded more than the others.

A Cumulative Model: Combining Three Types of Reputations over Time

Another mechanism by which a field-level reputation is achieved in French architecture is by combining three reputations. Combining reputations can be understood as a consensus among the three reputations as a coherent interplay within and among the three audiences. In line with Bowness's (1989) study, the data reveal that the three reputations develop in a specific order. First, the architects acquire an artistic reputation among their peers: They first have to be valued as talented to suggest new solutions for societal problems by their own profession:

> *"If you don't have first the positive acceptance from your peers, you can't get a high reputation. We architects work with competitions and committees: we quickly see who makes interesting things and who doesn't."*

After, architects start building their economic reputation with governments and cities. Once they have created one or two honorific buildings, they are considered able to manage important public projects, and so their reputation is no longer just artistic: They are also valued as operational architects.

Finally, after being reputed among peers and public clients, they begin to impact intelligentsia. They acquire a reputation among a broader cultural world, here called the intelligentsia, which ensures them a cultural reputation.[6] In contrast to their actions toward peers and public clients, architects do not generally engage in voluntarily dialogue with this wider audience:

> *"We do not try to publish in cultural journals; we only answer their solicitations."*

In this cumulative model, peers come before governments and cities because they act as key gatekeepers.[7] Indeed, even if clients need prestigious buildings, and thus organize public architecture competitions, expert architects advise those who run competitions about who to invite and pay attention to.

This combination of reputations over time is helped by such interrelationships between the audiences: The dialogue between them diffuses their admiration of certain architects, whose reputations thus grow by reflection (Figure 8.1). Attaining a reputation with the preceding audience helps getting onto the next one.

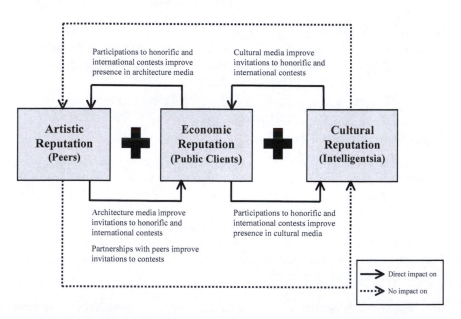

Figure 8.1. Combination mechanisms among artistic, economic, and cultural reputations.

An important channel for audiences to dialogue is architectural and cultural media. Such media build on the architects' accumulated actions and create paths between audiences so that critics, historians, and journalists dedicated to architecture participate in opinion-making and the creation of a collective mind about the architects among peers and clients (Jones 2010; Lang and Lang 1988). Moreover, as mentioned before, this connection is possible thanks to audiences' complementary logics that facilitate their consensus: Potential contradictory opinions don't emerge. Finally, as noted earlier, there is little interrelation between architects and the intelligentsia, and architects do not voluntarily act to establish a reputation with this wider audience. The latter, by diffusing but not prescribing, plays a role at the end of the construction of architects' field-level reputation and rely on public clients' validation over time to talk about architects: Public clients appear as intermediaries to create a consensus between peers and a broader cultural world. For instance, it is only when Architect 1 built several public buildings that cultural critics started to write books about Architect 1.

DISCUSSION

This study reveals the mechanisms by which reputations are built in creative fields: accumulation of traces for artistic, economic, and cultural reputations and a combination of these reputations over time.

This chapter's primary aim is to contribute to the stream of reputation-building research by shedding light on how its mechanisms operate within a creative field. First, in line with Bowness (1989), this study shows that audiences enter progressively into the construction of reputation: first peers, then clients, and finally intelligentsia. However, my results contradict Bowness's sequential model of reputation-building with regard to the necessity of 'dislocating' from one audience to 'relocate' in another. This chapter rather suggests that reputation-building is more a cumulative process than a sequential one, in that there are interactions among the several audiences integrated in the process. Some previous studies showed that an individual or a company can either have a local or a generalized reputation (Petkova et al. 2008). In contrast, I consider several kinds of reputation as not being incompatible if we integrate time and field mechanisms into the debate. Second, the results improve our understanding of reputation-building in a creative field by revealing how several reputations are combined over time. The data confirm that reputation is constructed by accumulating various traces over the years (Merton 1968; Petkova et al. 2008; Weigelt and Camerer 1988), but they also reveal that the artists' actions alone are not enough to achieve a reputation at the field level. In line with research about the importance of the artists' actions and context in building a career (Svejenova 2005; Svejenova et al. 2010), this study shows that the complementarities of audiences' logics and the field media both support the artists' actions to achieve a reputation at the field level (especially while dealing with the intelligentsia, with whom artists don't initiate the dialogue). A self-reinforcement within and among the three audiences is necessary to become reputed at a field level. Third, while Bowness considers media as another audience of this process, adding the organizational field perspective into the debate supports Deephouse's (2000) statement that media play an intermediary role in reputation-building, revealing that critics, journalists, and media are more properly understood as intermediaries of the field that help the combination of the various reputations and the dialogue among the audiences.

The results can also contribute to our understanding of how creative fields are structured. The model shows that three audiences—peers, clients, and populace at large—play roles in reputation-building within such fields. Peers are core actors whose activity is central to the field (DiMaggio 1988; Leblebici et al. 1991), whereas clients are more peripheral (Boutinot and Mangematin 2009); this study demonstrates that both core and peripheral actors play a role in constructing reputation within a field. So the establishment of prominent actors in a creative field is not determined only by those core actors themselves; other members of the field impact its structure and evolution. In this way, innovation in creative industries such as architecture needs to integrate the clients' expectations to be relevant for the field's topics.

CONCLUSION AND FUTURE RESEARCH

This chapter suggests a model of reputation-building in a creative field, which shows that a reputation in such a space can be built by accumulating and combining three reputations: artistic (among peers), economic (among clients), and cultural reputation (among intelligentsia). This chapter therefore contributes to a better understanding of how reputation in a field is achieved over time, and how the audiences and the field's mechanisms participate in the process.

I believe this study opens up a key issue for future research about reputation: The links among the three audiences, and especially their convergence, need to be examined in more detail. A quantitative study may be helpful here to learn more specifically how these self-reinforcing mechanisms work and how they may evolve over time.

NOTES

1. In this study, organizational reputation is considered synonymous with individual reputation. Individuals are the engines of creative sectors, not companies. Indeed, literature about organizational reputation can be used because the architects under study mostly created their own companies, which are based on their own talent and views on architecture, and they embody them completely.
2. Architectural contests are competitive mechanisms designed to facilitate the selection of an architect to design a building commissioned by a state

authority, a firm, or an individual. Such competitions can be open (any architect can participate in this kind of contest by sending a architectural proposal) or by invitation (where, generally, only four to six architects are invited by the contracting owner based on criteria such as the previous buildings they designed and their reputations).

3. M. Perruchione, an art historian working on the building industry, helped me to collect the huge amount of data and, thanks to her expertise, validated the way I chose to study the architects' lives.

4. Exhibitions and conferences were other events that occurred in the architects' trajectories. But they were removed from subsequent analysis because no official records were available and therefore such data proved difficult to gather.

5. The 100 most reputed French architects have been determined in a broader study I am currently conducting, in which the winners of the GPNA are included. I built on this list by adding the names of French architects mentioned positively at least twice in the top-five architecture French magazines between 2000 and 2008. For this chapter, so as to have a relevant sample of comparison, I only kept the non-GPNA winners who were practicing the profession in the same time as the 11 winners.

6. Cultural reputation differs from celebrity. Celebrity refers to an individual's ability to attract the attention of a large public (Rein, Kottler, and Stoller, 1987), not necessarily deserved and justified (McCracken, 1989); cultural reputation is established among a specific and an expert audience related to arts and culture and is the result of a legitimation process (Rao 1994).

7. I thank Chris Mathieu for helping me develop this idea and suggesting the term 'gatekeepers.'

REFERENCES

Anand, N., and M. R. Watson. 2004. "Tournament Rituals in the Evolution of Fields: The Case of the Grammy Awards." *Academy of Management Journal* 47: 59–80.

Ashforth, B. E., and F. Mael. 1989. "Social Identity Theory and the Organization." *Academy of Management Review* 14: 20–39.

Becker, H. S. 1988. *Les Mondes de l'Art*. Translated by J. Bouniort. Paris: Poche.

Boutinot, A., and V. Mangematin. 2009. "Surfing on Institutions by Temporary Peripheral Actors." *Academy of Management Proceedings* 1–6.

Bowness, A. 1989. *The Conditions of Success: How the Modern Artist Rises to Fame*. London: Thames and Hudson.

Caves, R. 2000. *Creative Industries: Contracts Between Art and Commerce*. Cambridge, MA: Harvard University Press.

Champy, F. 1999. "Commande Publique d'Architecture et Segmentation de la Profession d'Architectes." *Genèse, Sciences Sociales et Histoire* 37: 93–113.

Deephouse, D. 2000. "Media Reputations as a Strategic Resource, an Integration of Mass Communication and Resource-Based Theories." *Journal of Management* 26: 1091–1112.

Deephouse, D. L., and S. M. Carter. 2005. "An Examination of Differences between Organizational Legitimacy and Organizational Reputation." *Journal of Management Studies* 42: 329–60.

Deephouse, D. L., and M. C. Suchman. 2008. "Legitimacy in Organizational Institutionalism." In *The Sage Handbook of Organizational Institutionalism*, edited by R. Greenwood, C. Oliver, R. Suddaby, and K. Sahlin-Andersson, 49–77. London: Sage.

Delmestri, G., F. Montanari, and A. Usai. 2005. "Reputation and Strength of Ties in Predicting Commercial Success and Artistic Merit of Independents in the Italian Feature Film Industry." *Journal of Management Studies* 42: 975–1002.

DiMaggio, P. 1988. "Interest and Agency in Institutional Theory." In *Institutional Patterns and Organizations: Culture and Environment*, edited by L. G. Zucker. Cambridge, MA: Ballinger.

DiMaggio, P. J., and W. W. Powell. 1983. "The Iron Cage Revisited. Institutional Isomorphism and Collective Rationality in Organizational Fields." *American Sociological Review* 48: 147–60.

Fombrun, C. J. 1996. *Reputation: Realizing Value from the Corporate Image*. Cambridge, MA: Harvard Business Press.

Fombrun, C. J., N. A. Gardberg, and J. M. Sever. 2000. "The Reputation Quotient: A Multi-Stakeholder Measure of Corporate Reputation." *The Journal of Brand Management* 7: 241–55.

Fombrun, C. J., and M. Shanley. 1990. "What's in a Name? Reputation Building and Corporate Strategy." *Academy of Management Journal* 33: 233–58.

Greenwood, R., and C. R. Hinings. 1996. "Understanding Radical Organizational Change: Bringing Together the Old and the New Institutionalism." *Academy of Management Review* 21: 1022–54.

Greenwood, R., R. Suddaby, and C. R. Hinings. 2002. "Theorizing Change: The Role of Professional Associations in the Transformation of Institutional Fields." *Academy of Management Journal* 45: 58–80.

Jones, C., and M. Maoret. 2010, August. *Playing by the Rules: Social, Cultural and Symbolic Capitalin Achieving Distinction*. Paper presented at the annual conference of the Academy of Management, Montréal, Canada.

King, B. G., and D. A. Whetten. 2008. "Rethinking the Relationships Between Reputation and Legitimacy: A Social Actor Conceptualization." *Corporate Reputation Review* 11: 192–207.

Kraatz, M. S., and E. S. Block. 2008. "Organizational Implications of Institutional Pluralism." In *The Sage Handbook of Organizational Institutionalism*, edited by R. Greenwood, C. Oliver, R. Suddaby, and K. Sahlin-Andersson. London: Sage.

Lang, G. E., and K. Lang. 1988. "Recognition and Renown: The Survival of Artistic Reputation." *American Journal of Sociology* 94: 79–109.

Langley, A. 1999. "Strategies for Theorizing Process Data." *Academy of Management Review* 24: 691–710.

Leblebici, H., G. R. Salancik, A. Copay, and T. King. 1991. "Institutional Change and the Transformation of Organizational Fields: An Organizational History of the U.S. Radio Broadcasting Industry." *Administrative Science Quarterly* 36: 333–63.

McCracken, G. 1989. "Who Is the Celebrity Endorser? Cultural Foundations of the Endorsement Process." *Journal of Consumer Research* 16: 310–321.

Merton, R. K. 1968. "The Matthew Effect in Science." *Science* 159: 56–63.

Merton, R. K., M. Fiske, and P. L. Kendall. 1990. *The Focused Interview: A Manual of Problems and Procedures*. Second edition. New York: Free Press.

Petkova, A. P., V. P. Rindova, and A. K. Gupta. 2008. "How Can New Ventures Build Reputation? An Exploratory Study." *Corporate Reputation Review* 11: 320–34.

Rao, H. 1994. "The Social Construction of Reputation: Certification Contests, Legitimation and the Survival of Organizations in the Automobile Industry: 1895–1912." *Strategic Management Journal* 15: 29–44.

Rao, H., P. Monin, and P. Durand. 2003. "Institutional Change in Toque Ville: Nouvelle Cuisine as an Identity Movement in French Gastronomy." *American Journal of Sociology* 108: 795–843.

Rein, I., P. Kotler, and M. Stoller. 1987. *High Visibility*. New York: Dodd, Mead and Company

Rhee, M., and M. E. Valdez. 2009. "Contextual Factors Surrounding Reputation Damage with Potential Implications for Reputation Repair." *Academy of Management Review* 34: 146–68.

Rindova, V. P., A. P. Petkova, and S. Kotha. 2007. "Standing Out: How New Firms in Emerging Markets Build Reputation." *Strategic Organization* 5: 31–70.

Rindova, V. P., I. O. Williamson, A. P. Petkova, and J. M. Sever. 2005. "Being Good or Being Known: An Empirical Examination of the Dimensions, Antecedents and Consequences of Organizational Reputation." *Academy of Management Journal* 48: 1033–49.

Roberts, B. 2001. *Biographical Research*. New York: Open University Press.

Scott, W. R. 2001. *Institutions and Organizations*. Second edition. Thousand Oaks, CA: Sage.

Strauss, A. L., and J. M. Corbin. 1998. *Basics of Qualitative Research: Grounded Theory, Procedures and Techniques*. Newbury Park, CA: Sage.

Svejenova, S. 2005. "The Path with the Heart: Creating the Authentic Career." *Journal of Management Studies* 42: 947–74.

Svejenova, S., C. Mazza, and M. Planellas. 2007. "Cooking up Change in Haute Cuisine: Ferran Adrià as an Institutional Entrepreneur." *Journal of Organizational Behavior* 28: 539–61.

Svejenova, S., M. Planellas, and L. Vives. 2010. "An Individual Business Model in the Making: A Chef's Quest for Creative Freedom." *Long Range Planning* 43: 408–30.

Thornton, P. H., and W. Ocasio. 1999. "Institutional Logics and the Historical Contingency of Power in Organizations: Executive Succession in the Higher Education Publishing Industry, 1958–1990." *American Journal of Sociology* 105: 801–43.

Washington, M. and E. Zajac. 2005. "Status Evolution and Competition: Theory and Evidence." *Academy of Management Journal* 48: 282–296.

Weigelt, K., and C. Camerer. 1988. "Reputation and Corporate Strategy: A Review of Recent Theory and Applications." *Strategic Management Journal* 9: 443–54.

Yin, R. K. 2003. *Case Study Research, Design and Methods*. Third edition. Newbury Park, CA: Sage.

Table 8.A The 11 Architects' Biographical Information from Their Diploma in Architecture to the GPNA

Architects	Arch1	Arch2	Arch3	Arch4	Arch5	Arch6	Arch7	Arch8	Arch9	Arch10	Arch11	Means other architects
Date of diploma	1972	1969	1968	1978	1964	1963	1961	1966	1969	1976	1960	—
Date of the GPNA	1987	1992	1977	1993	1982	1979	1983	1989	1991	1990	1986	—
Date and place of company creation	1975, Paris	1980, Paris	2003, Paris	1981, Paris	1969, Paris	1963, Paris	1962, Paris	1973, Paris	1975, Paris	1976, Paris	1970, Paris	—
Number of honorific buildings	27	11	20	15	10	10	7	8	16	15	12	4
Number of public clients	25	10	18	13	8	8	6	7	16	12	12	2
Number of architects' writings	3	4	2	6	0	6	10	9	2	1	1	0
Number of publications in architecture media	83	34	29	102	22	46	20	19	18	27	21	14
Number of publications in cultural media	22	15	17	61	15	19	16	18	13	11	11	1
Number of awards	2	0	0	2	0	0	1	0	0	0	0	0
Number of honors	2	3	0	0	1	2	1	3	1	1	0	0
Number of partnerships	5	1	2	1	3	2	1	1	1	6	4	1

Part IV
Music

9 Transnational Careers in the Virtuoso World

Izabela Wagner

"Sociology is justified by the belief that it is better to be conscious then unconscious and that consciousness is a condition of freedom."

—Peter Berger

INTRODUCTION

According to common perception, the artistic world is the perfect example of an international environment in which all national/cultural[1] differences disappear. Following this romantic idea, artists are cosmopolitans—they are citizens of the world. This deep conviction seems to be shared by sociologists because there is not, to my knowledge, a specific literature dealing with a problem of cultural differences in art worlds. This chapter is a response to this significant absence. I analyze the international dimension of creative careers focusing on objective and subjective elements.

In order to avoid over-generalization in the following analysis, I focus on a chosen case—the creative careers of violin virtuosos as an example of one of the most internationalized specialties among the musical occupations. The chapter is based on ethnographic research of the violin virtuoso world, lasting for more than 10 years. This research is based mainly on qualitative methods developed by the Chicago School (Hughes 1971; Junker 1960) and carried out between 1996 and 2006. Ethnographic field work was carried out in soloist classes in France, Germany, and Poland, including participant observation in classes and more than 100 recorded in-depth interviews carried out in four languages: Russian, English, Polish, and French. I also conducted participant observations in master classes and competitions in these countries as well as Italy and Spain. During these 10 years of active research, I observed hundreds of violin lessons, and I was able to observe students' instrumental practice. My fieldwork also included informal interviews with and observations of at least 90 violinists, about 30 parents, 20 violin teachers, piano accompanists, violinmakers, and concert organizers. In this highly competitive world of virtuoso training, all forms of informal information are jealously guarded and hard to access. Through the accumulation of intersecting roles, I obtained not only unique access to different kinds of information but also the possibility to triangulate different perspectives. I held a rich and varied set of roles in relation to the topic beyond that of social researcher: translator, concert organizer, member of an association for young talents, host family during violin competitions, as well as mother of a young virtuoso. In this latter role, my situation was similar to Adler and Adler (1991, 1998) who studied their children's world.

Because of the geographic mobility of my participants, my study became the example of "multi-sited ethnography" (Marcus 1995). Field work was conducted in European countries, and I observed and interviewed people who were educated not only in the European Union (EU) but also in Russia, Asia, Israel, and the US. In my sample of the violin soloist population, the majority of participants originate from Eastern Europe and reside in Western Europe. Even if this sample consists of the elite musician world, the results and analysis provided here could be extended to other music specialties, environments, and to other examples of creative careers (Wagner 2006a).[2]

According to numerous studies, one of the most important characteristics of the professional elite[3] is the international aspect of their career (A.-C. Wagner 1995). This is strongly emphasized in the case of violin virtuosos' career because from the first stages of young musicians' socialization they are introduced to the international professional world. As a consequence of this specific education, we would expect that in such an environment national and cultural differences would be insignificant and people would ignore common stereotypes. This development was expected in the first years of the 20th century by Durkheim (1959/1928, 173–74) when he spoke about professional internationalism:

> [I]n our day an internationalism of an entirely new type has appeared— —professional internationalism. The rapprochement did not operate exclusively from people to people, but from one professional group to professional group of the same order. (. . .) In succession there were established international societies of scholars, artists, industrials, workers, financiers, etc, which went on specializing further as they multiplied, and which, because of the increasing regularity of their functioning, soon become an important factor of European civilization. (. . .) [P]rofessional sentiments and interests are endowed with a far greater universality. (. . .) Thus, national spirit encounters a formidable antagonist which it did not recognize until then, and as a result, conditions are exceptionally favorable for the development of internationalism.

Despite this international education and the process of the internationalization of careers, Durkheimian premonitions are not confirmed: the everyday life of virtuosos is far from the idyllic picture of cosmopolitanism. The virtuosos' nationalities and culture play an important, even crucial, role in their careers. We can observe this influence (positive for some, negative for others) during the selection processes, for example. This point is not so much related to citizenship and legal situation, through possession of a 'good' or 'bad' passport,[4] reflecting the objective status of a given person, which can facilitate or hinder work and prolonged stays in a given country. The crucial role of nationality and culture of origin, however, appears in the everyday interactions between participants. Because the professional training of virtuosos is based on these interactions, this has an influence and consequences on their education as well as their whole careers.

How do these rarely evoked determinants of virtuoso careers operate? How do these actors use the category of 'national/cultural origin' in their work? The response to these questions will help in understanding the following problems: Why does it seem that this cosmopolitan world is not free from national influenced cultures? In other words, are there some such preferences that can be observed in this elite milieu? Finally, why are creative careers dependent on national/cultural origin?

This chapter is divided into two parts. The first part is devoted to the presentation of the virtuosos' socialization process, with a short presentation of the basic concepts used in this chapter. In parallel, I show how this professional knowledge transmission is national/culturally determined and how the pattern of creative careers in this field is and has always been related to transnational experiences. Because I consider the career coupling process (Wagner 2006b) to be at the core of artistic socialization and the basis for the whole artistic career, I examine this process by focusing on the impact of 'national/cultural' elements on its dynamic.

The second part contains subjective dimensions of our topic. Here I discuss the question of the relationship between the culture of origin and creative career construction. The conclusion will bring the reader to the theoretical proposition and validation of the use of the term 'transnational' as a crucial adjective characterizing virtuoso careers as an exemplary case of a creative career.

SOCIALIZATION OF VIRTUOSOS WITHIN AN INTERNATIONAL PROFESSIONAL WORLD

The World of Young Soloists

The soloist elite constitute a small but significant part of the music world and the artistic world in general. This social group includes a select number of violinists who have attained a reputation as soloists.[5] Competition in this area is strong, and the race for this privileged position starts early—almost from the first steps in this education process. Newcomers to this environment are taught to aspire to uniqueness and individuality in order to be considered the best.[6] Because greatness in classical music usually means becoming known in several countries, this race occurs in different places, which requires geographic mobility. Young (less than 25 years is a general demarcation) and older soloists, just like the elites in many other professions, are mobile people who begin travelling internationally in their childhood (usually about 10 years of age) to participate in international young musician competitions. When we look at the origin of these students, we can understand why they are so mobile.

Young students enrolled in soloist classes are part of an extremely mobile population of transnational families in the evolving new, post-Communist Europe.[7] These specific historical, political, and economic contexts strongly influenced the composition of such classes at the end of the 20th century, and continue to do so. Virtuoso students come from socially homogenous backgrounds: 9 of 10 originate from musician families (Wagner 2006b). They are typically children of East European emigrants (in North American soloist classes, these would currently be children of Asian emigrants) (Lourie-Sand 2000), and the majority of them have an experience of multiculturalism. Consequently, their professional socialization within an international environment is doubled by their familial multicultural education. Few of them speak only a single language and multilingual functioning is the rule in this milieu.[8] This is why even from an early age, they are able to easily practice this intensive mobility. They travel around the world, alone or with their parents, following their famous teacher. They are mobile not because they are not able to get an established position in an orchestra. In this world, the elite path means intensive mobility, and a permanent position in the musical ensemble is perceived as failure. The young virtuosos are socialized with a perception at odds with that found in the majority of occidental societies, in which the stability of permanent positions in firms is preferred over international mobility as freelancers.[9]

The opportunities for mobility are abundant for the soloist students. During a single year, each young musician takes part in at least one international competition,[10] gives several concerts, participates in a master class taught by famous teachers, as well as attends their own teacher's master classes. All of these events may be organized anywhere throughout the world.

Numerous students from Europe take a master class at Keyshet Eylon, Israel, or at the Summer Academy of Aspen, Colorado, and American students come to Europe to participate in master classes in Sienna, Italy, or Tours, France. The international competitions for violinists (more than 300 were listed in the Geneva Guide for Competitions in 2005) are organized in Indianapolis in the US; in Montreal, Canada; Adelaide, Australia; Pretoria, South Africa; as well as in Europe: Brussels, Moscow, London, Helsinki, Monte Carlo, Geneva, Hannover, Poznan, and many other places.

This high mobility and international activity is organized by the networks built by teachers, who are powerful people in the world of classical music (Wagner 2004). Without the support of these networks, no one could attain a high-quality soloist education. One of the strong characteristics of these networks is its composition, generally organized with overrepresentation of people originating from the same geographic area. The following description is characteristic:

Professor Z. is a graduate of the Moscow Conservatory, and works in Paris. In his class around three-fourths of the students are from Eastern Europe (former Soviet Union and Central-Eastern countries) as first or second generation of immigrants. Two accompanists work with Z—both are Russian—graduates from USSR's Conservatories. His students have their violins repaired by violin-maker from Russia, and they buy their bows at Ukrainian bow-maker. Their recordings are made by a sound engineer who graduated from the Moscow Conservatory. Z is also a conductor of a chamber ensemble, which plays irregularly; almost all musicians in the ensemble are from Eastern Europe. The network of collaborators is composed of the people who studied at the same institution or in the same organizational universe (similar throughout Eastern Europe, very different from the French system). Their organization of work (for example working time, schedule of pauses, etc) and especially involvement in work are different from those observed in French ensembles. For example, musicians from Eastern Europe consider that when they meet for a rehearsal, they can take a short pause for lunch and work more than 14 hours also during the night if it is deemed necessary (this kind of schedule is possible with numerous groups, most improbable with French musicians).[11] Also, because some of them are not yet familiar with the language of the country in which they work, they frequently use Russian in professional communications. It is by reference to this particular way of organizing work as well as the high level of performance standards that the participants justify this kind of network composition—which is obviously culturally and linguistically determined. When they look for a new collaborator, they ask for 'someone from our side,' meaning someone originating from Eastern Europe. It is clear that the influence of national culture here is very important in the selection of collaborators and the construction of professional networks. (Wagner 2006b)

The soloists insist on the fact that this kind of organization based on networks is the result of musicians' traditions. It is easy to see the dominant presence of violinists originating from Eastern Europe and from a Jewish culture[12]; most of them were educated in classes conducted by Russian teachers. The opening of the borders of Eastern European countries starting in the 1980s made it possible for many musicians from these countries to travel. The young virtuosos followed their teachers, emigrating from former Soviet republics and other Eastern European countries to the Occidental world (Western Europe, the US, and Israel[13]). If the soloist class of a given teacher is frequently composed of students originating from the same country as their teacher, a situation during master classes looks different. The master class is the intensive learning during a short period of time (usually a week or two) with a famous teacher; usually each student has one hour of lesson per day (open to the public and sometimes even recorded by TV). During the master classes, teachers work with students who are not, in the most cases, enrolled in their classes for the whole year. Consequently, the composition of participants is more varied than in regular year-long classes: Students from the whole world attend master classes in order to work with another famous professor (someone other than their own teacher).[14]

The reputation of 'best virtuoso,' great musician,' or 'exceptional artist'—one of the most important elements of creative career—is accorded by those who impose the norms that dominate the music market at any given moment. The reputation of violinists who originate from a Russian tradition of violin playing in the international music market is, according to Schwarz (1983), the consequence of the imposition of norms concerning the virtuoso performance.[15] However, Russians were not alone in imposing these norms. Asian violinists, due to their strong involvement in technique preparation and extremely high level of playing technique, also progressively modify performance norms. With a significant number of Asian students pursuing violin training and participating in the selection processes of several violin competitions, the technical rigor of playing has increased.[16]

International aspects of the soloist environment are similar to the characteristics of foreign managers living in France and studied by Anne-Catherine Wagner. She suggests that "international culture can be considered as a form of capital" and further develops this idea: "The knowledge of foreign languages, cultures and foreign styles of life, the management of the geographic scattering of family and relationships, and the possibility to organize a professional career in several countries produce a kind of mixture of linguistic, cultural, social, professional, economic and symbolic capital" (A.-C. Wagner 1995, 12).

How do these international cultural elements influence face-to-face interactions? What kinds of relationships take place between the most important actors who constitute this specific world—teachers and their students? Finally, how do the participants perceive the influence of national culture on their careers?

CAREER COUPLING—THE BASIC PROCESS FOR SEVERAL TYPES OF CREATIVE CAREERS[17]

One of the surprising findings of my study is that despite an obvious power hierarchy in which teachers dominate students, there are ways in which teachers also need their own students. I deconstruct this mechanism of 'mutual dependence'—a special relationship between the teacher and the student, that I call 'Career Coupling.' The student–professor relationship is not an exclusive condition for the existence of career coupling relationship (Mathieu and Stjerne [Chapter 6, this volume] show in their work that this phenomenon also occurs between persons of equal status and different occupations), but this concept perfectly applies to the mentor–student relationship in the example analyzed here of violin virtuosos.

I use the concept of career in the interactionist tradition of the Chicago School (Becker 1970; Becker and Strauss 1956; Hughes 1971), defining the course of professional life as a series of stages, which differ in the quality of interactions according to the individuals who play a relevant role in their professional environment. Coupling means that the persons involved in this process build their careers jointly. Without this close collaboration, they do not evolve in their professional worlds. The teacher's career success depends only partly on his or her performances as a former violin virtuoso (because the majority of well-known teachers have stopped their intensive performance activity) but primarily on whether his or her students are successful musicians. Producing successful students enhances a teacher's reputation. This career relationship is built during long years of collaboration. That is why several Russian teachers who emigrated in the late 1980s and 1990s brought their best students with them to their new places of work and negotiated good working conditions for them. These protégés are 'business cards.' The point may be obvious but nonetheless worth making in this context: Although these professors' performance careers have subsided, their careers as teachers are under current development and evaluation. The common rule present in the musician's world, "You are as good as your last job" (Cameroon 1956; Faulkner 1983), is also available here. For teachers, the success of their students is a critical aspect of their career development as teachers and thus the crux of the mutual interdependence between teacher and student.

CULTURE OF ORIGIN AND THE QUALITY OF THE CAREER COUPLING RELATIONSHIP

There are three phases of career coupling, and completion of each phase is essential to be able to say that career coupling has taken hold. The first is the matching process: Students and teachers 'feel each other out' and decide whether their expectations, professional communication, habits of work, and personalities are compatible. This stage is a trial period in which both collaborators from the outset should understand each other without any problems. From the linguistic-sociological approach (Wierzbicka 1994), we can see that being from a similar culture helps collaborators' mutual understanding, especially if two factors interplay in given relationships. The first is the necessity for communication in the area of an unknown environment—creative and feeling related topics, which are everyday issues for musicians working on the 'interpretation of pieces.'[18] The quality of this work depends on feelings and understanding. According to Wierzbicka, the perception of feelings is strongly related to cultural patterns (Wierzbicka [1994] called it *scripts*). This is why during the typical violin lesson, understanding in teacher–student interactions is helped by both parties having the same mother tongue and originating from the same cultural area.

The second factor, which influences the quality of teacher–student communication, is related to the context of interaction—the stress accompanying violin lessons. According to the results of my study, this problem is related to the so-called 'hot time.' Two types of work organization are distinguished: quiet time and hot time. The first type takes place when the collaborators do not have an important public performance in the near future (this 'near future' is a flexible notion and depends on personal perception). The second type—hot time—occurs when the student is to soon play an important concert and is at the last stage of preparation for this event. In this period, the collaborators work under significant, competitive pressure (which is also a part of the professional training—public performances are always related to some level of stress). As Berger and Luckmann (1966) indicated, the primary education can take over the secondary education, and in such situations the emotions take over the professional 'adult' education. This situation happens during interaction, which occurs under stress. Then if the primary education is carried out according to differing cultural dispositions, the chances for coherent understanding between teacher and student (and conflict resolution) are weaker than in a situation where both collaborators have a similar cultural background.

When both parties are well matched and deeply devoted to their work, they have optimal conditions to pursue their career coupling process. On completion of the first phase, the second phase of the career coupling process—active collaboration—the fusion, can commence. This phase frequently lasts several years, during which almost daily contact forms the basis for their intensive work. The professional and private lives of both partners intertwine. Here again the culture of origin is important. Not so much in relation to professional communication (this is set at the first stage) but because of private life, which is almost always shared. Intensive training, preparation for competitions even during the summer, time spent together on rehearsals, and students traveling with teachers' families in order not to miss any lessons—all this contact provokes passionate relationships. Without it, it is difficult to obtain from both partners the high level of investment in soloist training necessary for excellence and success. The relationships are solidified by long days with several hours spent on intensive practice and several lessons (frequently unpaid—only a portion is remunerated), books discussed, hours spent in travel, competitions experienced, countries visited, and finally concerts prepared for and executed, and the rest time spent together. It is not at all exceptional that students live in the house or flat of their teachers (a famous example was Galamian—one of the most well-known teachers in the US in the 20th century—students lived for months in his Manhattan flat) (Schwarz 1983, 547–50). When people stay so close to each other, important cultural differences can be a problem, which can perturb the collaboration of both partners. When looking for fusion, this is no place for important misunderstandings or unpleasant situations provoked by cultural differences. The fusion relationship between master and student is the core of a successful process of career coupling and the necessary condition for accession into the elite milieu of soloists.

The third stage is called passive collaboration—passive because the intensive work together ends at the previous stage. But in order to maintain the image of the former relationship, the former partners symbolically underline their close relationship on many subsequent occasions. It is easy to learn about these bonds, for example, by reading artists' CVs, which always mention their mentor–student linkages. At this stage, culture plays a less important role than in previous periods. However, because this last stage occurs only as a succession of previous stages, by consequence this component of creative career analyzed here is still important.

In light of my results, the career coupling is the core process of career building in a virtuoso world. This is the basis for the construction of the networks. This study shows that the cultural origin of participants plays an important role in the career coupling process. Consequently, it is understandable that the professional networks in the global market could be dominated by persons from a particular culture (ethnicity). In the case of violin virtuosos, this domination is Russian or, more exactly, Eastern European. So for these students who are taught by the teachers belonging to the 'Russian' or Eastern European network (which is almost always the case of musicians educated in Eastern European conservatories), it is far easier to achieve a successful career. While the activity of these networks presently takes place in Occidental Europe (and in the US; only some teachers work in Asia), the students most often grow and realize their professional education in Western countries. But the situations that persons who possess all these characteristics experience are not so as conducive for their career promotion as we could expect. Why? Because even if Russian/Eastern European musicians are powerful—the agents, 'local' musicians, and other persons who participate in the organization of musical events can build obstacles in order to give priority to their own 'protégés' (i.e., young virtuosos originating from the country in which the event takes place). This phenomenon illustrates the following vignette, which concerns the persons whose life and career I followed during my research:

David was born in Moscow, but has since his early childhood lived in the EU. He was a typical example of a prodigy child—he performed several concerts, made TV performances, and won first place in the most important competitions before his 20th birthday. But rarely did he play in the country in which he was raised. Why? *"They are tired of the 'Russian Prodigy"* said his father. In every country around his new nation of residence he is a true star, but in the country he emigrated to, there is no need for imported gifted children or young soloist.

Similar situation occurred with Anastasia, who was presented to several conductors in her country of adoption: "we don't need more whizz-kids from Russia" they responded. At the same time some girls from this country (their physical appearance overlapping perfectly with the stereotype of the local beauty) were supported and developed their careers even if the quality of performances was largely inferior to Anastasia's. In addition to these informal slow-down or blockage actions we could add other practices: the official "nationally determined" supports such as loaning out violins from national collection not to the habitants of the country, but only to "citizens," and several situations of the negative selection provoked by possession of the "wrong passport."

What is the nature of the tension between these national/international or culturally determined elements that impact the careers of virtuosos?

THE PATHS OF EXCELLENCE: NATIONAL VERSUS INTERNATIONAL

Focusing on the international aspect of a soloist education, it is worth analyzing the opinion of students enrolled in soloist classes about what they call 'national' education—in opposition to the 'international.' Here the distinction between the local and global spaces for performance and the future career development related to the concert market is clear. For them, the violin education offered by the institutions of national reputation, such as, for example, the French–CNSMDP (Superior Conservatory of Paris), is not 'good enough' for preparing the international career. The soloist students and their teachers residing in France (25 persons in a formal interview that I conducted and more than 40 musicians expressed similar opinion in informal discussions) judged that 'entering into the CNSMDP' is not the goal nor it is a sign of success: "*The CNSMDP is not a place where international soloists are educated. It is a very good school if you want to get a job in France in an orchestra or in the conservatory. But for the violinist-soloists, the preparation is not good enough. It is very important for French people, but they actually don't prepare soloists there anymore.*"
(interview with a violin soloist and teacher—leaving 30 years in France and educated in the USSR).

This widely spread opinion is confirmed by the career pathways of the French violinist-soloists (born after 1945) who graduated from CNSMDP before definitively taking a place in the soloist market, needed to complete their education outside France.[19] However, this is not a similar path for soloist class students who graduated from the Julliard School, Curtis Institute, Bloomington University in Indianapolis (in the US), or Moscow and St. Petersburg conservatories. Finishing one's soloist education at these institutions entails not needing to complete their music study in another country.

When young French musicians speak to the media, pointing out their education with famous foreign musicians, they show that the most important aspect of their education is their collaboration with a master with an international reputation. In the French monthly music magazine *Diapason*, the journalist Y. Petit de Voize (1997) writes, "To the question of generation or of the strategy of the headlong rush, many cite their first French teachers and their education in the Conservatory of Paris. However, they insist a lot on their meetings and their master classes with international musical top brass."

Despite the fact that the soloist class students attribute a negative reputation to the Parisian Conservatory, some of them join this institution. For them, the education in this conservatory constitutes a strategic solution: This situation can afford them several support measures such as scholarships, violin loans, and easier access to the French concert stages, and foreign students may also benefit from staying and working in French territory.

Soloist students, in general, do not adhere to the French vision of excellence concerning instrumental education (violin). Their relationship to the French success path is different from French students educated in professional musical institutions.[20] Similar divisions between national and international paths of excellence were present in Poland, where students who decided to enter into a soloist class abroad frequently ignored passage through the customary national steps of musical education. Visibly, for members of my sample, these two paths are different. Which perception of such national/cultural differences do the participants have?

THE DISSONANCES AND THE CONSONANCES— INSIDE SOLOIST CLASSES

> *"If you have this mixture of blood—Russian, Polish, anyway, Slavonic, with Jewish culture, an Occidental passport, and you live in a Western metropolis, you have many chances of becoming a soloist. All great violinists have that."* **A soloist teacher originating from Moscow living in Germany, then in France.**

This quotation illustrates a common position of participants in my sample who believe that a causal link exists between one's place of origin and one's potential success. Different origins are mentioned as favorable to violin practice and a soloist's career. The 'Russians,' meaning those of Eastern European origin, are traditionally perceived by all actors as of 'a good origin.' A 29-year-old soloist (Polish origin, resident in Germany, educated partially in the US) recalls, "When I participated in competitions fifteen years ago, I had a strong and truly obsessive fear of Russian Passports. It was awful when I saw one. For me, he was a finalist, because all those (violinists) who they (the Soviet regime) allow to participate were strongly selected, and very good." This perception is so widely spread that frequently I heard the following anecdote while taking part in informal conversations: "The Japanese play in tune, the French with an important musicality, and the Russians do both."

Actually, some European teachers are fascinated by certain Asian students, as the following teacher (originated from former USSR residing in France) expresses in an informal interview: "Now, I take (in my class) almost only Asian students. They are exemplary. They never ask, why? How? They listen to me and immediately execute my advice; they have this extraordinary work ethic and this outstanding focus. Their progress is very quick, and what a great pleasure it is for each teacher to work with students like these."

There are innumerable similar examples in my data from informal conversations concerning the question of place of origin of the leading members of the soloist world. Musicians maintain that these differences influence, even determine, the possibility of success. In order to avoid the accusation that they are 'culturalists,' 'politically incorrect,' or strongly under the influence of easy stereotypes, they justify their opinions suggesting that a certain relationship exists between the nationality of soloists (students and adults) and their manner of working. This is a widespread opinion, which concerns not only attitudes toward working but also methods of practice and even physical aptitude for violin playing.

One of my informants relates his opinion about Asian violinists in his account of a master class:

> At the beginning when I came there, it was surprising for me that they were so numerous and there was almost no French or German students. They [Asian students] work very hard, but also those studying in EU, they are the best from their country. And I remember that I had this impression that they were very strong but it was not always like that. For example what is typical is their musical side. [reference to the 'musicality' which is near technique another criteria of a good music performance]. Frequently people say that they are a 'machine for playing' and frequently it is true (. . .) frequently they take a video of Oïstrakh for example and try to copy it. This method is not good at all, but some of them achieve . . . [means win the places in the international competitions] also they are very flexible [manual skills]—means. . . . I think that this is because of their physical morphology—and this is why they are technically so good.

INSIDER'S CATEGORIZATIONS

The informants in this study generally distinguish three principal categories that are determined by geographical origin: Asians, 'Russians,' and others. This last category is more detailed—Germans, French, Italian, and so on—while the former are more general, for example, the category of Russians contains not only people originating from Russia but from all Eastern and Central Europe countries (Poland, Hungary, Romania, Ukraine), and all stereotypes related to Russian musicians apply for the whole category. In comparison, it is found that life-science researchers in laboratories also provide similar categorizations but more detailed—'Asians' does not exist—because they use specifications pointing out that the culture of work for Chinese is different from Japanese and Korean, for example (Wagner 2011). In doing so, the scientists always precisely state the nationality of a given person, whereas musicians employ more general distinction. One of the reasons for this difference is that in the virtuoso world, it is frequently difficult to determine the exact national appurtenance because the number of multicultural people is very high. It is not exceptional that many have not only multicultural origins but also multiple citizenships (Wagner 2006b). The *'metissage'* is a phenomenon largely spread among virtuosos in the sense of mixing of the origins and cultures acquired in the experience of professional (and familial) mobility.

How can we explain the fact that this categorization is so frequently used by informants despite so many of them being culturally mixed? We need to look closer for the dominant culture in the studied milieu. In Eastern Europe, 'politically correctness' is not practiced as much as in Occidental countries, where regularly using such categorizations and expressing opinions that confirm popular stereotypes concerning the national differences are not openly allowed in several environments. This is not the case in the former USSR or Eastern Europe countries, where these types of opinions are widespread and openly expressed (Jasinska-Kania 1992; Kofta and Jasinska-Kania 2002). For the musicians, this categorization constitutes the tools for taking strategic decisions—the use of methods of practice, the amount of training time expected, and the competitions to prepare for.

For example, with regard to what kind of method of working to apply, there is a supposition that Asian and Occidental education differ and the methods of work differ (i.e., that copying the gestures of famous musicians playing simultaneously with the videos of great virtuosos is seen as an Asian specialty). The differences concerning the expected duration of practice is also believed to be culturally based—Occidental education makes a point out of work/private life balance, whereas Russian norms impose strong involvement in musical practice—even if this involvement is an obstacle for general scholastic education. Finally, several competitions include the prizes for citizens of various countries who place highest among their fellow nationals. In several interviews I conducted and observations of informal discussions showed, it is commonly perceived that in a given competition the violinist who is a native citizen of the host country will have stronger support and a better chance to advance to the final stage of competition.[21] This presupposition becomes a basis for students and their master teachers choosing to participate in some competitions over others.

All these suppositions factor into the strategies used in making decisions about the right direction to take in the career process. For the informants, it is clear that in their professional world, *international* does not mean a homogenous culture free of national elements, which is contrary to the image of Durkhemian 'international professionalism.' However, some components of this attractive conception exist. We can find them in the fundamental practices.

THE HOMOGENEITY OF PRACTICES

Even if the participants are convinced that the methods of work are determined by the culture of origin of musicians, when observing master classes, one finds similar behavior on the part of each student during the lesson.[22] In the situation of the master class (which is compared to years-long relationships between teachers and students in extreme cases) where people meet for the first time and work together for one hour, the participants act in such a singular manner with regard to communication and the student–master relationship. Their gestures, communication, and activity seem so similar. However, the personal characteristics of students and the language of communication are different from one person to another. Here is an excerpt from an observation of a master class conducted in Paris by a Russian emigrant to Germany:

At 9 AM, a Japanese 15 year old student takes his lesson in English. At 10 AM is a 10 years old girl born in Kazakhstan who immigrated with whole her family to Austria takes her lesson in Russian. At 11 AM an 18 years old boy born in Romania, proudly says that he originates from well-known Romany musician's family, living in Switzerland takes his course in German. The last person this morning is 12 years old. She came from Israel, and speaks Russian. Even if only the first student worked previously with this teacher, all disciples knew when to start and when to stop playing, how to apply the master's indications, when to replay expected fragments and from which note to start the repetition. Also the collaboration with Russian accompanist, who they met for the first time this morning, was not at all difficult for them. All students behave in a similar manner during their lesson and I could observe similar situations during the years of my study. They behave as if they were educated in the same environment, despite the fact that cultural origin, age (10 to 20), gender, the place of their previous training, and the language of study were different!

HOMOGENEITY OR DIVERSITY: SAME PRACTICE—DIFFERENT TERMS

In order to accomplish a given activity and share it with persons coming from such different parts of the world, participants must acquire the same model of behavior. This is one of the goals of professional socialization, which, in order to respond to the requests of the international universe, includes the elements of this international culture of work. In several professional environments, this process is related to the imposition of the unique language of work (in life sciences or business this is English, for diplomacy it was French). The members of the virtuoso world have to learn a standard and mutually intelligible language and pattern of behavior in order to make their collaborative work efficient. The question then arises: Does this homogeneity delete cultural differences?

In order to learn the cultural differences related to the core of their occupation, it is worth analyzing how the musicians call on their native language for their principal activity: the individual practice that allows the acquisition and maintenance of the highest technical level as well as learning the new program.

> When practicing, French virtuosos 'jouent' (play), sometimes only 's'exercent' (do themselve exercices) or 'travaillent leur instrument' (working their instruments); Germans 'spielen' (play) or like French 'uben' (doing exercise), Americans practice, Polish also 'ćwiczą' (practice) and Russians say 'zanimatsia' (take care on their selves or keeping busy themselves).

The interview passages concerning instrument practice confirm that the perception of this everyday activity differs depending on the cultural origin of violinists.[23] Here, according to my informal interviews conducted over almost 10 years, Asians declare to work the highest number of hours per day, followed by the students from Eastern Europe, and at the lowest end of the spectrum we find the violinists of Occidental origin. This was confirmed during master classes and also during the school year, when I observed and noted precisely the students working (individual practice between lessons) in the place of their learning. The violinists practice alone in rooms prepared for this activity, usually in the room for the master class or in its proximity; as an observer, I was able to hear from the corridor the music and to take notes about the working time of the students practicing in these rooms. In addition, I followed several persons who were hosted in my house during several weeks to 10 months, and I took notes about their working practices and time devoted to them. These relevant data show a close relationship between the time devoted to daily practice and culture of origin. Another important factor was the organization of general schooling (students who are enrolled in school by correspondence or reduced time in general school have more time for practicing). But in the group of students who had entire days for practicing, the Asians were among those who devoted the most time to playing violin, Eastern Europeans were also highly involved in their training, while the students of Western Europe origin worked less.

This conclusion brings us from linguistic and actual practice time-related data to the following question: Why does this difference appear? In order to respond to this question, we should interrogate more fundamental notions that are transmitted with the basis of each culture, the notions related with the beliefs about the musical 'talent.'

VIRTUOSO AND GENIUS AS IMPORTANT ELEMENTS OF CREATIVE CAREERS

The fundamental notions of genius and virtuoso belong to the *quasi* unconscious sphere—part of the culture of each individual, which is, according to Mead (1970), transmitted in the beginning of life. The notion of genius appears in the discourse of soloists animating their debate about creativity, individualism, performances, charisma, and virtuosity. In the Occident, the belief in 'artistic genius' is widely spread and integrated in the system of violin education; for example, the teachers often underlines that 'this one has extreme talent,' neglecting the importance of intensive training (which is less attractive to young students and their parents, too[24]). As the existence of genius is inscribed in Occidental culture, it is not surprising that the conviction that the talent is of the first importance in the musical career and the intensity of work is secondary. In Russia (and other neighboring countries), even if differences in potential among students are not denied, 'talent' or 'genius' is only the basis for hard work. At the beginning of a student's education, particular effort is paid to creating evidence of the causal relationship between intensive practice and virtuoso skills. Stoliarski Piotr Solomonovitch, a famous teacher, "demanded that his student take the violin out of its case immediately after breakfast and put it away just before going to sleep at night. All other activities, including general education, were expected to be cut to a minimum. The child's entire life had to be devoted to the violin" (Jelagin; cited in Schwarz 1983, 458). Here, hard work allows the 'talent' to appear. This is not the same in Asia (China, Japan). Among the students originating and educated in these cultures, the discourse about genius is absent. The person who is successful is a hardworking person. For Asian violinists, according to interviews I conducted with them as well as informal discussions I had with them, success depends on their quality and the quality of their practice.

The violinists who take their master-class lessons take the stage, play, and react to their teacher in a similar manner, despite coming from different parts of the world. But they perceive their activity completely differently! These cultural differences appear clear in the account provided by an Asian-American mother who engaged her daughter in intensive musical practice and wrote an interesting book, *Battle Hymn of the Tiger Mother* (Chua 2011). The core issue of this testimony is to explain to Occidental audiences (and American parents) the educational strategies typical for the Asian culture, which contrast highly with the American educational approach. Even if the author is not a social scientist and did not conduct a large amount of research on the question of cultural differences in the approaches to musical education, she provides an excellent case study showing the difference of perception of the same activity dependent on culture of origin.

This phenomenon constitutes a typical example of the complexity of the international dimension of the virtuoso professional culture.[25]

IS CULTURE IMPORTANT FOR CREATIVE CAREERS?

Speaking about professional behavior and cultural differences in the case of virtuoso socialization, we should always remind ourselves that we meet two opposite phenomena. First, culture of origin plays crucial role in the long-term collaboration and in the processes of coupling, which are fundamental for the creation of the next generation of virtuosos. Second, the culture of origin is not important in short-term collaborations (master classes, for example) when the participants are able to behave according to the specific rules, which are used in the internationalized professional universe. These rules are strictly related to professional practices (playing violin) and do not transcend the work context. This is not the same for career coupling relationships, where private life is also important. In such long-term contexts, the partners have more of a chance to develop successful career coupling when they come from similar cultures. I can provide some examples of breaking the process of career coupling at the beginning of the second stage of this relationship caused by cultural differences. After two years of work with her teacher, who was raised and educated in France, an Eastern European student in the informal interview complained about the private side of this relationship: "He is not taking care of me—never asked me if I had money for my living or even for food. Sometimes I am even hungry because my scholarship is never on time, and my parents in Russia are not able to help me. He does not care—he asks for performances, and my private life is not interesting for him. How can I work with him if he does not pay attention to me?" Indeed, the model relationship between a student and a music professor according to the Eastern European tradition requires some knowledge of the private lives of students (and teachers). They spend a lot of time not only working together but also sharing information about private issues. A professor of French origin was an excellent teacher, but the private life of his students was not important for him. Despite a good technical level of work, the student decided to start working with another professor who was interested in the non-musical side of her life—especially when it influenced the musical practice of the student and her well-being.

In a situation in which a student and their teacher are from similar cultures, it is much easier to adjust their mutual expectations—this is easy to do for a short period of time and it is more complex if it takes years. When a 13-year-old French student takes a master course with a Russian teacher, they work for 2 weeks intensively, and the student misses classes in his/her general education school. They focus on violin progress, and they communicate about pieces, technical correction, and the manner of playing. Acting according to the rule of professional culture (the course is in English), there is no need at this point for cultural proximity. When the same student is enrolled in this teacher's class for the whole year, the student is asked to drop full-time general educational schooling. According to the Russian culture of elite musical education, one of the most important expectations is that the young musician is always in the situation of partial schooling in order to be able to practice long hours each day. For a French family, this kind of solution runs the risk of being without a school leaver's diploma. Here we have a fundamental value conflict, which is provoked by cultural differences concerning the perception of the occupation of musician and its place in a given society (in France, being a musician is certainly not as 'desired' and prestigious an occupation as in Russia). This example indicates how in a long-lasting relationship (without which it is not possible to become part of the elite), sharing common values, having similar priorities, and focusing on the same goals are central.

CONCLUSION—TRANSNATIONAL CULTURE AND TRANSNATIONAL CAREERS

As I show in this chapter, the international professional culture is a space of intersection and interference of numerous nationally and/or ethnically informed cultures. This professional culture is constantly created through the interactions between people who participate in the everyday activities of this world (Sapir 1949). This play between universal and particular cultures is permanently present and constitutes the particularity of the international professional culture. In other words, the international professional culture is a hybrid determined by its elements, including the culture of persons who belongs to this professional environment. This culture is a dynamic phenomenon: Each moment is the result of an original and specific interaction creating a new effect.

The experts who analyze the international culture of work (in the world of business) define it as universal (Amadieu 1993; Huault 1998) or culturally determined (Hofstede 1980; Schneider and Meyer 1991; Zukin & DiMaggio 1990). As I showed in this chapter, the analysis of cultural influences should include the situational context that brings into light the variety of possible behaviors, considered as complementary and mutually enriching by the group of international professionals. Such crucial application of context to these analyses is possible only with the use of the method of participant observation. Consideration of these contexts brings more nuanced conclusions: As my results suggest, both groups of experts (universalists and culturalists) are right. Both interpretations could be correct because in everyday life, situations oscillate between the two extreme cases. The first—universalist situations—generally correspond to punctual activity (brief events, short-term collaboration). The second—culturally determined situations—generally relate to longer duration activities, such as several years of intensive collaborations—typical of the career coupling relationship. In such situations, the culture of the participants constitutes an important factor, which largely determines the collaboration.

Consequently, the international professionalism, which I studied in the violin virtuoso field, is not a homogenous phenomenon. A Durkheimian (like a cosmopolitan) definition could be nuanced by a Maussian proposition with regard to the term 'internationalism.' According to Mauss (1920), internationalism is contrary to cosmopolitism because in the latter the nation disappears, whereas internationalism denotes the *inter*-national, meaning the mutual influences of national elements. This definition of internationalism corroborates with the results obtained in this study. The national influences are present, and this is why the Maussian use of the term 'international' is a crucial adjective in characterizing the professional culture correctly. But because of the complexity and various definitions of the term 'international' (the majority of persons use the Durkhemian perspective), I use a more appropriate term to describe the features of the professional world of virtuosos—'transnational.' Ewa Morawska (2009, 11) defines the term 'transnational' as a sociological term appearing in the study of (im)migration, "referring to the civic-political memberships, economic involvements, social networks, and cultural identities of (im) migrants and their offspring extending across state-national boundaries and linking people and institutions in two or more nation-states in diverse, multilayered patterns." In my opinion, this concept perfectly matches with the situations observed among violin professionals: They are constructing their careers in several countries, they move and change their place of work and residence, and they maintain their relations with the persons and institutions whom they know from previous places of residence. More than just staying in touch, these mobile virtuosos prepare and realize artistic projects (the basis for their careers) by being present in several national spaces. Building their career simultaneously in several countries, the soloists construct their transnational careers, adapting their activity to the expectations of different publics, markets, and even artistic conventions. Enormous flexibility and astuteness are required for achieving such types of careers.

The study of professional transnational cultures and transnational careers is dynamic because these careers are ingrained in several cultures, and also, because they are continuously in permanent re-construction based on the interaction between participants. This is a particularly fruitful field for research. However, it is not easy to study such phenomena as nomadism, or *metissage*, especially with the use of the fixed concepts (Gruzinski 1999, 2004). Pieterse (2003) believes this to be the reason that only a few sociologists have studied these phenomena. In my opinion, the second reason for the lack of such deep and adapted studies is related to the fact that these topics dealing with behavior associated with culture (ethnicity) and national influence are quickly considered politically incorrect. However, this lack of study on the dynamics of transnational professional worlds, with all their creativity and complexity, should be undertaken because it holds important theoretical and practical potential—theoretical because we can come to understand how people's perceptions and practices are influenced by their cultural backgrounds, and practical because it will be increasingly important with the escalating internationalization of several human activities to help people understand each other when people originating from different cultures meet. Instead of proposing the ideology of cosmopolitism and homogenous global professional culture, such studies, through the cultural analysis of practice in the international professional environment, would be helpful and inspiring tools for improving the communication and quality of work not only for a virtuoso, but also for other creative occupations (for scientists, see Wagner 2011).

NOTES

1. The informants in this study use the adjective 'national' in order to name their country of origin as the important element that influences their career choices. The sociological term corresponding to this phenomenon would be 'national culture.' I maintained the double adjective in order to be as close as possible to the expression and meaning given by musicians to this issue.
2. This kind of extension, which is the application of findings from artistic fields to the study of other areas of professional work, is practiced by several sociologists and economists (Boltanski and Chiapello 2005 [1999]; Menger 2001; Wagner 2006a; Weinberg and Galenson, 2005).
3. Contrary to the absence of the studies about international aspects related to creative careers, the literature concerning international careers of businessmen is rich (Adler 1986; Hofstede 1980).
4. "Good" or 'bad' passport are the expressions used by informants to mark the potential difficulties in obtaining a visa for travel to or staying (permission of stay and work) in a given country.
5. I use the word 'soloist' as defined by D. L. Westby (1960, 225): "A soloist status—this term means here a self-employed entrepreneur, a free agent, not to the first men of the wind section, who are also referred to as soloists. Instead, such names as Menuhin, Heifetz, Serkin and Rubinstein come immediately to mind." Also, my work concerns people who are perceived by professionals in their fields as people who, by virtue of their occupation, are members of an international elite.

6. This phenomenon is not exclusive to musicians. In other examples of creative careers, we can observe similar mechanisms. Joseph Hermanowicz (1998, XIII), who studied researchers in physics remarks, "The scientist, like the artist or the athlete, follows a pantheon of immortals—figures who have achieved a place in history through exemplary performance. The achievements of these figures set a competitive standard for all those who embark on a given professional path. Who aspires to be a mediocre Johnny Unitas, a second-rate Beethoven, or a watered-down Newton? A desire for greatness—an imagined possibility of what one becomes—ignites a career and often sustains it." This citation applies perfectly to the soloist world.

7. The number of young soloists originating from Eastern Europe or who were educated in the classes of Eastern European teachers on European stages is large (for statistics on finalists in international competitions, see Wagner 2006b).

8. In addition to English, in the soloist world, the knowledge of 'rare' languages, such as Russian, is useful. This skill allows students to reach artistic intimacy and privilege with those teachers who originate from and/or have been educated in the former Soviet republics. Russian can also be useful during competitions, as during informal discussions between the members of the jury, during rehearsals, and in order to communicate with other students.

9. Some formerly mobile soloist have, after a period of extreme mobility, taken positions as concert performers in excellent orchestras or chamber ensembles, and frequently they also become professors for advanced students.

10. For this population, one of the most important events is the young virtuoso competitions. During these events, the main goal of which is the selection of the next generation of elite musicians, we can easily observe the career strategies and power relationships among the participants, most especially the teachers. In this game, national/cultural origin is one of the most important selection factors.

11. This phenomenon is present also in other areas of activity—for example, in the institutions working in other creative settings, such as engineering research (de Bony 2009).

12. This topic needs further explanation. In the beginning of the 20th century in Europe, among the Jewish bourgeoisie, playing violin was part of their regular education. The traditions of professional musical education were also well spread among Jewish families before WWII. Within my sample, several students who originated from Eastern Europe emphasized their 'Jewish roots.' This aspect was rarely pointed out despite its clear and structural origin, and the large presence of Jewish musicians in Easter Europe started under Tsarist jurisdiction. The members of Jewish communities were not allowed to live in the center of towns—except in rare cases. One of the exceptions was the enrollment of a child from a Jewish family in music conservatories. Immediately the whole family received the privilege of residing in the center of the city. That derogation was (in parallel with the great value placed on education) an important factor (for social and economical position, as well as physical safety as Jewish districts were under the constant danger of pogroms), which explains why so many bourgeois Jewish families offered their children the highest level of musical education (Milstein and Volkov 1990). For more than 100 years, the success of numerous children originating from Jewish families is, in part, due to the factor of extended hosting, such as having a network of relatives living in several places throughout the world. One of the most famous examples is the pianist Arthur Rubinstein, who, as a child, lived in Berlin in his aunt's house. This familial hosting network is efficient not only for Jewish students but also for those originating

from other cultures, which constitute ethnic diasporas (Armenian and post-1917 Russians). This crucial factor contributes to the high mobility of young children, which may lead to their later success in soloist careers.

13. The instances of Eastern European teachers who immigrated to Israel were significant in the 1960s and 1970s, which also explains the overrepresentation in the international environment of Russian musicians with Jewish roots—in 1970s and 1980, the emigration from the USSR was only allowed to people who could declare and prove Jewish origin (it was not an easy process, but for other USSR citizens, even traveling outside their country was almost impossible).

14. These professors are the powerful persons—not only are they frequently famous former virtuosos (few of them have active concert engagements at this point), but they also frequently are members of the jury at international competitions. Attending their class significantly raises the chances of being selected for a given competition's final stage. As a finalist, a virtuoso has better access to concert agencies, which is crucial in the race for the soloist position in the 'adult' concert market.

15. In his historical book, *Great Masters of the Violin*, Schwarz (1983) describes how the Russians came to impose their norm of playing in the early part of the 20th century.

16. Asian standards are not only the results of hard instrumental practice but above all the result of specific backgrounds: Asian ethnic music is based on smaller divisions of tones than is the case in European music. This difference provokes the highest skills in perception of the pitch, which is the basis of 'in tune' playing.

17. This specific relationship was observed in the case of life-science researchers (Wagner 2006a, 2011; intellectuals-sociologists, Wagner 2009; rock musicians, Marzec 2010).

18. See, for example, the inspiring study by Robert Faulkner (1983) about the interaction between two artists—a composer of music and a director of movies.

19. For example, Laurent Korcia went to the Royal College of Music in London with Felix Andrievski, Virginie Robillard studied at Julliard School in the US in Dorothy DeLay's class, Marie-Annick Nicolas completed her study in Moscow with Boris Bielinki and David Oistrakh, Pierre Amoyal worked with Yasha Heifetz in Los Angeles, and Renaud Capucon worked in Berlin with Thomas Brandys.

20. This difference is similar to the split between the points of view of international managers' families and French families about the 'grand ecoles' of French elites. According to A.-C. Wagner (1995, 550): "Scholar strategies and the international models of excellence are distinct from those of French scholar elites and the 'nobles of the State'. "

21. This phenomenon could be related to the specific organization of some competitions when the first selection is done by jury composed from musicians originated from the competition place country. Only next selections are performed by an international jury.

22. Playing the violin as a practice is limited by the instrument and for classical music; on each continent, a similar model of violin is used. This model certainly determines the manner of playing—the gestures. But this is not my purpose here. Instead I focus on the manner of 'taking the lesson,' which means reacting with a teacher, not so much by speaking with him but by executing the teacher's advice and remarks. In the context described here, this specific communication is between a teacher and students who are not his regular pupils.

23. A recent study conducted at Harvard focused on the cultural differences that are related to beliefs in the in-born origin of talent versus hard work in the

case of virtuosos. Research shows that the perception of the virtuoso performance differs significantly accordingly to the culture of origin of public (Tsay & Banaji 2011).

24. During a formal interview, one violin maker related the following anecdote: *"Etienne Vatelot who was the biggest violin maker in Paris said once—'the genius I never met, but the parents of geniuses, I speak with them each day in my office!'"*

25. In his book, *Art Worlds*, Howard Becker (1982, 63) remarks that, "[K]nowledge of professional culture, then, defines a group of practicing professionals who use certain conventions to go about their artistic business." Following Becker's analysis, the professional violinist's culture contains a particular *savoir-faire*, not only concerning techniques of playing and interpretation of pieces but also the knowledge of their social world.

REFERNCES

Adler, N. 1986. *International Dimensions of Organizational Behavior*. Boston: PWS-Kent Publishing Company.

Adler P. A., and P. Adler. 1991. *Backboards and Blackboards. College Athletes and Role Engulfment*. New York: Columbia University Press.

Adler P. A., and P. Adler. 1998. *Peer Power: Preadolescent Culture and Identity*. New Brunswick, NJ, London: Rutgers University Press.

Amadieu, J.-F. 1993. *Organisations et travail: cooperation, conflits et marchandage*. Paris: Vuibert.

Becker, H. S. 1970. *Sociological Work. Method and Substance*. Chicago: Aldine.

Becker, H. S. 1982. *Art Worlds*. Berkley: University of California Press.

Becker, H. S. and Strauss, A. L. 1956. "Careers, Personality, and Adult Socialisation." *American Journal of Sociology* LXII. pp. 253–63.

Berger, Peter. 1963. Invitation to Sociology. A Humanistic Perspective. Anchor Books, NY.

Boltanski, L., and Chiapello, E. 2005. *The New Spirit of Capitalism*. London, UK: Verso Books.

Bony de, J. 2010. "Project Management and National Culture: A Dutch–French Case Study." *International Journal of Project Management* 28: 173–82.

Cameron, W.B. 1954. "Sociological Notes on the Jam Session" *Social Forces* no. 33. no. 2 pp. 177–182.

Chua, A. 2011. *Battle Hymn of the Tiger Mother*. New York: The Penguin Press.

Durkheim, E. 1956. *Socialisme and Saint-Simon*. (C. Sattler, Trans.). London: Routledge & Kegan Paul Ltd. (Original publication 1928)

Faulkner, R. R. 1983. *Music on Demand. Composer and Careers in the Hollywood Film Industry*. New Brunswick, NJ: Transaction.

Gruzinski, S. 1999. *La Pensée métisse*. Paris: Fayard.

Gruzinski, S. 2004. *Les quatres parties du monde: Histoire d'une mondialisation*. Paris: Editions de la Martinière.

Grzymała-Kazłowska, A. 2004. "Three Dimensions of Tolerance in Poland and in Europe." In *Poles among Europeans*, edited by A. Jasińska-Kania and M. Marody, 152–72. Warsaw: Wyd. Naukowe Scholar.

Hermanowicz, J. C. 1998. *The Stars Are Not Enough-Scientists–Their Passions and Professions*. Chicago: University of Chicago Press.

Hofstede. G. 1980. *Culture's Consequences, International Differences in Work Related Values*. Newbury Park, CA: Sage.

Huault, I. 1998. *Le management international*. Paris: Ed. La Découverte.

Hughes, C. 1971. The *Sociological Eye: Selected Papers*. Chicago: Aldine.

Jasinska-Kania, A. 1992. (ed) Bliscy i dalecy. Studia nad postawami wobec różnych narodów, ras i grup etnicznych. Wyd. IS. UW. Warszawa.

Junker, B. 1960. *Field Work*. Chicago: University of Chicago Press.

Kofta, M., and Jasinska-Kania A., eds. 2002. *Stereotypy i uprzedzenia. Uwarunkowania psychologiczne i kulturowe* [Stereotypes and prejudices. Psychological and cultural factors]. Wyd. Scholar Warszawa.

Lourie-Sand, B. 2000. *Teaching Genius—Dorothy DeLay and the Making of a Musician*. Portland: Amadeus Press.

Marcus, G. E. 1995. "Ethnography in/of the World System: The Emergence of Multi-Sited Ethnography." *Annual Review Anthropology* 24: 95–117.

Marzec, H. 2010. *Relacja Mistrz-Uczeń w środowisku muzyków rockowych w Polsce*. Praca magisterska obroniona w czerwcu 2010 roku w Instytucie Socjologii Uniwersytetu Warszawskiego. [MA thesis in Polish] is.vw.warsaw

Mauss, M. 1920. "La nation et l'internationalisme." In *Communication en français à un colloque: "The Problem of Nationality,"* 242–51. Londres: Proceedings of the Aristothelien Society. accessible on-line: http://classiques.uqac.ca/classiques/mauss_mercel/oeuvres_3_15/nation_internationalisme.pdf last accessed September 2011.

Mead, M. 1970. *Culture and Commitment—A Study of the Generation Gap*. Garden City, NY: Doubleday.

Menger, P. 2001. "Artists as Workers: Theoretical and Methodological Challenges." *Poetics* 28: 241–54.

Milstein, N., and Volkov, S. 1990. *De la Russie à l'Occident Mémoires musicaux et autres souvenirs de Nathan Milstein*. Paris: Buchet/Chastel.

Morawska, E. 2009. "Badania nad imigracją/etnicznością w Europie i Stanach Zjednoczonych. Analiza porównawcza." *Studia Migracyjne—Przegląd Polonijny* 1.

Nederveen Pieterse, J. 2003. *Global Mélange: Globalization and culture*. Lanham, MD: Rowman & Littlefield.

Petit de Voize, Y. 1997. "Jeunes, talentieux et bucheurs, ils sont l'elite de la musique instrumentale francaise." *Diapason* 435 : 32.

Sapir, E. 1949. *Selected Writings in Language, Culture, and Personality*, edited by D. G. Mandelbaum. Berkeley; Los Angeles: California University Press.

Schneider, S. C., and Meyer de, A. 1991. "Interpreting and Responding to Strategic Issues: The Impact of National Culture." *Strategic Management Journal* 12: 307–20.

Schwarz, B. 1983. *Great Masters of the Violin*. New York: Simon & Schuster.

Tsay, Ch.-Y., and Banaji, M. 2011. "Child Prodigies, Maybe." *Harvard Gazette*, http://news.harvard.edu/gazette/story/2011/03/child-prodigies-maybe/, last accessed March 2011.

Weinberg, B. A., and Galenson, D. A. 2010. *Creative Careers: The Life Cycles of Nobel Laureates in Economics*. Working Paper 11799 2005, http://www.nber.org/papers/w11799, last accessed June 1, 2010.

Wagner, A.-C. 1995. *Le jeu du national et de l'international. Les cadres étrangers en France*. Thèse de doctorat de sociologie, EHESS Paris.

Wagner, I. 2004. "La formation de jeunes virtuoses: les réseaux de soutiens." *Sociétés Contemporaines* 56: 133–63.

Wagner, I. 2006a. "Career Coupling: Career Making in the Elite World of Musicians and Scientists." *Qualitative Sociology Review* 2: 78–98. http://www.qualitativesociologyreview.org /ENG/archive_eng.php, last accessed February 2010.

Wagner, I. 2006b. *La production sociale des violonistes virtuoses*. These de doctorat EHESS, Paris.

Wagner, I. 2007. "Kształcenie tożsamości członków międzynarodowych elit. Internacjonalizm zawodowy- pomiedzy dyskursem a praktyką." In *W Kręgu Socjologii Interpretatywnej—zastosowanie metod jakościowych. Ponowoczesność i tożsamość*, edited by J. Leoński and U. Kozłowska,116–38. Szczecin: Economicus.

Wagner, I. 2009. "Transnarodowy Profesjonalista i jego profesjonalna kultura." In *Mozaiki przestrzeni międzynarodowych. Teorie, metody, zjawiska*, edited by L. Krzyzowski and S. Urbanska, 155–171. Krakow: Nomos.

Wagner, I. 2011. *Becoming Transnational Professional. Mobilność i kariery polskich elit naukowych*. Warszawa: Wyd. Scholar Wydawnictwo Naukowe.

Westby, D. L. 1960. "The Career Experience of the Symphony Musician." *Social Forces* 38: 223–30.

Wierzbicka, A. 1994. " 'Cultural Scripts': A Semantic Approach to Cultural Analysis and Cross-Cultural Communication." *Pragmatics and Language Learning* (Monograph Series) 5.

Zukin, S., and DiMaggio, P. 1990. Structures of Capital: The Social Organization of the Economy. Cambridge, UK: Cambridge University Press.

10 Composing a Career
The Situation of Living Composers in the Repertoires of US Orchestras, 2005–2006

Timothy J. Dowd and Kevin J. Kelly

INTRODUCTION

Those individuals who author such things as music, literature, and film (i.e., creative personnel) face a number of challenges in securing professional careers that are both stable and long. Certain scholarship approaches these challenges by pointing to various stages in these careers, whereby movement from one stage to the next can be difficult if not unattainable for many (Craig and Dubois 2010; see Lincoln and Allen, Chaper 5, this volume; Pralong and Gombault, Chapter 11, this volume; Skov, Chapter 13, this volume; Stoyanova and Grugulis, Chapter 4, this volume). One important stage involves launching such professional careers. This is not as easy as it sounds because the number of hopefuls can far exceed the number of people who actually secure paid work (Menger 1999). Some handle this initial logjam by choosing to be amateurs rather than professionals, opting out of stages that mark a professional career (Jeffri 2008; Jeffri et al. 2011). For those who successfully negotiate the first stage, they still face a number of challenges in reaching another important stage—that of being 'established,' wherein they attain some regularity in their work opportunities (Craig and Dubois 2010). For instance, among those who help create a single film (e.g., actors, composers, directors), many never have the opportunity to create subsequent films—ending their professional careers shortly after 'breaking in' and never moving on to this second stage (e.g., Baker and Faulkner 1991; Faulkner 1983; Zuckerman et al. 2003).

Those who reach the stage of being established then face the uphill climb to becoming 'well established'—a stage at which they are widely known and highly regarded within *and* beyond their particular creative community (Craig and Dubois 2010; see Jones, Chapter 7, this volume). One stream of research finds that only a fraction of creative personnel attains widespread acclaim (e.g., Allen and Lincoln 2004; Schmutz 2005; see Lincoln and Allen, Chapter 5, this volume). This acclaim often depends on the actions of 'intermediaries' who stand between creative personnel and their ultimate audience—such as critics, academics, and organizations (e.g., museums, orchestras) that actively choose to elevate some creative personnel over others. The work of intermediaries can unfold across considerable stretches of time, and it can bear little relation to the original success of the creative personnel in question. Novelist Zora Neal Hurston enjoyed little financial or critical success during her lifetime, but decades later—due partly to the efforts of noted author Alice Walker and shifting standards of evaluation among academics—she is now considered a major figure in American literature (Corse and Griffin 1997). Similarly, among a cohort of visual artists from the 1910s, their odds of being featured a century later in university curricula increased greatly with the exposure provided by a particular intermediary—the Museum of Modern of Modern Art (MoMA): The number of exhibitions granted them by MoMA during the mid-1900s increased the number of pages devoted to these particular artists in 21st-century textbooks (Braden 2009). Thus, the acclaim of creative personnel can take years to grow, and it can extend beyond the lifespan of particular personnel.

The posthumous acclaim of creative personnel has a particularly great impact in fields that are described as 'high culture' (e.g., literature, orchestral music, opera, theater)—wherein the value of 'art for art's sake' purportedly takes precedence over entertainment and profit (Craig and Dubois 2010; DiMaggio 1982, 1992). This impact is fostered by the respective canons found in each high culture field. 'Canon' refers to ongoing explanations by important intermediaries about what constitutes great art. In offering such explanations—which are evolving, if not contested—these intermediaries often emphasize a select number of creators from an earlier era, showing how such individuals have both stood the test of time and have fundamentally shaped their art's historical development (DeNora 1991; Dowd 2011; Schmutz 2005). Within high culture fields, living personnel are not only jostling with their contemporaries for opportunities, they are also competing for the attention and resources that flow to the 'classic' works of a few creators from the (distant) past (Craig and Dubois 2010; Dowd 2011).

While much research has focused on each of the three broad stages listed earlier, relatively little addresses the implications that the well-established creators who are now dead hold for those established creators who are very much alive. This chapter fills that gap by addressing the US field of orchestral music—one in which challenges to the living are especially apparent and long discussed (Dowd 2011). The common moniker for this field ('classical music') suggests an overwhelming emphasis on such celebrated composers as Haydn, Mozart, and Beethoven—all of whom were active in the 18th century (Dowd et al. 2002). Composers and observers alike have noted the ramifications of this. "Musical art, as we hear it in our day, suffers if anything from an overdose of masterworks, an obsessive fixation on the glories of the past," wrote Aaron Copland (1963, 42), a famed composer. "This narrows the range of our musical experience and tends to suffocate interest in the present." Living composers, observed one musicologist, "have had to compete with the music of the past for performances and for the affection of players and listeners. It is a contest in which the reigning champions have an overwhelming advantage, for the orchestral repertoire is very crowded and the classics have enormous prestige" (Burkholder 2006, 410).

The American emphasis on the classics is not simply due to a dearth of living composers. While there is no exhaustive master list of orchestral composers, various sources indicate that they have numbered in the hundreds, if not the thousands, across the years. In the early to mid-1900s, the Eastman School of Music offered performances of more than a thousand compositions penned by some 400 US composers (Hanson 1951). Later that century, Felton (1978) identified and surveyed more than 1,500 active composers associated with the American Music Center—an organization representing the professional interests of composers engaged in 'serious' (rather than 'popular') music. Those composers authored some 1,500 compositions in 1974 alone, with more than 250 written for orchestras. At the turn of this century, the American Music Center represented more than 2,000 composers, while another entity—the American Composer's Forum—was associated with some 1,700 composers. Additional analyses revealed that such composer organizations likely represent about half of all serious composers active in the US during the early 2000s—with a substantial portion composing for orchestras (Jeffri 2008).

Composers in the US have long faced considerable difficulties in securing a full-time living from composition alone—despite often possessing relatively high levels of education and/or much specialized training (Copland 1933; Felton 1978; Jeffri 2008; Nash 1970). Among the 1,347 US composers surveyed by Jeffri (2008)—those characterized as 'serious' rather than 'popular'—three quarters of them self-identified as professional composers, with 90 percent of these professionals having college degrees and nearly 75 percent having graduate degrees. Yet only 10 percent of these professionals earned their income primarily from composition, with 8 percent earning all their income in that fashion. That income was not particularly great, with more than half of these professionals earning $60,000 a year or less and slightly more than 20 percent annually earning $20,000 or less. Despite such economic challenges, these professionals were more concerned, as a group, with getting their work out for consideration and with securing performances of their music than with the state of their finances. As Frank Zappa (1989, 197) once wrote after detailing the frustrations and costs he incurred in securing orchestral performances for his compositions, "Before an audience can tell whether or not it likes a piece, it needs to *listen* to it. Before it can listen to it, it has to know that it *exists*. In order for it to exist in a form in which it can be heard (not just on paper), it has to be *performed*."

Composers have not been passive in the face of such challenges. Aside from taking on additional work—for example, teaching, as nearly half of professional composers now do (Jeffri 2008)—some have collectively worked to promote their music. In the early to mid-1900s, for instance, they founded composer organizations, launched publishing endeavors, created festivals, and started periodicals that championed their music (Cameron 1996; Dowd et al. 2004; Oja 2000). Their efforts apparently had some success, as major orchestras of the day did occasionally perform the music of those still breathing—with a few notably championing the music of certain living composers (Arian 1971; Hanson 1951; Mueller 1951; Tawa 1984). Since the mid-1900s, some US orchestras have made a concerted effort to perform contemporary music. This includes the commissioning and/or debuting of new compositions, the securing of composers-in-residence, and outright specialization in new music (Craven 1987; Hart 1973; Jeffri 2008; Scholz 2001).

This attention to contemporary music can pose both benefits and costs for orchestras. For orchestras offering a broad range of musical works ('generalists'), incorporating new music into their repertoires allows them to claim both aesthetic vibrancy and relevance for contemporary life (DiMaggio and Stenberg 1985a; Gilmore 1993; Scholz 2001). For orchestras targeting a distinctive audience with a narrow range of works ('specialists'), a focus on new music fits easily with an avant-garde aesthetic, providing a well-specified mission and (possibly) a ready-made constituency found in and around universities and bohemian enclaves (Cameron 1996; Gilmore 1987, 1988; Oja 2000). However, when faced with unfamiliar works, orchestral musicians can require more rehearsal time than is the case for those classics with which they are well acquainted—particularly when the new music is challenging both stylistically and technically (Felton 1978; Gilmore 1993; Schuller 1962). In addition, new music can also involve higher costs for copyright and printed music (Felton 1978; Tawa 1984). Finally, new music can be costly given its potential for alienating those audiences who are expecting the familiar (Arian 1971; Felton 1978; Maitlis and Lawrence 2003).

These benefits and costs are relevant for the careers of living composers—particularly for becoming widely known ('well established') like their deceased counterparts (see Jeffri 2008). What Copland (1933, 88) wrote many years ago arguably applies to the present: "Contemporary music could only find its way to the larger musical public through the agency of the symphony orchestra." Thus, this chapter quantitatively analyzes a range of factors that could shape the extent to which orchestras feature the music of living composers. We do so by considering the repertoires that US orchestras offered during the 2005–2006 season. While most of these 313 orchestras still feature composers who are long dead, certain factors facilitate their attention to living composers—including their programming strategy (generalist vs. specialist). But first we discuss scholarship that offers a number of hypotheses regarding which types of orchestras are likely to follow this emphasis on the past and which ones are likely to innovate by way of contemporary music.

ORCHESTRAS AND COMPOSERS IN THE CURRENT US

Our focus resonates with studies that address the programming choices of performing arts organizations (e.g., symphony orchestras, opera companies, resident theaters). As Boerner (2004) notes, their choices unfold along three dimensions—the extent to which an organization offers programming that is distinctive from its counterparts (originality vs. conformity), the extent to which it offers a broad range of programming (specialization vs. generalism), and the extent to which it emphasizes recent works and creators (contemporary vs. classic). The studies mentioned next each grapple with one or more of these dimensions. Consequently, we draw on them for hypotheses—which we group into three broad categories—regarding the types of orchestras amenable to the performance of living composers.

Community Context and Innovation

Symphony orchestras and other performance arts organizations can face the difficult, if not contradictory, missions of celebrating the classics while also introducing audiences to contemporary creators—with the latter an important type of innovation but one that runs the risk of alienating the audience (DiMaggio and Stenberg 1985a; Martorella 1977; Pierce 2000). Hence, DiMaggio and Stenberg (1985b, 112) lament, "Case studies of performing arts organizations have illustrated vividly the extent to which such organizations may become prisoners of audience demand, mortgaging their participants' artistic aspirations in the interest of organizational survival."

Yet DiMaggio and Stenberg (1985b) expect that certain types of communities are more conducive to adventuresome programming than others. They hypothesize that innovative arts organizations are found in locales containing a large population, a sizable number of highly educated individuals, and a large share of individuals engaged in managerial and professional occupations. Their predictions make sense given research on arts audiences. For instance, Flanagan (2008) finds that attendance at US orchestra concerts is positively associated with population size: The bigger the city, the bigger the audience. Meanwhile, high-status individuals—those with much education and/or much occupational prestige—have historically formed the core audience for performing arts organizations in the US (DiMaggio & Useem 1978). In a similar vein, others hypothesize that locales conducive to innovation are marked by high levels of resident income (another marker of high-status individuals) and a large share of residents who are students, as the latter provide a ready audience for the educational missions of many performing arts organizations (Blau 1989; O'Hagan and Neligan 2005; Pierce 2000). Considering next the attributes of a *single* American locale, DiMaggio and Stenberg (1985b) hypothesize that New York City is unusually conducive to adventuresome programming given its unique confluence of a sizable and educated audience base, a large supply of creative personnel, and a vast range of performing arts organizations—all of which provide an infrastructure supporting experimentation that is unmatched elsewhere in the US. O'Hagan and Neligan (2005) offer a similar hypothesis when noting that London likely fosters more innovative programming than elsewhere in the UK.

Despite their intuitiveness, these hypotheses have faced problems when applied in empirical research. Studies of programming originality among resident theaters (Blau 1989; DiMaggio and Stenberg 1985b; O'Hagan and Neligan 2005) and opera houses (Pierce 2000) do not find statistically significant support for all the community hypotheses. When one or more do prove significant, they nevertheless offer little explanatory power and have led to mixed results (Castaner and Campos 2002). For instance, DiMaggio and Stenberg (1985b) and Pierce (2000) both find that central cities (New York and London, respectively) foster innovative programming more than other locales, whereas Blau (1989, 122) finds that this central city effect disappears when considering residents' income for all communities in which theaters are located. As she asserts, "Rich people, not rich cities foster innovation." Finally, all of these studies do not examine how the number of competing organizations in a given community could also shape programming choices (Castaner and Campos 2002).

Organizational Attributes and Innovation

If community context shapes how performing arts organizations balance both classic and contemporary offerings, so may particular attributes of those organizations. Researchers typically approach this possibility by considering two general types of attributes. On the one hand, some performing arts organizations are less reliant than others on ticket sales (i.e., earned income). Such 'autonomy from the market' may help arts organizations avoid being captive to conservative audience demand (DiMaggio and Stenberg 1985b). Some offer this hypothesis in light of national comparisons—positing that relatively low public funding for the arts leads to less innovative programming in the US than in Canada or Europe (Heilbrun 2001; Martorella 1977, 1985). Others offer it while pointing to the financial situation of individual organizations. For instance, adventuresome programming may flourish among organizations receiving a healthy amount of unearned income, such as government funding (Blau 1989; DiMaggio and Stenberg 1985b; O'Hagan and Neligan 2005; Pierce 2000). Such innovation may also occur for individual organizations that are not freestanding but 'embedded' in larger organizations (e.g., university orchestras), having substantial financial support beyond the box office (DiMaggio 2006; Martorella 1985). On the other hand, some performing arts organizations are more established than others.

Given their resources and reputations, one hypothesis is that those organizations could have more freedom to innovate than their less established counterparts; for instance, they may be able to absorb costs associated with contemporary works, and they may be able to persuade loyal audiences to tolerate the unfamiliar (DiMaggio and Stenberg 1985b; Pierce 2000). However, another hypothesis is that established organizations are more conservative rather than innovative in their programming choices. This is because the process of becoming established—what DiMaggio and Stenberg (1985b) label "institutionalization"—involves such things as 1) age, whereby older organizations are less attuned to recent creators and developments than their younger counterparts; and 2) size, whereby larger organizations have commitments (e.g., filling vast venues) that make innovation risky (Blau 1989; DiMaggio and Stenberg 1985a, 1985b; Martorella 1977, 1985; O'Hagan and Neligan 2003).

Research on contemporary arts organizations has not addressed another organizational attribute—productivity. Historical research finds that as US orchestras performed more works in a season, they greatly expanded the range of composers addressed, adding new composers to their repertoires; however, many of these 'new' composers were deceased composers receiving their debuts in America (Dowd 2011; Dowd et al. 2002; Kremp 2010). Given this historical pattern, we hypothesize that heightened productivity for contemporary orchestras will result in increased attention to composers of the past rather the present.

The testing of these organizational hypotheses is not without problems. This is partly because market autonomy and institutionalization are complex attributes that are not likely to be captured by a single indicator. Consequently, researchers have relied on a variety of indicators to assess the respective impact of both attributes on programming choices. However, these indicators have provided little explanatory power, with many of them proving to be insignificant predictors of innovation. Some speculate that this is because the indicators are intertwined (e.g., highly correlated) and, in turn, capturing similar things while sometimes rendering each other statistically insignificant (Blau 1989; O'Hagan and Neligan 2005). For instance, the size of a performing arts organization may well capture both its autonomy from the market and its extent of institutionalization (DiMaggio and Stenberg 1985b). Problems also flow from the mixed results that have occurred (Castaner and Campos 2002). While some studies find that large opera houses, orchestras, and theaters are less innovative than small ones (DiMaggio and Stenberg 1985b; Gilmore 1987, 1988; Martorella 1977, 1985; O'Hagan and Neligan 2005), one study of opera companies finds the opposite (Pierce 2000). Furthermore, while short-lived orchestras and resident theaters may be more innovative in programming than their long-lived counterparts (DiMaggio and Stenberg 1985a; Heilbrun 2001), some find that it is not aging per se that leads to conservative programming (Blau 1989; DiMaggio and Stenberg 1985a, 1985b).

Programming Strategies and Innovation

Innovation may also be shaped by the strategies by which performing arts organizations operate (see Dowd 2004). Heeding such strategies may help overcome the difficulties associated with the previous hypotheses. However, many of the studies cited earlier are more suggestive than revealing on this point. This chapter moves into new terrain by examining the respective impact of programming strategies on a particular type of innovation—the performance of living composers.

Two hypotheses deal with strategies (i.e., programming choices) that Boerner (2004) identifies—conformity and specialization. DiMaggio and Stenberg (1985b) suggest that institutionalization also entails conformity for performing arts organizations: As they become established, they likely adhere to field-wide expectations regarding how to operate and what to perform. While they and other researchers treat performance conformity as an outcome to inspect (Heilbrun 2001; O'Hagan and Neligan 2005; Pierce 2000), we use it here as a predictor. In particular, we hypothesize that orchestras that are conformist in their programming strategies will also feature relatively few performances by living composers. This makes sense given the orchestral field's longstanding emphasis on the past rather than the present (see Dowd et al. 2002; Kremp 2010). DiMaggio (2006) notes an entirely different strategy—the specialization that makes performing arts organizations distinct from others in their field. In terms of orchestras, this distinctiveness manifests not only in unusual ways of operating but also in a propensity to feature underemphasized, if not 'risky,' music that many organizations do not address—especially that of contemporary composers who are not yet well established (Gilmore 1987, 1988; Khodyakov 2007). We thus hypothesize that orchestras pursuing specialist strategies will also feature relatively more performances of living composers. That said, we recognize that some orchestras may specialize not in contemporary music but, instead, in music from an earlier time.

Two hypotheses stem from research addressing the situation of contemporary US orchestras—particularly in how they seek to engage audiences via their programming. Gilmore (1993) argues that some orchestras strategically use premieres to balance the programming of the classic and the contemporary. Their spectacle allows orchestras to show that they are aware of cutting-edge developments and to generate goodwill among audiences, as the latter know that the performance of a new piece is a special, yet passing, occurrence. Hence, we hypothesize that the more orchestras make use of the premier strategy, the more they will perform the works of living composers. Other observers note another strategy that has apparently grown pronounced in recent years—that of miscellany (DiMaggio 2006). Some orchestras supposedly pursue this strategy to draw in audiences—hoping to entice them by relying on well-known excerpts, mixing the classics with popular works, and/or combining the old with the new as part of 'themed' concerts (Dowd 2011; Glynn 2002; Peterson and Rossman 2008). This miscellany strategy could limit the opportunities provided to serious composers, especially if they are competing for attention with Hollywood soundtrack composers, jazz musicians, and others—as well as with the well-established composers of years gone by.

DATA AND METHOD

To test our hypotheses—and thus learn about career opportunities for living composers—we turn to repertoire data generously provided by the League of American Orchestras (LAO). Formerly known as the American Symphony Orchestra League, it is the preeminent body representing orchestras on the continent (see Hart 1973; League of American Orchestras 2011). The League supplied us with information about the performances of more than 70,000 pieces from the 2000–2001 and 2006–2007 seasons—including the title of the piece, the composer and orchestra responsible for performance, as well as the type (e.g., university orchestra) and budget classification of each orchestra. Because this is the first installment in a larger project, we begin here with a single season before complicating matters by dealing with temporal patterns across multiple seasons—following the example of DiMaggio and Stenberg (1985a, 1985b). Due to data issues in certain seasons—such as missing performance data for some major orchestras and spotty coverage of smaller orchestras—we focus on the one we deem to be most complete in its coverage, the 2005–2006 season.[1] Once we selected that season, we further pruned the performances that we consider. Sensitive to national differences in funding for the arts (Heilbrun 2001; Martorella 1977, 1985), we included neither seven Canadian orchestras reporting during this season nor a Swiss orchestra touring in the US. We did not include seven orchestras performing only a single piece because we need multiple performances to distinguish specialization from generalism. Finally, we did not include a music festival. Thus, we eventually assessed 7,570 performances by 313 orchestras during the 2005–2006 season.

The LAO repertoire data are notable for their sheer coverage—ranging from a host of small orchestras to those majors that have been in operation for years. This represents a considerable step forward over past studies addressing only the repertoires of major orchestras (Dowd et al. 2002; Kremp 2010). That said, we still had to supplement these repertoire data for the purposes of our study. The LAO data do not provide any biographical information on the composers performed. To assess the situation of living versus dead composers, we had to track down the birth and death years of the 639 performed during the season—relying extensively on such sources as the *Grove Music Dictionary*, the *Oxford Music Dictionary*, as well as a host of textbooks, periodicals, websites, and the like. Following Heilbrun (2004), we also categorized deceased composers as '20th century' if born after 1880, '19th century' if born after 1780 and before 1881, and '18th century' if born after 1680 and before 1781.

We also turned to other data sources to assess the community context in which orchestras reside for the 2005–2006 season. Given that the season spans two years—with no reported performance occurring earlier than September—we draw on the 2005 American Community Survey (ACS) compiled by the US Census Bureau. After identifying the standard metropolitan area (or micro-area) in which each orchestra is located during the 2005–2006 season, we used the ACS to gauge the 1) population size of that area, 2) percentage of the population having at least a bachelor's degree, 3) percentage of the workforce ages 16+ employed in managerial and professional occupations, 4) median household income of that area, and 5) percentage of the population enrolled in school of any type. The only difficulty occurs in terms of managerial-professional occupations: The 2005 ACS does not provide information for the smallest communities; hence, those percentages are missing for 11 orchestras. After gathering this community information from the ACS, it was easy to identify the number of orchestras operating in the New York City metropolitan area and the number of orchestras 'competing' in a given metropolitan area. Note that in our analysis, we take the natural log of both population size and median income to address issues of skewness (Neter et al. 1983).

The LAO repertoire data say little about the organizational attributes of orchestras. While it would be helpful to have direct financial information (e.g., extent and type of nonearned income), this information can be hard to access given reasons of confidentiality (Heilbrun 2001). As was the case with an earlier study of LAO repertoire data (Heilbrun 2004), we too lack the type of detailed funding information that some studies have for performing arts organizations (e.g., O'Hagan and Neligan 2005).[2] Nevertheless, we can address two types of orchestras that are somewhat removed from the pressures of the box office: university-college orchestras and youth orchestras. Both are notable in that their musicians are not salaried, and both are self-identified in the LAO repertoire data. While the LAO data reveal the orchestra responsible for the performance of each piece during 2005–2006, they are silent on the age of orchestra. We found this information by resorting to various sources (e.g., journalistic accounts, webpages of orchestras). While we are not able to identify the ages of 6 of the 313 orchestras, we do fare better than some studies that lack age information for all the arts organizations considered (e.g., O'Hagan and Neligan 2005). The LAO data are better suited for assessing another aspect of institutionalization—size. During the 2005–2006 season, the LAO classified orchestras into 'tiers' on the basis of their annual operating budget and other related factors. In general, Tier 1 and Tier 2 orchestras have budgets that range from more than $5.5 million to nearly $15 million in the 2005–2006 season, whereas all other tiers have smaller budgets, sometimes dropping to less than $15,000 (personal correspondence, 2008). We combine Tiers 1 and 2 into a group denoting 'large' orchestras and Tiers 3 through 8 marking 'small' ones. Finally, we measure productivity by simply noting the number of pieces performed by each orchestra, which the LAO data nicely provide.

The advantages associated with the LAO data come to the fore when addressing programming strategies—especially as they allow for rigorous measurement and comparison. We measure conformist strategies by way of an index used in previous studies (DiMaggio and Stenberg 1985a, 1985b; Heilbrun 2001; O'Hagan and Neligan 2005). Conceptually, this index measures the extent to which a given orchestra overlaps with others in terms of composers performed. Statistically, for all composers performed by a given orchestra, the conformity index is the average number of times that other orchestras perform those composers. High values for this index indicate that many orchestras are performing the exact same composers as a given orchestra (conformity), whereas low numbers indicate that a given orchestra is distinctive in terms of composers performed (originality). We measure it in two fashions—a conformity index for the large orchestras only and a conformity index for all the orchestras in the sample, both large and small. We do this because large organizations typically serve as a reference group for each other while also defining the field that small organizations confront (Dowd 2004). We measure specialist strategies by way of the Herfindahl index (see DiMaggio and Stenberg 1985a; Dowd et al. 2002; Heibrun 2001). Conceptually, this index gauges the extent to which a few composers dominate the repertoire of a given orchestra. Statistically, it does so first by calculating the percentage of performances devoted to each composer (e.g., 40 percent, 40 percent, 20 percent); squaring those percentages and summing them (e.g., 1,600 + 1,600 + 400 = 3,600); and finally dividing the sum by 100 (e.g., 36). Thus, a high Herfindahl value indicates a heavy reliance on a few composers if not a single composer (specialization), whereas a low value indicates that a given orchestra features a wide range of composers (generalism). From the LAO repertoire data, we gauge the miscellany strategy by coding as such any performance whose title includes the terms 'excerpt,' 'selection,' and 'medley'—capturing specific 'snippets' of works performed along complete works. We assess premiere strategies by drawing on the LAO's website that lists all the national and world premiers occurring among its members during the 2005–2006 season.

Our main outcome of interest—our dependent variable—is the percentage of performances that each orchestra devotes to living composers in the 2005–2006 season. Given its continuous and cross-sectional nature of this dependent variable, we rely on OLS regression for assessing the relative impact of the various independent variables. This technique also allows for an easy assessment of explanatory power offered by a collection of predictors (via the adjusted-R^2 measure) and ways to ensure that particular independent variables are not highly correlated (via the VIF measure) (Neter et al. 1983).

RESULTS

What constitutes 'classical music' in the US is not fixed in stone, yet it nevertheless shows some stability across the decades—raising barriers for those living composers who seeking performance by orchestras (Dowd 2011). Table 10.1 supports this view. When comparing the most performed composers of the 2005–2006 season to those most performed in the early to mid-1900s (Dowd et al. 2002; Table 2), there is little change—other than a slight shift in the rankings (e.g., Mozart now topping Beethoven and Shostakovich now replacing Wagner among the Top 5). Furthermore, the Top 5 in the early 21st century collectively account for roughly the same percentage of performances as they did in the middle decades of the 20th century (Dowd et al. 2002; Table 2). Additional calculations show that 88.5 percent of all performances in 2005–2006 are devoted to dead composers. What counts as the 'past' is growing increasingly long as well. Although a slight presence in current repertoires, the Top 5 pre-18th-century composers somewhat rival the Top 5 living composers in terms of performance (1.4 percent vs. 2.3 percent), and the top composer of this ancient group (Vivaldi) receives 67 performances in 2005–2006, whereas the top living composer (Tower) receives only 59.

Perhaps Table 10.1 reveals favorable conditions for living composers—as the 313 of them comprise nearly half of all performed composers. As Heilbrun (2004) notes, such large numbers are actually not as positive as they appear because the field of orchestral music has long engaged in a process of winnowing out a few from the many living composers (see Mueller 1951; Weber 2001). Thus, the top 18th-century composers in Table 10.1 do not exhaust all of those once active but instead represent the tiny number (31) still receiving attention centuries later. The same process will likely play out for the 313 living composers, leaving but a fraction in the later orchestral repertoires. Considerable differences in opportunities are also at play. Of the 639 composers performed during the 2005–2006 season, 291 receive only 1 performance, and the average number of performances is 12; in contrast, Mozart accounts for 813 performances and Beethoven for 528. The situation is more daunting for the living—particularly as they compete with the well-established composers from the past. More than half of the living composers (176) receive only one performance during this season, whereas their average number of performances is three.

Barriers do exist for living composers, but they are not insurmountable, as suggested by Table 10.1. First, the prominence of 20th-century composers shows that living composers can gain their way into concert halls. Although the Top 5 of this group are now deceased, they did enjoy some success while alive, and they continue to be a presence in the decades following their demise—now approaching the consideration that orchestras devote to the Top 5 of the 19th century (8.4 percent of performances vs. 14.2 percent). They also have gained renown that extends beyond the concert

Table 10.1   Types of Composers Receiving the Most Performances by US Orchestras During the 2005–2006 Season

Type of Composer	Top 5 composers of a given type and their respective percentages of all performances	Combined percentage for top 5 composers of a given type
All composers	Mozart (10.7), Beethoven (7.0), Tchaikovsky (4.3), Brahms (3.6), Shostakovich (2.4)	28.0
Pre-18th-century composers	Vivaldi (0.9), Corelli (0.2), Cacinni (0.1), Gabrieli (0.1), Purcell (0.1)	1.4
18th-century composers	Mozart (10.7), Beethoven (7.0), Haydn (1.7), J.S. Bach (1.6), Handel (1.2)	22.3
19th-century composers	Tchaikovsky (4.3), Brahms (3.6), Dvorak (2.3), R. Strauss (2.1), Ravel (1.9)	14.2
20th-century composers	Shostakovich (2.4), Prokofiev (1.8), Stravinsky (1.7), Copland (1.6), Gershwin (1.0)	8.4
Living composers	Joan Tower (0.8), John Adams (0.5), John Williams (0.5), John Corigliano (0.3), Jennifer Higdon (0.3)	2.3

The above percentages are in reference to 7570 performances by 313 orchestras. The total number of "All composers" = 639, "Pre-18th century" = 13, "18th century" = 31, "19th century" = 136, "20th century" = 453, and "Living composers" = 313.

hall. In addition to winning the prestigious Pulitzer Prize and Guggenheim Fellowship, Copland enjoyed some exposure as a Hollywood soundtrack composer—earning an Academy Award nomination for *Of Mice and Men*, as well as an award from the National Board of Review (Bick 2005; Bishop 2005). The other Top 5 of the 20th century secured widespread recognition, too—with Gershwin and Stravinsky even finding their way into Bourdieu's (1984) famous survey of French tastes. Second, the Top 5 of the living composers reveal that such things as critical accolades, funding, and affiliations—while not guarantees of success—can nevertheless help.[3] For instance, they too have collectively secured such things as the Pulitzer (Adams, Corigliano, Higdon), the Guggenheim (Corigliano, Higdon, Tower), grants from the National Endowment for the Arts (Corigliano, Tower), and Grammy Awards (Adams, Corigliano, Higdon, Tower, and

Williams). Tower likely secured the top spot in 2005–2006 because of funding received for her composition, *Made in America*—which debuted in 2005 and involved the LAO and Ford Motor Company (among others), as well as contributions from 65 orchestras (Jeffri 2008). Corigliano, Higdon, and Tower all have academic positions, which likely connect them to the serious music scene (see Gilmore 1987, 1988), and Adams has served as a composer-in-residence with the San Francisco orchestra (among other things). While Corigliano extends the tradition of serious music composers being involved in film soundtracks—such as *Altered States* and *The Red Violin*—the presence of John Williams among the Top 5 raises a cautionary note. Arguably the leading soundtrack composer in recent decades (see Faulkner 1983), he is in the Top 5 mostly because of numerous performances of *E.T.*, *Harry Potter*, *Raiders of the Lost Ark*, *Star Wars*, and other filmic music. Thus, he may be the best anecdote for the presence of miscellany in contemporary repertoires—whereby orchestras mix Hollywood with Haydn, Hindemith and Higdon.

While traits of individual composers play a role in the attention that they receive—such as their awards and connections—other factors do as well. Indeed, we posit that the patterns contained in Table 10.1 can, and should, also be explained by considering what types of orchestras are disposed to feature the music of living composers. Before testing those hypotheses, we offer two points of information. First, in our preliminary analysis, we find that one organizational attribute—orchestral size—is relevant not simply on its own but also in how it combines with other factors (see DiMaggio and Stenberg 1985b). Consequently, we do not treat it as a single variable; instead, we split the analysis into one examining large orchestras (budgets exceeding $5.5 million) and another on small orchestras. This allows us to disentangle aspects of size from other aspects of the orchestras (e.g., their age). Second, in exploring our dependent variable—the percentage of living composers performed by a given orchestra—we find it helpful to compare this outcome to other types of composers performed. In terms of our main dependent variable, Table 10.2 shows that all large orchestras address the works of living composers—but are limited in the degree to which they do so. In contrast, some small orchestras completely ignore the music of living composers, while other small orchestras play nothing but the most recent music. This shows the merit of splitting the analysis by size and, of course, the merits of explaining the choices of these intermediaries.

Table 10.3 presents our regression analysis for the large orchestras. Each vertical column contains a distinct regression model, while reading from left to right allows a comparison of how a given predictor impinges on the performance of various types of composers—with significant effects denoted by stars and bold font. Table 10.3 reveals two important omissions: the lack of nearly all the community context variables (except NYC) and the absence of the organizational age variable. First, apart from the NYC variable, none of the community context variables attains significance either

Table 10.2 Repertoire Choices of US Orchestras, 2005–2006

	Minimum	*Maximum*	*Average*
Large orchestras: (N = 50)			
Percentage of living composers	2.83	26.09	11.39
Percentage of pre-18th-century composers	0.00	5.97	0.58
Percentage of 18th-century composers	9.09	64.52	24.84
Percentage of 19th-century composers	12.90	66.67	44.19
Percentage of 20th-century composers	15.52	50.00	30.37
Small orchestras (N = 263)			
Percentage of living composers	0.00	100.00	14.28
Percentage of pre-18th-century composers	0.00	31.37	1.16
Percentage of 18th-century composers	0.00	100.00	20.66
Percentage of 19th-century composers	0.00	100.00	44.26
Percentage of 20th-century composers	0.00	100.00	33.59

individually or in combination with all of the variables in Tables 10.3 and 10.4. Furthermore, their respective insignificance did not result from high correlations among them and other variables. While past studies of arts organizations find limited effects of community context on programming choices (e.g., DiMaggio and Stenberg 1985b), we join Heilbrun (2004) in finding no effect of such factors on recent orchestral repertoires—with the exception of our NYC variable. For the sake of parsimony, we do not include these consistently insignificant variables in Tables 10.3 and 10.4. This is not to say that community context has no relevance for the operation and programming of orchestras, but rather it has little to offer in explaining the specific types of programming considered in these two tables. Second, we find that organizational age has no bearing on the programming choices of large orchestras, but it does play out in various ways for small orchestras. Thus, we only include it in Table 10.4.

Table 10.3 shows a number of factors that significantly predict the performance of both living and dead composers. The explanatory power it contains compares favorably to previous studies—with models explaining some 17 to 42 percent of the variation. Consistent with predictions regarding the importance of a central city for innovation (DiMaggio and Stenberg 1985b; O'Hagan and Neligan 2005), large orchestras located in the New York metropolitan area are distinctive in featuring a higher percentage of living composers. However, being located in NYC has no significant bearing on any other programming choice—including the percentage of

Table 10.3   OLS Regression on the Repertoire Choices of Large US Orchestras, 2005–2006

	Percentage of living composers	*Percentage of pre- 18th-century composers*	*Percentage of 18th-century-composers*	*Percentage of 19th-century composers*	*Percentage of 20th-century composers*
Community context:					
NYC locale	.290*	.219	-.001	-.085	.066
Organizational attributes:					
Productivity (# of pieces)	-.720**	.225	.416**	-.047	-.515**
Programming Strategies:					
Conformity (large Orchs.)	-.691**	-.240	-.058	.548**	-.538**
Specialization	-.257*	-.086	.721**	-.539**	-.270*
Premieres	.141	-.354**	-.121	.190	-.011
Miscellany	-.134	.015	-.040	.194*	-.182
Number of Orchestras	50	50	50	50	50
Adjusted R²	29.3%	24.8%	42.1%	41.9%	16.7%

$p < .05;$ *$p < .01$** (one-tailed tests)
Standardized coefficients shown to facilitate comparison

20th-century composers. The impact of this locale is thus not about the performance of relatively recent music composed by the dead and living (e.g., Copland and Corigliano), but instead it is specifically about the performance of music by the living. This is consistent with the view of New York City as a vibrant and up-to-the-minute scene for serious music (see Gilmore 1987, 1988; Oja 2000). But this view is complicated by the finding that large, rather than small, orchestras are conduits for this scene: The NYC variable, like all the other context variables, has no significant bearing on the programming choices of the small orchestras (see Table 10.4).

While one organizational attribute (age) is insignificant for large orchestras, another one (productivity) shows palpable effects in Table 10.3. In fact, the standardized coefficient (–.720) indicates that productivity has the strongest impact: The more performances a large orchestra offers during the season, the less it features the music of living composers. Looking to the right of the table (the–.515 coefficient), it is clear that increased productivity also dampens the performance of 20th-century composers (both living and dead)—indicating that productivity moves large orchestras away from contemporary works, in general, and toward 18th-century composers, as shown by the .416 coefficient in column 3.

Table 10.3 also shows the utility of heeding program strategies. As large orchestras make programming choices that conform with the choices of their counterparts, that leads them away from both living and 20th-century composers, as shown by the negative coefficients in the first (−.691) and last (−.538) columns. Meanwhile, increasing conformity among large orchestras leads them toward relatively more performances of 19th-century composers, as shown by the positive coefficient in the fourth column (.548). If this conformity is a sign of adhering to field-wide expectations, as DiMaggio and Stenberg (1985b) suggest, those expectations are clearly concentrated on the past for large orchestras—although not to the extent that it is for small orchestras (see below). The large orchestras are not as specialized as their small counterparts (see Table 10.2). Nevertheless, to the extent that they do focus on particular composers in their programming, that too pushes them away from living composers, as shown by the significant coefficient of−.257. Interestingly enough, increasing specialization also reduces the relative number of performances they give to both 20th- *and* 19th-century composers (see the coefficients of−.270 and−.539, respectively). Instead, as the coefficient in the third column shows (.721), specialization for these large orchestras entails a greater share of 18th-century composers—celebrating the likes of Bach, Beethoven, Handel, Haydn, and Mozart. The remaining strategies have no significant relationship with the percentage of living composers performed, but they are revealing in other ways. A rising number of premieres, be they national or world, does not boost performances for recent music, but it does work against the already limited share of performances that large orchestras devote to the oldest group of composers (see−.354 in column 2; see also Table 10.2). Meanwhile, the use of excerpts and snippets seems to be a way that large orchestras can bolster their emphasis on 19th-century composers (see the .194 coefficient in column 4).

Whereas Table 10.2 shows that small orchestras are quite varied in their programming choices, Table 10.4 shows that organizational attributes and programming strategies do fairly well in accounting for that variety—as shown by adjusted R^2s that range from 17 to 43 percent. While age has no relevance for whether they perform living composers, those small orchestras that are older do feature a great proportion of 19th-century composers (.163 in column 4) and a lesser proportion of pre-18th- and 18th-century composers (−.116 and−.157, respectively). Like their large counterparts, increased productivity among small orchestras reduces the share of performances given to living composers (−.180 in column 1) and 20th-century composers (−.211 in column 5). However, its effects are somewhat more consistent for this group—with rising productivity stimulating the percentage of performances devoted to the composers of the distant past—both pre-18th- and

Table 10.4   OLS Regression on the Repertoire Choices of Small US Orchestras, 2005–2006

	Percentage of living composers	Percentage of pre- 18th-century composers	Percentage of 18th-century composers	Percentage of 19th-century composers	Percentage of 20th-century composers
Organizational Attributes					
Univ/College Orchestras	-.048	.093	.105*	-.033	-.073
Youth Orchestras	-.008	.063	-.099*	.111*	-.024
Age	.058	-.116*	-.157**	.163**	.001
Productivity (# of Pieces)	-.180**	.432**	.464**	-.273**	-.211**
Programming Strategies:					
Conformity (all Orchs.)	-.535**	-.185**	.490**	.118*	-.495**
Specialization	.294**	.206**	.259**	-.355**	-.057
Premieres	-.259**	-.095	.085	-.192**	.132*
Miscellany	-.059	-.146**	-.035	.081	-.029
Number of Orchestras	257	257	257	257	257
Adjusted R²	42.9%	15.7%	40.2%	16.6%	27.0%

p< .05;*p< .01** (one-tailed tests)
Standardized coefficients shown to facilitate comparison. We are missing information on the age of six orchestras—hence, the N is 257, not 263.

18th-century (.432 and .464, respectively), while restricting this percentage for all composers who come after the 18th century. As for autonomy from the market—captured by those orchestras embedded in institutions of higher education, as well as those for amateur youth—it is not associated with innovation. In fact, neither type of orchestra has a significantly higher share of performances devoted to living composers, let alone to 20th-century composers. Instead, university orchestras emphasize a higher share of 18th-century composers (.105), whereas youth orchestras gravitate toward 19th-century composers (.111) and away from 18th-century composers (–.099). Perhaps the educational mission of these orchestras matters more than their autonomy from the market—with both emphasizing the classics for instructional purposes (see Arian 1971).[4] Of course, lacking any detailed information on non-earned income for both large and small orchestras, the present results are far from definitive in terms of market autonomy.

Programming strategies prove to be important predictors for small orchestras as well. To the extent that they conform to the choices of all other orchestras, that works against the share of performances that they provide for living composers (–.535 in column 1) and 20th-century composers (–.495 in column 5)—as well as for 'ancient' composers (–.185 in column 2). Instead, their conformity means that they offer a large share of those classics at the core of the field—the composers of the 18th and 19th centuries (.490 and .118, respectively). However, small orchestras are distinct from large orchestras in terms of their various types of specialization. This is particularly important for living composers—as specialization by small orchestras leads them to perform a greater share of those individuals (.294 in column 1). That is not the only type of specialization: When some small orchestras emphasize a limited range of composers, that can also be associated with either a greater share of 18th-century composers (.259 in column 3) or of pre-18th-century composers (.206 in column 2). Regarding the latter, small orchestras are more involved in the music of these ancient composers than the large orchestras, so their specialization is particularly important for that group of composers (see Table 10.2). Meanwhile, specialization has no impact on the performance of 20th-century composers. The latter group is aided, however, by premiere strategies among small orchestras—with a rising number of national/world premieres leading to a greater share of performances afforded 20th-century composers, in general, and living composers in particular (.132 and .259, respectively). The use of the premier strategy, in turn, takes performances away from 19th-century composers (–.192 in column 4), whereas the use of excerpts and other miscellany take performances away from the composers of the most distant past (–.146 in column 2).

CONCLUSIONS

There is no shortage of writings about individual composers. Those texts—which include (auto)biographies, academic and journalistic articles, and encyclopedia entries—give important insights into the trajectories of their lives and, and as a result, give some sense of how they respectively navigated their creative careers. While important and instructive resources, such writings run two risks. First, they often focus on those composers who are deemed important in some form or fashion—be it aesthetically, critically, and/or historically. Consequently, they can give a perspective on creative careers that underemphasize the challenges that prevent many from becoming novice professionals or that prevent movement into stages of being established and well-established professionals (Braden 2009; Craig and Dubois 2010; Menger 1999). Second, those writings on individual composers can sometimes gloss over the supra-individual factors that are at play in the broader field—such as classifications that favor a particular type of creator (e.g., the 'classic') and the collective enactment of those classifications by important intermediaries (Allen and Lincoln 2004; DeNora 1991; Roy and Dowd 2010; Schmutz 2005).

We offer this chapter not as a replacement for biographies and other writings on composers—but as a complement. In doing so, we seek to highlight how particular intermediaries can provide tremendous opportunities for some and extremely limited ones for others, examining the repertoires of 313 American orchestras during the 2005–2006 season. Given the historical classification of 'classics' in this field, these orchestras tend to favor deceased composers overwhelmingly. Indeed, there is a tremendous convergence among both large and small orchestras in terms of programming choices; the more that a particular orchestra adheres to such collective choices, the greater the share of performances that it devotes to either 19th-century composers (large orchestra) or to 18th- and 19th-century composers (small orchestras). For orchestras of both sizes, such conformity also results in a smaller share of performances given to composers of the recent past (the 20th century) and to those who are still alive. A similar pattern occurs in terms of productivity. As both small and orchestras expand the number of pieces that they perform, the additional numbers benefit the performance of 18th-century composers (large orchestras) or pre-18th- and 18th-century performers (small orchestras). Meanwhile, for orchestras of both sizes, such enhanced productivity actually dampens the share of performances devoted to living composers. These results reveal the zero-sum competition that can occur between living and dead composers—with orchestral resources flowing to well-established composers of the past at the expense of living composers. Small wonder, then, that 313 living composers account for some 12 percent of all performances during 2005–2006, whereas 326 dead composers account for 88 percent.

While the orchestral field as a whole may seem completely aligned against the interests of living composers, our analysis reveals factors that could help novice and established composers become well established, which we summarize in terms of suggestions. Regarding location, there is no particular region of the country that is particularly conducive to the orchestral performance of living composers nor are bigger cities superior to small cities in this regard. The one exception is that New York City is more receptive to living composers than any other place in the US—most notably, the three large orchestras that are located in that metro area. Getting their recognition would be particularly beneficial. As for large orchestras outside of the NYC metro area, living composers should approach those that perform relatively few works and that proclaim a distinctive approach that diverges from the common offerings of other major orchestras. Other than such large orchestras, certain types of small orchestras are especially amenable to contemporary music—and it does not matter whether they are located within or beyond New York City. What does matter is that they too pursue a mission of distinctive programming, that they specialize in contemporary music, and that they have a healthy number of national and world premieres. Finding a small orchestra that does all three is especially useful.

Yet even if living composers follow all these suggestions, there still is the well-known issue of repeat performances. Most of the living composers enjoyed only one performance during the 2005–2006 season. Here, then, is where individual attributes likely come into play. While our focus in this chapter has been on aggregate patterns, we did make mention of certain things that could facilitate multiple performances—including the securing of critical accolades and crucial connections within the orchestral field and beyond (Allen and Lincoln 2004; Schmutz 2005; see Jones, Chapter 7, this volume; Lincoln and Allen, Chapter 5, this volume). Of course, such attributes as gender, race, and nationality can matter greatly (Braden 2009; Roy and Dowd 2010; see Eikhof et al., Chapter 3, this volume; Wagner, Chapter 9, this volume). For instance, the majority of US orchestral performances from 1842 to 1969 (93 percent; Dowd 2011)—as well as during the 2005–2006 season (84%)—were devoted to composers from beyond the US. Moreover, living composers associated with universities may experience different career opportunities and trajectories than do those without an academic post (see Gilmore 1987, 1988) The next phase of this project, then, will address that type of interplay between orchestras and composers—noting which types of living composers are most likely to move beyond the single performance. Until then, we encourage consideration of how creative careers are not only shaped by what individual creators do during the course of their lives but also by what others do with the works during and beyond the lives of these creators.[5]

NOTES

1. Flanagan (2008) notes that orchestras can fail to report in a given year when undergoing 'extraordinary circumstances' (e.g., labor difficulties or management change).
2. One important study does gain access to financial information contained in confidential LAO reports (Flanagan 2008). However, it only has that information for the large orchestras and it lacks the repertoire data.
3. This discussion partly draws on the personal webpages of the composers. Half of the living composers in our dataset have personal webpages.
4. There are examples of youth and university orchestras performing the music of living composers. So, it is not necessarily beyond their technical abilities to do so (e.g., Jeffri 2008; Smith 1983).
5. We thank the League of American Orchestras for provision of their repertoire data and Rob O'Reilly for his assistance on data management. For helpful comments and suggestions, we thank Flemming Agersnap, Trine Bille, Doris Ruth Eikhof, Sonal Nalkur, Bill Roy, and participants in the Careers in Creative Industries Conference. Special thanks go to Chris Mathieu for all he has done.

REFERENCES

Allen, M. P., and A. E. Lincoln. 2004. "Critical Discourse and the Cultural Consecration of American Films." *Social Forces* 82: 871–94.

Arian, P. 1971. *Bach, Beethoven, and Bureaucracy.* Tuscaloosa: University of Alabama Press.

Baker, W. E., and R. R. Faulkner. 1991. "Role as Resource in the Hollywood Film Industry." *American Journal of Sociology* 97: 279–309.

Bick, S. 2005. "'Of Mice and Men.'" *American Music* 23: 426–72.

Bishops, P. J. 2005. Patronage of Composers in the United States. MA Thesis; College of Fine Arts, Boston University.

Blau, J. 1989. The Shape of Culture. Cambridge, UK: Cambridge University Press.

Boerner, S. 2004. "Artistic Quality in an Opera Company." *Nonprofit Management & Leadership* 14: 425–36.

Bourdieu, P. 1984. *Distinction.* Cambridge, MA: Harvard University Press.

Braden, L. 2009. "From the Armory to Academia." *Poetics* 37: 439–55.

Burkholder, P. J. 2006. "The Twentieth Century and the Orchestra as Museum." In *The Orchestra*, edited by J. Peyser, 409–32. Milwaukee: Hal Leonard.

Cameron, C. M. 1996. *Dialectics in the Arts.* Westport, CT: Praeger.

Castaner, X., and L. Campos. 2002. "The Determinants of Artistic Innovation: Bringing in the Role of Organizations." *Journal of Cultural Economics* 26: 29–52.

Copland, A. 1933. "The Composer in America, 1923–1933." *Modern Music* 10:87–92.

Copland, A. 1963. *Copland on Music.* New York: W.W. Norton.

Corse, S. M., and M. D. Griffin. 1997. "Cultural Valorization and African American Literary History." *Sociological Forum* 12: 173–203.

Craig, A., and S. Dubois. 2010. "Between Art and Money." *Poetics* 38: 441–60.

Craven, R. R. 1986. *Symphony Orchestras of the United States.* New York: Greenwood.

DeNora, T. 1991. "Musical Patronage and Social Change in Beethoven's Vienna." *American Journal of Sociology* 97: 310–46.

DiMaggio, P. 1982. "Cultural Entrepreneurship in Nineteenth-Century Boston." *Media, Culture & Society* 4: 33–55 and 303–22.

DiMaggio, P. 1992. "Cultural Boundaries and Structural Change." In *Cultivating Differences*, edited by M. Lamont and M. Fournier, 21–57. Chicago: University of Chicago Press.

DiMaggio, P. 2006. "Nonprofit Organizations and the Intersectoral Division of Labor in the Arts." In *The Nonprofit Sector*, edited by W. W. Powell and R. Steinberg, 432–61. New Haven, CT: Yale University Press.

DiMaggio, P., and K. Stenberg. 1985a. "Conformity and Diversity in the American Regional Stage." In *Art, Ideology and Politics*, edited by J. Balfe and M. Wyszomirski, 116–40. New York: Praeger.

DiMaggio, P., and K. Stenberg. 1985b. "Why Do Some Theatres Innovate More Than Others?" *Poetics* 14: 107–22.

DiMaggio, P., and M. Useem. 1978. "Social Class and Arts Consumption." *Theory & Society* 78: 141–60.

Dowd, T. J. 2004. "Concentration and Diversity Revisited." *Social Forces* 82: 1411–55.

Dowd, T. J. 2011. "The Production and Producers of Lifestyles." *Kölner Zeitschrift fur Soziologie und Sozialpsychologie* Special Issue 51.

Dowd, T. J., K. Liddle, K. Lupo, and A. Borden. 2002. "Organizing the Musical Canon." *Poetics* 30: 35–61.

Dowd, T. J., K. Liddle, & J. Nelson. 2004. "Music Festivals as Scenes." In *Music Scenes*, edited by A. Bennett and R. A. Peterson, 149–67. Nashville: Vanderbilt University Press.

Faulkner, R. R. 1983. *Music on Demand.* New Brunswick, NJ: Transaction Press.

Felton, M. V. 1978. "The Economics of the Creative Arts." *Journal of Cultural Economics* 2: 41.

Flanagan, R. J. 2008. *The Economic Environment of American Symphony Orchestras*. Report to Andrew W. Mellon Foundation. http://www.gsb.stanford.edu/news/packages/pdf/Flanagan.pdf

Gilmore, S. 1987. "Coordination and Convention." *Symbolic Interaction* 10: 209–27.

Gilmore, S. 1988. "Schools of Activity and Innovation." *Sociological Quarterly* 29: 203–19.

Gilmore, S. 1993. "Tradition and Novelty in Concert Programming." *Sociological Forum* 8: 221–42.

Glynn, M. A. 2002. "Chord and Discord." *Poetics* 30: 63–85.

Hanson, H. 1951. *Music in Contemporary Civilization*. Lincoln: University of Nebraska Press.

Hart, P. 1973. *Orpheus in the New World*. New York: W. W. Norton.

Heilbrun, J. 2001. "Empirical Evidence of a Decline in Repertory Diversity among American Opera Companies 1991/92 to 1997/98." *Journal of Cultural Economics* 25: 63–72.

Heilbrun, J. 2004. "The Symphony Orchestra Repertoire." *Journal of Arts Management, Law and Society* 34: 151–55.

Jeffri, J. 2008. *Taking Note—A Study of Composers and New Music Activity in the United States*. New York: Research Center for Culture and the Arts.

Jeffri, J., D. D. Heckathorn, and M. W. Spiller. 2011. "Painting Your Life:." *Poetics* 39: 19–43.

Khodyakov, D. M. 2007. "The Complexity of Trust-Control Relationships in Creative Organizations." *Social Forces* 86: 1–22.

Kremp, P.-A. 2010. "Innovation and Selection." *Social Forces* 88: 1051–82.

League of American Orchestras. 2011. "About the League." http://www.americanorchestras.org/about_the_league.html

Maitlis, S., and T. B. Lawrence. 2003. "Orchestral Manoeuvres in the Dark." *Journal of Management Studies* 40: 109–39.

Martorella, R. 1977. "The Relationship between Box Office and Repertoire." *Sociological Quarterly* 18: 354–36.

Martorella, R. 1985. *The Sociology of Opera*. New York: Praeger.

Menger, P.-M. 1999. "Artistic Labor Markets and Careers." *Annual Review of Sociology* 25: 541–74.

Mueller, J. H. 1951. *The American Symphony Orchestra*. Westport, CT: Greenwood Press.

Nash, D. 1970. "Challenge and Response in the American Composer's Career." In *The Sociology of Art and Literature*, edited by M. Albrecht, 256–65. London: Duckworth.

Neter, J., W. Wasserman, and M. J. Kutner. 1983. *Applied Linear Regression Models*. Homewood, IL: Richard D. Irwin.

O'Hagan, J., and A. Neligan. 2005. "State Subsidies and Repertoire Conventionality in the Non-Profit English Theatre Sector." *Journal of Cultural Economics* 29: 35–57.

Oja, C. 2000. *Making Music Modern*. New York: Oxford University Press.

Peterson, R. A.. and G. Rossman. 2008. "Changing Arts Audiences." In *Engaging Art*, edited by S. J. Tepper and B, Ivey, 307–342. New York: Routledge.

Pierce, J. L. 2000. "Programmatic Risk-Taking by American Opera Companies." *Journal of Cultural Economics* 24: 45–63.

Roy, W. G., and T. J. Dowd. 2010. "What Is Sociological about Music?" *Annual Review of Sociology* 36: 183–203.

Schmutz, V. 2005. "Retrospective Cultural Consecration in Popular Music." *American Behavioral Scientist* 48: 1510–23.

Scholz, L. B. 2001. "Across the Private Policymaking Process: The Case of the American Symphony Orchestra League and Americanizing the American Orchestra." *Journal of Arts Management, Law and Society* 31: 137–48.

Schuller, G. 1962. "American Performance and New Music." *Perspectives of New Music* 1: 1–8.

Smith, W. A. 1983. "Leopold Stokowski." *American Music* 1: 23–37.

Tawa, N. E. 1984. *Serenading the Reluctant Eagle*. New York: Schirmer.

Weber, W. 2001. "From Miscellany to Homogeneity in Concert Programming." *Poetics* 29: 125–34.

Zappa, F. 1989. *The Real Frank Zappa Book*. New York: Poseidon Press.

Zuckerman, E. W., T.-Y. Kim, K. Ukwana, and J. von Rittmann. 2003. "Robust Identities or Nonentities." *American Journal of Sociology* 108: 1018–74.

Part V
Visual Arts and Fashion Design

11 Unpacking Unsuccess
Sociocognitive Barriers to Objective Career Success for French Outsider Artists

Jean Pralong, Anne Gombault, Françoise Liot, Jean-Yves Agard, and Catherine Morel

INTRODUCTION

Contemporary art worlds are full of unsuccessful outsiders (Becker 1963, 1982). Few artists achieve objective success compared with the mass who attempt it. Others experience difficult professional and personal conditions in their lives. While artists' career success has been widely investigated from economic and sociological points of view, few studies have focused on unsuccessful artists and barriers to their success. Unsuccessful visual artists are defined here as those artists who are not able to value their work despite a high level of personal investment in the practice of their art. They are on the periphery of the art worlds; they are not able to enter any structured world, but nor are they successful in producing a new world for themselves. While they are not truly at the margins of society, in the sense that they are quite a long way from those we would generally call the outcasts of society, even though they may be living in precarious situations, they have nevertheless become sidetracked from the contemporary art worlds, and this can basically be defined as a characteristic of intra-artistic deviance. In 2009 and 2010, a broad qualitative action-research project investigating unsuccessful visual artists' careers was conducted in a French region. The general research question was: what are the barriers to success for these artists? This chapter presents results from this research, focusing on specific sociocognitive barriers. The theoretical framework is built around a multi-disciplinary literature overview combining boundaryless career framework with the sociological 'art worlds' perspective.

Generally, career success is objective and subjective (Boudreau et al. 2001, 25–50). The literature in the creative field tends to focus on untypical career outcomes: intrinsic interest in work, search for autonomy, challenge, passionate commitment. Subjective, psychological success, which comes in many forms and can be defined as a 'feeling of pride and personal accomplishment that comes from achieving one's most important goals in life' (Hall 1996), appears as the key reward. Objective success indicators such as compensation, progression, and job security, which for an artist correspond to gaining recognition for his art (Bowness 1989; Moulin 1992) and making a living from it, would be less relevant (Bridgstock 2008a; Caves 2000; Throsby 1994; Throsby and Hollister 2003) to successful career development. The overriding theme of our chapter is to focus specifically on objective unsuccess in an artist's career as the population observed in the study is much more concerned with objective than subjective success (i.e., with the fact that they do not gain recognition from the art worlds for their art and do not make their living from it).

THEORETICAL FRAMEWORK: SHAPING OBJECTIVE UNSUCCESS IN VISUAL ARTISTS' CAREERS

Career theory and sociology of arts literature have documented career success. Both frameworks are reviewed here and combined in order to construct the general theoretical framework mobilized to interpret empirical data about barriers to objective career success for visual artists. Boundaryless careers demonstrate the relevance of project enactment to achieve success and provide the notion of frame of reference (Weick 1995). Sociology of arts shows that artists have to cope with art worlds, a hybrid paradoxical environment combining stable conventions and entrepreneurial requirements.

Career Enactment and Career Frame of Reference

Since the 1990s, a stream of organizational changes in industry has led to major changes in employment relations. Weakened organizations are unable to set boundaries for career paths (Arthur and Rousseau 1996). Careers are driven by projects rather than by bureaucratic rules. This has led to major theoretical changes in career theory. The definition of success and the process to achieve it have changed. Individual behavior now has a dramatic influence. Career success should be defined in subjective rather than in objective terms. Because there are no organizational rules to put boundaries on careers, individuals have to build their own paths according to personal, subjective rules. These idiosyncratic rules define career success and the way to achieve it. Within such boundaryless, post-organizational paths, career success (Arthur et al. 2005) derives from an individual's ability to become an entrepreneur of the self and to enact his/ her environment (Littleton et al. 2000; Weick 1995, 1996). DeFillippi and Arthur (1994) claim that individuals should learn how to accumulate portfolio skills and enact them into new projects. This enactment process is key to understanding career success and unsuccess (Littleton et al. 2000). Weick (2007) notoriously illustrates what enactment is with the story of an incident during military maneuvers in Switzerland. The reconnaissance unit of a small Hungarian detachment was sent into an unexplored icy area of the Alps. After two days of uninterrupted snow-storms, the unit was still missing and was obviously lost. Finally, on the third day, the unit returned. How had they been able to find their way back in unknown territory? One of them had finally found a map in his pocket and was able to use it to find the way. However, the Lieutenant of the detachment finally discovered that this was a map of the Pyrenees, not a map of the Alps, and so this happy but astonishing ending raises the possibility that, in a weak environment, any map will do. The more ambiguous the situation, the weaker the environment, the fewer individuals are able to interpret it. Ambiguity leads to a myriad of personal interpretations and enactment opportunities. Once they begin to act, people generate tangible outcomes and enact what occurs and what should be done next. Action creates environment. Finally, enactment provides self-fulfilling prophecies. When extended to career success, Weick's anecdote means that individuals enact the situations and understandings of their environment and of their own dispositions and backgrounds. Improvisation and 'making do' are the order of the day. People spend less time in planning than in acting and developing projects. This ongoing interaction generates histories, project opportunities, and the 'interminable series of experiments and explorations' that characterize new careers (Hall 1976). However, enactment is a process rooted in the cognitive properties of individuals. Enacted representations of the environment are memorized as a frame of reference (Weick 1995). Individuals must constantly use such frames to make sense of further situations. The notion of a career frame of reference describes the frames that are involved in career and vocational behavior.

Art Worlds as a Complex Dual Organizational Context to Develop Artists' Careers

The creative industries (or new cultural economy) paradigm (Caves 2000; Throsby 2001), which observes the growing link between art and business and its economic impact, ironically emphasizes the romantic 'cultural ideology' (Chiapello 1998) that artists' career success is not defined by career standards, and even goes so far as to say—contrary to the romantics—that the artist is isolated from the rest of the *bourgeois* society. In this new careers approach, there are no stable organizational environments or hierarchical progression to constrain artists' careers in art worlds. They are directly exposed to markets in an unpredictable economy: because artistic creation produces only prototypes, it is impossible to predict customer reaction. Caves (2000) described this property of artistic markets as the 'nobody knows (anything)' property, which makes the artistic career a highly risky one. In the same way, Menger (2001, 2003, 2009) focuses on the high level of uncertainty in which an artist has to work in order to succeed and develop a career. Artists' career environments seem weak because there is not really an organizational structure to moderate the effects of these unpredictable art markets. Entrepreneurship, self-employment, and employment in small-to-medium sized organizations are common features of their work. In such contexts, stable employment and traditional hierarchical progression are virtually impossible (Bridgstock 2005). From one period to another, artists cross the traditional boundaries between jobs: the traditional rules of promotion and upward mobility disappear. Artists' careers unfold in networks rather than in organizations. Thus, artists' career development relies first and foremost on individual responsibility and work (Menger 2009). Artists must make decisions by themselves about opportunities to be constructed or career tactics to be developed (O'Mahoney and Bechky 2006). Such environments and characteristics seem to be common to most post-industrial paths. In recognition of this new aspect that careers are acquiring, a new literature has emerged. Not everyone's career is 'boundaryless,' but artists' careers are perfect examples of 'new careers' (Arthur and Rousseau, 1996; DeFillippi and Arthur 1994), which involve creativity, innovation, and renewal. Artists have to cope with highly competitive, selective, and "weak environments" (Weick and Berlinger 1989). Their careers depend dramatically on the tactics that they develop. The oversupply of artists in a tight market generates intense competition where only the few most skilled artists will be successful (Bridgstock 2008b; Menger 2009). Singular trajectories no longer characterize only artistic excellence (Heinich 1998) but also diverse and renewable skills and a strong adaptability (Menger 2009) as this new type of success unfolds through the discontinuity of professional paths.

However, far away from the romantic 'cultural ideology' (i.e., 'art for art's sake' with its antagonism toward the rest of the capitalist *bourgeois* society) (Caves 2000; Chiapello 1998) and from this boundaryless career trend, sociological literature has clearly demonstrated that artists' careers are not made only from individual talents and skills. They are embedded in socially constructed contexts, defined by Becker (1982) as 'art worlds.' In Becker's modern perspective of creation, art is a collective product. Art worlds do not result from the activity of a single artist but from the coordinated work of a social network of cooperating actors playing various roles (artists, collectors, patrons, institutions, critics, media, amateurs, general public, etc.), cooperating through social conventions—or game rules. These shared conventions are embodied in knowledge, techniques, working practices, and categories of perception. Conventions arise within an art world, known only to those on the inside, and knowledge of these conventions defines its outer borders. All artists have to cope with an art world, although there are different types. Even if they tend toward conservatism, art worlds are in constant change, sometimes faster, sometimes slower. These changes happen when revolutionary outsiders challenge the conventions of the art worlds and push at new ones, thus becoming the 'avant-garde' (Becker 1963, 1982). In spite of their informal intra-organizational hierarchies, 'art worlds' are artistic communities that assess art works and artists' creativity, and this recognition mechanism is essential in artists' careers (Bowness 1989; Heinich 1998). Art worlds spend a lot of time deciding what is or is not art and fighting over this question. Bourdieu (1977) clarified this with his analysis that artists are fighting for the limited resources of the art world. So, in order to build their projects, artists need to be aware of the influence of structural boundaries. Agents of art worlds—art galleries, critics, collectors, museums, media, audiences, –and so on—play an essential role in helping artists with this awareness and defining where boundaries are; hence, it is important that artists should be close to the agents.

Visual Artists' Objective Career Success or Unsuccess

On the one hand, like a boundaryless careerist, contemporary artists evolve more and more through temporary, self-designed, and short-lived projects (Heinich 1998), projects that either have to develop within the existing art worlds or develop a new one. On the other hand, recognizing the influence of art worlds, actors, and conventions, even if it is in order to break through them, is a key to success in artists' careers (Becker 1982; Bowness 1989; Heinich 1998; Menger 2003; Moulin 1992). Art worlds seem weak and driven by unpredictable markets, but they are in fact highly structured by major institutions and actors (various agents, etc.) In summary, artists have to cope with this paradox (i.e., to enact their careers through temporary projects and self-designed organizations within a highly structured industry).

Although it is undeniable that there are contextual obstacles to a tight market, the main barriers lie in the artists' inability to achieve a clear vision of the context, and this is what often happens in the absence of any clear guidelines as to what an artist's career path and skills should be (Liot 2009). Not only is there no career type, but in addition the art worlds have no clearly defined contours despite the fact that the conventions that regulate them are strong indeed—which makes it particularly difficult to construct a professional identity. For some artists, for example, it is not entirely obvious that a salon of amateurs is not a professional workplace given that one can sell one's work there. The very nature of the skills an artist needs is vague, whether for producing works or for the accompanying knowledge required. Thus, success in artistic careers depends on how artists understand and accept art worlds and their specific firm and tacit rules, including the entrepreneurial system. Contemporary visual artists' career successes unfold through self-designed projects in weak yet highly socially structured art worlds. Even in this complex dual environment, however, patterns of competencies, progression, and behaviors are necessary. Objective career success comes from the capacity to develop sustainable projects in such worlds.

METHODOLOGY: INVESTIGATING ARTISTS' CAREER UNSUCCESS IN A FRENCH REGION

Research Goal and Question

This chapter presents the first step in a wider program of innovative action-research conducted in Aquitaine, a French region, during fall 2009. Almost 100 visual artists participated over three months in a 24-hour training program organized by the Arts, Culture, and Management in Europe Chair of the BEM Bordeaux Management School. They were all volunteers for this career development training, funded by the regional authority, which wanted to help these unsuccessful artists market their art production and so develop their careers. The artists had been identified as unsuccessful by the French employment services according to the employment administration criteria: employment seekers or those receiving the social integration minimum income, declaring themselves to be professional artists, and with some form of production to back this up. This training program was an excellent opportunity for the research team to observe these art world outsiders in order to better understand their barriers to career success. Our research goals were to describe and analyze artists' objective unsuccess and the content of their career frame of reference. Objective career success implies the individual's ability to enact an understanding of events, recognize opportunities, and produce appropriate behavior. The career frame of reference is involved in this process. So we ask: What are the career frames of reference of unsuccessful artists?

Data Production

According to a comprehensive goal, our work is based on an empirical qualitative study, using an anthropological approach, to carry out an in-depth investigation over a two-year period. The first phase of this specific longitudinal research was to 'densely describe' (Geertz 1973) artists' barriers to objective success in an identified, stable group of individuals involved in regular voluntary social interactions in specific locuses (i.e., group of artists in the Aquitaine region (France) taking part in the training program).

Field access was achieved via triangulated paths before, during, and after the training sessions: focus groups, participant observations, immersion in the artists' context of actions.

Four group interviews of 10 artists each were organized as preparation before the training began. A purposive sample of interviewees was designed.

The recruitment process, based on expert advice, included three main categories of artists with a specific set of problems and preoccupations according
to the sociology of the Aquitaine region (Liot 2004): urban artists from the
Bordeaux area (one group), peri-urban artists from the greater Bordeaux area
(one group), and rural artists from other parts of the Aquitaine region such
as Dordogne and Landes (two groups). All group interviews were composed
of outsider visual artists from a variety of disciplines (painting, photo, video,
sculpture, poetry, theatre, storytelling, dance). Artists from so many different
art forms could be aggregated as they were all outsiders confronting the same
situation of objective unsuccess. Ages ranged from young adults to artists in
their 50s. Interviews were held in an environment that was supposedly non-
hostile for the artists (i.e., art galleries, an art collective, and a Bordeaux art
and media university in the heart of an arts district). Three researchers carried out the group interviews: one as main group interviewer (anthropologist),
one as secondary interviewer (sociologist), and one as note-taker (management scientist). In the meantime, each group interview was filmed and sound
recorded *in extenso*. Each interview lasted about two hours, starting with the
artists describing their 'professional expectations.' Next, three main conversa-
tion topics were launched to encourage each individual to speak freely:

- *As artists, tell us something about your professional aspirations.*
- *Tell us about what has held you back in your career path toward
  becoming an artist.*
- *Tell us about what has helped you in your career path toward becoming an artist.*

Their career frame of reference was investigated next, with questions about
what could 'impede' and 'favor' artists' careers. Interviewers took the opportunity to reformulate and interact to ensure that all participants expressed
their views. An informal meeting followed the group interviews. These
moments of deep exchanges and observation were also used as sources for
narratives and facts for an understanding of the cross-contexts.

In situ participant observations of the volunteer artists took place during
the training sessions, which means that observation started in the socialization period preceding the training time (informal welcome phase) and continued throughout the training time (lectures, debates, case studies, etc.), the
breaks, and during the group arts marketing projects proposed as 'action-
oriented' participative assignments. Seven projects were carried out and
observed, including '1 *Château for 1 Artist*' (art exhibitions open to large
audiences sponsored by the wineries of the area during the summer season)
or '*Portraits of Aquitaine Artists*' (self-marketing communication project
about artists in the city) and other projects.

Deep immersion took place in the artists' areas of activity (i.e. exhibitions, happenings, artistic events, mail exchanges, and live interactions
with the training session organizers [researchers]). This involved multiple

meetings, with significant periods spent with the artists in professional and social (formal and informal) exchange situations.

These observation situations were collected in ethnographic reports, with particular care taken in describing the following elements: actors, sites, close and wider surroundings, material organization, interferences, and sequence of events. The actors' perceived emotional states, body language, attitudes, and posture were also noted when possible.

Content Analysis and Validation

The analysis method used was a classical thematic content analysis designed as a qualitative analysis of qualitative data. This technique was initiated at a first empirical level to reduce the amount of data, and an empirical thematic dictionary was compiled. The collected data were categorized into themes. This categorization process was all the richer because the data obtained came from diverse sources of group interviews, participant observations, and immersion in the artists' context of action. Using abductive logic, a theoretical content analysis of these empirically reduced data was started in order to create the theoretical dictionary. This step was particularly original and rich due to the high level of cross-disciplinarity in the backgrounds of the researchers, who were all from different disciplines (i.e., psychology, social anthropology, sociology of art, and management sciences [organizational behavior, arts management, and marketing]).

Consequently, due to the specificity and richness of the field and the deep and dense contextual descriptions provided by the data production and analysis methods, the methodology cross-validates the findings from multiple perspectives. The aim was to use these methods to interpret data within a definite context, in the stream of social discourse, leading to far-reaching conclusions, with less likelihood of falsification.

EMPIRICAL RESULTS: OBJECTIVELY OUTSIDE THE ART WORLDS

Using the empirical content analysis, we were able to start compiling an empirical dictionary around the most important categories or themes mentioned by the artists in relation to their careers, their professional paths, and factors that have facilitated and hindered their evolution. A classification of the themes they identified provided a basis for interpretation. These themes describe the career frame of reference of the artists studied.

Uncertainty in a Risky Environment

For these artists, their careers have had to cope primarily with uncertainty. This meta-theme appears as a frame, a context, and a background in all the discourses: uncertainty of creation, uncertainty of incomes, and uncertainty of career. The artist has to find his own unique way, one that matches his specific artistic project and production process. He has to create his own social demand in a highly competitive environment. The famous 'Nobody knows (anything)' property of creative industries as formulated by Caves (2000) is here plainly illustrated.

> A sculptor: *Personally, I think that there're too many artists for the market. There're a profusion of people who are making interesting things, but there's no public.* [. . .] *The problem is that those people, we have them dream, we train them and 80% of them are on RMI* [French minimum social revenue]. *At last year's meeting, everybody was expressing his ill-being* [preparatory meeting for the project], *because they can't make a living. There's not enough market.*
>
> (Focus group extract)

A Quest for Economic Balance

The next most salient theme is the quest by each artist for 'economic balance' in his everyday life. Earning money from artwork is not a required condition for considering oneself to be an artist. Nevertheless, all of them position themselves around this 'economic balance': to sell their art, to have a secondary job, or to live on the social minimum revenue. Many prefer this solution to the constraints of marketing art or of a secondary job: Ordinary work constraints would be an obstacle to creation. Artists' economic adaptability versus their social marginality is at stake here.

A discussion between painters:

> - *I, personally I had a parallel job for 20 years. It's difficult to manage*;
> - *It depends, you cannot generalize. It depends according to the period, The 'Maison des Artistes'* [literally: 'House of the Artists', a structure helping artists to have economical status for their activity], *it is difficult to get into it, to stay with them and to get out of it; because, it is very administrative. You have to comply with a specific frame.*
> - *I, since I understood that I can make a living from my art, I am doing something else, cartoons, wine bottle labels. Personally, nowadays I need this kind of change. It can even be an advantage, because those who only make a living from painting may repeat themselves . . . Here, I've found a rhythm for my life, a way to organize my work.*
> - *It changes everything if you are compelled to create at a specific time of the day.*
>
> (Focus group extract)

Awareness of Key Success Factors in Art Worlds

Even in a difficult situation, artists are well aware of key success factors in art worlds (Becker 1982): reputation, social networks, supply marketing, other technical resources like a space in which to work and spaces to exhibit, access to collectors, donors, and audiences in general. They explain their difficulties perfectly clearly by the fact that they do not have the managerial competency or the financial resources to provide themselves with these key factors. They do not know how to do it and with whom.

> A dancer: *For about 5, 6 years, we have been doing shows for youngsters or very young public. The support: it is ourselves . . . and the main problem is that we don't know how to sell ourselves. We do it very badly, and we can't afford an administrator.*
>
> A visual artist: *During the school of Beaux Arts* [Fine Arts school], *if we had had professors who explained what to do, or what not to do, it would prevent us wasting too much time. Go and see the advisory office for plastic arts, how to build up a book, etc. I learned empirically.*
>
> A painter: *Artists are isolated, they lack everything, critics, agents.*
>
> (Focus group extract)

Outsiders in Search of Recognition

The artists feel excluded from the institutionalized art worlds. They remain on the periphery, as 'outsiders' (Becker 1963). Finally, they all describe a lack of recognition of their work, either by these art institutions, their audiences, or society in general.

> A 'cartoonist': *It is very complex* [public grants for creation] *and we have the impression that the dice are loaded. The impression we have is: that it is not for us!*
>
> A dancer: *There is another obstacle, more sociological, it concerns recognition* [. . .] *you always have to justify yourself, explain what you are doing.*
>
> A visual artist: *Let's have recognition from the institutions! In the group of local communes* [smallest French territorial divisions] *it is the same, they are looking elsewhere for famous people, why should we not have a little share of the local people* [local artists] *as well.*
>
> (Focus group extract)

Agents Wanted

All the artists think that others would achieve more than they can. They need intermediaries, agents, to market and sell their work through fundraising, pricing, promotion, publicity, and audience development. However, the artists explain that they do not have easy access to agents, nor do they know whether this kind of professional really exists in their local environment. They complain extensively about the role of art galleries and their operational rules. For them, galleries are mainly oriented toward the international and national art markets, much more than toward local creations.

> A sculptor: *No, if I had to talk about my professional path, personally it would be to find a broker, an agent who will put me in touch with the few collectors who might be interested. The real problem, it is the connection. With the small amount, a small elite of people who appreciate my work. My only request would be for an agent who would be in touch with people I cannot contact myself.* [. . .] *I introduced myself to Parisian galleries with a book. I made a choice already, but a gallery job does not correspond to my profile. Gallery owners need artists who are continuously producing, they are merchants, consequently they take artists who are producing all the time.* [. . .] *With an agent, it is better.*
>
> An art photographer: *If we, we could create, and someone could deal with all the rest.*
>
> (Focus group extract)

Fatalism or Pragmatism

The main question for these 'unsuccessful artists' is how to move from this position: how to manage art worlds and become an insider. There are two basic attitudes: fatalism and pragmatism.

The fatalists simply observe how impossible it is for them to change their situation, to sell or economically value their artwork. It is too demanding for them, both psychologically and in terms of time consumption. They have clearly understood that art is a market and that they have to cope with it, but this leads to two problems. First, they never thought they would have to take on a business role. They describe their lack of skills and training. Second, and more important, having to cope with art as a market, and artists as a network, is detrimental to their ideas about art and artists. It seems impossible to draw the line and to solve the conflict between art as a creation and art as a business, so they find other solutions. Most rely on minimum social revenue and/or another job as their main source of revenue and/or for some women on their husband's income. For some, even the other job could be difficult to bear. It is perceived as an obstacle to creation or as an unbearable reminder of their failure to get an artistic position. This perception is especially true if the job is in an art organization (e.g., a security guard in a museum). The *fatalists* are the oldest artists in the sample. They have accepted their lack of success.

The pragmatists, on the contrary, regularly set a variety of tactics in motion, even if it is sometimes rather clumsily done. From the one-shot attitude and the everyday 'making do' around various sources of relationships and revenues to proactive behavior: the artist as an entrepreneur, the artist as his own agent or producer, the artist as a simple worker who has to sell his art to survive and who is trying a wide range of means to achieve this. These artists described the range of the hurdles to be climbed in order to be recognized as an important artist by their art world. Artists with this capability were a minority, however, in the groups studied.

> A designer: *I am laying down mark stones. I am going forward; it is all about encounters, things like that that favored my trajectory.* [. . .] *I met someone from Sud-Ouest* [the local leading newspaper in the region], *lucky me, he appreciated my work. An architect contacted me. He's in charge of renovating a Coffee-bar in the square "la Bourse"* [famous up-market square in Bordeaux]. *He is interested in my work. The miracle recipe, I don't know it. I brazen it out; I did not do anything exceptional.*
> A painter: *You pull out a thread and it leads to another.*
> An art photographer: *I, personally, I had financial help for creation from the DRAC* [French State institution promoting culture and art] *which turned into a catalogue. There're institutions, there're networks; you have to find help in order to produce.*
>
> (Focus group extract)

During training, the best evidence of the artists' lack of ability to move and open up a successful path in the art worlds, showing that they were either fatalists or even pragmatists, could be seen through their behavior toward the training environment and the projects. Concerning the training environment, when they actually entered the business school each week over the two-month period, they always behaved like strangers in an ambiguous and a potentially hostile environment. As for the projects, two specific behaviors were observed. First, they had tremendous difficulty in clearly formulating their artistic project in order to produce an action plan to validate it. In particular, they were unable to position their project in the hierarchy or conventions of contemporary art worlds. Even those who had more awareness of their work were all totally unable to imagine any relevant action to market it. Second, when they were offered a project during the training period, ready to go, including funding, they reacted rather timidly.

> *Every session ended with the presentation of a project. These projects systematically put an artist (or groups of artists) in contact with the economic world. First of all, this required involving the artists immediately in putting into action the theoretical points covered and initiating actors from the local economic world to embark on a productive cooperation project with the artists (BEM, agencies, galleries, wine chateaux, etc.). The participating artists, all volunteers, joined these projects alone and sometimes in groups. This transition to a phase of activity, which required commitment, which sometimes meant giving up some time, was never immediate, open and massive. We noted that they needed time to think, to see what the others were doing. The dynamics did not usually get going until the next session, at the instigation of 2 or 3 leaders, and repeated reminders by the organizers or the cultural representatives involved in the session. Given that these projects were very well supervised, with financial support, we were surprised to note a reticence, a lack of daring, even distrust.*
>
> (Training observation report extract)

ANALYSIS AND DISCUSSION: SOCIOCOGNITIVE BARRIERS TO SUCCESS IN THE ART WORLDS

The analysis was conducted with two objectives: to describe the unsuccessful visual artists' career frames of reference, and explore the links between career frame of reference and objective career unsuccess.

Career Frame of Reference and the Art Worlds: Unsuccessful Artists are Aware Outsiders

These empirical data confirmed the most recent observations in the sociology of arts and management literature about artists' careers. In the risky environment in which they evolve, artists have to 'manage uncertainty' (Menger 2009) as they have always had to do. They have to cope with the tacit rules of functioning in a highly institutionalized art market (Becker 1982; Moulin 1992), and if they do not, they remain excluded from it and feel this exclusion strongly. In this context, stable careers are impossible (Bridgstock 2005). However, in spite of their position as contemporary outsiders to the art worlds, they can clearly see what the key success factors for entering this art market are. This awareness marks the recent reconciliation between arts and business logics due to the socioeconomic transformation of these two worlds analyzed by Chiapello (1998). Even precarious artists are no longer in the romantic paradigm of 'art for art's sake' with a strong ideological opposition to management as a '*bourgeois* capitalist tool.' The unsuccessful visual artists observed are clearly aware of the pragmatism required by contemporary art worlds and are looking for ways to manage their own project, accepting the entrepreneurial nature of their activity. As a consequence, they would very much like to be more open minded and more creative to value their work, even if their managerial learning is still not developed. They may have moved beyond the romantic paradigm of pure art versus impure business and market tasks, but the boundaries between art and business still seem insurmountable.

Career Frame of Reference and Objective Career Unsuccess

The frame of reference is the resource that artists use to make sense of their environment and to manage art worlds. This process provides opportunities and empowers individuals or, on the contrary, defines barriers.

All artists in the sample studied were aware of the key factors for success in art worlds, but few seemed to be able to draw pragmatic lines between such goals and action. They frame artwork so that it has an intrinsically double activity, one part being the creation of art works, and the other part being project management and marketing these art works. This split frame is a consequence of the boundaries experienced by unsuccessful artists between art and business. It prevents them from enacting opportunities and developing skills. Their capability (Sen 1999) (i.e., their capacity to act) is limited by this frame. *Fatalists* seem to be the least able to make links between art and business. For them, managing art works as entrepreneurship projects is too demanding. They are simply not able to do it and are not able to find agents to do it for them. They stand back from involvement in any part of business. *Pragmatists* seem to be more able to make links. They have developed a minimal ability to reconcile art as creation and art as business, even though this may often be done in a rather clumsy fashion. Nevertheless, their better capability does not necessarily mean that they will find the right path to evolve successfully.

Unsuccessful artists in our sample frame art worlds in a way that prevents them from applying efficient tactics. Their career frame of reference is unable to lead them to appropriate behaviors. One of their basic mistakes, for instance, is to remain isolated and not to seek out useful actors in the world of art because of their mixed fear of uncertainty, the market, and competitors. Because they are isolated, they are too far away to be assessed, even by insiders in the art worlds, in accordance with the conventions of this world, or to challenge these conventions that are reinforced by the power positions of these insiders through allegiances and the sharing of dominant beliefs. Generally speaking, there is no acculturation of these artists to the conventions of the art worlds, and the strangeness of these worlds is almost total. Nevertheless, cognitive frames have a potential for change and development. Weick (2001) claims that frames may change through reframing or revolution. Pragmatists' frames can luckily be changed through reframing. These artists are actively searching tactics through action, even though their actions may be rather clumsy and have little chance of success. Yet they do explore several ways of moving from being outsiders to being insiders. Such a search may lead to a virtuous circle: The discovery of new means of acting leads to reframing. The new frames open up new possibilities and so on. Fatalists, on the contrary, can hardly overcome the boundaries between arts and art management. They seem to enact a vicious circle: Their lack of capability to act leads them to avoid initiatives and may even lead them further toward radicalization. Individuals then identify themselves as definitive outsiders. In such cases, change can only come from a cognitive revolution.

CONCLUSION: DESTROYING ARTISTS' CAREER MYTHS

This chapter presents results from qualitative action research describing and analyzing the objective career unsuccess of visual artists in a French region. The central contribution made here is specifying the sociocognitive barriers to successful careers for these artists. A key theoretical point of this contribution is to establish links between literature on arts careers and literature on boundaryless careers. Art worlds are complex because of their dual nature, forming this socially structured environment where singular career trajectories are highly sought after. Our results show that unsuccessful visual artists are unable to make sense of the art worlds. Their frame of reference for these worlds, making a clear division between art and arts business, leaves them unable to take the right action when the opportunity arises. In their frame of reference, these artists do not reject this business side of the contemporary art worlds, nor are they unable to recognize it as key to success; they are simply unable to enact it in order to develop consistent behaviors. Thus, their career frame of reference leads to their objective career unsuccess. They are total outsiders—producing art for which they receive neither recognition nor payment—and they are therefore totally desocialized from any kind of professional environment and are very much aware of it.

These results are also interesting in other ways. First, if it still needed to be done, they completely destroy the romantic myth of the artist's career shaped by a 'cultural ideology' (as analyzed by Chiapello 1998), proof that even unsuccessful outsiders to contemporary art worlds are aware of the business tasks required to succeed as an artist. Second, they relativize the modern theories of Becker (1982) and Bourdieu (1977), who show that it may be possible to succeed outside the art worlds by re-creating other conventions. While this may be true for a minority of maverick artists, who are perfectly comfortable with single trajectories and are able to share knowledge, there remains a mass of artists who find themselves blocked at the periphery of the art worlds, with little possibility of moving forward. Unsuccessful visual artists are in the position of 'losers lose' (Gombault et al. 2011); they are firmly excluded from art worlds because they have not assimilated the conventions.

Furthermore, these results suggest some points about the boundary-lessness of artists' careers. First, the characteristics of the art worlds demonstrate that artists' career environments are apparently both weak *and* highly normative. Individuals are not free to create or enact projects. Their behaviors are assessed by the social worlds in which individuals behave. Second, the classical artist's quest for subjective career success does not ignore the relevance of objective career success. New career theoreticians suggest that a lack of objective career success does not necessarily deprive individuals of experiencing subjective career success. The results of this research show that objectively unsuccessful artists do not take advantage of this situation; they are unable to experience subjective career satisfaction. These two points need further investigation. A final and more pragmatic point from this research is that it sheds light on unsuccessful visual artists and their need for help. Results show that representations that limit career success will be difficult to change without external help; therefore, if any training is to be provided for this artist population, it should primarily target changing their career frame of reference.

REFERENCES

Arthur, M., and D. Rousseau. 1996. *The Boundaryless Career: A New Employment Principle for a New Organizational Era.* New York: Oxford University Press.

Arthur, M., S. Khapova, and C. Wilderom. 2005. "Career Success in a Boundaryless Career World." *Journal of Organizational Behavior* 26: 177–202.

Becker, H. 1963. *Outsiders: Studies in the Sociology of Deviance.* New York: The Free Press.

Becker, H. 1982. *Art Worlds.* Berkeley; Los Angeles: University of California Press.

Boudreau, J., W. Boswell, T. Judge, and R. Bretz. 2001. "Personality and Cognitive Ability as Predictors of Job Search among Employed Managers." *Personnel Psychology* 54: 25–50.

Bourdieu, P. 1977. "La production de la croyance: contribution à une économie des biens symboliques." *Actes de la Recherche en Sciences Sociales* 13: 3–43.

Bowness, A. 1989. *The Conditions of Success.* New York: Thames and Hudson.

Bridgstock, R. 2005. "Australian Artists, Starving and Well-Nourished: What Can We Learn From the Prototypical Protean Career?" *Australian Journal of Career Development* 14: 40–48.

Bridgstock, R. 2008a, June 25–27. *"Follow Your Bliss" or "Show Me the Money"? Career Orientations, Career Management Competence and Career Success in Australian Creative Workers.* Paper presented at the Creative Value Conference hosted by the ARC Centre of Excellence for Creative Industries and Innovation, Brisbane, Australia.

Bridgstock, R. 2008b. *Success in the Protean Career: A Predictive Study of Professional Artists and Tertiary Arts Graduates.* Unpublished doctoral dissertation, Queensland University of Technology, Kelvin Grove.

Caves, R. 2000. *Creative Industries: Contracts between Art and Commerce*. Cambridge, MA: Harvard University Press.

Chiapello, E. 1998. *Artistes versus Managers*. Paris: Métailié.

DeFillippi, R., and M. Arthur. 1994. "The Boundaryless Career: A Competency-Based Perspective." *Journal of Organizational Behavior* 15: 307–24.

Geertz, C. 1973. *The Interpretation of Cultures: Selected Essays*. New York: Basic Books.

Gombault A., F. Liot, J. Pralong, J.-Y. Agard, and C. Morel. 2012. "Losers Lose: les vrais outsiders des mondes de l'art contemporain." In *Howard Becker et les mondes de l'art*, edited by P.-J. Benghozi and T. Paris. Cerisy: EcolePolytechnique.

Hall, D. 1976. *Careers in Organizations*. New York: Goodyear Publishing.

Hall, D. 1996. *The Career Is Dead, Long Live the Career*. San Francisco: Jossey-Bass.

Heinich, N. 1998. *Le triple jeu de l'art contemporain: sociologie des arts plastiques*. Paris: Les Editions de Minuit.

Liot, F. 2004. *Le métier d'artiste: les transformations de la profession artistique face aux politiques de soutien à la création*. Paris: l'Harmattan.

Liot, F. 2009. "Collectifs d'artistes et action publique." In *L'artiste pluriel: démultiplier l'activité pour vivre de son art*, edited by M.-C. Bureau, M. Perrenoud, and R. Shapiro, 51–64. Lille: Presses Univ. Septentrion.

Littleton, S., M. Arthur, and D. Rousseau. 2000. "The Future of Boundaryless Careers." In *The Future of Career*, edited by A. Colin and R. Young, 101–14, Cambridge, UK: Cambridge University Press.

Menger, P.-M. 2001. "Artists as Workers: Theoretical and Methodological Challenges." *Poetics* 28: 241–54.

Menger, P.-M. 2003. *Du labeur à l'œuvre:portrait de l'artiste en travailleur*. Paris: Seuil.

Menger, P.-M. 2009. *Le travail créateur: s'accomplir dans l'incertain*. Paris: Seuil.

Moulin, R. 1992. *L'artiste, l'institution et le marché*. Paris: Flammarion.

O'Mahoney, S., and B. Bechky. 2006. "Stretchwork: Managing the Career Progression Paradox in External Labor Markets." *Academy of Management Journal* 49: 918–41.

Sen, A. 1999. *Un nouveau modèle économique: développement, justice, liberté*. Paris: Odile Jacob.

Throsby, D. 1994. "A Work Preference Model of Artists' Behaviour." In *Cultural Economics and Cultural Policies*, edited by A. Peacock and I. Rizzo, 69–80. Dordrecht: Kluwer Academic Publishers.

Throsby, D. 2001. *Economics and Culture*. Cambridge, UK: Cambridge University Press.

Throsby, D., and V. Hollister. 2003. *Don't Give Up Your Day Job: An Economic Study of Professional Artists in Australia*. Sydney: Australia Council for the Arts.

Weick, K. 1995. *Sensemaking in Organizations*. Thousand Oaks: Sage.

Weick, K. 1996. "Enactment and the Boundaryless Career: Organizing as We Work." In *The Boundaryless Career: A New Employment Principle for a New Organizational Era*, edited by M. Arthur and D. Rousseau, 40–57. Oxford: Oxford University Press.

Weick, K. 2001. *Making Sense of the Organization*. Oxford: Blackwell.

Weick, K. 2007. "Nowhere Leads to Somewhere." *The Conference Board Review* 44: 14–15.

Weick, K., and L. Berlinger. 1989. "Career Improvisation in Self-Designing Organizations." In *Handbook of Career Theory*, edited by M. Arthur, D. Hall, and B. Lawrence, 313–28. Cambridge, UK: Cambridge University Press.

12 Education and Becoming an Artist
Experiences from Singapore

Can-Seng Ooi

When Charles Landry introduced the idea of the creative city two decades ago, he was advocating a place for people to think, act, and live with imagination, so they can seek out opportunities and manage urban challenges (see Landry 2008). A culture of creativity underpins the creative city. The concept of the creative city has moved on, with the emphasis on the promotion of creative industries, such as the culture and the arts, advertising, architecture, and movies (Florida 2003; Hospers 2003; Howkins 2001). A creative city is also a magnet for the creative class (Florida 2003). Creativity goes beyond solving urban problems. A creative individual is seen to celebrate innovation and design and accept, even embrace quirkiness and diversity. Today, cities from Seattle to Shanghai, Århus to Adelaide, are boasting their creativity credentials, which include vibrant cultural scenes, efficient urban design, dedicated creative business clusters, art festivals, museums, and art schools. These manifestations are evidence of artistic industry, but it is questionable whether they constitute a true culture of creativity. It is also debatable whether these manifestations demonstrate reverence for creativity in wider society, beyond the cognoscenti.

This chapter takes Singapore as a case study and looks behind the claim that Singapore is developing its arts and culture sector and art professionals are being nurtured in the education system. It examines Singapore's creative economy policies, as well as public attitudes toward art, as conditioned through the education system, for the purpose of understanding the position and career path of the homegrown fine artist.

In contrast to the official celebration of Singapore as an emerging cultural city, many fine artists interviewed lamented on the challenges they face in their jobs and careers. Beyond the difficulties in selling their works, gaining recognition in society, and getting state support for their art activities, they face a more fundamental challenge, namely, a general indifference toward their art—or the value of their art—by the public. As is explained, the education system plays a large part in the shaping of these attitudes. Within this context, this study seeks to unearth the values and mores inculcated into my respondents and into society via the Singaporean education system with regard to the arts.

Data for this study were collected since April 2007 through various means, including documents, media reports, observations, and in-depth interviews with 66 stakeholders in the Singapore art world.[1] The 66 respondents include 35 practicing artists, 10 of whom are also art teachers and another 10 have other jobs to supplement their income; 13 respondents are administrators, decision markers, or curators in the public sector (Singapore's Ministry of Information, Communications and the Arts, state-supported museums and schools), 15 persons run private art spaces (galleries and art complexes) or write art reviews, and 3 are art collectors. Where permission was granted, actual names are used. Respondents who chose to remain anonymous are referred to by random strings of letters.

SETTING THE SCENE: CULTURAL POLICY AND SOCIETY

Singapore, a former British colony, became an independent state less than 50 years ago. It has little to no cultural tradition that is unique. Being a settler colony, what 'indigenous' art forms it can claim are transplants from regional cultures that reflect the diversity of its migrant population. In Singapore, the population is divided into three ethnic groups: Chinese (77 percent), Malay (14 percent), and Indian (8 percent). There is a miscellaneous category of 'Others' (1 percent). This is the CMIO model (Benjamin 1976; Ooi 2005; Siddique 1990). The ancestries of the Chinese, Malay, and Indian communities are broadly defined as from China, Malaysia/Indonesia, and the Indian sub-continent, respectively. Officially, the diversity in Singaporean society is always defined along these ethnic lines, rather than along social class or political lines.

The promotion of the arts in Singapore started in earnest after the release of the 1989 *Report of the Advisory Council on Culture and the Arts* (Advisory Council on Culture and the Arts 1989). Based on this report, among other things, the National Arts Council (NAC) was formed in 1991, more support was given to art groups, and schools started offering art programs. To further develop the 1989 recommendations, the Singapore Tourism Board (STB, formerly Singapore Tourist Promotion Board [STPB]) and the Ministry of Information, Communication and the Arts (MICA, formerly Ministry of Information and the Arts [MITA]), took the initiative to make Singapore into a 'Global City for the Arts' in 1995 (Ministry of Information, Communication, and the Arts and Singapore Tourist Promotion Board 1995).

Over the years, cultural infrastructure and institutions mushroomed in the city-state to tap into the cultural industries, attracting tourists and skilled foreign labour (Ooi 2010). To demonstrate that Singapore is culturally vibrant, in the mid-1990s, the Singapore Art Museum and the Asian Civilizations Museum opened and the National Museum of Singapore was extended. New cultural festivals, including the Singapore Biennale, Singapore Arts Festival,

Singapore Writers Festival, and Singapore Film Festival, were established over the years. The Esplanade, a state-supported world-class performance center, hosts hundreds of free concerts annually. Between 2003 and 2009, ticketed attendance of performing arts events increased from 1 million to 1.4 million (Ministry of Information, Communication and the Arts 2010). Non-ticketed attendances increased from 11 million in 2006 to 19 million in 2009 (Ministry of Information, Communication and the Arts 2010). The number of visitors visiting museums in Singapore tripled from 2 million in 2003 to 6.7 million in 2009 (Ministry of Information, Communication and the Arts 2010). Apparently, art and cultural activities have not only become more abundant but have also become more accessible.

Following the footsteps of internationally recognized cultural cities such as London and New York, the plan is for Singapore to develop its art trading sector, get world famous artists to perform, and attract established art companies to its shores. The aim then, and still is, to make Singapore the art and cultural capital of Southeast Asia (Ooi 2008). A natural assumption from these indications would have been that there are many career opportunities in the arts. But many Singaporeans, including artists, think otherwise. These developments may be visible and measurable indications that the cultural economy is actively promoted in Singapore, but foreign performance productions are more prominent in the city-state, for instance. Many prominent sculptures in public places are not local. Instead, expensive Dalis, Boteros, and Lichtensteins are used to brighten up the concrete jungle in the financial and shopping districts. Local artists interviewed complain that public funding for the arts often goes to foreign artists and art businesses. As a representative of the arts community, then nominated Member of Parliament, Audrey Wong, voiced this concern in response to the increase in arts funding in the 2011 Singapore government budget. Building on her observations from previous years, Wong said (Yen 2011):

> There is a concern that the additional funding will go towards international events like the recently concluded art fair, Art Stage, or attracting foreign productions to our shores.

Furthermore, the arts are largely art-as-commerce, with one eye on the bottom line (Lee 2006). The cultivation of local art talents and productions is encouraged, but many artists and art lovers do not feel that the cultural scene is bubbling with a culture of creativity and innovation.

Since 2000, MICA has pushed the 1995 initiatives further in successive plans that envisage Singapore as a 'Renaissance City' (Ministry of Information and the Arts 2000; Ministry of Information, Communication, and the Arts 2008). The authorities saw the arts and culture as necessary to: "enrich us as persons," "enhance our quality of life," "help us in nation-building," and "contribute to the tourist and entertainment sectors" (Ministry of Information and the Arts 2000). The latest plan further elaborates their ambition in three ways: 1) produce distinctive art and cultural contents, 2) produce a dynamic art and culture ecosystem, and 3) cultivate an engaged community as part of the nation-building process.

The language of creativity is rife in these ambitions, but art and culture can only flourish if there is a receptive audience. Many artists I interviewed described the public as being unsympathetic toward art and artists. For instance, a furor broke out between the fine arts community and the general public in 2007. The arts community was incensed that public art installations were destroyed during building renovations and renewals of public spaces. One was the removal of four of six stoneware water features, an art installation by Delia Prvacki, by Singapore Power, a statutory board that provides public utilities, from its headquarters (Chew 2007). Not only was the public disrespectful, government boards were also nonchalant toward art works. In order to understand this lack of enthusiasm, one must consider the way society has been disposed toward the arts through their exposure to it in the education system.

ART, ARTISTS, AND THE SINGAPORE EDUCATION SYSTEM

Broadly, art education in Singapore takes place at two levels. At one level, art is offered as a hobby-like subject at the earliest stages of the general education system. There is no scholastic examination at this stage, and if there is, the obtained grade is not factored into how pupils progress to the next year. At the second level, art training is a dedicated program through which selected children can further cultivate their artistic talents. For pre-tertiary art education, talented children can audition and join the School of the Arts (SOTA); older students can choose to receive tertiary art education at the Nanyang Academy of Fine Arts (NAFA) or the LASALLE College of the Arts (LASALLE).

When interviewed, the artist respondents described their career journeys as challenging, and they pointed out that many of their school peers have given up on the professional artist ambitions. In fact, the local education system does not encourage children to become artists. This point is elaborated next.

ART IN GENERAL EDUCATION

From a structural functionalist perspective, an education system serves many functions in society (Haralambos and Holborn 2004). They include the transmission of values, the allocation of social roles in society, and dividing labor. Many education systems around the world identify talented and gifted children to nurture and realize their potentials (Colangelo and Davis 2002).

Structured on the British system, Singapore has devised an elaborate education system that streams pupils. The segregation broadly mirrors C. P. Snow's (1960) ideas of polarization between 'the two cultures'—'the sciences' and 'the humanities'—in modern society. From the age of 10 (Primary School, Year Four), pupils are grouped according to academic ability to facilitate more efficient learning. At the age of 14 (Secondary School, Year Two), the more academically successful pupils are selected for the 'science stream,' where they concentrate on science subjects such as physics, chemistry, biology, and more advanced mathematics; these are the subjects that they will be evaluated in for their GCE 'O' levels. Those pupils with poorer grades are streamed into the 'arts stream' (i.e., 'the humanities'), where they will take subjects such as basic mathematics, literature, history, geography, and art. In order to progress to higher education at the university level, pupils must, after clearing their GCE 'O' levels, obtain appropriate GCE 'A' level qualifications in junior colleges (equivalent to grades 11–12 in the American education system). Junior college students are also streamed into the science and arts streams; science students from secondary schools can cross over to become arts students in junior colleges but not vice versa. The former also have more options when they enter university in terms of choosing subjects and disciplines. The system therefore inherently maintains the view that 'the sciences' are more desirable, and because the best of the talent pool is channelled into it, science students come to be perceived as more able than arts students.

In this rather complex system of segregating pupils, art as a subject is provided. However, pupils seldom learn anything more than simple drawing and craftwork in primary and secondary school. The subject does not contribute to the promotion of a pupil to the next level. Art appreciation, by way of introduction to classic or well-known works, is rarely a component of art lessons. Without such experiences, students are limited in their opportunities to develop an aesthetic faculty. Art, therefore, faces the challenge of being taken seriously.

The Singapore Ministry of Education (MoE) nevertheless boasted that its education system is ranked best in the Global Competitiveness 2007/2008 Report, "in terms of the ability to meet the needs of a competitive economy" (Ministry of Education 2009). That the education system has overwhelmingly favored schooling in 'the sciences' may be attributable to a calculation that 'harder' technical skills were required for the industrialized economy of the 1960s and 1970s. With the emergence of the knowledge economy and the ascendance of the creative class, this emphasis is being moderated.

Member of Parliament, Ong Kian Min, pointed out (Parliament Hansard, March 9, 2010):

> PE [physical exercises], art and music, being non-core and non-academic subjects, tend to get sidelined by other subjects, like mathematics and science. In schools, the temptation to use art, music and PE periods for other subjects, especially around examination time, is strong.

If we are serious about providing our children with quality PE, music and art education, we should have teachers who have in-depth knowledge and are specially trained to teach in these areas. Precious time is wasted and interest lost if children do not receive instructions from specialists in these areas who can give a better insight into their area of specialty and are more likely to infect and inspire the children with their enthusiasm.

At the middle stages of education, when art is offered as a graded, scholastic subject (at the GCE 'O' and 'A' levels), it is considered a 'soft option.' Art as a subject is generally seen as academically less taxing and easier. Curiously, even at this level, there is a tendency for art to be studied in isolation as a hobby craft, without investigation or exploration into the progeny of art. Art education, as provided, is thus fragmentary and ill conceived. For instance, WWH trained art teachers at the National Institute of Education lamented the isolation of art theory and history from art practice:

> I feel that they should come up with a system or program with theory that is better integrated with studio practices. Right now, I am doing it on the side [for my trainee teachers].

WWH also observed that art teachers are not interested in art history and theory. He complained that these teachers do not encourage their pupils to select art history and theory electives. Two secondary school art teachers, KLP and PS, reasoned why they are not encouraging their pupils to do art theory during an interview. KLP said:

> Pupils are doing Math and Geography already. They do not want [Art as] another academic subject.

Generations of Singaporeans have gone through this education system that systematically marginalizes the importance of art as a subject. With the perception that art is an easy subject and that it is often chosen only by academically weaker pupils, the system does not encourage pupils to become artists. As a result, while there are many children who are good in academic subjects and are also artistically talented, they face the pressure of going into the science stream and not nurture their artistic skills.

This tendency is not lost on the government. Over the years, attempts are made to encourage artistically talented children to cultivate their skills. So, for instance, an option for artistically talented pupils is to do the 'art elective program' in secondary school and pre-university, regardless of whether they are in the arts or science stream. The 'art elective program' is a more rigorous and in-depth training in the arts, but these pupils still face the persistent view that other academic subjects are more important. These pupils receive diminished social support as many of their peers and teachers perceive art dimly. Hoh

Chung Shih, a composer and then Head of Aesthetics in Raffles Institution, a top school in Singapore, observed that most of his pupils would not pursue an art career because these pupils also excel in other fields, even if they have strong passion and remarkable artistic talent. He also reasoned that "many parents do not know the scope of careers possible in the arts. And Singapore being a young nation still lacks convincingly 'successful' role models."

SCHOOLS DEDICATED TO THE ARTS

In 2002, SOTA was founded. It is Singapore's only arts school at the pre-tertiary level, and it is under the purview of MICA, not MoE. Pupils with special talents in art have the opportunity to study there. Unlike normal schools, SOTA gives due attention to art education, together with other academic subjects. The acting Minister for MICA, Lui Tuck Yew, explained the uniqueness of SOTA in the Singaporean education system (Singapore Parliament Hansard, March 12, 2010):

> SOTA's unique proposition lies in the pedagogy which makes meaning-ful connections between the arts and academic subjects to provide an enriched learning and teaching experience for those who are talented in the arts. The distinctive curriculum and learning environment have attracted highly-qualified teachers with teaching and industry experi-ence, and prominent artists, into SOTA's arts faculty as well as full-time practitioners who teach on a part-time or adjunct basis.

Interest in SOTA seems strong. In 2009, for instance, about 1,000 children auditioned for 200 places. The school offers a six-year program, leading up to the International Baccalaureate (IB). A good IB qualification will allow school leavers to enter university or other tertiary-level education. In terms of curriculum development, faculty, and student exchanges, SOTA partners with a number of established international arts institutions, including the Chicago Academy of Art and the Shanghai Conservatory of Music Middle School in China. It is prestigious to study at SOTA because the pupils are recognized to have special artistic talents; they are specially selected and not streamed there by default. They must also prove to be good in other school subjects before they can enter SOTA. This is a significant develop-ment for the arts in the Singaporean education system.

There are two tertiary-level art schools in Singapore: LASALLE and NAFA. The Nanyang Academy of Fine Arts, or better known as NAFA, was founded in 1938. It offers programs in fine art, music, dance, inte-rior design, fashion design, video production, 3D design, advertising, ani-mation and interactive media, among others. LASALLE College of the Arts, popularly known as LASALLE, was set up in 1984, with the aim of providing contemporary art education in fine art, design, media, and performing arts.

In the context of its fine art education, NAFA, with its historical links to the Chinese segment of the population, is known to emphasize traditional art techniques and skill training. LASALLE is associated with contemporary art approaches and takes a more open approach to art making. Both art schools offer diploma programs and are recognized as polytechnic-level educational institutions by MoE. Their cooperation with foreign universities, such as the UK Open University for LASALLE, University of Huddersfield, Purchase College (State University of New York), Loughborough University, University of Wales, and Singapore Institute of Management University for NAFA, has allowed them to offer degree courses. By studying just one more year after attaining the diploma, students can obtain a bachelor degree. For instance, at LASALLE, after passing their GCE 'O' levels, candidates apply to take a one-year preparatory foundation course before they pursue a two-year Diploma program, and they will be awarded a degree if they continue into the third year. This is a four-year fast track to obtaining a bachelor degree, as compared to obtaining one's GCE 'A' levels (two years) before studying in the local state-supported universities such as the National University of Singapore and Nanyang Technological University (three years). While the academic entry requirements are relatively low for NAFA and LASALLE, each potential student has to build and present a portfolio during his/her application for entry.

There is an apparent tendency for students who do well in the first-year foundation course to enter the more commercially oriented applied arts programs, such as animation, graphic design, and fashion. Singapore has pursued a pragmatic and neo-liberal economic model in the last five decades (Chan 2005; Chua 1995; King 2006; Low and Johnston 2001). This message is prevalent at all levels of society, including in the education system. It would seem that however puristic the artistic instinct, socialization by this line of thinking predisposes students to position themselves toward the more gainful, if not lucrative, careers.

Artists who graduated from these institutions also revealed an inherent prejudice against pursuing the fine arts even in the art schools; the fine arts curriculum is a 'residual' program for students who do not qualify for the others. Respondents teaching these students often shook their heads when they spoke of these prejudices. Artist respondents who were good students and committed themselves to the fine arts in NAFA and LASALLE found it exhausting to continuously respond to these preconceptions. Regardless, for those who end up in the fine arts program, a fine arts diploma or degree from NAFA or LASALLE provides a formal recognition of the person as a trained artist.

CULTURAL CAPITAL OUTSIDE OF SCHOOLS

Challenging the view that a meritocratic school system offers equal opportunities to all, Bourdieu (1973) argued that socialization outside of school has an impact on pupils' achievements in school. French children acquire

'cultural capital' at home. Children who have been introduced and participated in 'high culture' such as classical music, art, and literature will do
better in the French education system because the education they receive
also promotes and celebrates high culture (Bourdieu 1973). Studies from
around the world (see Buchmann 2002; De Graaf et al. 2000; Kaufman
and Gabler 2004; Yamamoto and Brinton 2010) have similarly shown that
pupils advance faster in the school education system when endowed with
different types of cultural capital, including embodied ones (e.g., dispositions of the mind and body) and objectified ones (e.g., books, dictionaries,
and art objects) (Bourdieu 1986). As a result, the school system engages in
social and cultural reproduction. Following Bourdieu's arguments, while
certain interests and values are reproduced through the education system,
some interests and values are also marginalized and even disparaged.

Parents respond to the demands of the education system by attempting to
increase the cultural capital of their children by sending them for extramural tuition. In Singapore particularly, extramural tuition in mathematics,
science, and languages is common. Being knowledgeable and artistically
cultivated is nice, but excelling in the more academic subjects takes precedence. This may be seen as another consequential effect of the neo-liberal
economic model; to have an edge in an increasingly competitive world has
become a major impetus for individuals to hone from an early age the 'hard
skills' necessary for the more lucrative careers offered by 'the sciences.' In
contrast to Bourdieu's observation in France, high culture may be appre-
ciated by the middle class, but it may not readily translate into cultural
capital in Singapore's education system. Instead, the Singaporean education
system socially and culturally reproduces groups of people who value 'the
sciences' over 'the humanities.'

Moreover, the message that the arts and culture are important in one's
personal development is not translated into Singapore's education system; the
promotion of creativity and the regulation of the arts is under the purview of
MICA, whereas education in the arts falls under the MoE. The two do not
necessarily work in concert. There are contradictory policies and messages
that dampen the aspirations of children who want to become artists.

THE POSITION OF THE FINE ARTIST

Social Engineering

Fine artists trained by institutions assimilate to various degrees the ethos
celebrated or preserved by those institutions, in either the form or the
spirit of the learned discipline. It has been pointed out by some that an
educational system can be a socializing agent, with the social engineering
intention of generating social cohesion through the promotion of value
consensus, for example, patriotism (Erickson 2005; Neo and Chen 2007;

Shpakovskaya 2009). Art, as taught, can be co-opted for such purposes. In fact, and as described earlier, one of the functions of art and culture, as explicitly elaborated by MITA in their plan to make Singapore a 'Renaissance City,' is to "help us in nation-building" (Ministry of Information and the Arts 2000).

In line with such social engineering messages, fine arts students in Singapore tend to be directed toward traditional, international, and 'indigenous' Asian art forms, such as drawing, oil painting, pottery, Chinese ink brush painting, and Malay batik. Art forms and their combinations that fit into the official multicultural CMIO model, described earlier, constitute the bulk of this work. It would be observed that the natural and essential emphasis of these traditional art forms is on the picturesque, and that adherence to tradition means that their employed themes are mostly historical and trite. Even for more contemporary or polemical forms, the championed messages are often based on the official views of Singaporean history and how Singaporean society is constituted. Art in these forms seldom rises above pageantry but as a purely aesthetic work may be displayed and viewed by all with little controversy. The educational process directs budding artists toward making works that are considered 'safe' and acceptable in society. This may explain why the fine arts receive limited public attention. Even for more ambitious contemporary fine artists who gravitate toward newer media, such as video and cinematography, which are more open to innovation and 'edginess,' few of their works are politically controversial.

In other words, many Singaporean artists, as trained, tacitly or inadvertently perpetuate the social engineering messages of the state. As a collective, many artists in Singapore forge an identity tied through the set values they have internalized through various social engineering mechanisms, including the education system. While the CMIO social engineering message is ingrained in art training in Singapore, the emergence of current social and political criticisms in works is discouraged and even trampled on. For instance, in challenging the orderly environment of Singaporean society, a second-year student at LASALLE was expelled for stenciling graffiti on the new campus (Singh 2007). The school's spokesman justified the harsh action: "Our institution respects and promotes the freedom of creative expression but always in a responsible way, without damage to the property of others." The expelled student described himself as "a free radical who loves exploring new avenues for artistic expression" (Singh 2007). In another similar example, in the build-up to the first ever Youth Olympic Games in Singapore, 2010, SingPost—the main local post service provider—devised a viral marketing stunt by 'vandalizing' some of its post boxes with graffiti. The result backfired as the public lodged complaints to the police. SingPost apologized for the alarm caused (Thomas 2010). While this example encapsulates the view that the public is still ambivalent about art works that are contentious, the authorities have also maintained that Singaporeans are not ready for controversies.

This does not, however, mean that artists are not interested in engaging with and criticizing the authorities; they are wary of such attempts because they have not been emboldened in art school. Revealed by teachers and graduates in NAFA and LASALLE, critical social and political commentaries exist in student works, but these works are not publicized and would be received cautiously by most art teachers and classmates. For instance, an art teacher and practicing artist jokingly said to me when we were discussing candidly on including critical social political art in the curriculum: "Hey, you want the ISA [Internal Security Agency or Singapore's secret service] to come get you?" Critical social and political statements in art can result in reprimands from the authorities (Ooi 2010).

Social Stratification

Closely related to the previous point, the education system also communicates tacit messages and inculcates values that stratify society. Bowles and Gintis (1976) argued that inherent in any educational system, there is a hidden curriculum. For instance, the idea of a meritocratic education system is a myth to justify the continuation of an unequal society. Based on their study in the US, the education system there produces a subservient workforce, generates an acceptance of hierarchy, teaches pupils to be motivated by external rewards, and fragments knowledge through individually insulated school subjects. Scholars have argued against Bowles and Gintis, stating that the formal curriculum is also important, and that school children also acquire skills to be critical (e.g., Reynolds 1984). But Bowles and Gintis highlighted the importance of identifying what is not formally taught but insidiously ingrained into children.

The Singaporean education system advocates a neo-liberal economic view of society and establishes the importance of being economically independent and of the need to constantly better oneself. Wealth generation and advancement in society are major and common preoccupations. Many artists find that they need public support for their projects, and, consequently, artists may feel that they are dependents in society.

These real-world Singaporean challenges are daunting to the artist who has not yet established himself or herself. From the perspective of gallery managers, they find Singaporean art works not very saleable even though these artists may hold qualifications from local art schools. Works from Indonesia, the Philippines, Vietnam, and China are popular with customers. They give several reasons for this phenomenon. One is that Singaporean artists are too expensive for the quality they produce. To some gallery managers, local artists are less loyal, and therefore they are reluctant to invest their efforts in local artists. According to a few gallery managers, there are too few good Singaporean artists to generate the excitement for Singaporean art in the market. A damning observation against local art schools is that most graduates from the schools are technically and conceptually inferior to their foreign counterparts; three gallery owners whispered this view when interviewed. Local artists, in contrast, lamented that galleries are unprofessional and not supportive of them. The galleries do not consistently champion their works and do not develop their careers; instead the galleries are obsessed only with profit, not art. These conflicts arise partly because the art schools do not educate their students on career management. Essentially, as a former teacher of LASALLE and practicing conceptual artist, HW stated that students were given little idea about what it takes to become a professional artist:

> If you are a professional artist, how should you behave? How do you position your career? All these are very important. [The government's approach] is just like I give you time, space and school to develop your skills and that's it.

New art school graduates felt unprepared for their career. Reflecting a number of artist respondents laments, JHT, a professional artist and graduate of LASALLE, said:

> There were many art competitions while we were in LASALLE. Companies and statutory boards invite us to submit our works. We were busy preparing and submitting our works then. After we graduated, we are left on our own. We don't even know where to start!

Many fine arts graduates ended up being art teachers, with little time to make art themselves. Many of their classmates became real estate agents and insurance agents as these jobs have lower entry barriers.

Singapore's education system implicitly communicates the message that doing art and being an artist belongs to the lower echelons of society. Having to seek public support despite the policy to promote the arts, careers in making art are not well regarded in Singaporean society. Many artists in Singapore, while developing their careers, have to overcome the prejudices against them and struggle to show that they also contribute economically and usefully to society.

Cultural Compass

Art history and art theory are scantily covered in the local art education. Students are said to be uninterested. For instance, YMU, a professional artist and graduate from NAFA and LASALLE, observed that most of her classmates were not interested in art history, the single academic course she attended in these art schools. She did well in the course and self-admitted that she is academically oriented; she holds a bachelor degree in business administration before she took the step to becoming a professional artist by joining NAFA and then LASALLE. She is also a free-lance writer. YMU finds the art history course important to her career because it provides the foundation for her to situate her works in different art movements.

Art students who limit their exposure to art theory and history are somewhat limiting themselves, as they do not acquire a broad enough knowledge of art to learn to embed societal contexts and historical roots into their art practice. While many of my artist respondents have taken it on themselves to practice art in a theoretically, historically, and socially engaged manner, they also complained about the fragmented approach to art making in school. Studio work and theory are not integrated. They also lamented that their education had not prepared them for becoming a professional practicing artist. They were not guided on developing a successful career in art.

That said, with the emergence of new media and new technologies, ideas and inspirations coming from everywhere, questions have been raised not only on what is art, but how useful an art school education is (see Madoff 2009). In other words, inspirations for art making and for becoming an artist do not come singularly from art school. Art schools and their curricula not only fragment the training needed for an artist career, they generate a false sense of having been trained and being qualified to be a professional artist. As discussed earlier, graduates of the art schools soon found that they were unable to situate their practice in theory and history, and they were unprepared for the grubby business of developing a career as a professional artist.

Art does not necessarily reflect reality, but many works can communicate the emotional voices of the people in society (Kavolis 1964). By being the emotional voices of the masses, artists engage with society and become salient and relevant mouthpieces for sections of the population. But except for a few theater groups in Singapore, most artists in Singapore are not ready to step into the role of becoming the emotional voice of the society. They do not engage in a manner that makes them relevant and central in society. Many artists in theater and film who make critical social and political statements have gotten themselves into trouble (Ooi 2008; Tan 2007).

IN SUMMARY

The existence alone of art schools and art programs cannot be used, such as they are, as indicators of how serious a city takes culture and creativity. As this chapter shows, such indicators must be evaluated more critically.

Art training and art school education carry explicit and hidden curricula that do not necessarily match. In Singapore, one explicit message is that art training helps develop the 'soft skills' of pupils; they will make for a more intellectually rounded and gracious populace in the future (Singapore Parliament Hansard, March 9, 2010). The many initiatives to promote the arts and culture also show that the cultural economy is important, and artists are central in the emerging scheme of things. But the streaming processes in the Singaporean education system perpetuate a low status for artists in Singapore and, by association, a low regard for art in general. The education system socially reproduced a system that better respects the sciences and professions that require good academic performance in school. Going to art school is not considered prestigious. Many Singaporeans still think that most persons who have taken up an art education are lousy in school and their choice of an art education is forced on them. Thus, children are given a negative impression of becoming a professional artist. The system continues to rank the career of an artist lowly. With the limited recognition from society, many professional artists inevitably feel deflated at times. If art in school and art schools do not train artists, what do they do? The system continues to perpetuate the CMIO social engineering messages of Singapore, and many practicing artists inadvertently continue the message. Artists are not encouraged to take risks for fear of overstepping the boundaries of public morality set by the authorities. The current situation does not inspire students to become artists with the aspiration of mobilizing people emotionally and speaking up for the masses. The art education discourages that. Even for those who are successful and can make a living from their art making, they question how useful their art education was.

NOTES

1. This study is part of the project, Creative Encounters, supported by the Danish Strategic Research Council.

REFERENCES

Advisory Council on Culture and the Arts. 1989. *Report of the Advisory Council on Culture and the Arts*. Singapore: Singapore National Printers.

Benjamin, G. 1976. "The Cultural logic of Singapore's 'Multiculturalism'." In *Understanding Singapore Society*, edited by O. J. Hui, T. C. Kiong, and T. E. Ser, 67–85. Singapore: Times Academic Press).

Bourdieu, P. 1973. "Cultural Reproduction and Social Reproduction." In *Knowledge, Education, and Cultural Change*, edited by R. K. Brown, 71–112. London: Tavistock.

Bourdieu, P. 1986. "The Forms of Capital." In *Handbook of Theory and Research for the Sociology of Education*, edited by J. G. Richards, 241–58. New York: Greenwood Press.

Bowles, S., and H. Gintis. 1976. *Schooling in Capitalist America*. London: Routledge, Kegan Paul.

Buchmann, C. 2002. "Getting Ahead in Kenya: Social Capital, Shadow Education, and Achievement." In *Schooling and Social Capital in Diverse Cultures*, edited by B. Fuller and E. Hannum, 133–59. Oxford: Elsevier Science.

Chan, C. B. 2005. *Heart Work: Stories of How EDB Steered the Singapore Economy from 1961 into the 21st Century*. Singapore: Singapore EDB.

Chew, D. 2007, April 19. "Where Art Thou?" *Today*, April 19.

Chua, B. H. 1995. *Communitarian Ideology and Democracy in Singapore*. London: Routledge.

Colangelo, N., and G. A. Davis. 2002. *Handbook on Gifted Education*. Boston: Allyn & Bacon.

De Graaf, N. D., P. M. De Graaf, and G. Kraaykamp. 2000. "Parental Cultural Capital and Educational Attainment in the Netherlands: A Refinement of the Cultural Capital Perspective." *Sociology of Education* 73: 111.

Erickson, F. 2005. "Arts, Humanities, and Sciences in Educational Research and Social Engineering in Federal Education Policy." *Teachers College Record* 107: 4–9.

Florida, R. 2003. *The Rise of the Creative Class*. New York: Basic Books.

Haralambos, M., and M. Holborn. 2004. *Sociology Themes and Perspectives*. London: Harper Collins Publishers Limited.

Hospers, G. J. 2003. "Creative Cities: Breeding Places in the Knowledge Economy." *Knowledge, Technology, & Policy* 16: 143–62.

Howkins, J. 2001. *The Creative Economy: How People Make Money from Ideas*. London: Penguin Books.

Kaufman, J., and J. Gabler. 2004. "Cultural Capital and the Extracurricular Activities of Girls and Boys in the College Attainment Process." *Poetics* 32: 168.

Kavolis, V. 1964. "Art Content and Social Involvement." *Social Forces* 42: 467–72.

King, R. 2006. *The Singapore Miracle: Myth and Reality*. Inglewood, Australia: Insight Press.

Landry, C. 2008. *The Creative City: A Toolkit for Urban Innovators*. London: Earthscan.

Lee, T. 2006. "Towards a 'New Equilibrium': The Economics and Politics of the Creative Industries in Singapore." *Copenhagen Journal of Asian Studies* 24: 55–71.

Low, L., and D. M. Johnston. 2001. *Singapore Inc. Public Policy Options in the Third Millenium*. Singapore: Asia Pacific Press.

Madoff, S. H. 2009. *Art School (Propositions for the 21st Century)*. London: MIT Press.

Ministry of Education. 2009. *Education in Singapore*. Singapore: Author.

Ministry of Information and the Arts and Singapore Tourist Promotion Board. 1995. *Singapore, Global City for the Arts*. Singapore: Author.

Ministry of Information and the Arts. 2000. *Renaissance City Report: Culture and the Arts in Renaissance Singapore*. Singapore: Author.

Ministry of Information, Communication and the Arts. 2008. *Renaissance City Plan III*. Singapore: Author.

Ministry of Information, Communication and the Arts. 2010. *Singapore Cultural Statistics in Brief* Singapore: Author.

Neo, B. S., and G. Chen. 2007. *Dynamic Governance: Embedding Culture, Capabilities and Change in Singapore*. Singapore: World Scientific.

Ooi, C.-S. 2005. "The Orient Responds: Tourism, Orientalism and the National Museums of Singapore." *Tourism* 53: 285–99.

Ooi, C.-S. 2008. "Reimagining Singapore as a Creative Nation: The Politics of Place Branding." *Place Branding and Public Diplomacy* 4: 287–302.

Ooi, C.-S. 2010. "Political Pragmatism and the Creative Economy: Singapore as a City for the Arts." *International Journal of Cultural Policy* 16: 383–97.

Reynolds, D. 1984. *Constructive Living*. Honolulu: Kolowalu Books.

Shpakovskaya, L. 2009. "The Soviet Education Policy: Social Engineering and Class Struggle" (English). *Journal of Social Policy Studies* 7: 39–64.

Siddique, S. 1990. "The Phenomenology of Ethnicity: A Singapore Case Study." In *Understanding Singapore Society*, edited by J. H. Ong, C. K. Tong, and E. S. Tan, 107–24. Singapore: Times Academic Press.

Singh, K. 2007, September 7. "LaSalle Student Expelled for Campus Graffiti." *The Straits Times*, http://global.factiva.com, Document STIMES0020070906e3970000t

Singapore Parliament Hansard. 2010, March 9. *Singapore Parliament Hansard*, Vol. 86, Sitting 22, Singapore Parliament, Singapore.

Singapore Parliament Hansard. 2010, March 12. *Singapore Parliament Hansard*, Vol. 86, Sitting 25, Singapore Parliament, Singapore.

Snow, C. P. 1960. *The Two Cultures*. Cambridge, UK: Cambridge University Press.

Tan, K. P. 2007. "In Renaissance Singapore." In *Renaissance Singapore? Economy, Culture, and Politics*, edited by K. P. Tan, 1–14. Singapore: NUS Press.

Thomas, S. 2010, January 7. "SingPost Apologises for Publicity Stunt." *The Straits Times*, http://global.factiva.com, Document STIMES0020110228e7310001b

Yamamoto, Y., and M. C. Brinton. 2010. "Cultural Capital in East Asian Educational Systems: The Case of Japan." *Sociology of Education* 83: 67–83.

Yen, F. 2011, March 1. "Budget for the Arts Should Fund Local Talent." *The Straits Times*, http://global.factiva.com, Document STIMES0020110228e7310001b

13 'It Was a Huge Shock'

Fashion Designers' Transition from School to Work in Denmark, 1980s–2000s

Lise Skov

Michael Arthur's concept of boundaryless careers is an inherently ambivalent notion (Arthur 1994; Arthur and Rousseau 1996; Sullivan and Arthur 2006). In bringing together 'physical' inter-firm mobility with the 'psychological' development of competences, it zooms in on the two-way interrelationship between industry and individual. On the one hand, structural labor market changes affect the individual's sense of agency and competence; on the other hand, employee mobility affects organizations. Looking at fashion designers through such a lens is appropriate because they have never sat well in organizations (McRobbie 1998).

This chapter examines the way Danish fashion designers start their careers on the basis of two assumptions. The first one is that it is essential to the success of a boundaryless career that it starts off with some jobs that offer learning opportunities that increase an individual's competences. The second assumption is that an individual must be able to find paths through the labor market that lead to new opportunities. These concerns are expressed in two common conceptions of careers. The first is to view a career as an accumulative process; for example, Bird (1996, 150) defines careers as 'accumulations of information and knowledge embodied in skills, expertise and relationship networks that are acquired through an evolving series of work experiences over time.' The second is to see a career as a thread weaving itself into the texture of other careers' at the inter-firm level, to form 'a changing tapestry of industry regions' (Arthur 1994, 303). Following Tim Ingold (2007), I see a career as a unity of movement and perception that cannot be reduced to 'connecting the dots' between different jobs. It is a trail that the individual travels *along*. On the basis of these two metaphors, we generate the questions that guide the following analysis: how are fashion designers' careers launched? How do first work experiences shape and foreshadow subsequent career trajectories? How does the subjective perspective—what the individual knows, wants, and can control—interact with the objective conditions in the labor market at different stages of (de)industrialization?

These questions are answered on the basis of an interview study of the careers and life stories of 45 Danish fashion designers conducted in 2009–2011. Informants have been chosen among fashion or apparel design graduates from the three leading Danish design schools. Informants are divided into three cohorts based on their year of graduation (mid-1980s, mid-1990s, and mid-2000s) so that we were able to meet informants, respectively, 25 years, 15 years, and 5 years into their working lives. Interviews were conducted in an unstructured format, asking informants to chronologically tell the story of their choice of profession, school, and work lives. Data have been analyzed on the basis of themes deduced from existing research, quantitative data, and explorative interviews combined with inductive methods based on grounded theory.[1]

We have also conducted exploratory interviews with design school teachers and other resource persons, both about individual graduates and about changes in education and the labor market. In order to increase reliability, we have held these findings up against quantitative data of fashion designers' employment, although this admittedly tends to be richest with regard to the younger two age groups. Descriptive statistics were used to corroborate the overall trends in the qualitative data material in terms of fashion designers' jobs, social status, and income. Surveys conducted by the schools and the Ministry of Culture were also used to discuss explanatory models. For example, it is estimated that it takes a Danish design school graduate four to five years to gain a foothold in the labor market (Danmarks Statistik Kulturministeriet 2009; Kulturministeriets Rektorer 2008). But the notion of a 'foothold' is somewhat vague and perhaps misleading in giving a sense of a limited phase. Many informants in the youngest cohort do not face any prospect of full-time paid employment five years after graduation. In the older cohorts, many still experience a high degree of job uncertainty. Some continue to go through periods of unemployment, and many have experienced their opportunities shrinking as a result of the 2008 financial crisis.

The analysis presented in this chapter is, to use Peacock and Holland's (1993, 369) term, a 'life-focused approach' (as opposed to a story-focused approach) in the sense that we use the life story material as a 'window on the objective facts of historical and ethnographic events.' One of the 'objective facts' that we look at through the career stories is the industrial transformation of the fashion sector. Paradoxically, we find that although Danish fashion is now acknowledged to have sustained growth during deindustrialization, it is actually harder for fashion designers to launch their careers now than it was 20 years ago when the industry was considered to be in a crisis. The total dependence on outsourcing, which characterizes the Danish fashion sector today, has brought with it an extensive industrial restructuring that has also reconfigured the role of fashion designers. Their supporting role in manufacturing has been replaced by a focus on collection development at an ever-increasing pace. In spite of the industry transformation, the fashion sector's time-honored autocratic management style still holds sway, so that employers tend to perceive themselves as purchasers of fashion designers' creative capabilities for as long as the employment contract lasts, rather than as facilitators of extended careers.

To analyze the individual's transition from school to work in the context of industry transformation, each cohort's experience is represented by an informant's story. Their names, Anna (1984 graduate), Martin (1994 graduate), and Tammie (2004 graduate), are fictive, but their stories are real and supplemented with additional examples from their cohorts. Anna and Tammie are typical for those who have had a career in the industry (as opposed to couture or costume designers), whereas Martin exemplifies how the original intention of working in the industry can lead along a serendipitous route to, in his case, a teaching job.

From the onset, we were aware that transition from school to work was a difficult time for the informants. But we could not have predicted that a large number of them would describe their first job as a 'shock', or that we would hear so many metaphors of physical violence and trauma when informants talked about their first encounters with the labor market. In research on emotions at work, attention has been paid to stress and burn-out as a reaction to long-term strain (Barbalet 2002; Fineman 2000). But the shock of a stressful transition from one environment to another has received little attention. A shock can be defined as the impact of a sudden forceful blow. Wolfgang Schivelbusch (1987), who has written the history of the shock, from the medieval 'mounted shock combat' of two knights galloping against each other to railway accidents in the 19th century, documents a shift from a focus on the immediate physical impact of a shock to an extended or a delayed emotional reaction. Even though the shock experienced by fashion designers is of the latter kind, the imagery of a physical clash still appears meaningful as fashion designers tend to describe physical symptoms.

Based on the designers' accounts of their shocks, I therefore suggest envisioning the fashion industry as a high-speed merry-go-round, which alters a person's orientation in time and space. Designers describe working in the industry as 'fun,' as 'being on a high,' and as being 'paid to do their hobby.' It requires that they make priorities to accommodate long working hours with limited remuneration, which on the whole they willingly do. But working in fashion industry involves a risk of burn-out and of being the victim of the jealousy and mudslinging, which they commonly describe as characterizing interpersonal relations in the workplace.

But while the description of the fashion industry as a parallel reality was a consistent theme in all our interviews, we also heard different qualities of shock from the oldest to the youngest cohorts. Of course, we would expect the transition from school to work to be a particularly vulnerable theme for the recent graduates, who are still uncertain about what paths their careers will take and what opportunities they will find, whereas the older cohorts would be more detached about past hardship. But the different patterns we found cannot be explained only by distance in personal history. Instead, the explanation can be found in the changing industry structure.

The mid-1980s graduates found it tough to hold their own in their first jobs, but they were given responsibilities through which they learned important skills that brought them further. The mid-1990s graduates experienced that their way into the industry was blocked, and they went into different niches, including some dead ends. The mid-2000s graduates experienced the job market as a hostile environment in which paid jobs, offering few learning opportunities, had to be supplemented by unpaid 'work experience.' In this respect, we trace a change in the quality of the shock from the oldest cohort, which was able to overcome the shock by actively facing up to the challenges, to the youngest cohort, which passively suffered the shock without really being able to develop competences that could bring them along in their careers.

This finding is important because studies of creative industries so far have tended to emphasize the differences among industries rather than changes in industry organization and work processes over time. As Susan Christopherson (2008) points out, the notion of the creative person as an individualistic self-expressive entrepreneur may block the understanding of structural changes in the production environments that shape the opportunity structures. When it comes to the famous fashion designers whose names are known from books and magazines, the clash between individual and structure invariably tilts in favor of the subjective perspective. They are the ones who have managed to impress their perception on the environment. Fashion designers working in the industry face the same task of reconciling the opposing forces of their creative ethos and the organizational environment, but the objective constraints are much more likely to act as an ongoing pressure that limits possibilities and redirects career trajectories.

The outline of the chapter is as follows. After an overview of fashion designers' jobs under different industrial conditions, I discuss fashion design education and the dilemmas faced by the educational institutions. This is followed by a presentation of the data through the stories of Anna, Martin, and Tammie, leading to a discussion of how the objective and subjective perspectives of fashion designers' careers are refracted against each other.

FASHION DESIGNERS AND INDUSTRY TRANSFORMATION

Job functions of fashion designers are extremely varied due to the highly segmented and geographically dispersed nature of the clothing and textile industries (Djelic and Ainamo 1999; Fine and Leopold 1993; Green 1997). However, it is useful to distinguish between two types of fashion designers, associated with different stages of industrialization, even though they both continue to exist today. The first has grown out of craft-based manufacturing and represents a unified vision of and control over all aspects of production. Historically, this is the oldest type, exemplified by the founders of Paris haute couture from the mid-19th century, who were essentially clothing manufacturing entrepreneurs. Their role as creative leaders was not separate from their responsibility for managing the company and overseeing the production process. This model has been formed by tailors and dress-makers, typically catering to upper class clients. In Denmark, where the couture tradition has been marginal, such designers have also worked with traditions of craft-based artistic dress, which in the 1960s were companions to Scandinavian Design furniture and interior. A few in the oldest cohort in our study started out with their own dress-making shops. But the Danish designer fashion sector that emerged in the 1990s is entirely based on outsourcing, enabled by the increasingly sophisticated suppliers in India and China, rather than by owner-managers in control of all aspects of production.

The second type of fashion designer is closely linked to the maturation of the clothing industry. Because the clothing industry is highly sensitive to increases in labor costs, due to its dependence on the manual assembly of garments, mature industries invariably experience a strong pressure to increase the value of their production (Fine and Leopold 1993). Under such conditions, fashion designers are employed in manufacturing and retail companies in order to interpret market trends through product development. Such designers tend to be anonymous or, at least, only known to industry insiders. American manufacturers and retailers were the first to employ fashion designers in this function as early as the 1940s (Lipovetsky 1994). In Denmark, professional fashion designers only came to play a central role in the clothing industry in the 1960s (Melchior 2008), at the same time as fashion design education, and design education in general, was formalized and expanded.

The industrial transformation taking place in the last two decades has complicated the polarization between the two types of designers. These days it is not only luxury conglomerates such as the French LVMH and PPR that own a portfolio of designer brands; the Danish multibrand firm IC Companys also includes two local designer brands, such as 'By Malene Birger' and 'Designers Remix' (by Charlotte Eskildsen). In high-end fashion, owner-managers are few and far between, and many 'name' designers consider being bought up as the most desirable way to ensure financial backing. Although this economic setup is rare, it feeds the dream that fashion designers, simply by being extremely creative, can attract investments, much in the same way as a creative musician can hope to land a contract with a record company.

Outsourcing has obviously changed industry conditions. In Denmark, practically all manufacturing facilities were closed down by the late 1990s. What until then had been the designers' core competences in calculating and minimizing production costs for each individual style were no longer needed. At first this was welcomed as creative freedom—the most popular Danish brands of this period generously used embroidery and sequins that would have been prohibitively expensive to produce in Europe. But in the longer term, there are increasing concerns that designers who are unfamiliar with industrial production cannot assert their ideas vis-à-vis suppliers or control that price calculations, based on material use and labor cost, are correct (TEKO 2009). Ultimately, the fear is that innovation capability is so closely linked to manufacturing that it is not only the lowest paid manual jobs that are lost but also the highly paid knowledge-intensive jobs.

In the same period, the pace of fashion cycles has been speeded up. As the number of annual collections increased from 5 or 6 to an ideal of 24, time for product development has decreased in proportion. Fast fashion, exemplified by the much-publicized two-week production cycle of Spanish chain store Zara, is based on a near-continuous supply of new products. Rather than develop new products from scratch, designers modify existing products based on an analysis of market data. This requires, first, that the work of fashion designers is increasingly anonymous, and second, that the production process or value chain in the company is completely reorganized. Both factors make it harder for young fashion designers to find first jobs with good learning opportunities. First, the range of creative freedom is carefully described and the product development process much faster and less independent than in the past. Second, the struggle of fashion companies to match the speed of the fast fashion celebrity brands creates a lot of internal stress. In several of the cases described to us, Danish companies have simply increased their number of annual collections without any major restructuring by making the designers work harder.

Under conditions of deindustrialization, the Danish fashion industry has actually increased its turnover and has remained one of the biggest (re) exporters among the manufacturing industries, even though its domestic workforce has shrunk to half of what it was in the 1980s (Høgenhaven 2003). For this reason, the clothing industry has become politically interesting as a high-performing sector. Unlike earlier industry policy, the fashion business was now the object of cultural industry policy, jointly initiated by the Ministries of Culture and of Economic and Business Affairs (Melchior et al. 2010). The template for this was the UK government's inclusion of designer fashion among 13 creative industries defined as 'activities which have their origin in individual creativity, skill and talent and which have the potential for wealth and job creation through the generation and exploitation of intellectual property' (quoted from Flew 2002, 3). But although in the public image it is the designer fashion sector that emerged in the late 1990s that symbolizes the international recognition Danish fashion (Melchior 2008), as a beneficiary of cultural policy, designer fashion has not been set apart from the rest of the sector.

According to the political and media discourse, it is creative fashion designers who are driving the success of the industry. But this image is at odds with the humdrum work and long hours, the modest remuneration, close to the average of the population as a whole, and the limited career opportunities documented by our study.

FASHION DESIGN EDUCATION

The present study includes the three leading schools that offer bachelor- and master's-level degrees in fashion or apparel design: Danmarks Designskole (DKDS), Designskolen Kolding (DK), and TEKO. Even though two of the schools have longer roots, they were all molded in their current form in the late 1960s. The former two originated as schools for applied arts, developed from an emphasis on life drawing and sketching for arts and crafts to design, including product design, graphic design, and more recently also digital and visual design. DKDS, located in Copenhagen, was founded in 1967 as a result of a merger of several vocational schools, including a school for the artistic education for women, founded in 1875, a direct precursor for the woman-dominated education in fashion design. DK was founded in the same year in a small town in Jutland in Western Denmark. Both schools, guided by the humanistic ideal of individual creativity, have sought to unite the Scandinavian approach to design as 'giving form' with social visions for the improvement of life. However, courses in fashion and apparel have been relatively isolated, perhaps due to the perception that fashion was 'too feminine' to match the modernist connotations of the design concept (Melchior 2008; cf. McRobbie 1998). The design schools perceive themselves as direct rivals. DKDS has the advantage of being located in Copenhagen, whereas DK makes up for its provincial location through an intense and committed learning environment. In terms of labor markets, DKDS graduates tend to find employment in the Copenhagen area, whereas DK graduates are scattered across Jutland (Kulturministeriets Rektorer 2008). This finding reflects the geographical clustering of the Danish fashion industry.

The schools are not overly worried about the fact that their graduates find it hard to enter the labor market. The educational programs pride themselves on their autonomy in relation to industry needs. They argue further that a four- to five-year transition period is only slightly longer than that of humanities graduates from the universities (Danmarks Statistik 2009; Kulturministeriets Rektorer 2008). This comparison is particularly relevant because the design schools in 2010 completed academic accreditation, which will give them status as universities. Statistical data also indicate that transition time is highly dependent on economic trends (Danmarks Statistik Kulturministeriet 2009; Kulturministeriets Rektorer 2008). The fact that industry conditions at the time of labor market entry shape and constrain individual career trajectories is corroborated by our interviews in which the three cohorts have distinct career patterns.

Surveys conducted among alumni document that many graduates feel that the transition from school to the labor market is difficult and that they would like a better connection between the two (Designskolen Kolding 2008; Danmarks Designskole 2008).[2] Looking back, graduates would have liked two additional elements in their education: knowledge of CAD programs and internships. They find they are simply not considered for jobs until they have completed after-school courses in Illustrator, Photoshop, or In-Design. The problem with internships applies to DKDS graduates in particular because the school did not include any internships in the study program until 2006. Students and teachers alike agree that this led to an unfortunate arrogance on the part of the students vis-à-vis potential employers. However, even those who have gone through internships during their education often need to seek more unpaid 'work experience' in order to build up qualifications for paid employment. In general, the alumni report that they lacked skills in how to put an application together and present oneself at a job interview. Most find their first job through personal networks rather than through advertisements.

The third school, TEKO, has a history that goes back to 1944 as a technical training institute for the clothing industry. In 1968, it was reorganized under its current name, an abbreviation of 'TExtil' and 'KOnfektion,' to offer full-time education. Compared with similar technical schools in Europe, it has been known as a visionary school. For example, in addition to technical skills, the students have been taught visual arts and psychology. Today TEKO offers specializations in fashion buying and retailing in addition to fashion design. Located in the provincial town of Herning, the heartland of the old manufacturing industry, teachers take pride in the fact that all student projects are realistic, that students can make business plans and design for specific target groups, and that they monitor the industry's educational needs in regular surveys. The educational program at TEKO has come to include a range of topics from product development and construction to CAM-CAD, collection development, and communication. TEKO occupies a difficult position as the educational partner of an industry that does not place much value on education. For example, it is only recently that the school first raised a critical voice to say that companies should not merely demand that fresh graduates provide them with a customized bundle of skills to their requirements but also be prepared to invest in continued education for employees (TEKO 2009).

In addition to these schools, there are a few other educational programs related to fashion design in Denmark, including both non-degree courses in design technology and craft and design primarily based on domestic science. Other schools also offer short skill-oriented courses in CAD, fashion forecasting, and similar, the latter taken by many design school graduates who need to supplement their degree.

MID-1980s: 'THROWN IN AT THE DEEP END'

Anna, who represents the oldest cohort, graduated from TEKO in the mid-1980s at the age of 21 and went immediately to work for a branded fashion company, specializing in navy blue women's sports jackets. Her job was to make and (size) grade patterns, make the first sample, and order materials for the whole batch. These tasks required precision and overview, and if she made a mistake, it had consequences for subsequent stages in the production. Although she came from a school known for being industry-oriented, she had not been prepared for such technical challenges. But on her first day, she was asked to get started without any supervision. 'I was thrown in at the deep end. I thought it was super cool,' she recalls. In talking about her early experience, she also indirectly expresses the qualities she values in a fashion designer—a passionate self-motivated person who can overcome any obstacle. 'If you have the right attitude there is no barrier to what you can do,' she says.

Two years later, she was employed at Daells Varehus, Copenhagen's major low-end department store, which at the time was trying to reposition itself as a fashion-forward store, a strategy that eventually failed but for some years engaged many young fashion designers and marketing people. Still in her early 20s, Anna was employed as a product developer and trend forecaster, a job that combined the technical task of making grading tables with extensive travel to fairs in Europe's metropolitan cities. To support her assertiveness in relation to 'ancient buyers who had been working in the store for 30 years,' the management sent her to a communication training course, where she learned to 'emphasize her words and visualize in different ways. It helped a lot.' Anna's experience is exceptional in that it is one of the few examples we have of a company providing after-school training for its employees.

Through her first jobs, Anna acquired competences that led to the next steps in her career. 'I had no idea how much I learned in those days. But I sat in on negotiations with suppliers and would say, "If we remove that pocket what would the price be?",' she says. She adds, 'Almost without knowing I built up a huge knowledge. At the time I did not know that I would be using this knowledge for anything. I just wanted to be a designer. But I grew interested in the trade in a different way because I was allowed to be part of the whole process.' Anna's learning was both technical—in terms of clothes construction and production planning—and organizational—how fashion is produced collectively with input from different people. This in turn shaped the direction of her future career as a product manager who has worked with a wide range of designers and companies. Anna's progression from a creative to a technical job function—by one informant termed 'a half designer'—represents a career path that involves an accumulation of knowledge and typically also an increase in salary and job security. Yet many designers are ambivalent about leaving the creative processes of product development behind.

Anna's story is comparable to that of other 1984 graduates. Their first jobs involved a lot of responsibility because they performed upgrading functions that were of strategic importance to the firms that employed them. At that time, fashion designers were actually driving wide-ranging organizational changes in different firms. Looking back, informants value the facts that they were given 'a free rein' and that they were in charge of 'the whole process' from idea to market. Many had the experience of being the first, and only, designer employed in a company. However, for some, this was also a lonely position in an organization.

Many informants in this cohort express a preference for change and variety. They show a high degree of inter-firm mobility. Anna, for example, has changed jobs on average every two years, except for a seven-year period when she ran her own company. Looking back, the only thing she really regrets was having to close down her company as a consequence of divorce. On the surface, fashion designers explain their frequent moves with phrases such as, 'I needed a change' or 'I didn't like the atmosphere and the nylon carpets.' But it is not always clear whether these job-hopping trajectories represent inherent restlessness or blocked opportunities. When designers talk about mobility, they do not describe it as a process of accumulation, at least not in the sense of learning opportunities that enable them to progress to a management position. Nor does it represent genuine horizontal mobility, which leads them to greater expertise. In fact, specialization may lead to a dead end in a highly volatile industry. One designer, who began work for a lingerie company almost 20 years into her career, explains her commitment by saying, 'It was the only thing in fashion I had never done before.' Developing all-around competences is a method of safeguarding opportunities.

When we look a bit deeper, it seems that many job changes are brought on by insufferable working conditions. The colorful examples from our data include a company that collapsed because of the owner's drug abuse and a woman who had to conceal her identity because she was being stalked by her ex-boyfriend. But the overwhelming majority of changes are caused by poor interpersonal relations and poor organizational relations. For example, Anna describes how, in one company, she was asked to develop a new line in swimwear, and when she did well the first year, an envious colleague arranged for her to take over next year's collection. In another company, a designer confirmed the suspicion that the sales personnel were getting at her for personal reasons when for a presentation she swapped her work with that of a colleague and found that they were still criticizing her work. A third designer described how she used to argue with the sales director about good taste, and when he became managing director, he took his revenge for many a lost argument. Summarizing such experiences, one designer said that the dominant management style in the fashion business is 'management by fear,' characterized by managers going to great lengths to remind employees that it is a privilege to work in the fashion business, and that there are dozens of people waiting to take over their jobs. Even at the best of times, fashion designers rarely experience that their contribution is openly acknowledged and valued in the company. This image of the fashion business, structurally a fragmented sector dominated by autocratic and exploitative owner-managers, is richly supported in the literature (e.g., Fine and Leopold 1993; Gamber 1997; Green 1997; Lee 1998; Skov 2002; Yanagisako 2002).

MID-1990s: 'THIS IS NOT THE WAY FOR ME'

When the mid-1990s graduates look back on their student days, many remember preparing for employment in the large companies in the industry. But the fact that this cohort was more career-minded than their older colleagues does not seem to have helped them much in getting a foothold in the industry. In the mid-1990s, outsourcing was so extensive that several designers started their first jobs by being sent to factories in China to work with local designers. The days were over when a fresh graduate could be allowed to perform an independent role in a Danish company. DKDS graduate Martin's work life started with a job interview that did not go as expected. But unlike most job interviews, which end with the dismissal of the applicant, it was Martin who dismissed the potential employer, a multibrand company, and with that the career path that he had planned to enter. 'I remember sitting in the company's reception thinking, "This is completely wrong. This is not the way for me," ' he told us.

Informants from the older cohort had also been put off by potential employers. One of the older TEKO graduates told a similar story of how she decided after her first job interview that she would never seek employment in the Danish fashion industry. Instead she set up a design-services company operating from her home, which quickly had enough customers to keep her in business. But in the mid-1990s, the industry did not open many doors to fashion designers, as either employees or self-employed consultants. So designers like Martin did not experience the momentum of the older cohort. Their first jobs, or customers, did not lead straight to the next. Martin developed quite diverse interests, including costume design, which gave him work in the theatre; problem solving as a design method, which led to collaboration with an industrial designer; and sustainability, at the time an emerging concern that brought him consultancy and research-oriented jobs. For some years, he patched his work life together from different irregular jobs. Four years after graduation, he began to reconcile his diverse interests when he began to teach fashion at the design school, a job that he eventually came to hold full time. Although Martin describes himself as less focused than some of his classmates, several of the informants in the 1990s cohort felt that in response to the blocked opportunities in the industry, they had to redirect their efforts into different areas of specialization.

Another difference from the older cohort is that many of the 1990s graduates have had ongoing problems with securing a regular income. Strikingly, Martin presents his need for financial security, not as a reasonable expectation, but almost as a personal weakness. When he describes his job uncertainty as a costume designer, he says, 'I couldn't sleep at night if my bank account was in the red. But I could see that my colleagues were better at handling it. They simply didn't care. I had to realize that living with such an enormous uncertainty was not for me.'

The 1990s graduates who have found their way into the industry show the same pattern of job-hopping as the older cohort. Yet it seems that more of them have been repeatedly laid off or hit dead ends. Extensive outsourcing has also changed their opportunities and risks. For example, one informant describes how, in the early years of the new millennium, his newly started company was approached by East European buyers who were interested in placing a large order. After consulting with lawyers and banks, the designer increased his investment considerably and made the first delivery—only to find that the customer disappeared without paying. He spent the next five years working, mostly in manual jobs outside the fashion business, to pay off his debts.

The late 1990s were also the breakthrough of Danish designer fashion, with the establishment of the CPH Vision Fair in a redeveloped industrial building in the old meat-packing district as the up-market alternative to the commercial Copenhagen Fashion Week, and the international recognition of Danish designer brands (Melchior 2008). For the design school graduates, this opened up a new route of setting up one's own brand, thus bridging couture design and industry employment. Some of the best-known Danish name designers, including Naja Munthe and Karen Simonsen (of Munthe plus Simonsen) and Rikke Baumgarten and Helle Hestehave (of Baum und Pferdgarten), are former students of Kolding Design School. There are also a few name designers among the 1990s graduates in our study. But for all the other designers, conditions have changed in that they recognize that there are different success criteria for a fashion designer's career. Implicitly and explicitly, they compare themselves to a glamorous image that was not even mentioned by the older cohort. One informant says, 'I am not a designer with long red finger nails flashing myself in the press. If you choose to have your own company you need to brand yourself publicly. But I don't need to be famous. I don't care as long as I can do a job that is fun.'

MID-2000s: 'LIKE A COLD TURKEY'

The upsurge of the Danish designer fashion sector helped change the industry's image from a 'sunset industry' to a dynamic creative industry with long-term significance for the national economy. No doubt this has affected the mid-2000s graduates who tend to hope that they will be able to unite the 'commercial' with the 'creative' by primarily hoping their creativity will attract investors. In spite of apparent objective opportunities, this cohort seems to be more alienated and confused than previous cohorts. Tammie, a DKDS graduate, feels that the school taught the students to mistrust business. 'So we came out with an attitude like "we know best" compared to how things really function. It is not very smart to go to a job interview and indirectly criticize the company. We had needed an interface with the trade. Instead the transition from education to reality has been like a cold turkey.'

In designating the labor market 'reality,' she implicitly criticizes her education as an escapist dream. Such disillusionment is also typically found in the design schools' alumni surveys (Danmarks Designkole 2008; Design-skolen Kolding 2008). The phrase 'cold turkey' has entered the Danish language as a direct translation from the English, connoting the physical withdrawal symptoms following drug rehab, but also used metaphorically, as Tammie does. But what struck me by her use of the term was not only that it was dramatic and exaggerated, but that it exemplified a tendency by many fashion designers to describe complex conditions in terms of concrete bodily states.

Tammie is committed to carving out a career for herself as a fashion designer in the industry. But she explains that 'the only commercial jobs you can get in the beginning are the ones where you feel like you have to prostitute yourself as an artist. It is a huge shock.' By the first decade of the 21st century, newly graduated designers have been employed as assistants to senior designers. They are no longer given 'a free rein' but have to find their place in a design team. Their job content is typically CAD-based generation of styles, details, or color combinations. For Tammie, the alternative to paid employment is unpaid internships, which she sees as creative and 'give you something for your CV and insight into the trade.' As for many others of her cohort, her experience includes both unpaid internships and paid employment. For older designers, internships also provided valued learning opportunities and international experience. Yet there is a difference in the way the youngest graduates see internships as essential and strategic steps to a meaningful career. Five years after graduation, Tammie is still preoccupied with positioning herself for career take-off. She has not yet begun to see her career either as an accumulation of competences or a thread that weaves itself into the organizational fabric. Finding the right mix of paid work and unpaid 'work experience' requires intellectual effort and creative skill. Without any successful models to emulate, she and others in her cohort experience a great deal of uncertainty. Several informants have their income from low-paid service sector jobs unrelated to the fashion industry.

Tammie is acutely aware that she also needs paid work on her CV in order to move on to more interesting jobs in the industry. She has worked for two years as an assistant designer for a designer label owned by one of the major Danish multibrand companies. She describes herself in that period as 'totally paralyzed, as if I had been chained.' This has to do with the overall working environment, with rivalry between women designers and assistants, which she experiences as 'cat fights.' In addition, she has felt oppressed by the control exercised over her appearance and ideas. She fought to keep her own clothing style, rather than wear the company's products only, and she carefully kept her personal plans and side projects from her employer and colleagues for fear that she would be fired if they found out about them. With the concept of boundaryless careers, Michael

Arthur has shown how factors outside the firm—such as professional networks, extra-firm information flows, and family life—impact careers. In the study of fashion designers in the deindustrialised fashion sector in Denmark, extra-firm extra-economic factors, including internships and part-time projects, are so important that careers are potentially delinked from the labor market.

Compare Tammie's guarded approach with the story of a contemporary TEKO graduate who threw herself into her work for a large multibrand company in a period when the number of annual collections grew from 5 to more than 16. Fast fashion benchmarks, such as Zara and H&M, have publicized the organizational changes that enable them to speed up collection development on the basis of templates that are moderated in response to market data so that designers no longer work from scratch (Hilger 2010). However, this company increased its production pace without changing the designers' work process, so the TEKO graduate was sucked into a frenzy of long work hours, no overtime pay, and where it was an everyday occurrence that she and her colleagues would 'cry into the computer because of stress and pressure.' She had thought this would provide her with a good learning experience, which would lead her on to more interesting jobs. But after two years, she had to go on long-term sick leave, and when we met her three years later, she was still unable to return to the labor market. Looking back, she says, 'I could have done with some guidance after I finished school. I didn't know what I could do, but I still believed that when I was employed I should show the world—or the company—that they couldn't do without me. So I worked so hard for a three-month trial period, and thought when I had permanent employment I could calm down. Then they would know what I could do. But by that time I had created an identity as the girl who was always there. My advice to fresh graduates is this: find out what role you want to play, and play it from day 1.'

These two stories point to the fact that there are no viable coping strategies to deflect the shock of entering the labor market. The industry jobs for young fashion designers are no longer associated with product upgrading or organizational change, but with generating content variety at a fast pace. Neither the self-important DKDS graduates nor the eager-to-please TEKO graduates are prepared for this. They enter an industry that is set up to bring in young designers and make them work hard for a few years before they are replaced by others. For the designers, creating themselves in such an exploitative work environment—by patching together their CVs and by impression management—are their primary line of defense. This is a major difference from the experience of the older cohorts for whom one experience led to the next. For the youngest fashion designers, finding and sustaining a position for themselves in the labor market is a task that continues to require their creative problem-solving skills.

CONCLUSION: TRANSITION AND TRANSFORMATION

The stories of Anna, Martin, and Tammie show a multidimensional world in the way in which the threads of individual trajectories, weaving themselves into the tapestry of industry regions, change over time. The changes that have affected the Danish fashion industry in the period in question—outsourcing, speeding up of fashion cycles, new CAD technology, emergence of a designer fashion sector, and growing political interest in fashion as a creative industry—cannot be explained merely as exchanges between industry and individuals. In this respect, the Danish fashion industry must be understood as responding to global conditions—even promotion of local designers has its counterparts in many other countries—and, as far as we can judge, the Danish industry has not come up with any unique solutions. On this basis, we can arguably draw from the present analysis some general points about fashion designers' careers under conditions of deindustrialization.

The leifmotif of this analysis is the shock experienced by designers when they first enter the fashion industry. Yet the stories of designers' transition from school to work in, respectively, the 1980s, 1990s, and 2000s, have brought out different qualities of shock. The oldest cohort had a shock because they were given too much responsibility. We do not wish to paint a rosy picture of the older cohort's experiences. They were overwhelmed by the responsibility for technical details, which are central to industrial clothing production, and they were also humiliated by colleagues and bosses. They also report that they felt dull and numb and sorry for themselves. No doubt the distance in time helps them recall their early hardship in a humorous matter-of-fact way. In allowing themselves to be shaped by their encounter with the 'reality' of the industry, they developed the toughness, detail orientation, and no-nonsense approach that represent some fashion designers' professional traits.

Some of the designers in the middle cohort had similar experiences. But they entered the industry at a time when product development processes had to be standardized because of outsourcing, and this gave them fewer opportunities to shape their own work environment. More of them entered design teams emotionally characterized by 'mudslinging' and 'cat fights', and objectively characterized by a fast turnover of creative personnel. All designers know the phrase, 'Let someone else pay for your mistakes,' expressing an ideal career that builds on the learning of the first years of employment to establish an independent company. However, it has become increasingly difficult for young designers to heed this advice. The shock experienced by the youngest cohort is brought on by the fact that it is so hard for them to find meaningful learning opportunities. What is new is not merely the fact that it is harder to construct themselves as fashion designers but that their professional identities only partially overlap with paid work. Too much employment has actually become a threat to sustaining a career as a fashion designer. Summarizing the changing transition experiences, we can say that the shock of the oldest cohort enabled them to fight back and pick up the knowledge and opportunities they needed to move on, whereas the shock of the youngest cohort leaves them with few openings and paths to the next level.

The biggest paradox in our findings is this: in the late 1980s, when the fashion industry was seen to be in crisis, entry-level jobs allowed fashion designers to accumulate competences that helped them advance. But in the first decade of the 21st century, when the fashion industry was recognized as a national success, entry-level jobs did not give fashion designers the learning opportunities they needed to move forward. There are probably two interrelated reasons for this. The first one is the fact that competence and creativity in fashion design are closely associated with clothing manufacturing. Many of the skills that the older designers have developed as a matter of course—calculating production costs of a style, suggesting alternative ways of cutting a pattern, and understanding how different fabrics can be used, and so on—are inaccessible for the younger designers because they are not directly involved in the manufacturing processes. Thus, behind the recent success of Danish fashion, there is an industrial and craft-related deskilling that may undermine it in the long term.

The second reason is that the fashion industry is dominated by owner-managers who first and foremost see themselves as traders. The value chain of the fashion business operates on small margins, making cost cutting a priority at all levels. Yet our data also include numerous examples of managers trying to increase the profits by replacing materials with inferior substitutes, simplifying production, or simply undercutting suppliers to the point that deliveries are uncertain. From the designers' unanimous description of their working conditions in an extreme low-trust environment, we also heard many examples, first, of how fashion designers would suggest ways of minimizing waste and improving product development processes, and second, how their voices were overruled in the organizations. In this respect, we can say that the fashion industry still needs to wake up to the fact that it has been reclassified as a creative industry and to begin to approach product development as well as organizational processes as an object of design.

To complement the analysis of industry transformation, I wish, finally, to turn to what Peacock and Holland (1993) call a story-focused approach (as opposed to the life-focused approach) by examining the way in which fashion designers present themselves. It is obvious that all three cohorts share a positive valuation of the traits of fashion designers, which we associate with a particular dynamic form of romantic individualism. Because an important element of the latter is the willful misrecognition of environment and the refusal to accept obstacles, we can say that there is a dynamic clash between subjective and objective understandings of careers in creative industries. In the sociology of emotions, we tend to meet the assumption that emotions caused by macrostructural conditions are also addressed as macrostructures

(Barbalet 2002; Turner and Stets 2005). But fashion designers are not sociologists in the sense that they look for structural explanations or collective solutions. They accept the conditions of the industry as a given, and they fully endorse the individualistic ethos as self-motivated creative people. In Anna's words, fashion designers 'feel that they have a lot to give.' When tired or disappointed, they themselves take on the responsibility for regenerating their productive capacity. Many of the older and some of the younger designers have been through periods of 12 months or longer of stress and stress-related illness. The data from 45 life story interviews reveal what is not visible at the individual level; in fact what many individuals have actively tried to conceal from their former classmates and potential employers in terms of hardship. Yet the analysis would not be adequate without also describing the designers' ability to recover and reconcile themselves with negative experiences. Accepting adversity as a normal condition, fashion designers embody Arthur's notion of 'career actors that perceive a boundaryless future regardless of structural constraints' (Sullivan and Arthur 2006, 20). As one designer puts it, 'Everything is connected with everything. And I wouldn't have come to here if I hadn't experienced those thousands of disappointments and been sacked many times.'

In the beginning of this chapter, I stated two assumptions for the success of boundaryless careers—that they start off with some jobs that offer learning opportunities, which increase their competences, and that individuals are able to find trajectories that lead to new opportunities. The analysis of Danish fashion designers has shown that for this highly educated group of professionals in the fashion business, it is hard to sustain a middle-class income and to find career opportunities that lead to vertical or horizontal advancement. We therefore end with a question for reflection: how far can we extend the notion of boundaryless careers? When is it appropriate to consider that young fashion designers' attempts at putting a work life together are so far removed from the organizational opportunity structure that they no longer represent boundaryless careers but careers out of bounds?

NOTES

1. The project was headed by Lise Skov, and interviews were conducted by research assistants Andre Amtoft and David Sausdal. Data analysis was done by Lise Skov and David Sausdal.
2. In addition to the two reports, we had access to the raw survey data from Designskolen Kolding.

REFERENCES

Arthur, M. 1994. "The Boundaryless Career: A New Perspective for Organizational Inquiry." *Journal of Organizational Behavior* 15: 295–306.

Arthur, M., and D. Rousseau, eds. 1996. *The Boundaryless Career: A New Employment Principle for a New Organizational Era*. Oxford: Oxford University Press.

Barbalet, J, ed. 2002. *Emotions and Sociology*. London: Blackwell Publishing, The Sociological Review.

Bird, A. 1996. "Careers as Repositories for Knowledge: Considerations for Boundaryless Careers." In *The Boundaryless Career: A New Employment Principle for a New Organizational Era*, edited by M. Arthur and D. Rousseau, 150–68. Oxford: Oxford University Press.

Christopherson, S. 2008. "Beyond the Selfexpressive Creative Worker: An Industry Perspective on Entertainment Media." *Theory, Culture and Society* 25 (7–8): 73–95.

Danmarks Designskole. 2008. *Beskæftigelsesrapport 2008: Danmarks Designskoles dimittendundersøgelse 2008*.

Danmarks Statistik & Kulturministeriet. 2009. *Beskæftigelsesrapport 2009: Dimittender fra de kunsteriske og kulturelle uddannelser under Kulturministeriet*.

Designskolen Kolding. 2008. *Beskæftigelsesrapport: Designskolen Koldings egen undersøgelse af kandidaternes arbejdssituation 2008*.

Djelic, M.-L., and A. Ainamo. 1999. "The Coevolution of New Organizational Forms in the Fashion Industry: A Historical and Comparative Study of France, Italy and the United States." *Organization Science* 10: 5.

Fine, B., and E. Leopold. 1993. *World of Consumption*. London: Routledge.

Fineman, S, ed. 2000. *Emotion in Organizations*. Second edition. London: Sage.

Flew, T. 2002. *Beyond ad Hocery: Defining Creative Industries*. Paper presented at Cultural Sites, Cultural Theory, Cultural Policy conference, Wellington, New Zealand.

Gamber, W. 1997. *The Female Economy: The Millinery and Dressmaking Trades, 1860–1930*. Champaign: University of Illinois Press.

Green, N. 1997. *Ready-to-Wear and Ready-to-Work; A Century of Industry and Immigrants in Paris and New York*. Durham, NC: Duke University Press.

Hilger, J. 2010. "The Apparel Industry." In *Berg Encyclopedia of World Dress and Fashion, Volume 8, West Europe*, edited by L. Skov, 111–18.Oxford: Oxford University Press.

Høgenhaven, C. 2003. *Sammenligning af danske og udenlandske rammebetingelser og innovationsystemer indenfor modebranchen*. FORA Working Paper http://www.foranet.dk/upload/mode-_og_bekl%C3%A6dning.pdf.

Ingold, T. 2007. *Lines: A Brief History*. London: Routledge.

Kulturministeriets Rektorer. 2008. *Beskæftigelsesrapport 2008: Dimittender fra de kunsteriske og kulturelle uddannelser under Kulturministeriet*.

Lee, C.-K.1998. *Gender and the South China Miracle: Two Worlds of Factory Women*. Berkeley: University of California Press.

Lipovetsky, G. 1994.*The Empire of Fashion: Dressing Modern Democracy*. Princeton, NJ: Princeton University Press.

McRobbie, A.1998. *British Fashion Design: Rag Trade or Image Industry?* London: Routledge.

Melchior, M. 2008. *Dansk På Mode: En undersøgelse af design, identitet og historie i dansk modeinudstri*. Unpublished doctoral disseration, Danmarks Designskole: 209–228.

Melchior, M., L. Skov, and F. Csaba. 2010. "Translating Fashion into Danish." *Culture Unbound* 3. doi:10.3384/cu.2000.1525.113209

Peacock, J., and D. Holland. 1993. "The Narrated Self: Life Stories in Process." *Ethos* 21: 367–83.

Schivelbusch, W. 1987. *The Railway Journey*. Berkeley: University of California Press.

Skov, L. 2002. "Hong Kong Fashion Designers as Cultural Intermediaries: Out of Global Garment Production." *Cultural Studies* 16: 553–69.

Sullivan, S., and M. Arthur. 2006. "The Evolution of the Boundaryless Career Concept: Examining Physical and Psychological Mobility." *Journal of Vocational Behavior* 69: 19–29.

TEKO. 2009. *What's Coming? TEKO-analysen 2009.*

Turner, J., and J. Stets. 2005. *The Sociology of Emotions.* Cambridge, UK: Cambridge University Press.

Yanagisako, S. 2002. *Producing Culture and Capital: Family Firms in Italy.* Princeton, NJ: Princeton University Press.

Contributors

Jean-Yves Agard, PhD in Sociology from Sorbonne University, is currently Professor of Sociology at BEM-Bordeaux Management School and researcher in the ACME (Arts, Culture, and Management in Europe) Chair. His research interests focus on diversity management, identity, and socialization in organizations. Along with his socioanthropological academic background, his research covers qualitative ethnographical approaches ranging from international mobility for executives and scholars to artistic careers in creative industries. In a current research project, he questions the links among cultural identity mobilization (role of idiom), social cohesion (feeling of belonging), creativity, and territory development in traditional 'clustered' territories (Périgord, France).

Michael P. Allen is Professor of Sociology at Washington State University and Conjoint Professor of Sociology at University of Newcastle (Australia). His research interests focus on the creation of symbolic value in various fields of cultural production. He is currently writing a book on the American film industry as a field of cultural production, which is titled *Good Movies: Talent and Art in Hollywood.*

Trine Bille is Associate Professor, PhD at Copenhagen Business School, Department of Innovation and Organizational Economics, and Senior Researcher II at Telemarksforskning, Norway. She got her PhD from University of Copenhagen, Department of Economics. Her main research interest is cultural economics, and she has published many books and articles within this field, recently in *International Journal of Cultural Policy, Journal of Cultural Economics*, and *Handbook on the Economics of Arts and Culture* (Series Handbook of Economics, Elsevier Science). Among other things, she is a co-editor of the *Nordic Journal of Cultural Policy*, she is on the Executive Board of Imagine . . . Creative Industries Research, CBS, and she has been active on the Executive Board of ACEI, the Association of Cultural Economics International.

Amélie Boutinot, got her PhD in October 2011 in Management Science at Grenoble, France. Her dissertation tackles the problem of reputation-building in creative industries and, more specifically, in French architecture. She also teaches Innovation Management and Organizational Theory courses at Grenoble Ecole de Management, France.

Timothy J. Dowd is Associate Professor of Sociology at Emory University and was the Erasmus Chair for the Humanities as Erasmus University Rotterdam (2007–2008). He specializes in cultural sociology, with much of his research focusing on such issues as the construction of the orchestral canon in the US, the extent of diversity in popular music, the careers of musicians, and the state of music sociology. He and Susanne Janssen are currently editors in chief of *Poetics: Journal of Empirical Research on Culture, Media, and the Arts*. Recently, he taught an advanced seminar on the sociology of music with Robert Spano, conductor of the Atlanta Symphony Orchestra.

Doris Ruth Eikhof, PhD, is Lecturer in Work and Organisation Studies at Stirling Management School, University of Stirling. She researches creative work and enterprise, women's work and work–life boundaries. She has published internationally and is co-editor of *Creating Balance? International Perspectives on the Work-Life Integration of Professionals* (Springer 2011) and *Work Less, Live More? Critical Analyses of the Work–Life Relationship* (Palgrave 2008).

Anne Gombault, PhD in Management Science from Bordeaux University, Professor of Organizational Behavior and Strategic Management, is the founder and present holder of the ACME (Arts, Culture, and Management in Europe) Chair at BEM-Bordeaux Management School. Her research interests focus on organizational identity, behavior and strategy of arts, culture, and creative industries. She has researched for various organizations, including the Louvre Museum, the French Ministry of Culture and Communication, French regions, arts organizations, and creative industries. Her work has been published widely in both France and internationally. Since 2004, she has developed the ACME Chair, a network of 15 researchers producing and sharing knowledge in European management of arts, culture, and creative industries.

Irena Grugulis is Professor of Employment Studies at Durham Business School, University of Durham, AIM/ESRC Services Fellow, and an associate fellow of SKOPE. Her research focuses on all areas of skill and has been funded by the ESRC, EPSRC, and EU. Her recent projects have covered the retail sector, film, and TV and an ethnography of a computer games company. She has published widely and recent publications with Dimitrinka Stoyanova cover skills, recruitment, and discrimination in film and TV, as well as a review piece on "Skill and Performance" in the *British Journal of Industrial Relations*. Books include *Skills, Training and Human Resource Development* (Palgrave 2006). She is currently joint Editor in Chief of *Work, Employment, and Society*.

Axel Haunschild is Professor of Work and Employment Studies at Leibniz University of Hanover, Germany. He held Visiting Professorships at Royal Holloway College, University of London and at the University of Innsbruck, Austria. His research interests include changing forms of work and organization, creative industries, the institutional embeddedness of work and employment, CSR from an industrial relations perspective, organizations and lifestyles and organizational boundaries. He has published in journals such as *Human Relations, Journal of Organizational Behavior, British Journal of Industrial Relations* and *International Journal of Human Resource Management* and he has recently co-edited *Work Less, Live More? Critical Analysis of the Work-Life Boundary* (Palgrave 2008).

Candace Jones is Associate Professor in the Organization Studies Department at Boston College. Her research focuses on careers, social networks, and institutional processes within creative industries and professions. She has published in *Administrative Science Quarterly, Organization Science, Academy of Management Review, Organization Studies*, and *Journal of Organizational Behavior*, as well as numerous book chapters. She is currently co-editing with Mark Lorenzen and Jonathan Sapsed for Oxford University Press, *The Handbook of Creative Industries*. She serves on the Editorial Review Boards for *Organization Science, Strategic Management Journal*, and *Journal of Management Studies*, and she has been a Senior Editor for *Organization Studies* from 2008 to 2011. She was Rep at Large for the OMT Division of the Academy of Management from 2008 to 2010.

Kevin J. Kelly received his BA and MA from Emory University and was the Bobby Jones Scholar at St. Andrews University. His research interests include the impact of collective solidarity on sporting venues and team performances, as well as the fate of the orchestral canon in the contemporary US. Since graduation, among other things, he has worked at Emory University and has traveled far and wide.

Anne E. Lincoln is Assistant Professor of Sociology and Director of Markets and Culture at Southern Methodist University. Her research explores organizational change, educational and labor market outcomes, gender, and culture, with particular interest in attraction, retention, and attrition from science careers. Current projects involve science awards and prizes and scientists' work–family balance. Her research in the sociology of culture focuses on stratification processes in the production of culture: the influence of critical discourse on the collective memory of American film, 'double jeopardy' of age and gender in film acting careers, and awards and prizes in cultural labor markets.

Françoise Liot, PhD in Sociology from Bordeaux University, is currently Professor of Sociology at the Emile Durkheim Research Center, Bordeaux Segalen University. Her research interests focus on analysis of cultural public policies and the sociology of artistic careers. Her work has been published widely in French sociology journals and books: the book based on her dissertation, *Le métier d'artiste* (l'Harmattan 2004) or more recently the article"Collectifs d'artistes et action publique" in *L'artiste pluriel: démultiplier l'activité pour vivre de son art*, edited by M.-C. Bureau, M. Perrenoud, and R. Shapiro, 51–64 (Presses Univ. Septentrion 2009).

Chris Mathieu is Associate Professor at the Department of Organization at Copenhagen Business School and Director of the master's program in Human Resource Management. He has researched and written on gender issues in the IT industry, and his current research focuses on the Danish film industry with regard to creativity and inter-professional collaboration in on-set production, evaluative practices, project selection, and career development.

Catherine Morel, PhD in Marketing from Sheffield University, is currently Director of the MA in Creative Industries and the Creative Economy at Kingston University (London) and Associate Researcher in the ACME (Arts, Culture, and Management in Europe) Chair. Prior to this, she worked at Sotheby's Institute of Art, London, where she taught marketing in the MA in Art Business. Her research interests focus on the role of intermediaries in contemporary art worlds. She also specializes in relationships between business organizations and art worlds. With the ACME Chair, she is currently researching corporate sponsorship in France for the Ministry of Culture and Communication.

Can-Seng Ooi, PhD, a Singaporean, is Associate Professor at Copenhagen Business School. His art world research compares situations in Singapore, Denmark, and China. Besides art education and career development, he investigates cultural policies, creative processes, and cultural tourism. He publishes extensively on these subjects, including in the *International Journal of Cultural Policy, Culture Unbound*, and *Place Branding and Public Diplomacy*.

Jean Pralong, PhD in Management Science from ESCP Europe, is Professor of Human Resource Management at Rouen Business School, Head of the

'New Careers' Chair and Researcher in the ACME (Arts, Culture, and Management in Europe) Chair at BEM-Bordeaux Management School. He previously headed HR Development at Groupe Vedior France. His research interests focus mainly on critical HR, employment relationships, and careers. He has published articles in various French journals, as well as chapters in collective books on careers. His recent research concentrates primarily on career success in post-industrial organizations and generational influences on career expectations.

Franziska Schößler is Professor of German Literature at the University of Trier and Principal Investigator of "Repräsentationen von Juden in der deutschsprachigen Literatur des 19. Jahrhunderts," a project within the Collaborative Research Center 600 'Fremdheit und Armut' funded by the DFG (German research association). She studied in Bonn, Freiburg, Paris, London and Brisbane, received her PhD in 1994 and obtained her Habilitation in 2001. Her work focuses on interdependencies of Literature and Economy (with emphasis on Antisemitism), Theatre (especially Contemporary Drama) and Cultural and Gender Studies. Recent publications include *Augen-Blicke. Erinnerung, Zeit und Geschichte in Dramen der neunziger Jahre* (Tübingen 2004, Forum Modernes Theater) and *Börsenfieber und Kaufrausch: Ökonomie, Judentum und Weiblichkeit bei Theodor Fontane, Heinrich und Thomas Mann, Arthur Schnitzler und Émile Zola* (Bielefeld 2009).

Lise Skov is Associate Professor of Creative Industries at Copenhagen Business School. She has done extensive research on fashion, fur and other creative industries in Asia and Europe, and has published in a variety of academic journals and books. She is the Editor of the *Berg Encyclopedia of World Dress and Fashion*, West Europe volume, and the Editor (with Marie Riegels Melchior) of *Dreams of Small Nations in a Polycentric Fashion World*, themed issues of *Fashio Theory*, 2011.

Iben Sandal Stjerne has a master's degree in Human Resource Management from Copenhagen Business School. Her thesis, "Career Structures in the Danish Film Industry," analyzes career success in the Danish film industry. She has worked as a scientific research assistant on the "Creative Encounters" project at Copenhagen Business School, which provided the foundation for the chapter by Mathieu and Stjerne in this book. Prior to working at CBS, she worked for Toyota Morocco analyzing the implementation of Japanese work and corporate values in a Moroccan context.

Dimitrinka Stoyanova is Lecturer in Management at St. Andrews School of Management and Associate Researcher at the Institute for Capitalising on Creativity at St. Andrews University. Her research interests are in the area of work and employment in the creative industries, creative careers, learning and skills development, and free lance work. Her latest research focuses on film and television industries, and her publications discuss issues related to skills development, learning, communities of practice, and social capital.

Izabela Wagner is a former music teacher (MA in Music Pedagogy from the University of Music in Poznan/Poland). In 1997, she became a sociologist. Her research focuses on the careers of virtuoso musicians (PhD at EHESS in France). Since 2003, this study was extended to the world of life-science scientists. Currently, she is Associate Professor at Warsaw University in the Institute of Sociology and Associate Researcher at the Center for Study of Social Movements at EHESS in Paris. In 2010/2011, she was visiting researcher at Harvard University (the Department of the History of Science), where she conducted a project devoted to the careers of scientists, supported by the Kosciuszko Foundation. She is the author of the book *Becoming Transnational Professional* and several articles about career and mobility of artists and scientists, their international culture of work, and transnational professionalism.

Index